BRITISH ARMY MUSIC

IN THE

INTERWAR YEARS

CULTURE, PERFORMANCE, AND INFLUENCE

Copyright © 2020 Major David B Hammond

All rights reserved. No part of this publication may be reproduced or transmitted in any form or by any means, electronic or mechanical including photocopying, recording or any information storage or retrieval system, without prior permission in writing from the publishers.

The right of Major David B Hammond to be identified as the author of this work has been asserted by him in accordance with the Copyright, Designs and Patents Act 1988

First published in the United Kingdom in 2020 by
The Cloister House Press

ISBN 978-1-913460-05-1

www.getpsychedup.co.uk

BRITISH ARMY MUSIC

IN THE

INTERWAR YEARS

CULTURE, PERFORMANCE, AND

INFLUENCE

MAJOR DAVID B HAMMOND

FOREWORD

BAGSHOT PARK

The Corps of Army Music has been in existence for twenty-five years, but music has been an integral part of the British military for centuries. Those who have witnessed the great military pageants of the twentieth and twenty-first centuries will be aware of the role of music in The Queen's Birthday Parade and other state events, but military bands have had a much larger involvement in the military and musical history of our nation, providing an essential link between military and civil societies, both at home and abroad.

British army bands have always had the capacity to project military strategy in a less threatening manner, enabling the accomplishment of objectives through peaceful means. Yet despite the important role of music in the army there has been very little written about what this has meant for the military and society in general. This book is the first to address the subject from the perspective of the interwar years, bringing together many themes to analyse the role of military music of the period, and providing a unique insight into the work of military musicians in one of the most fascinating periods of our nation's history.

HRH The Countess of Wessex GCVO
Colonel-in-Chief, Corps of Army Music

PREFACE

This book aims to identify how British army bands in the interwar years were a primary stakeholder in the music industry and to explore their role in projecting soft power for the British military. There were approximately 7,000 full-time bandsmen serving in the British army, which was about a third of the total number of musicians in the music profession in the United Kingdom. The War Office was the largest employer of professional musicians in the country and yet there has been very little acknowledgement of the contribution made by this body of musicians, both to the music industry and to the effectiveness of army operations. This book uses models from the business and management literature to interrogate the position of British army music within the context of military structures and the music industry in the interwar years. It reveals the extent that residential institutions were organised to provide young boys for recruitment into the army as bandsmen and how these boys became an integral part of the music industry. It explores how army music set the standard for training and performance while creating sustainability for the music industry, which relied upon the existence of army bands for its business. The book then exposes the tempestuous relationship army bands had with the BBC and recording industry, as well as the function the military played in the adoption of an international standard of musical pitch. Finally, it uncovers the effective role and soft power influence of British army bands and their music in the maintenance of British imperial authority, at home and overseas, and the tragic consequences of operating at the forefront of the military campaign in Ireland.

I should like to thank all those people who have helped me through the whole process of researching for this book. I acknowledge the assistance of John Ambler, Frank Andrews, Captain Fergal Caroll, Art Cockerill, John Curtis, Colin Dean, Graham Gordon, Janet Kelsey, Esther Mann, Lieutenant Colonel Neil Morgan, Major Richard Powell, Dr Joseph Ryan, Alan Shellard, Janet Snowden, Major Roger Swift, and Major Hugo White.

I am grateful to the the Corps of Army Music for allowing me the flexibility to spend time researching. Thank you to staff at The British Library; The National Archives; London Metropolitan Archives; the Museum of Army Music; Band of the Grenadier Guards; The Open University Library; The Royal Hampshire Regiment

Museum; Cornwall's Regimental Museum; Soldiers of Gloucestershire Museum; The Foundling Museum; Royal Archives, Windsor Castle; Prince Consort Library, Aldershot; Richmond Museum Archives; The Rifles Office, Pontefract; Household Cavalry Museum Archives; Hampshire Cultural Trust, Aldershot Military Museum Archives; The Irish Army No. 1 Band and Defence Forces School of Music; Military and civilian staff at Headquarters Corps of Army Music and the Royal Military School of Music, Kneller Hall; The Royal Marines Band Service; Royal Academy of Music Museum; RTÉ Documentaries on One; The Sandhurst Collection and Library; International Military Music Society; The Band of The Royal Yeomanry (Inns of Court & City Yeomanry). The front cover pictures are all from the archives of the Museum of Army Music. Pictures throughout the book are individually acknowledged.

From the Open University I should like to express gratitude to Professor Catherine Tackley and Dr Fiona Richards for their help, and I am particularly grateful to my principal supervisor, Professor Trevor Herbert, whose encouragement and inspiration made this project possible.

I am eternally indebted to my wife Kate, and our two daughters, Jane and Elizabeth, who have given me all the support I could wish for, as well as the companionship, patience, and forebearance to see me through.

This book is dedicated with love and respect to my parents, Brian and Sheila Hammond, who set me on the path to discovery, and to whom I shall be forever thankful.

CONTENTS

Foreword v

Preface vii

Contents ix

Chapter 1: Introduction 1
   Aim 2
   'Cheating between the wars': Background and context 3
   Rationale 5
   Methodology: the models 15
   Scope 22
   Structure 25

Part 1: Culture 33

Chapter 2: The gentlemen of the regiment:
Musicians in the regular army 35
   The structure of British army bands 37
   The hierarchy of army bands 42
   Unofficial and part-time bands 44
   The role of bandsmen 46
   The way we do things around here: the culture of
   soldier-musicians 50
   Training 61

Chapter 3: 'Breaking in' the young hands:
The dependence on band boys 67
   Structural issues and motivations of institutions 69
   The relationship between the army and residential
   institutions for children 73
   Specialist band institutions 81
   The military boarding schools 84
   'Civilian' band boys 89
   Band boy training 93
   Social changes and recruiting 96

Part 2: Performance 107

Chapter 4: Seaside, ceremonial, and an unhappy union: Bands and live performance 109
    Ceremonial 110
    Remembrance and commemoration 116
    Tattoos and pageants 123
    Regimental duties 127
    Civilian funded engagements 131
    Instrumentation and repertoire 141
    Orchestras 159
    Controversy and competition 165

Chapter 5: A clear and homogenous sound: Performance practice and recording 173
    The suitability of military bands for recording 175
    The military band sound 177
    The influence of recording managers 179
    The naming of military bands 183
    The demise of military band recordings 187

Chapter 6: 'Tonic' music and discord with the BBC: Repertoire and broadcasting 191
    Repertoire 192
    Kneller Hall and BBC grading systems 207

Part 3: Influence 215

Chapter 7: Kneller Hall and the pitch battle with the War Office 217
    The impetus to change 219
    Developing interest and pressure on the War Office 223
    The order to change 231

Chapter 8: Punching above their weight: Soft power influence of British army bands overseas 241
    Military band soft power influencing activities 245
    British army band service overseas 249
    India 251
    Shanghai 1927 260
    Southern Africa 1931 265

Chapter 9: The Youghal 'outrage': Political appropriation of military bands and the founding of the Irish Free State.. 273
    The context of music appropriation................................ 274
    The conflict environment 276
    The National Anthem.. 278
    Recruiting for the British army....................................... 280
    Band identity and political allegiance 282
    Bands as targets 285
    The Youghal 'outrage'... 288
    The military music of the Irish Free State 297

Appendix 1: Broadcasts (excluding outside broadcasts) by staff bands from January 1932 to September 1933....... 305

Appendix 2: Colonel Somerville's list to the BBC of army bands graded 'outstanding' by Kneller Hall in 1933. 307

Appendix 3: Colonel Jervis's 'order of merit' army band list sent to the BBC in 1934, notable for its absence of staff bands.. 309

Appendix 4: Walton O'Donnell's BBC audition reports for three bands in Northern Ireland. 311

Appendix 5: Internal 1941 BBC memo rejecting the Kneller Hall band grading system. 317

Appendix 6: Army Council Instruction – 544: Pitch of Instruments of Army Bands 318

Appendix 7: An anonymous humorous poem about the change to low pitch published in *The Leading Note* in 1929... 322

Bibliography 325
    Archives... 325
    Books, articles, and other printed sources...................... 327

The author 351

BRITISH ARMY MUSIC

IN THE

INTERWAR YEARS

CULTURE, PERFORMANCE, AND

INFLUENCE

CHAPTER 1

INTRODUCTION

The military has been the largest single employer of musicians in the United Kingdom of Great Britain and Ireland since the late eighteenth century. Despite social changes at the conclusion of World War One the regimental band system remained intact in the interwar years, maintaining military bands at the forefront of music making in the British Isles. Throughout this period military musicians were much in demand, with musical ensembles around the country, such as theatre and cinema orchestras, employing a significant number of ex-Servicemen, as well as those still serving. Central to the training of these musicians was the Royal Military School of Music at Kneller Hall, on the outskirts of London, established in 1857 to instruct bandmasters for the British army, and continuing to produce bandmasters and bandsmen for the regular army throughout the twentieth century.[1] It was distinctive amongst conservatoires in that it trained musicians for a specific job, being rated as 'one of the most important [music] institutions' in the country by the popular music press.[2]

In the interwar period Britain saw a great deal of social, technological, economic, and political change ('STEP').[3] Social transformation was taking place after the First World War with extra demands on the fledgling welfare state, including Asquith's pre-war Liberal reforms that had started to materialise, votes for women, and several unprecedented housing booms. Following demobilisation, the

---

[1] Bandsman (Bdsm) was the designation given to a regimental band-trained soldier in the rank of Private (Pte), with the exception of the Household Division and Royal Artillery, where members of the band were known as Musician (variously abbreviated to Mus, Musn or Msn). In 1994, when the Corps of Army Music was formed, all band-trained personnel, male and female, in the rank of Pte were redesignated Musician (Musn). In the interwar years women were not permitted to serve in army bands.
[2] J. Greig (ed.), *The Musical Educator: A Library of Instruction by Eminent Specialists: Volume The Fifth* (Edinburgh: T. C. & E. C. Jack, Grange Publishing, 1895), p. 194.
[3] L. Fahey and V. K. Narayanan, *Macroenvironmental Analysis for Strategic Management* (St Paul: West Publishing, 1986).

focus of Government moved away from the military, creating an introspective culture for those who remained in the army. Momentous social fractures were never very far away with warning signals from Russia, Germany, Spain, and the threat of severe civil strife in France being a constant reminder of the potential of substantial social upheaval. There was not any significant threat of revolution in Britain in 1919, but within the United Kingdom, Ireland was moving towards an increasingly violent transition to partition and a civil war which heavily involved the British army.

There was technological innovation, with the advent of broadcasting and new forms of audio recording, as well as the huge rise in the use of the motor car, and the expansion of the national grid, which all contributed to the way music was received amongst the population. Economic issues saw the decline in heavy industries, causing huge fluctuations in the labour market, and currency changes with the abandonment of the gold standard; the resultant redirection of the budget away from the War Office contributed to the military's difficulties. In politics, the rapid rise of Labour and a split in the Liberals, the birth of the Irish Free State, the pressures of a sprawling Empire, and the rise of Germany and Japan, were to have an effect on the government's relationship with the military.

Despite these transformational events British army bands endured throughout the period, ensuring thousands of musicians were employed in the biggest state-sponsored music project the country has ever witnessed.

Aim

The main purpose of this book is to explore the state of military music in the dynamic environment of social, technological, economic, and political change in the interwar years of 1919 to 1939, assessing the implications on the culture of bands, their performance practice, and how they acted as a soft power lever of influence on civilian institutions as well as to national and international events. The study adopts an innovative approach using business and management models to identify salient issues that shape the nature of the discussion. The analysis explores whether military bands made a significant contribution to the social world of music-making in interwar Britain and what this meant for the military and the nation as a whole.

'Cheating between the wars': Background and context

The British army emerged from the First World War victorious, but battered and bruised, and just as with previous major conflicts it soon needed to shed large numbers of soldiers to return to a peacetime footing. This was done relatively quickly with a swift withdrawal to barracks and the pre-war social stratum re-affirmed as the hastily commissioned white-collar workers of the Kitchener battalions were demobilised. Widespread public revulsion of the war resulted in the army becoming more secluded, but it was not unhappy about retreating into the regimental system and re-entrenching the divisions between officers and other ranks. Regular army officers had tended to view Kitchener subalterns to be not 'proper officers…for the duration only' and saw the re-establishment of pre-war class divisions as a natural occurrence.[4] 'The officer/man relationship of the 1930s simply reflected prevailing social attitudes' was how one officer of the 5th Inniskilling Dragoon Guards described the situation,[5] and this state of affairs was to remain up until the Second World War.

In a short space of time the army became the poor relation as the Royal Navy retained its status as the popular senior service with a strong lobbying power that enabled effective influence over the political leadership. The newly formed Royal Air Force had the image of the modern technical service and retained a novelty status. The army, however, had been relegated to the image of the cartoonist David Low's caricature of Colonel Blimp, a representation that became the public's perception of the army.[6]

This was at a time when the British army had a great responsibility, assigned by the state to be the 'Imperial Police' and constantly engaged in protecting the Empire's possessions and communications. Planning for the armed forces had quite naturally focused on preparation for war, but preparation for peacetime proved

---

[4] Quoted in A. Mallinson, *The Making of the British Army: From the English Civil War to the War on Terror* (London: Bantam, 2009), p. 323.
[5] Quoted in M. Carver, *Britain's Army in the 20th Century* (London: Macmillan, 1998), p. 160; There is an anecdote about the class divisions at this time provided by Maj (retd) Roger Swift who recalls being told about how guests were treated at a regimental open day with a sign outside each respective mess tent: 'Officers and their Ladies'; 'Sergeants and their Wives'; 'Other Ranks and their Women'. (R. Swift. Personal Communication. 15 November 2012.)
[6] B. Bond and W. Murray, 'The British Armed Forces, 1918-39', in A. R. Millett & W. Murray (eds), *Military Effectiveness Volume 2: The Interwar Period*, new (2nd) edn (Cambridge: Cambridge University Press, 2010), p. 107.

to be a far more important aspect of Service planning.[7] The British Empire had become bigger than ever after the First World War, comprising different types of dependencies, and there was a need to protect it, but with a huge decrease in military personnel. Britain also had commitments to what is referred to as the 'informal Empire', territories under the influence of Britain, either for the defence of vital strategic points, such as Egypt, as a source of natural resources, such as parts of Persia, or trade, such as Shanghai in China.[8] The obligation to these informal territories could vary considerably, as in Shanghai, where a British Division, under the name of the Shanghai Defence Force, was deployed in 1927 in support of the threatened International Settlement. Nevertheless, the addition of greater responsibilities over a large part of the globe did not bring with it the corresponding increase in power as resources were decreasing, leading Howard to describe the sprawling Empire as a 'gouty giant', and Beloff, 'a brontosaurus with huge, vulnerable limbs which the central nervous system had little capacity to protect, direct or control.'[9] Harris goes as far as to say that perhaps no army has ever had to face such a complex challenge as the British army did between the two world wars, with the demands of politicians not being backed up with the resources for the tasks.[10]

Whether deployed throughout the Empire or distributed across the British Isles in barracks, army units were short of kit and equipment and there was a lack of strategic direction, which did not help the image of the army. The feeling of those serving is summed up by one former officer who recounts that the interwar period was known by those in the cavalry as the 'era of the green and white flag' because when they went on manoeuvres they carried police rattles instead of machine guns, and green and white flags instead of anti-tank rifles: 'No one who did not serve can appreciate the frustration of the army

---

[7] R. Higham, *Armed Forces in Peacetime: Britain, 1918-1940, a case study* (London: G. T. Foulis & Co, 1962), p. 162, fn. 1.
[8] M. Banton, *Administering the Empire, 1801-1968: A Guide to the Records of the Colonial Office in The National Archives of the UK* (London: Institute of Historical Research/The National Archives, 2008), p. 5.
[9] Quoted in B. Bond, *British Military Policy between the Two World Wars* (Oxford: Clarendon Press, 1980), p. 10.
[10] J. P. Harris, 'Obstacles to innovation and readiness: the British Army's experience 1918-1939', in W. Murray and R. H. Sinnreich (eds) *The Past as Prologue: The Importance of History to the Military Profession* (New York: Cambridge University Press, 2006), p. 215.

between the two wars'.[11] Within a strained and demoralising environment for the army, accurate shooting and proficiency on manoeuvres suffered, but there was still great emphasis on faultless drill, immaculately groomed horses, and polished boots.[12]

Ranson's statement that the army was 'cheating between the wars'[13] is perhaps no better demonstrated than through its ceremonial image, with bands at the vanguard of the army's public relations, accompanying the regiments wherever they were posted, usually with one battalion serving at home and the other overseas.[14] This projection of 'soft power' resources allowing Britain to punch above its weight was of great significance for military music for several reasons. Firstly, one way the army kept itself in the public eye in Britain was to utilise regimental bands in order to re-establish and re-assert the authority of the military. They did this by by staging huge public displays of military music (tattoos) in garrison towns such as Aldershot, Tidworth, and Colchester, in addition to public duties and state ceremonial in London. Secondly, bands performed around the country on bandstands and were quite often the only form of professional live concert music that audiences would hear. Thirdly, by doing the same overseas, albeit on a smaller scale, performing around the world wherever their regiment was stationed, and sometimes on a separate band tour. And fourthly, as a symbol for re-stating British nationhood. These functions were not necessarily new but took on a greater significance after the shock of the First World War, the lack of resources available, and the withdrawal of the army from society. The British army managed to cheat by using its bands, usually unwittingly, to assert its authority through soft power, without the superior force and greater resources that would normally have been required.

Rationale
The interwar years have been chosen as the period for this study for three main reasons: it follows on from Herbert and Barlow's

---

[11] R. J. T. Hills, *The Royal Horse Guards (The Blues)* (London: Leo Cooper, 1970), pp. 93-94.
[12] *Ibid*, p. 125.
[13] E. Ranson, *British Defence Policy and Appeasement Between the Wars, 1919-1939* (London: The Historical Association, 1993), p. 5.
[14] Infantry regiments comprised two battalions.

investigation of military music in the long nineteenth century[15]; it is a period flanked by momentous events that changed society, and described by some as being a 'heyday' for military music[16]; and most importantly, there is no published material that seriously considers the role and impact of military music in the interwar years.

Hector Sutherland, a Life Guards musician who left the army in 1923, publishing his memoirs in 1959, seems to have realised that he was part of something special. He witnessed the rise of jazz in London and Paris and met and performed with famous musicians, but in general he worked with musicians 'whose names now, like my band, are all just memories'[17] – the silent majority of performers who made up the backbone of the British music scene. He concludes his memoirs with the rather quaint, yet inviting appeal: 'as I bring these recollections to a close, I would like to think that their experiences may be recorded by some musical historian.'[18] He follows this with a tantalising statement:

> We can't all be Louis Armstrongs and Krieslers, and if these pages have given a certain pleasure and interest, it may prove that lesser mortals can live the lives of colour and background worthy of mention.[19]

The musicians he referred to are not quite what Finnegan calls 'The Hidden Musicians'[20] – military musicians were full-time professional musicians – but they are the forgotten musicians, and the realisation by Hector Sutherland that he was part of something important served as an impetus for this research.

Anecdotal reports of military bands in the interwar period, like Sutherland's, suggest that there was a segment of the military and music profession whose activities had gone unreported. Not only was it apparent that these soldier-musicians had been neglected by military historians, but that musicologists had also overlooked the significance of the contribution to the music industry of

---

[15] T. Herbert and H. Barlow, *Music and the British Military in the Long Nineteenth Century* (Oxford: Oxford University Press, 2013).
[16] J. Curtis, *Bands of Hope: A Study of Military Bands in the Twentieth Century*. Unpublished Manuscript, 2010.
[17] H. Sutherland, *They Blow Their Trumpets* (London: P. R. Macmillan, 1959), p. 150.
[18] *Ibid.*
[19] *Ibid.*
[20] Predominantly amateur community musicians. R. Finnegan, *The Hidden Musicians: Music-Making in an English Town*, rev. edn (Middletown: Wesleyan University Press, 2007).

approximately one third of its number. Any literature review will confirm that while a number of studies referred to military bands in the period, none recognised the impact they had on both the music profession and the military, and this will become apparent below.

In the interwar period military bands were an integral part of the national music scene, making recordings and broadcasts, and performing large numbers of public concerts. Military bands were also major stakeholders in the instrument manufacturing and music publishing industries, and yet military music has until recently not attracted much attention in either military or music research fields. The most important study is Herbert and Barlow's *Music and the British Military in the Long Nineteenth Century*, but as the title suggests the period studied ends at the First World War. From the military perspective, bands have been completely ignored, with a focus being on the hard power influence tools of 'Fires' and 'Manoeuvre'.[21] Even then, the overall study of the army in the interwar period has been neglected by military historians in contrast to the interest in the expansion of the newly formed Royal Air Force and the detailed writings on the Royal Navy's albeit rather inactive period.[22] The single exception has been the focus on mechanised warfare and the dominance of the writings of Fuller and Liddell Hart by, for example, Luvaas,[23] but other than the Royal Tank Corps there is very little known about recruitment, training, and doctrine.[24] Keegan's plea in 1972 for more research has unfortunately remained unheeded, particularly in the areas of the sociology of the army and

---

[21] Influence can be described as utilising the best combination of actions and words to achieve desired outcomes. This may be by using Fires (causing physical destruction), Manoeuvre (placing strength against identified vulnerabilities in time and space to gain advantage), Information Activities (such as media operations and community relations), and Other Activities (such as support to governance). In general Fires and Manoeuvre are types of hard power because they involve physical influence, and Information and Other Activities are types of soft power because they rely on information and services. See I. Harrison, 'Achieving Unity of Purpose in Hybrid Conflict – HQ ARRC: Capability Experimentation: Part 1', *British Army Review*, No. 148, Winter 2009/2010, p. 55.

[22] See R. Higham, 'The Development of the Royal Air Force, 1909-1945', in R. Higham (ed.), *A Guide to the Sources of British Military History* (London: Routledge & Kegan Paul, 1972), pp. 422-451; J. Keegan, 'The Interwar Years', in R. Higham (ed.), *A Guide to the Sources of British Military History*, pp. 452-469.

[23] J. Luvaas, *The Education of an Army: British Military Thought, 1815-1940* (London: Chicago University Press, 1964), pp. 331-424.

[24] Bond, *British Military Policy*, p. 9.

civil-military relations,[25] two fields especially relevant to the study of music in the army. Even though some works on these topics have emerged over the last few years they tend to cover broad periods.[26]

The main focus of music research on interwar military bands so far has been on the music of Holst, Vaughan Williams, Grainger, and other high-profile composers,[27] but while they had an important part to play in the development of wind band repertoire, their contribution was limited and the main catalogue of military band music remained transcriptions of light orchestral works and popular music, and marches. Light music had the power to bring in big revenues – Albert Ketèlbey was Britain's first millionaire composer[28] – but military bands' association with middle-of-the-road popular music that was originally written for other ensembles is probably the reason why its musical contribution has not been deemed worthy of evaluation, and the music it can call its own, the march, has received scant attention, possibly because of its association with other types of, what Richards refers to as, 'the peoples' music': the ballad, hymn and music-hall song.[29]

The exasperation of the military music profession to this state of affairs was well summed-up by the nineteenth-century bandmaster, J. A. Kappey[30]:

> The music of the people has been passed over with almost contemptuous indifference, and it seems as if they were, so to say, ashamed to mention the poor cousin who found inspiration in the open air, or went 'a-soldiering'.

---

[25] Keegan, 'The Interwar Years', p. 462.
[26] For example, R. Holmes, *Soldiers: Army Lives and Loyalties from Redcoats to Dusty Warriors* (London: HarperPress, 2011).
[27] See for example W. M. Rapp, *The Wind Band Masterworks of Holst, Vaughan, and Grainger* (Galesville: Meredith Music, 2005); F. Fennell, *Basic Band Repertory: British Band Classics from the Conductor's Point of View* (Evanston, Ill: The Instrumentalist, 1980); J. C. Mitchell, *From Kneller Hall to Hammersmith: The Band Works of Gustav Holst* (Tutzing: Verlegt Bei Hans Schneider, 1990).
[28] See J. Sant, *Albert W. Ketèlbey 1875-1959 From the Sanctuary of his Heart: Reflections on the life of the Birmingham born composer* (Sutton Coldfield: Manifold, 2000).
[29] J. Richards, *Imperialism and Music: Britain 1876-1953* (Manchester: Manchester University Press, 2001), p. 525.
[30] J. A. Kappey, *Military Music: A History of Wind-Instrumental Bands* (London: Boosey and Co, 1894), p. 1.

This frustration is understandable and although there were examples of composers revealing an interest in the influence of military music, the dialogue was limited. Debussy, for example, when writing in 1903 had shown that he understood the power of military music in society and was envious that orchestral music did not have the same hold on people:

> Why is the adornment of our squares and boulevards left solely to military bands? Isn't military music meant to relieve the tedium of long marches, and to bring joy to the streets? It expresses the patriotism that burns in every heart, and it unites the quiet soul of the little pastry cook with the gentleman who thinks of nothing but the Alsace-Lorraine question, yet never talks of it.[31]

Writing in *Open-Air Music*, Debussy goes on to recognise the political role of military bands: 'the music of the Republican Guard…is practically an instrument of diplomacy'.[32] Debussy identifies several critical points here, particularly that of diplomacy, but the problem with Debussy's appreciation of military music is that while he recognises the social and political influence, his comments firmly place the role of bands as providing outdoor music, relegating its status to that of incidental melodic music. This reveals that part of the issue was how military band music was written about.

The context of Kappey's gripe and Debussy's observations was recognised by the composer, conductor, and critic, Constant Lambert, who identified in 1939 that there had been a split in the styles of writings about music: on the one hand he asserted that academic technical writers on music were far too complicated for the lay reader to understand and thus disaffected them, and on the other he noted that those writing more popular generalist texts on music tended to lack the technical knowledge and were not taken seriously by professionals.[33] Wood's 1932 book *The Romance of Regimental Marches* would be an example of the latter,[34] and may have been the

---

[31] Quoted in R. L. Smith (ed), *Debussy on Music* (London: Secker and Warburg, 1977), p. 93.
[32] C. Debussy, 'Open-Air Music', in *Three Classics in the Aesthetics of Music: Monsieur Croche the Dilettante Hater*, trans. B. N. Langdon Davies (New York: Dover, 1962; repr. of 1928 edn), p. 32.
[33] A. Motion, *The Lamberts: George, Constant & Kit* (London: Hogarth, 1987), p. 198.
[34] W. Wood, *The Romance of Regimental Marches* (London: William Clowes, 1932).

type of publication that influenced where military music was positioned. Another example would be Chapter IV of Galloway's *Musical England* from 1910, which describes the nature of 'Music in the Army and the Navy.'[35] Galloway's intent was to look at the cross-class British public's interest in and attraction to music. As a businessman and politician he could take a different view of music without having to rely on professional music opinion and for this reason he openly states the worth and influence of military bands on the musical tastes of the nation.

Technical writers were not concerning themselves with military music matters and after the Second World War music critics seem to gradually abandon military music as an idiom altogether. The remaining literature only really includes general educational pamphlets, such as Gaskell's *Everybody's Musical Companion*,[36] where equal status is given to the symphony orchestra, military, and brass bands, with a list of British regimental marches alongside that of operas. The single exception is Farmer, whose writing on military bands is important, as discussed below, but his *History of the Royal Artillery Band*, published by the Royal Artillery Institution in 1954, only had limited circulation.[37]

The trend in the marginalisation of military music away from that of art music probably started in the nineteenth century with the ascendancy of a refined and established art music that resided in an institutional culture, creating a canon and critique associated with it. Art music became more exclusive and developed cultural associations that were different to those of military music; military music became an enclosed category of music that established its own traditions and was performed in a particular way. As music education improved, civilians were able to start making a living as musicians and the art music world began to rely more and more on professional musicians to fill its orchestras. By the interwar period the order and hierarchy

---

[35] W. J. Galloway, *Musical England* (London: Christophers, 1910), pp. 66-87.
[36] G. Gaskell, *Everybody's Musical Companion: Containing Interesting Facts on Instruments of the Full of Symphony Orchestra. The Military Band. The Brass Band. National Anthems. Some Music Journals. Tales of the Tunes. Diplomas and Certificates. Do You Know? Opera. Regimental Marches. The World's Great Musicians* (Southport: Hugh Rigg, 1949).
[37] G. H. Farmer, *History of the Royal Artillery Band 1762-1953* (Woolwich: Royal Artillery Institution, 1954).

of cultures, as described by Levine's 'Highbrow/Lowbrow',[38] became more established, but the relationship between military music and art and popular music was still not yet clear cut. For example, the Bournemouth Symphony Orchestra had started off as the *Bournemouth Royal Italian Band* and it was not until Dan Godfrey Jnr took over as conductor in the 1890s of the renamed *Corporation Military Band* that bandsmen were required to double-up on stringed instruments,[39] although there was still a separate corporation military bandmaster in 1924.[40] Furthermore, the wind section of the City of Birmingham Symphony Orchestra in the 1920s originally comprised members of the Birmingham Police Band.[41] Nevertheless, military music, and its performers, did not fit comfortably into either camp and so the various approaches to research, both military and musical, have not dealt with the state sponsorship of military music in the interwar years – remarkable by the fact that there were at least 7,000 full-time musicians employed by the War Office at the time.

Confusion over the status of military music has led academic writers on popular and light music to skirt around the discussion of military bands with, for example, Russell's *Popular Music in England*, Nott's *Music for the People*, Frith's *Performing Rites*, and Self's *Light Music in Britain since 1870*, all making only cursory reference to military music.[42] It is possible that the reluctance to engage has been due to researchers being apprehensive about

---

[38] L. W. Levine, *Highbrow/Lowbrow: The Emergence of Cultural Hierarchy in America* (Cambridge, Massachusetts: Harvard University Press, 1988), pp. 169ff.
[39] S. Street and R. Carpenter, *The Bournemouth Symphony Orchestra: A Centenary Celebration* (Wimborne, Dorset: Dovecote, 1993), pp. 10-15.
[40] S. Lloyd, *Sir Dan Godfrey: Champion of British Composers* (London: Thames, 1995), p. 53.
[41] R. Nettels, *The Orchestra in England: A Social History* (London: Jonathan Cape, 1946), p. 270; T. Grimley, 'Celebrating 90 years of musical memories', <http://www.cbso.co.uk/?page=birthday/past.html> [accessed 12th May 2013].
Nettels maintains that the Birmingham Police Band was the forerunner of the City of Birmingham Symphony Orchestra (CBSO) but Grimley states that the bandsmen were used to supplement the orchestra that had been assembled by Appleby Matthews, the conductor of both bodies.
[42] D. Russell, *Popular Music in England, 1840-1914: A social history*. 2nd edn (Manchester: Manchester University Press, 1997); J. Nott, *Music for the People: Popular Music and Dance in Interwar Britain* (Oxford: Oxford University Press, 2002); S. Frith, *Performing Rites: Evaluating Pop Music* (Oxford: Oxford University Press, (1996); G. Self, *Light Music in Britain since 1870: A Survey* (Aldershot: Ashgate, 2001).

entering into the seemingly daunting world of regimental life, with its bewildering number of exclusive customs and rituals, denying the 'civvy' outsider an understanding of its workings. There may also be political motives with some academics not wishing to be associated with a 'complicity in war', and even the glorification of war and conflict, through music.[43] For example, the correlation between violent insurrection and the broadcasting of military music on the radio has presented an unsavoury but frequent image, with Lapado calling it 'a global trend' and at least twenty-four examples from preliminary research.[44] Olatunji notes that the broadcasting of martial music in Nigeria during military rebellions was 'almost synonymous with "another military take over".'[45] It is hard to disassociate military music from these events and so the connection between music and the military can be distasteful. On the other hand, for some researchers it is this very connection with the military that makes it so attractive, particularly for enthusiasts and writers from within the military who tend to have a positive bias towards the army and its bands.[46]

There has been a recent attempt to consider military music in the political sphere by Khan,[47] but unfortunately a significant amount of the material presented as fact is spurious, and there is too much reliance on questionable secondary sources. Furthermore, some of the speculations are too far fetched to take seriously – a 'third world war' on military bands for example. This is regrettable as there are some interesting considerations of soft power in the text.

---

[43] D. A. Wilson, 'Consequential Controversies', *The Annals of the American Academy of Political and Social Science*, Vol. 502 (Universities and the Military), March 1989, pp. 47-49; see also 'Chapter 6 The Military Mind' and 'Chapter 7 The Academic Mind' in H. J. Howard, *Military Brass vs. Civilian Academics at the National War College: A Clash of Cultures* (Lanham, Maryland: Lexington Books, 2011), pp. 87-121.

[44] O. A. Ladapo, 'Martial Music at Dawn: Introit for Coups d'État', in M. J. Grant and F. J. Stone-Davis (eds), *The Soundtrack of Conflict: The Role of Music in Wartime and in Conflict Situations* (Hildesheim, Germany: Georg Olms, 2013), pp. 200-201.

[45] M. Olatunji, *European styled Military Music in Nigeria: Its Theme, Style and Patronage System* (Saarbrücken, Germany: VDM, 2011), p. 97.

[46] See for example *Band International* and *Journal* of the International Military Music Society <http://www.imms-uk.org.uk/> [accessed 5 June 2013].

[47] S. S. Khan, *When Military Wages Peace: Military Bands in Diplomace, War & Statecraft* (New Delhi, India: Pentagon Press, 2019).

Introduction   13

This positioning of military music on the periphery of conventional discussions of both music and the military leaves a gap in the literature, leading to the overarching research question of this book: What was the role and impact of military music on the music industry, the military, and society in the interwar years? To help answer this question, the study is also guided by a series of sub-questions: Why has military music in the interwar period not been considered important? Who were the performers? When did they perform their music? What was their role? Where did they fit within the music industry? And how should the position of military music in the interwar period be investigated?

A starting point to answer these questions requires consideration of extant research material available. An early endeavour to collate a military band bibliography was made by Paine in 1928,[48] but despite his enthusiasm for what he considered a large amount of available research material, Paine's list has hardly developed since. Bannister's more recent (2002) critical review of military band literature is useful but, with only a few exceptions, it does not consider primary source material.[49] As already mentioned, Herbert and Barlow's study of military music in the nineteenth century is the most important recent contribution, but the dearth of new writing on military bands has meant that two names – both on Paine's list – have remained the main sources in academic writing: Jacob Kappey and Henry George Farmer. While their work is significant it is in urgent need of updating.

Bandmaster Jacob Kappey's *Military Music: A History of Wind Instrumental Bands* (1894) was the main reference for military music in the early twentieth century, but Henry Farmer was probably the first significant researcher to consider military music as having made a meaningful impression on the musical establishment, with his writings spanning from Edwardian times until his death in 1965. Farmer's work is most interesting because he combined it with a lifelong career as a practising musician as well as study in the fields of Arab and Scottish music.[50] Farmer was on the executive committee of the Musicians' Union and a member of the British Broadcasting

---

[48] J. Paine, 'A Bibliography of British Military Music', *Journal of the Royal United Service Institute*, Feb 1, 73, 1928, pp. 334-341.
[49] R. Bannister, 'How are we to write our music history? Perspectives on the historiography of military music', in *Musicology Australia*, 25:1, 2002, pp. 1-21.
[50] For a complete list of his work see C. Cowl and S. H. Craik, *Henry George Farmer: a Bibliography*, (Glasgow: Glasgow University Libraries, 1999).

Corporation's (BBC) Musical Advisory Board, and his interests extended to writing on philosophy, politics, and religion. Furthermore, he had been a military musician himself before the First World War – 'Sometime 2nd Band Corporal Royal Artillery Band'[51] – and had participated in many of the important parades at the turn of the nineteenth and twentieth centuries, providing him with an insight into the workings of the military and its culture. Herbert describes Farmer's work as 'the starting place for new schematic research of the history of military music',[52] and so it would be appropriate to reassess Farmer's four related research themes[53]:

1. Military music and its response to changes and developments in military regulation
2. The function of music in specific and routine military ceremonial
3. Individual military bands as quasi-independent institutions
4. The associated relationship between military music and other musical traditions

Herbert and Barlow's study into nineteenth-century military bands can be broadly allied to these themes, but even though they provide a sound starting point they are in need of updating in order to incorporate issues pertinent to the twentieth century, such as broadcasting, recording, and the political employment of military bands. In order to re-calibrate the research areas, two further themes should be added to complement those by Farmer:

5. The position of military music in the music industry
6. Military music in marketing, propaganda, and diplomacy, at home and abroad

While the current study follows on in the manner of Herbert and Barlow's research, its main contribution to musicology is twofold: to fill the gap in research on military bands in the interwar period; and to address this research using analytical models relevant to the twentieth century.

---

[51] Farmer, *History of the Royal Artillery Band*, p. iii.
[52] T. Herbert, 'Farmer's Contribution to the Study of Military Music', in Cowl and Craik, *Henry George Farmer*, p. xxi.
[53] *Ibid*, p. xx.

To structure the analysis, key models from the business and management literature have been drawn upon, particularly from work on organisational theory and strategy. While most of the models have been used for the analysis of commercial business they can equally be applied to not-for-profit and government organisations and, with some adaption, there is significant relevance in applying the models to the historical analysis of military music.

Methodology: the models

There are several models that could have been selected, but as a preliminary investigation it was decided to use accepted standard models associated with three interrelated areas that have an impact on how organisations operate: the far external environment, with Fahey and Narayanan's 'STEP' model; the near external environment, with Porter's 'five forces'; and the internal environment, with Johnson's 'cultural web' (Fig. 1.1).

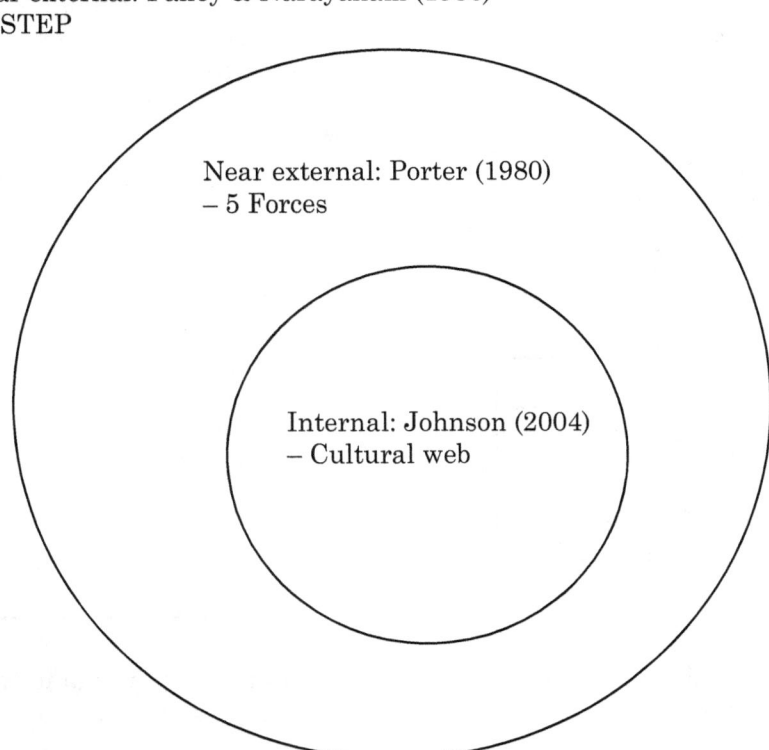

Figure 1.1
The three environments and the relevant models for analysis

Although military music is not a single entity, for the purpose of this study the associated functions and composition of military bands will be considered similar enough to regard them as a distinctive organisational structure.

For the far external environment Fahey and Narayanan's model deconstructs the social, technological, economic, and political domains (known as 'STEP' and already referred to above).[54] Exploration of these domains reveals the outside influences on organisations that will affect the way they operate, such as conflicts, elections and changes in social structures, with those factors affecting military bands in the interwar years shown in Fig. 1.2. It is rare that organisations have an immediate impact on these domains, but they can have an influence over time.

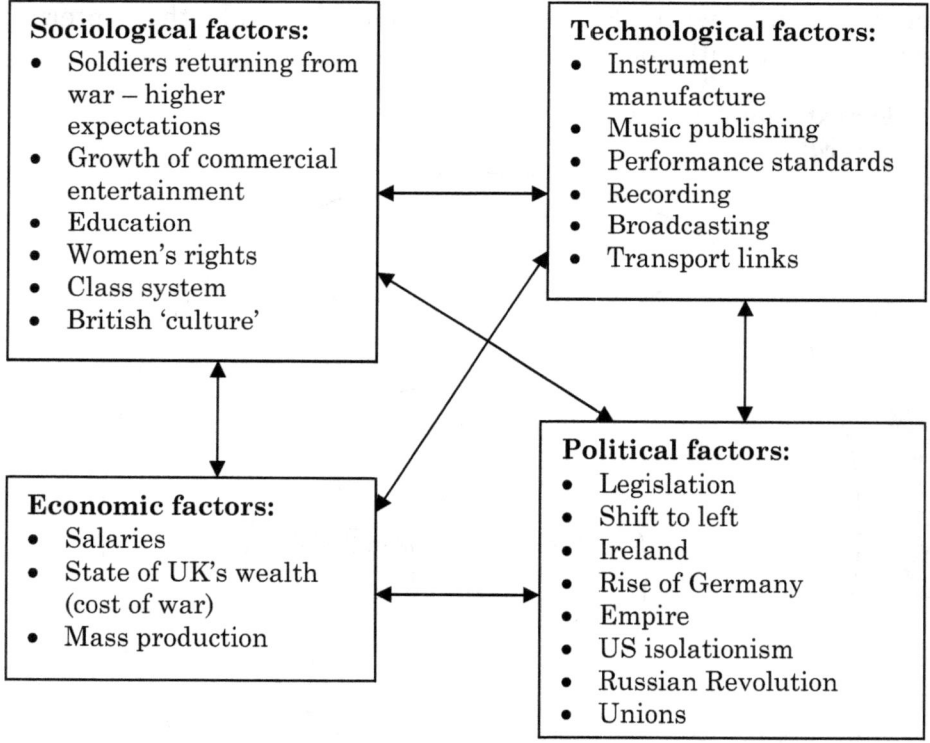

Figure 1.2
'STEP' analysis of factors in the interwar years that affect organisations from the external environment

---

[54] Fahey and Narayanan, *Macroenvironmental Analysis*.

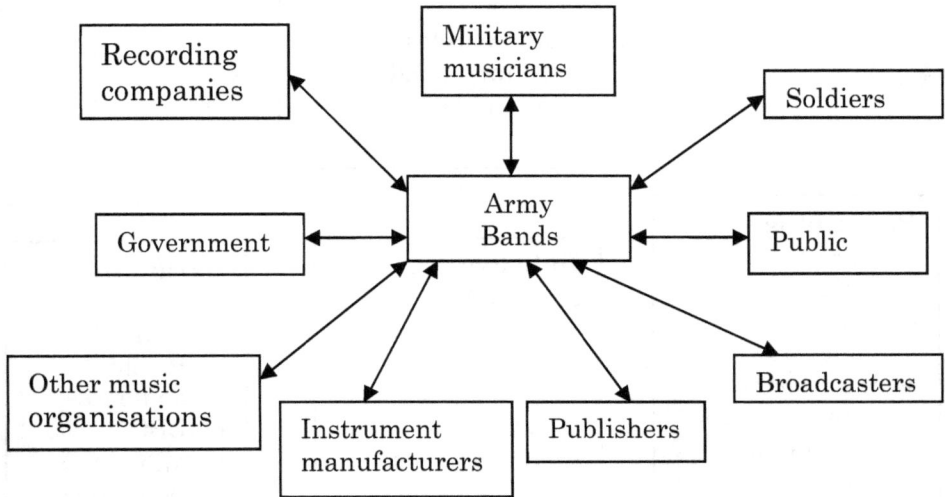

Figure 1.3
Stakeholders associated with army bands

The near external environment is concerned with forces that directly impact the way organisations function and comprise a number of stakeholders – those that had a legitimate interest – with stakeholders associated with interwar military bands shown at Fig. 1.3.[55]

Porter's 'industry structure' or 'five forces' model considers these stakeholders as customers, suppliers, substitute devises, and new entrants to the market, and how they interconnect with the industry structure,[56] in this case the music industry, illustrated in Fig. 1.4.

---

[55] Stakeholders can be described as 'any group or individual who can affect or is affected by the achievement of the organisation's objectives'. See R. E. Freeman, *Strategic Management: A Stakeholder Approach* (Boston, MA: Harper Collins, 1984); R. K. Mitchell, B. R. Agle, and D. J. Wood, 'Towards a theory of stakeholder identification and salience: defining the principle of who and what really counts,' *Academy of Management Review*, 22, 4, 1997, pp. 853–86.
[56] M. E. Porter, *Competitive Strategy: Techniques for Analysing Industries and Competitors* (New York: The Free Press, 1980).

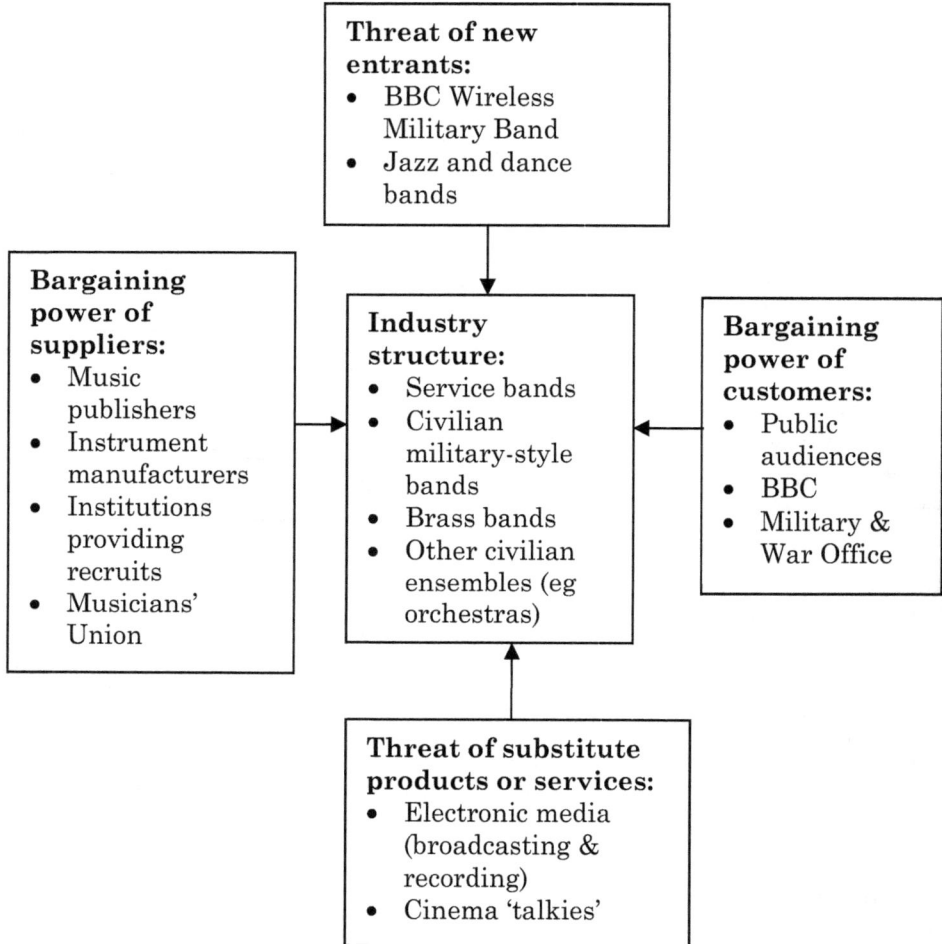

Figure 1.4
Porter's five forces affecting army bands in the interwar near external environment

The music industry in Britain changed considerably in the twenty years of the interwar period with several major episodes, such as the development of gramophone recording and broadcasting, having significant bearing on the way the industry operated. There were also other less forcible, yet significant, issues that swayed the industry's evolution, such as the merging of instrument manufacturing companies,[57] and the move towards a standard musical pitch.[58] All the issues were in some way interconnected and their influence on the industry depended on the relative salience of the stakeholders involved (Fig. 1.3), the appetite for various markets to receive them,[59] and the resources available to achieve change. This dynamic process was contingent on the interaction of five different forces: the structure of the industry, the customers, the suppliers, the threat of new entrants, and the availability of substitute products or services (Fig 1.4).[60]

The structure of the music industry was based around those who performed music, comprising professional musicians employed as performers in the military, orchestras, theatre and cinema ensembles, as well as the various amateur groups, including brass bands and part-time military bands, who were working in comparable markets. Customers were not only the consumers who listened to the music performed, but also stakeholders who used military music as a platform for ceremonial and entertainment (the military and War Office) or for broadcasting (the BBC), for example.

The industry could not operate without suppliers and this force comprised those who provided products or services that enabled the musicians to perform, including instrument manufacturers, music publishers, and the institutions that provided many of the boys who were to become recruits. As a trade body for musicians in the industry, the Musicians' Union can also be counted as a supplier of services.

New entrants in this case were predominantly musicians providing the same service but in a different context, such as the BBC Wireless Military Band, but also jazz and dance bands who were responding to changes in musical tastes. Substitute products entering the market had an enormous effect on the way musicians carried out their work. This was particularly evident with the

---

[57] For example, Boosey & Company merged with Hawkes & Son in 1930, creating a single instrument manufacturing concern.
[58] During the 1920s and 30s British army bands changed the pitch of their instruments from 'high' or 'Old Philharmonic' to the civilian standard 'low' or 'New Philharmonic' pitch.
[59] M. Christopher, A. F. T. Payne, and D. Ballantyne. *Relationship Marketing: Bringing Quality, Customer Service and Marketing Together* (Oxford: Butterworth Heinemann, 1991). Christopher, *et al*, suggest that there are six markets: customer, supplier, recruitment, referral, influencers, and internal.
[60] See Porter, *Competitive Strategy*.

challenge to live music performance when commercial recording became viable, broadcasting changed listening habits, and the cinema organ and 'talkies' reduced the demand for musicians performing live for films, which by 1932 had probably put 12,000 to 15,000 musicians out of work in one fell swoop.[61]

The internal environment concerns the conditions, events, and entities that influence the tactical and strategic choices an organisation makes; what might be called the culture. There have been many attempts to define culture but one of the more practical, advocated by organisational management theorists in the 1960s, expressed it as 'the way we do things around here'.[62] This simple description helps to identify some of the idiosyncrasies of military band culture, particularly as Gregory points out, 'one can only begin to understand the music of another culture if one understands the culture'.[63] Johnson's 'cultural web' model aptly provides a focus for discussion in this environment (Fig 1.5).[64]

The six cultural 'artefacts',[65] as Johnson calls them, all influence the paradigm which is described as 'the core set of beliefs and assumptions which fashion an organization's view of itself and its environment'.[66] Like all environmental issues they change over time with some artefacts gaining greater salience at different times. For example, the influence of power structures could depend on personalities involved, and in the case of the Royal Military School of Music (RMSM), where various Directors of Music and Commandants had differing priorities, and bands' perception of their relationship with the RMSM could affect their manner of performance.

---

[61] C. Ehrlich, *The Music Profession in Britain since the Eighteenth Century: A Social History* (Oxford: Clarendon, 1985), p. 210.
[62] M. Bower, *The Will to Manage: Corporate Success Through Programmed Management* (New York: McGraw-Hill, 1966), p. 22.
[63] A. H. Gregory, 'The roles of music in society: the ethnomusicological perspective', in D. J. Hargreaves and A. North (eds), *The Social Psychology of Music* (Oxford: Oxford University Press, 1997), p. 138.
[64] G. Johnson, 'Managing Strategic Change: Strategy, Culture and Action,' in S. Segal-Horn, (ed.) *The Strategy Reader* (Malden, MA: Blackwell, 2004), pp. 279-292.
[65] *Ibid*, p. 281.
[66] *Ibid*, p. 282.

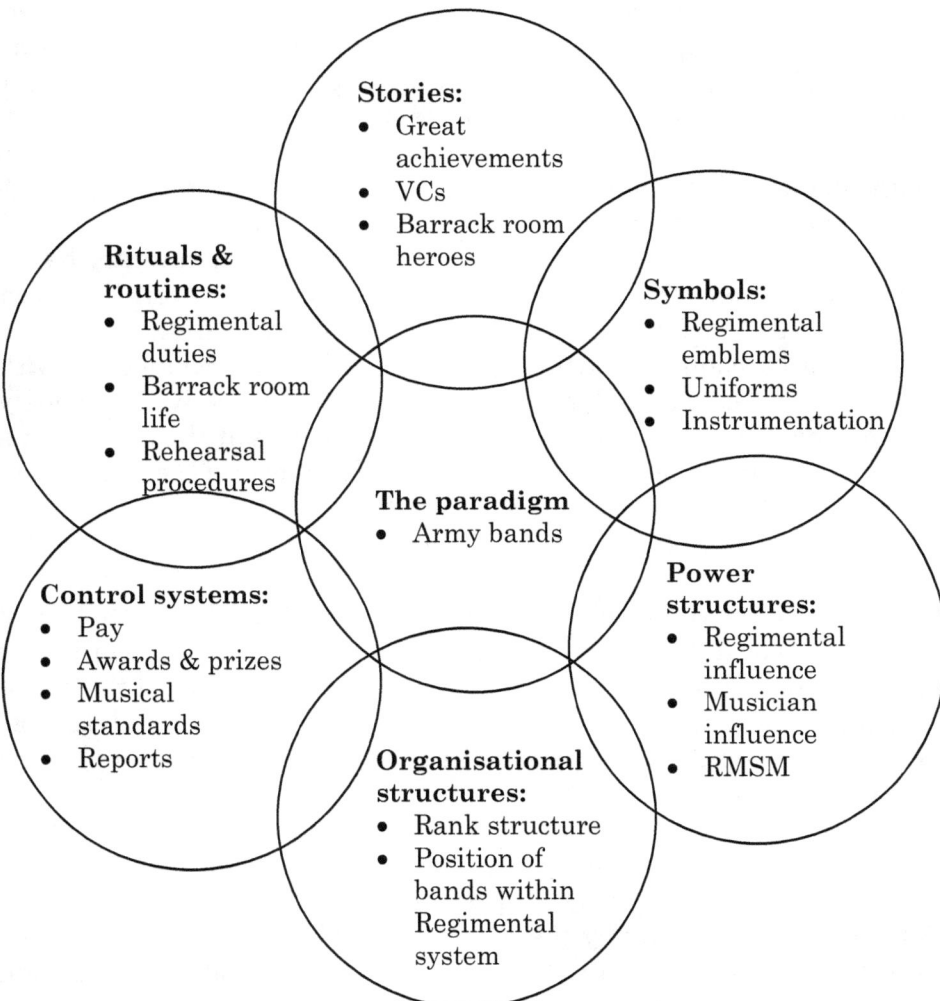

Figure 1.5
The army band 'cultural web' in the interwar years

In order to help understand these relationships one source is first-hand accounts, available either published as memoirs, or as audio files from archives such as the Imperial War Museum.[67] But Higham provides a word of caution about military autobiographies, particularly after the First World War, in that they 'are generally written by those who were exceptional or non-conformist....Few

---

[67] Imperial War Museums Collections <http://www.iwm.org.uk/collections> [accessed 23rd October 2017].

memoirs or biographies deal with ordinary garrison life in the interwar years, unfortunately.'[68] Ex-bandsman Norman Wisdom's autobiography[69] is certainly that of an exceptional person – he was to become a famous actor and comedian – but there are several additional first-hand accounts that corroborate his story by other ex-bandsmen, and Higham's concerns probably do not apply to bands as they were not part of a directly recruited officer corps.

One of the additional considerations for analysing military bands has been that the research material crosses several subject boundaries. Without sacrificing the depth of research, this has been taken into account as much as possible, such as the connection with leisure studies, particularly as military band music was so widely experienced by lower- and middle-class audiences at the seaside at a time of thriving leisure activities, despite the effects of the Depression in the 1930s.[70]

Scope

The term 'interwar' would suggest a set period bounded by the end of the First World War in 1919 and beginning of the Second World War in 1939 and these parameters have been broadly adhered to, except for some cases where pre-First World War background analysis was deemed appropriate. This is also the case for the occasional reference to occurrences beyond 1939.

A clarification of terminology is required. Throughout the book the terms 'military' and 'army' are used and they are occasionally interchangeable, but 'army' is specific in that it excludes all those not employed in the army by the War Office. 'Military', while generally referring to the army can also mean military-like, such as a civilian military-type band which performs and dresses in a similar fashion to the army. Where clarity is required it is explained in the text.

In this study there is little reference to the army's part-time military bands, for two reasons: first, their way of operating was much more akin to civilian bands, and second, it is extraordinarily

---

[68] Higham, *Armed Forces in Peacetime*, p. 42, fn. 3 & p. 90, fn. 4. This was also the case in previous periods, with one or two notable exceptions. See for example J. Crook, *The Very Thing: The Memoires of Drummer Richard Bentinck, Royal Welch Fusiliers, 1807-1823* (London: Frontline Books, 2011).
[69] N. Wisdom and W. Hall, *My Turn* (London: Arrow, 1992).
[70] P. Bailey, 'The Politics and Poetics of Modern British Leisure', in *Rethinking History*, 3:2, 1999, p. 135.

difficult to discover anything about these bands, with only a few anecdotal articles available.[71] On occasion they are referred to in the text when a particular instance is considered appropriate, but this is an area ripe for further study as there is almost no mention of the Territorial Army bands in music or military histories, including Beckett's otherwise comprehensive *Britain's Part-Time Soldiers*.[72]

Writers often interchange the terms brass and military bands and so it can be unclear what they mean. This may seem insignificant but the traditions were different and this book does not consider the role of brass bands, although they are referred to on occasion when they were employed as Territorial Army battalion bands. Similarly, corps of drums, bugles, pipes and drums, and regimental trumpeters, do not come under the remit of this study as they grew from a separate tradition.[73] These instrumentalists had a different role to bandsmen in the army in the interwar years, although often performing alongside bandsmen for larger events. Their tasks were decided at a regimental level and could vary from close attachment to a band, to operating as a separate entity. Tanner's *Instruments of Battle* provides a fine history of British army drummers and buglers, with Norris's *Marching to the Drums* being a less thorough text.[74] For the role of pipes in the army, Murray's *Music of the Scottish Regiments* affords a very thorough account and also considers the regimental bands, but there is little on the period that is the main focus of this book.[75]

The bands of the Royal Navy, Royal Marines, Royal Air Force, and police are not examined in this study except where issues have specific relevance to the army. With the opening of the Royal Air Force School of Music in 1918, and the development of the Royal Naval School of Music, this further increased the pool of musicians schooled in a Service state-funded institution and their stories are linked to those of army bands, as they experienced similar issues in

---

[71] For example, A. W. Selth, 'Territorial Bands', *The Leading Note*, October, 1928, p. 11.
[72] I. F. W. Beckett, *Britain's Part-Time Soldiers: The Amateur Military Tradition 1558-1945*, 2nd edn (Barnsley: Pen & Sword Military, 2011).
[73] See Chapters 1 and 2 of Herbert and Barlow, *Music and the British Military*.
[74] J. Tanner, *Instruments of Battle: The Fighting Drummers & Buglers of the British Army from the Late 17th Century to the Present Day* (Oxford: Casemate, 2017); J. Norris, *Marching to the Drums: A History of Military Drums and Drummers* (Stroud: Spellmount, 2012). Both books have almost nothing on the interwar years.
[75] D. Murray, *Music of the Scottish Regiments* (Edinburgh: Mercat, 2001 [1994]).

the interwar period, but there are enough differences for them to deserve separate research projects. Literature on the Royal Navy and Royal Marines includes three volumes by Ambler,[76] and the rather outdated (1923) but useful series of articles, *Notes on the Development of Bands in the Royal Navy*, by W. G. Perrin.[77] For the Royal Air Force, two books recount the forming and development of it bands: Singleton's *Music in Blue*, and Kendrick's *More Music in the Air*.[78]

There appears to be only scant information on police bands except in a few isolated chapters, including Wright and Newcomb's *Bands of the World*. They comment that 'the majority of police bands are organized along military lines',[79] and this would appear to be the case for the interwar years, with retired army bandmasters and directors of music taking up positions in the police.[80] This is another area for further research.

There is one large-scale media source that is rarely exploited in this study, that of newsreels. This might seem an unjustified omission as although the viewing of newsreels at cinemas was predominantly a working class activity, in terms of numbers attending they were at least as popular as the buying of newspapers or listening to the radio, and by 1933 the equivalent of a feature film was made every week by the industry.[81] Nevertheless, the newsreel industry should be considered as a journalistic enterprise, with competition between the five main producers more about the scoop rather than the quality or accuracy of material and, as a source of information, it can be unreliable: newsreel companies always combined actual footage with stock footage and so it is difficult to tell

---

[76] J. Ambler, *The Royal Marines Band Service*. Special Publication Number 28 (Southsea: The Royal Marines Historical Society, 2003); J. Ambler, *The Royal Marines Band Service: Volume 2*. Special Publication Number 37 (Portsmouth: The Blue Band, 2011); J. Ambler, *World War I Remembered: Royal Marines Buglers and Musicians at War*. Special Publication Number 47 (Portsmouth: The Royal Marines Historical Society/The Royal Marines Band Service, 2019).
[77] W. G. Perrin, 'Notes on the Development of Bands of the Royal Navy', *The Mariner's Mirror*, six articles from Vol 9, No 1 to Vol 9, No 7, 1923.
[78] G. Singleton, *Music in Blue* (Maidenhead: Eagle & Lyre, 2007); I. Kendrick, *More Music in the Air: The Story of Music in the Royal Air Force* (Ruislip: RAF Music Services, 2011). First edition originally published as I. Kendrick, *Music in the Air: The story of music in the Royal Air Force* (Baldock, Herts: Egon, 1986).
[79] A. G. Wright and S. P. Newcomb, *Bands of the World* (Evanston, Illinois: The Instrumentalist, 1970), pp. 39-48.
[80] *Ibid.*, p. 43.
[81] N. Pronay, 'British Newsreels in the 1930s: 1. Audience and Producers', in *History (Film Section)* (ed. J. A. S. Grenville), 1971, Vol. 56(188), pp. 412-416.

if the film being watched contains footage from the story being referred to by the commentator, or from a previous event.[82] Even so, it was decided that carefully selected sound and video archives from *British Pathé* could be utilised when appropriate.[83]

Perhaps the most significant exclusion from this study is that of the role of women, but that is because in the interwar period the military establishment did not consider there to be any place for women in its bands. Regrettable as it may be, this state of affairs should be considered within the context of attitudes and constraints of society at the time as the exclusively male military band career was established from a young age at the residential institutions for destitute children. This was the recruiting ground for army bands, but girls were denied the opportunity of being accepted, being mostly placed in domestic service: 'The boys had their band and the girls their sewing, singing and cooking'.[84] There is, however, some material for future research in this area which might consider the relationship of the suffragette composer, Ethel Smyth, with military bands, especially the occasions when she conducted military bands, and in particular her involvement at the 1924 British Empire Exhibition.

Structure

The methodological approach has influenced the overarching framework but as aspects of the three environments overlap, and are linked in many ways, their relevance to each section does not bound them to be treated as discrete areas for discussion. They do, however, have more significance to some chapters and so the study is presented according to subject area, rather than chronologically. Many, but not all, of the issues identified in the above models are addressed in the study but due to limitations of space it was deemed appropriate to focus on issues that were most pertinent. There are three parts – culture, performance, and influence – each comprising several chapters.

'Part 1 – Culture' is broadly analogous to Farmer's first and third research themes (military music and its response to changes and developments in military regulation; individual military bands as quasi-independent institutions). Comprising chapters two and three,

---

[82] N. Pronay, 'British Newsreels in the 1930s: 2. Their Policies and Impact', in *History (Film Section)* (ed. J. A. S. Grenville), 1971, Vol. 57(189), p. 70.
[83] British Pathé <http://www.britishpathe.com/> [accessed 5 Jul 13].
[84] G. Pugh, 'London's Forgotten Children: Thomas Coram and the Foundling Hospital'. Transcript of lecture given at Gresham College, 12 March 2012, p. 7.

the analysis models from the internal and near external environment are most relevant when examining matters around the people involved, where they came from, and how they interacted with the military.

Chapter 2 'The Gentlemen of the Regiment' considers the personnel who made up the bands and their relationship with the army. There has been very little work in this area, with the exception of Boyle's focus on Australian bands and Bannister's earlier work, also looking at Australian bands.[85] Several books are useful sources on charting the number of bands, including their names and personalities involved, particularly Turner and Turner's three volumes on military bands.[86] Furthermore, official documents such as *The King's Regulations and Orders for the Army* and other written orders, such as Army Council Instructions (ACIs), as well as regiments' own Standing Orders, provide details of the inner workings of a regiment, including the regimental band. For example, *Regimental Standing Orders of The Manchester Regiment, 1930*,[87] provides specific instructions on the duties of the band. Care has been taken when referring to these official documents, however, as there is considerable evidence from photographs and first-hand accounts that they were commonly ignored, but they provide initial references for policy.

Similar sources are used for Chapter 3 "Breaking In' the Young Hands: The Dependence on Band Boys', with Charles Nalden's *Half and Half: The Memoirs of a Charity Brat*,[88] and three of Spike Mays'

---

[85] S. Boyle, 'Organizational Identity or Esprit De Corps? The Use of Music in Military and Paramilitary Style Organisations', paper presented at the 3rd International Critical Management Studies Conference, Lancaster, 7-9 July 2003, <https://www.mngt.waikato.ac.nz/ejrot/cmsconference/2003/proceedings/music/boyle.pdf> [accessed 17th September 2017]; S. Boyle, 'And the Band Played On: Professional Musicians in Military and Service Bands', *International Journal of Arts Management*, 6, 3, Spring, 2004, pp. 4-12; R. Bannister, 'Watching Paint Dry: Musical Meaning in a Military Ceremony', *Australian Defence Force Journal*, No. 106, May/June, 1994, pp. 33-40.

[86] G. Turner and A. Turner, *Cavalry and Corps: The History of British Military Bands, Vol. 1* (Staplehurst, Kent: Spellmount, 1994); G. Turner and A. Turner, *Guards and Infantry: The History of British Military Bands, Vol.2* (Staplehurst, Kent: Spellmount, 1996); G. Turner and A. Turner, *Infantry and Irish: The History of British Military Bands, Vol. 3* (Staplehurst, Kent: Spellmount, 1997).

[87] *Regimental Standing Orders of The Manchester Regiment: By Order of The Colonel Commanding, 1st June, 1930* (Aldershot: Gale & Polden, 1930).

[88] C. Nalden, *Half and Half: The Memoirs of a Charity Brat 1908-1989* (Tauranga, New Zealand: Moana Press, 1989).

collection, *Fall Out the Officers*, *The Band Rats*, and *The First and the Last*,[89] providing a good starting point – but there are several others listed in the references. Many documents have been accessed at the London Metropolitan Archives (LMA),[90] and aural accounts have come from the Imperial War Museum, as stated above. British *Hansard* Parliamentary reports from the twentieth century have also been used for relevant debates in the House of Lords and the House of Commons.[91] Some work on boy musicians has already been carried out in the area of band boys, but they deal with specific periods or institutions, such as Sheldon's 'The Musical Careers of the Poor',[92] which concentrates on pre-First World War institutions, and Gledhill's 'Coming of Age in Uniform',[93] focusing on a single institution, the Foundling Hospital. Furthermore, other work into the role of boy soldiers tends not to consider the role of band boys as a discrete vocation, referring to them all as drummers.[94]

'Part 2 – Performance' relates to Farmer's second and fourth research themes, and also the fifth supplementary theme (the function of music in specific and routine military ceremonial; the associated relationship between military music and other musical traditions; the position of military music in the music industry). Made up of chapters four, five, and six, it is based around models from the near external environment, considering the nature of the music played by military bands, the different circumstances encountered, and the variety of audiences that were exposed to bands.

---

[89] S. Mays, *Fall Out the Officers* (London: Eyre & Spottiswoode, 1969); S. Mays, *The Band Rats* (London: Peter Davies, 1975); S. Mays, *The First and the Last* (London: Janus, 1975).
[90] London Metropolitan Archives <https://www.cityoflondon.gov.uk/things-to-do/london-metropolitan-archives/Pages/default.aspx> [accessed 23rd October 2017].
[91] Historic Hansard (House of Lords)
<http://hansard.millbanksystems.com/lords/C20> [accessed 23rd October 2017];
Historic Hansard (House of Commons)
<http://hansard.millbanksystems.com/commons/C20> [accessed 23rd October 2017].
[92] N. Sheldon, 'The musical careers of the poor: the role of music as a vocational training for boys in British care institutions 1870-1918', *History of Education*, Vol. 38, No. 6, November, 2009, pp. 747-759.
[93] J. Gledhill, 'Coming of Age in Uniform: the Foundling Hospital and British Army Bands in the Twentieth Century', *Family and Community History*, Vol. 13/2, November, 2010, pp. 114-127.
[94] For example, R. van Emden, *Boy Soldiers of the Great War*, rev. edn (London: Bloomsbury, 2012).

Russell has argued that subcultures in music can show support to the formal power structures,[95] and this is one of the subjects discussed in Chapter 4 'Seaside, Ceremonial, and an Unhappy Union: Bands and Live Performance'. Sources for this chapter have included military bands' involvement in State ceremonial as recorded in Dean and Turner's *Sound the Trumpets Beat the Drums*,[96] and also the comprehensive programme lists for the annual Queen's/King's Birthday Parades itemised by Dean.[97] For band concerts there are many programmes at the archive of the Museum of Army Music (MAM), Kneller Hall,[98] and it is possible to track the changes in programming over the two decades of the 1920s and 30s. Occasional private publications, such as Wilson's *Regimental Music of the Queen's Regiment*,[99] are important for understanding the musical aspect of regimental tradition. King's College London (KCL) Basil Liddell Hart Archives and the Aldershot Military Museum have provided some background on tattoos.

There are several notable omissions of army bands from the academic music literature in this area, such as Range, who does not refer to the role of miltary music in his studies on music at British coronations and royal and state funerals, apart from the most cursory mention of bands lining the routes.[100] Moreover, there is no attempt to consider the role of the fanfares played by the Household Cavalry State Trumpeters, who played for the sovereign's arrival and departure, or the Kneller Hall trumpeters, who played at the very moment the crown was placed.[101]

---

[95] Russell, *Popular Music in England*, p. 149.
[96] C. Dean and G. Turner (eds), *Sound the Trumpets Beat the Drums: Military Music through the 20th Century* (Tunbridge Wells: IMMS/Parapress, 2002).
[97] C. Dean (ed.), *Music Programmes from the Sovereigns' Birthday Parades Trooping the Colour 1864-2008* (n.p.: International Military Music Society, 2008); C. Dean (ed.), *Supplement to Music Programmes from the Sovereigns' Birthday Parades 1864-2008* (n.p.: n.d.).
[98] Since 1994 Kneller Hall has been home to Headquarters Corps of Army Music (HQ CAMUS) and the Royal Military School of Music (RMSM). The Museum of Army Music archive comprises material not only from the RMSM but also from field army bands. See Museum of Army Music
<http://www.army.mod.uk/music/23294.aspx> [accessed 23rd October 2017].
[99] L. M. B. Wilson, *Regimental Music of the Queen's Regiment* (n.p., 1980).
[100] M. Range, *Music and Ceremonial at British Coronations: From James I to Elizabeth II* (Cambridge: Cambridge University Press, 2012), p. 13.
[101] M. Range, *British Royal and State Funerals: Music and Ceremonial since Elizabeth I* (Martlesham: Boydell & Brewer, 2016).

Jeffrey Richards, on the other hand, in his *Imperialism and Music: Britain 1876-1953* has several chapters on the significance of the role of military music in promoting the idea of Empire, particularly in chapter seven, which chronicles the Aldershot Tattoo.[102] Richards' discussion of the military band and its music leads to the supposition that there was a military band style and genre all of its own that was sometimes replicated on the piano or by the orchestra, but he does rely almost entirely on a single source for each section: Trendell for Kenneth Alford, and Oakley for Sir Vivian Dunn.[103] Furthermore, Lieutenant Colonel Mackenzie-Rogan's autobiography, *Fifty Years of Army Music*,[104] is fascinating but Mackenzie-Rogan's self-aggrandisement means that it may not be fully reliable as a single source for Richards' material.

Chapter 5 'A Clear and Homogenous Sound: Performance Practice and Recording' addresses the contribution of military bands to the recording industry and why the military band sound was particularly suitable for recording in the early years. There is also consideration of the reasons why military band recordings became less popular in the 1930s. The important re-issue of some recordings from the 1920s and 30s carried out by the British Military Music Archive are used for this chapter,[105] as well as other recordings. But apart from the recordings themselves, the two main written primary sources for this chapter have been by recording managers who worked with military bands in the studio: Joe Batten and Fred Gaisberg.[106]

Chapter 6 "Tonic' Music and the Discord with the BBC: Repertoire and Broadcasting' tracks the temperamental relationship between the BBC and military bands, notably the authorities at Kneller Hall, and reveals how personalities at both organisations were responsible for shaping the nature of broadcast military band music. The main primary sources for this chapter have come from the large number of

---

[102] J. Richards, *Imperialism and Music: Britain 1876-1953* (Manchester: Manchester University Press, 2001).
[103] J. Trendell, *Colonel Bogey to the Fore: A Biography of Kenneth J. Alford* (Dover: Blue Band, 1991); D. Oakley, *Fiddler on the March: A Biography of Lieutenant Colonel Sir Vivian Dunn KCVO OBE FRAM Royal Marines* (London: Royal Marines Historical Society, 2000).
[104] J. Mackenzie-Rogan, *Fifty Years of Army Music* (London: Methuen, 1926).
[105] British Military Music Archive <http://www.bmma.org.uk/> [accessed 23rd October 2017].
[106] J. Batten, *Joe Batten's Book: The Story of Sound Recording, Being the Memoirs of Joe Batten, Recording Manager* (London: Rockliff, 1956); F. W. Gaisberg, *Music on Record* (London: Robert Hale, 1946).

military band files at the BBC's Written Archives Centre at Caversham (BBC WAC).[107]

'Part 3 – Influence' primarily corresponds to the supplementary fifth and sixth themes (the position of military music in the music industry; military music in marketing, propaganda, and diplomacy, at home and abroad). Comprising chapters seven, eight, and nine, through a series of case studies it considers issues relevant to the far and near external environments, investigating areas that highlight the part military bands and their music played in shaping events in the music industry, as well as in the national and international political arenas.

Chapter 7 'Kneller Hall and the Pitch Battle with the War Office' investigates the final stages of military bands' eventual shift to low pitch, how the military went about it, and what this meant to the music industry. There has been some research into the issue of pitch, referred to in the chapter, but none considers the process of change that the military underwent in the 1920s and 30s. Much of the primary source material for this chapter has come from files at the National Archives in London (TNA).[108]

Both Chapter 8 'Punching Above Their Weight: The Soft Power Influence of British Army Bands Overseas',[109] and Chapter 9 'The Youghal 'Outrage': Political Appropriation of Military Bands and the Founding of the Irish State', use case studies to uncover how bands participated in, and influenced, various military and diplomatic episodes through direct involvement, and also as a reputational asset and symbol of power. There has been some debate in this area, notably in the journal *Diplomatic History*, including Statler's *The Sound of Musical Diplomacy*.[110] Other research has been Gienow-Hecht's *Sound Diplomacy*,[111] essays in *Music and Diplomacy from the*

---

[107] BBC Written Archives Centre <http://www.bbc.co.uk/informationandarchives/access_archives/bbc_written_archives_centre> [accessed 23rd October 2017].

[108] The National Archives <http://discovery.nationalarchives.gov.uk/> [accessed 23rd October 2017].

[109] An earlier version of this chapter has been published in *The RUSI Journal*: D. B. Hammond, 'Soft Powering the Empire: British Military Bands, Influence and Cultural Imperialism in the Twentieth Century', *The RUSI Journal*, Vol. 158, Issue 5, 2013, pp. 90-96.

[110] K. C. Statler, 'The Sound of Musical Diplomacy', *Diplomatic History*, Vol. 36, No. 1, January, 2012, pp. 71-75.

[111] J. C. E. Gienow-Hecht, *Sound Diplomacy: Music and Emotions in Transatlantic Relations, 1850-1920* (Chicago: Chicago University Press, 2009).

Early Modern Era to the Present,[112] and work by the research group *Music, Conflict and the State*,[113] but they address the role of civilian musicians and rarely, if at all, mention the significance of military bands in the diplomatic arena. More recently, there has been some fascinating research on the military music of the Balkans during the First World War by Vasiljević, particularly on how bands from Serbia were utilised as a symbol of national identity.[114]

In this study it is argued that influence through persuasion and attraction make culture and values the key elements of soft power, and Chapter 8, which assesses military band activity in India, Southern Africa, and China, particularly draws upon Nye's work on the concept of soft power.[115] The National Archives have provided a rich source of information for these chapters, especially for British military intelligence reports from Shanghai, but also documents from the Irish Military Archives (IMA)[116] for Chapter 9. One single particular source has been George Miller's diaries held at the Museum of Army Music. For all the chapters documents have been obtained from the British Library (BL).

The distinct conclusions drawn from these chapters is that during the interwar years British army bands and their music had a significant impact on the musical, military, and political life of the British Isles and farther afield. Firstly, in exploring the internal environment, it will be argued that British army bands maintained a

---

[112] R. Ahrendt, M. Ferraguto, and D. Mahiet (eds), *Music and Diplomacy from the Early Modern Era to the Present* (New York: Palgrave Macmillan, 2014).

[113] Research Group Music, Conflict and the State <https://www.uni-goettingen.de/en/84354.html> [accessed 7th October 2017].

[114] See for example, M. Vasiljević, 'A 'Quiet African Episode' for The Serbian Army in the Great War: The Band of the Cavalry Division and Dragutin F. Pokorni in North Africa (1916–1918)', *New Sound*, 43, I, 2014, pp. 123-156; M. Vasiljević, 'Stanislav Binički (1872–1942) in the Great War: Preserving National Identity and Musical Links with the Homeland', in Milanović, B., (ed.), *On The Margins of the Musicological Canon: The Generation of Composers Petar Stojanović, Petar Krstić and Stanislav Binički* (Belgrade: Serbian Musicological Society, 2019), pp. 301-319; M. Vasiljević and V. Abramović, 'Cultural Diplomacy, Preservation and Construction of National Identity: Dragutin F. Pokorni in North Africa During the Great War', in B. Andrić (ed.), *Proceedings from the International Conference "Elite in the Great War", Novi Sad 27-28. October 2016* (Novi Sad, 2016), pp. 542-553; M. Vasiljević and H. Dajc, 'Between Courtly, Civil and Military Service: Military Musicians in the Principality and Kingdom of Serbia, *Istraživanja, Journal of Historical Researches*, 28, 2017, pp. 118-133.

[115] J. Nye Jr, *Soft Power: The Means to Success in World Politics* (London: Public Affairs, 2004).

[116] Defence Forces Ireland Military Archives <http://www.militaryarchives.ie/en/home/> [accessed 23rd October 2017].

quasi-independent status from the rest of the army, despite War Office attempts to change this, resisting limits on numbers, and maintaining an important social link with residential children's institutions.

In the near external environment, the key points are that bands were a conduit for the army to advance its brand in specific and routine ceremonial events, particularly evident through the involvement in military tattoos and state ceremonial. Although there were disputes with the Musicians' Union and the BBC, British army bands produced a musical product that set the highest standards for wind playing, and through relationships with recording companies and local municipalities, they propagated middlebrow repertoire to diverse audiences. Furthermore, the military adoption of low pitch impacted on key stakeholders in the music industry by forcing them to re-focus their business strategies in order to face the challenges of new entrants to the market from abroad.

Analysis of the far external environment brings into focus how military music was exploited as a soft power influencing tool in response to diplomatic tensions, both to encourage allegiance and as a demonstration of power. Its impact was highly effective in terms of resource cost to the British army, and this source of power was leveraged by the Irish Free State authorities who embraced Irish military music as a powerful cultural brand.

The assessment of these diverse contributions of military bands makes this book a meaningful and original contribution to musicological research of the early twentieth century.

PART 1

CULTURE

CHAPTER 2

THE GENTLEMEN OF THE REGIMENT: MUSICIANS IN THE REGULAR ARMY

Before the First World War army bands had been indelibly linked to the regimental system, with each cavalry regiment and infantry battalion having its own band.[1] The First World War saw a substantial increase in the number of battalions and significant changes to the configuration of army music but, after demobilisation in 1919, the pre-war structure gradually returned. In the immediate post-World War One era regimental establishments were reduced, with the size of the infantry battalion cut from over 1000 officers and men in 1919 to twenty-two officers and 664 men in 1935.[2] There was also the re-assertion of class distinctions that had been prevalent in Edwardian times and the gulf between ranks widened once more.[3] Although men were given a pay increase with a cost-of-living bonus, the Services had their pay reduced by the Anderson Committee in 1923 and, after the financial crisis, pay was further reduced by 15% by the National Emergency Cabinet in 1931 for men who had enlisted after 4 October 1925.[4] Despite the initial pay rise, the regular (full-time) army lacked appeal in a pacifist era and was 8,000 below its establishment by 1931. Barracks were sub-standard and it took boys to far flung parts of the Empire for seven years at a time, away from girls and pubs.[5]

In spite of these drawbacks, the army still comprised a substantial force and, until remobilisation in the late 1930s, the regular army's strength stood at around 135 battalions of infantry, of which half were commonly overseas. This number varied slightly throughout the period but, in general, they were located in the United Kingdom (sixty-seven), India (forty-five), Egypt and the Sudan (eight), the Far

---

[1] R. Holmes, *Soldiers: Army Lives and Loyalties from Redcoats to Dusty Warriors* (London: Harper Press: 2011), p. 477.
[2] R. Higham, *Armed Forces in Peacetime: Britain, 1918-1940, a case study* (London: G. T. Foulis & Co, 1962), p. 100.
[3] Higham, *Armed Forces*, p. 89.
[4] *Ibid*, pp. 92, 137-140 & 142.
[5] *Ibid*, pp. 92 & 235.

East (five), the Mediterranean (four), and on the Rhine (eight). The Cavalry and Royal Artillery were distributed in the same proportions but the Royal Tank Corps stayed in the United Kingdom.[6] In these circumstances, there were approximately 180 official bands, employing some 7,000 full-time musicians.

The significance to the music industry of this large corpus of full-time army musicians has largely been overlooked, probably because they were considered primarily as musicians (and not soldiers) by the military, and as soldiers (and not musicians) by the music profession. For the regular army, the percentage of musicians was around 3% of the 223,599 total army strength,[7] but while this was a small proportion, their profile and status ensured greater prominence. As a segment of professional musicians in Britain, however, the proportion was much higher. A cursory inspection of British census figures reveals that military musicians were a primary stakeholder group in the music industry. The 1921 census discloses that there were 21,000 declared musicians (not including music teachers)[8]; if, at the very least, all military musicians pronounced their occupation in the census to be 'soldier', the most conservative estimate would deduce that the 7,000 military musicians comprised about a quarter of the music profession at the time.[9]

The British army regimental system has been described as 'a collection of warring tribes',[10] highlighting the continued emphasis on individual regimental customs and traditions. The bands and their musicians were a part of this culture who nonetheless maintained

---

[6] J. Keegan, 'The Interwar Years', in R. Higham (ed.), *A Guide to the Sources of British Military History* (London: Routledge & Kegan Paul, 1972), p. 459; The *Army Estimates* and *General Annual Report* were published anually by the War Office and contain the exact figures for 1920-39; The regular army comprised full-time professional soldiers.

[7] *The General Annual Report on the British Army for the Year Ending 30th September, 1923, with which is incorporated the Annual Report on Recruiting, Prepared by Command of the Army Council. Presented to Parliament by Command of His Majesty, 'Section II. – Part I. – Establishment and Strength of the Regular Army, Army Reserve, Militia, Territorial Army, etc.; and of the Militia and Volunteers in the Channel Islands, Malta and Bermuda, on the 1st October, 1923.'* (London: HMSO, 1924), p. 10.

[8] C. Ehrlich, *The Music Profession in Britain Since the Eighteenth Century: A Social History* (Oxford: Clarendon 1985), pp. 193 & 236.

[9] If military musicians logged their profession as 'musician' then the proportion would no doubt have been higher.

[10] Quoted in A. Beevor, *Inside the British Army* (London: Chatto & Windus, 1990), p. 5.

their identity as musicians. Notwithstanding the fact that bandsmen were employed by the War Office, and bound by its rules and regulations, most army bandsmen considered themselves musicians rather than soldiers first. But the soldier-musician relationship was a dilemma for bandsmen as they were expected to maintain the standards of both professions, which were not always fully compatible. Who were these soldier-musicians? And how did they go about their business?

This chapter is associated with Farmer's first and third research themes: military music and its response to changes and developments in military regulation; and individual military bands as quasi-independent institutions. Using a number of artefacts from Johnson's 'cultural web',[11] it considers the relationships involved with organisational structures, power structures, and control systems, that affected the soldier-musician balance, the position of military bands in the army, and also with the role of the Royal Military School of Music (RMSM) as a training establishment and standard setter. Symbols, stories, and rituals and routines are underlying factors in the discussion on the day-to-day business of bands and also the transition from the war-time requirements of bands to that of an interwar footing.

The structure of British army bands

The number of military personnel assigned to regular army bands was clearly expressed in *King's Regulations and Orders for the Army* (KRs)[12]:

> The establishment of a regiment of cavalry and of a battalion of infantry includes for service in the band – 1 bandmaster, 1 sergeant, with for infantry, 1 corporal and 20 privates, and for cavalry, 15 privates, in addition to the establishment of trumpeters, buglers, drummers, fifers and pipers. The N.C.O.s and men will be effective soldiers, perfectly drilled, and liable to serve in the ranks. The numbers stated will not be exceeded. Boys enlisted by special authority for training as musicians, but not included in the establishment, may be clothed like bandsmen, provided that expense to the public is not caused thereby.[13]

---

[11] Johnson, 'Managing Strategic Change'. See p. 21 for the six cultural web artefacts.
[12] In the interwar period there were three updated versions of *The King's Regulations and Orders for the Army* published: the 1912 edition was superseded in 1923, 1928, and 1935.
[13] *The King's Regulations and Orders for the Army* (1912, 233, para 1113); *The King's Regulations and Orders for the Army* (1923, 349, para 1434).

This instruction is clear with the only ambiguity of numbers concerning the recruitment of boys. Nevertheless, from contemporary accounts and photographs it is evident that bands often contained about twice the maximum number prescribed; a practice that had started in the nineteenth century but become increasingly prevalent.

The War Office began to recognise the reality of the size of bands and made an amendment to *King's Regulations* in 1924 removing the specific numbers, and just referring to 'the respective establishments'.[14] An important revision was then made in the *King's Regulations* of 1928,[15] retained in 1935,[16] when it was acknowledged that bands were appointing musicians over the agreed establishments, so that 'band numbers may be temporarily augmented by the inclusion of soldiers from within the unit's establishment' – although the use of the word 'temporary' was optimistic.

Not only did the War Office not know the size of its bands, but in the 1920s it did not know how many bands there were. In 1920 the Deputy Director of Personal Services (Army) (DDPS(A)) indicated that there were 197 regular army bands, but this number was uncorroborated.[17] A further attempt to gather information on bands in 1928 led to a survey put out to regiments and corps asking for details,[18] but only 82 responses were received.[19] This rather perplexing state of affairs meant that the War Office had to overlook the indifference regiments showed towards regulations, as extra band personnel continued to be routinely taken from the strength of each infantry company or cavalry squadron. The Royal Artillery Band had many attached personnel in order to recruit over its establishment, and when 'Bunnie' Mason joined the band in 1907 he was on the establishment of the Royal Garrison Artillery 'attached to the Royal

---

[14] *The King's Regulations and Orders for the Army* (1923 (AO 23, 1924, 8, 750) para 19).
[15] *The King's Regulations and Orders for the Army* (1928, 372, para 1359).
[16] *The King's Regulations and Orders for the Army* (1935, 424, para 1397).
[17] TNA WO/32/3920. Note from Deputy Director of Personal Services (Army) (DDPS(A)) to Director of Personal Services (Army) (DPS(A)), 1920.
[18] TNA WO/32/3915. Letter to the Secretary of State for War from the organising committee of the Federation of British Music Industries, dated 10th December 1925.
[19] TNA WO/32/3916. 'Circular to the Officers Commanding All Units at Home' dated 23rd October 1928, Colonel Dalrymple, Commandant, Royal Military School of Music.

Artillery Band'.[20] The 1st Battalion the King's Own Yorkshire Light Infantry (KOYLI) had a band of forty-two (excluding boys); a number that had not changed a great deal from 1874 when the Band of the 51st King's Own Light Infantry comprised forty-nine instrumentalists, one bandmaster and the addition of twenty buglers.[21] Another band, the Coldstream Guards, increased from thirty-two to sixty-six between 1896 to 1920.[22]

Charles Nalden, who served both as a bandsman and bandmaster in the interwar years, was well aware of the situation:

> As a conservative estimate, I would say that during the second and third decades of the present [twentieth] century, even allowing for the fall of the 'Geddes Axe', there averaged about 6000 bandsmen distributed between upwards of 140 army bands.[23]

Nalden's reckoning is not far off. Even allowing for thirty-five musicians per band would put the total figure around 3,000 full-time musicians, but as regular army bands could be made up of any number from twenty-one to 100 players the number of full-time musicians employed by the army was probably more like 7,000. For example, the Band, 2nd Battalion Hampshire Regiment is pictured at Bordon in 1923 with thirty-five musicians plus four band boys (Fig. 2.1),[24] and similarly a photograph of the Coldstream Guards Band in 1921 shows them with 63 musicians (Fig. 2.2).[25] Other sources, such as Farmer, also describe bands being far larger than established, reporting the Border Regiment Band as sixty strong in 1930, and the

---

[20] H. B. Mason, *Memoirs of a Gunner Bandsman: 1907-1932* (Orpington: Mason, 1978), p. 5.
[21] W. K. Grainger, *The Life and Times of a Regimental Band: A History of the Bands of the King's Own Yorkshire Light Infantry*. The Rifles Office, Pontefract, 1995, MS, pp. 5-7.
[22] *The Musical Times,* 'Obituary: John Mackenzie-Rogan', Vol. 73, No. 1069 (Mar. 1, 1932), p. 272.
[23] C. Nalden, *Half and Half: The Memoirs of a Charity Brat 1908-1989* (Tauranga, New Zealand: Maona, 1989), p. 205. The so-called 'Geddes axe' was the round of public sector cuts made by the the Committee on National Expenditure, chaired by Sir Eric Geddes, in 1921-22; see, for example, A. J. P. Taylor, *English History 1914-1945* (Harmondsworth: Pelican, 1970), pp. 240-241.
[24] The Hampshire Regiment Museum archives, Sgts' Mess Scrapbook.
[25] MAM archive, miscellaneous band group photographs.

numbers in the Royal Artillery Band at eighty-six plus fourteen boys under training, in 1936.[26]

Another problem with estimating the number of military musicians was the title given to the different ranks. The only clear designation is 'Bandsman' (or 'Musician' in the Household bands and Royal Artillery), which was equivalent to the lowest army rank of 'Private.'[27] It becomes more complex once a bandsman was promoted, however, as he would become 'Corporal' and then 'Sergeant', and it is only occasionally possible to discern musicians at a higher rank when 'Band' is prefixed, as for 'Band Corporal' or 'Band Sergeant'. For example, in 1936 the Royal Artillery Band was established for six Band Bombardiers,[28] but the prefix 'Band' was not always used and so it is difficult to track when musicians were being referred to.

The size of bands was also confused by the addition of various corps of drums, trumpets, bugles, fifes, and pipes, all performing on musical instruments but not part of the band establishment. The DDPS(A) at the War Office did not even attempt to delve into this area of regimental music when trying to find out about bands as it was a topic 'about which I am not quite clear'.[29] This was understandable as these soldiers were not trained as full-time musicians but were maintained as a relic of their eighteenth- and nineteenth-century roles as the signal and discipline platoon. Commanding Officers preferred to keep them as sometime performers to add to the prestige of the regiment, and collaboration between these groups and bands varied between regiments. But the decisive factor in determining the size of bands depended upon where it was positioned in the hierarchy of army bands.

---

[26] H. G. Farmer, *History of the Royal Artillery Band 1762-1953* (London: Royal Artillery Institution, 1954), pp. 359 & 369.

[27] Privates in other branches of the army could be known by other names such as 'Gunner', 'Sapper' or 'Trooper', depending upon the regiment or corps. Farmer relates that 'Musican' was actually a separate rank in the Royal Artillery, see H. G. Farmer, *Memoirs of the Royal Artillery Band: Its Origin, History and Progress* (London, Boosey & Co, 1904), pp. 53 & 171.

[28] Farmer, *History of the Royal Artillery Band*, p. 359. 'Bombardier' was the Royal Artillery equivalent of 'Corporal'.

[29] TNA WO/32/3920. Note from Deputy Director of Personal Services (Army) (DDPS(A)) to Director of Personal Services (Army) (DPS(A)), 1920.

The Gentlemen of the Regiment 41

Figure 2.1
The Band of the 2nd Battalion The Hampshire Regiment at Bordon in 1923, re-formed two years after an Irish Republican Army attack (The Royal Hampshire Regiment Museum)

Figure 2.2
Band of the Coldstream Guards, 1921 (MAM)

The hierarchy of army bands

There was always a seniority of regiments and a definite hierarchy of bands that was most clearly articulated in the difference between 'staff' and 'line' bands. It is difficult to find official recognition of the differences and it is only with the BBC, when assessing the quality of army bands in the 1930s, that the differences are made clearer:

> In regard to the term "Staff" Bands, this name is applied to those Bands which have a permanent base instead of being moved about every two years or so, which is bound to occur with most Line regiments. Secondly, the Bands themselves are on a slightly different footing. Whereas in Line regiments each battalion has, more or less, its band – good or indifferent as the case may be – without there being one specially identified with the name of that regiment, "Staff" Bands are definitely identified with the name of the regiment they bear. Thus when we speak of "The Grenadiers" we have in mind only one Band, although such a crack regiment will surely have others. It is certain that in the case of Staff Bands great care and attention is bestowed on them, and their members are regarded not merely from a military angle but also from a musical one.[30]

This description by the BBC is fairly accurate and reveals something of the BBC's view of military bands (see chapter 6). One misleading point is the assumption that staff bands would have more than one band whereas a more precise account would state that the band would be split into smaller ensembles to undertake different engagements. This was not limited to staff bands as most line bands who would often have a 'playing out' band to perform at seaside resorts, made up of the best players, and a 'depot' band comprising new recruits, boys, and those not required.

In 1934, the BBC listed the bands it recognised as 'staff':[31]

Household Brigade: Grenadier Guards, Coldstream Guards, Scots Guards, Welsh Guards, Irish Guards
Household Cavalry: Life Guards, Royal Horse Guards
Royal Engineers, Royal Artillery
Royal Marines
Royal Air Force

---

[30] BBC WAC R27/209/1 Music General Military Bands File 1A 1933-1934. 'BBC Internal Circulating Memo: Military Bands.' From A Buesst to M. E., dated 14th June, 1934.
[31] BBC WAC R27/209/1 Music General Military Bands File 1A 1933-1934. 'Staff Bands.'

The following year this list was revised:³²

> The Life Guards.
> Royal Horse Guards.
> R.A. Band, Woolwich.
> R.A. Band, Portsmouth.
> R.E. Band, Chatham.
> Grenadier Guards.
> Coldstream Guards.
> Scots Guards.
> Welsh Guards.
> (We use the R.A.F. and Royal Marines too, of course, but these are not <u>Army</u> bands).
> The remainder are all non-Staff bands.

Significantly, the Irish Guards have been removed from the list, but this reveals that the BBC's criteria for giving bands 'staff' status was through their own assessment of performance standard and not bands' status within the army. This view is further clarified:

> They [staff bands] have a practically permanent personnel of experienced musicians, and a <u>certain</u> <u>standard</u> of performance can normally be expected. Even then some are definitely better than others and we are not likely to use those which are less good.
>
> [N]on-Staff bands suffer from shifting personnel of young players who have neither the experience, playing physique nor continuity of band service ever to make a <u>really</u> reliable combination.³³

The BBC's fluid description of staff bands is slightly misleading because of its infatuation with standards, but it does highlight that there was a hierarchy of bands in the army and that the reputation of bands and their bandmasters rested on the musical quality of the bands. While there was some confusion both inside and outside of the army about the number, size, and status of regular army bands, the situation becomes even more complicated with the status of unofficial and part-time bands.

---

³² BBC WAC R27/209/1 Music General Military Bands File 1B 1935. 'BBC Internal Circulating Memo: Army Bands.' From Music Ex. To Ent. Ex., dated 23ʳᵈ May 1935.
³³ *Ibid.*

Unofficial and part-time bands

As well as the bands that were supposedly accounted for in *Kings' Regulations*, there were also some unofficial full-time bands. It is hard to put a number to the unofficial bands because all members were manned from misemployed regimental ranks and funded solely by officers. One such band was the Army Service Corps (ASC) Voluntary Band, Aldershot, who were maintained as a full-time private venture.[34] Bandsmen were recruited straight to the band, with the difference from other regular army bands being that they received no funding from the War Office and they technically held positions in the ASC as driver or loader. Unofficial bands, like the ASC Band, carried out the same sort of engagements as the official bands, and in many respects were a continuation of the system of officers' private regimental bands in existence in the early nineteenth century, with a civilian bandmaster in charge. The ASC Band, allowed by the War Office to be raised on a voluntary basis in 1892, finally received official sanction in 1938 'by a reluctant treasury', probably because the Secretary of State for War at the time, Hoare-Belisha, had been a part-time Territorial Army ASC officer.[35]

Even more elusive are the details of bands of the irregular forces and the War Office had not even attempted to calculate the number of these bands, with the DDPS(A) acknowledging that 'no Yeomanry, Militia or Territorial bands (all unauthorised) are included'.[36] Part of the issue was that the re-defining of regular and reserve regiments had created problems for the identification of bands. The extraordinarily complicated changes in the nineteenth and twentieth centuries to the status of the Royal Monmouthshire Royal Engineers (Militia) (R MON RE(M)) shows how regiments were re-roled with

---

[34] J. Sutton (ed.), *Wait for the Waggon: The Story of the Royal Corps of Transport and its Predecessors 1794-1993* (Barnsley: Leo Cooper, 1998).

[35] H. M. Whitty (ed.), *The Story of the Royal Army Service Corps 1939-1945* (London: G. Bell and Sons, 1955), p. 7; S. Ambler, *A Musical Ride: The Story of the Staff Band of the Royal Corps of Transport. With a concise history of the Band's predecessors* (Stilton: MRA Publishing, 2010), pp. 2-6.

[36] TNA WO/32/3920. Note from Deputy Director of Personal Services (Army) (DDPS(A)) to Director of Personal Services (Army) (DPS(A)), 1920. Militias had been absorbed into the Special Reserve in 1908 but the term was officially revived in 1921 with the Territorial Army and Militia Bill (HL Deb 10 August 1921 vol 43 cc371-90) <http://hansard.millbanksystems.com/lords/1921/aug/10/territorial-army-and-militia-bill> [accessed 2nd May 2013].

changing establishments.[37] The regimental archives show that the R MON RE(M) had a band of some sorts from at least 1803 to 1965,[38] with the band being re-established as the regiment evolved,[39] but beyond the regiment itself, little would have been known about this band, particularly by the War Office.

There were also part-time bands that had long associations with their regiments, such as The Duke of Lancaster's Own Yeomanry which had a band since at least 1818. Reformed after the First World War it is clear that musicians were recruited directly from the civilian music profession. The bandmaster in 1922, Mr Henry Mortimer, had studied the clarinet at the Royal Manchester College of Music and played in the Hallé Orchestra under Sir Hamilton Harty.[40] The rank and position of the bandmaster varied considerably as while some bands had civilians in charge, others, such as the Band of the Northumberland Hussars was led by a commissioned officer, Captain H. G. Amers.[41]

Territorial Army Bands usually included non-enlisted men who would wear the uniform but only be paid from the band fund, and invariably be 'most willing to accept a remunerative engagement but dodge regimental duties',[42] which would understandably cause problems for bandmasters. The informal nature of the Territorial Army bands is described by Harry Chapman who served with the 9th

---

[37] 'Letters Confirming the Date of Formation and Precedence of the Regiment' <http://www.monmouthcastlemuseum.org.uk/more/articles/seniority2/page24.html> [accessed 2nd May 2013].

[38] 'The Regimental Archive of the Royal Monmouthshire Royal Engineers (Militia): Rae, James; attested 1803-05-25; Band (horn player)' <http://www.monmouthcastlemuseum-archives.org.uk/regsearch.php?dirsearchterm=Band&submit=Search> [accessed 22nd June 2013]; 'Programme for concert by the band of the RMonRE(M) to celebrate the 550th Anniversary of the Battle of Agincourt', DP34/5, 1965 <http://monmouthcastlemuseum-archives.org.uk/uploads/dp34.pdf> [accessed 22nd June 2013].

[39] The band was eventually subsumed into The Band of The Welsh Volunteers in 1967 which in 2006 became The Regimental Band of The Royal Welsh (<https://www.army.mod.uk/infantry/regiments/30236.aspx> [accessed 22nd June 2013]).

[40] J. Brereton, *Chain Mail: The History of The Duke of Lancaster's Own Yeomanry* (Chippenham: Picton, 1992), p. 196.

[41] J. W. Pegg, *Newcastle's Musical Heritage: An Introduction* (2003), pp. 68-69 <https://www.newcastle.gov.uk/wwwfileroot/legacy/educationlibraries/tbp/historyofmusic.pdf> [accessed 21st November 2017].

[42] A. W. Selth, 'Territorial Bands.', *The "Leading Note" The Journal of The Royal Military School of Music, Kneller Hall*, October, 1928, p. 11.

Battalion The Manchester Regiment from the age of 15 in 1930 as a cornet player. His father had been in the regiment as a clarinettist and his two cousins were also clarinettists in the band. The band practised twice a week, Sunday morning and Thursdays with a 'professional conductor' Mr Shaw. Harry recalls that they often played 'something like Aida…We only did music'. There was no weapons training or stretcher bearer training, and although the band was 'taught how to drill', he reiterates that 'we only did music'. While the 9th Battalion Band was a military (wind band), the 5th (Wigan) Battalion was a brass band,[43] probably a local brass band. Harry's experiences were typical of the bands of the irregular forces and were a continuation of practices that had been going on since the nineteenth century.

There were also numerous civilian bands that modelled themselves on the military format and the symbols and structures of the military band culture proved alluring to those who wanted to replicate not only the sound, but also the look and function of the military band. The civilian City of Ely Military Band began life as the Ely City Band in 1909, taking over the functions of the disbanded Band of the 4th (Militia) Battalion The Suffolk Regiment.[44] The employment of retired army bandmasters by bands such as the Ely band ensured that the military training and culture of these conductors extended into the civilian musical world. Even in the radical Nationalist environment of Southern Ireland in the 1920s, the 'Barrack Street Band', a civilian military band from Cork, employed a former British army bandmaster.[45]

The role of bandsmen

There had been some debate about the role of bandsmen in wartime but other than the general view that bandsmen should be medics

---

[43] H. Chapman, Interviewed by P. M. Hart July 2004. Imperial War Museum Sound Archive (Oral History), 27038, Reel 1 (incorrectly labelled Reel 3).
[44] L. Green, *City of Ely Military Band: Golden Jubilee Celebrating 50 musical years 1962-2012* (Ely: SHBB Publishing, 2012).
[45] R. T. Cooke, *Cork's Barrack Street Silver and Reed Band: Ireland's oldest amateur musical institution* (Cork: Quality Books, 1992), p. 243.

there seems to have been no official policy,[46] which was derided in the popular press (Fig. 2.3).[47]

Figure 2.3
'Facing the Music'. This cartoon from *Punch* in 1906 highlights the debate about the use of military bands in war time

There were many bandsmen who remained working as musicians during the First World War, particularly the staff bands and those in the Household Brigade, which did cause some friction with the Musicians' Union (see chapter 4), but most bandsmen were subsumed into regimental duties, mainly as medical auxiliaries.[48] The decision was not well-liked, however, and the popular press, as well as some

---

[46] See for example 'First-Aid to Wounded in the Army.', *House of Commons Debate*, 9th November 1908, Vol. 195, c1683,
<http://hansard.millbanksystems.com/commons/1908/nov/09/first-aid-to-wounded-in-the-army#S4V0195P0_19081109_HOC_103> [accessed 20th November 2017].
[47] The caption reads: 'It is proposed, with a view to economy, that military bandsmen in future shall become combatants.'
[48] P. L. Binns, *A Hundred Years of Military Music: being the story of the Royal Military School of Music Kneller Hall* (Gillingham, Dorset: The Blackmore Press, 1959), p. 122.

48   British Army Music in the Interwar Years – Culture

famous personalities, such as Rudyard Kipling, argued for the role of military band music in wartime to be maintained (Fig. 2.4).[49] They were partially successful in their arguments and eventually Divisional bands were created by the War Office.[50]

Figure 2.4
Punch in 1915, quoting Kipling, questioned the decision to reduce the bands in the First World War

---

[49] The caption reads: 'A band revives memories, it quickens association, it opens and united the hearts of men more surely than any other appeal can, and in this respect its aids recruiting perhaps more than any other agency.' Mr. Rudyard Kipling at the Mansion House meeting promoted by the Recruiting Bands Committee.
[50] See D. Jones, *Bullets and Bandsmen: The Story of a Bandsman on the Western Front* (Salisbury: Owl Press, 1992).

Prior to this, and in the habit of ignoring War Office regulations, regiments had begun recruiting their own bands alongside the reserve battalions that had been created to maintain the war effort. Some of these were probably civilian bands recruited directly into the local battalion and it was not uncommon for brass band conductors to join the army in the First World War to become bandmasters of battalion bands. Mr. Thomas Valentine, conductor of the Kingston Mills Band, served as bandmaster of the 2nd Battalion Monmouthshire Regiment throughout the war and continued in that position with the battalion at least until 1925, as reported in *The Bandsman*.[51]

Similarly, Mr. R. W. Davison, having been solo cornet with the J. H. Amers Royal Exhibition Band, Southport Corporation Band, and as solo trumpet with the Moody Manners Opera Company, became Bandmaster of the Liverpool Scottish during the First World War, giving him a stepping stone for future civilian bandmaster appointments after the war.[52] In Cornwall, the Band of the 7th Battalion the Duke of Cornwall's Light Infantry had the distinction of being the last military band to play troops into battle when it performed the regimental march for the 5th Battalion as it went forward with bayonets fixed at St Quentin, in 1918.[53] Their bandmaster Sergeant Wynne had been killed earlier in 1918,[54] and the band was almost certainly a locally raised band. Another typical example was the Band of the 2nd/5th Battalion Gloucestershire Regiment which probably comprised musicians from local brass bands, and a few others, including the composer/poet, Ivor Gurney, as second baritone player (Fig. 2.5).[55]

---

[51] 'Bandmaster of the Month: Mr. Thomas Valentine', *The Bandmaster*, Vol. 1, No. 6, 15th August 1925, p. 91.
[52] 'Bandmaster of the Month: Mr. R. W. Davison', *The Bandmaster*, Vol. 1, No. 7, September 1925, p. 107.
[53] H. White, *One and All: A History of the Duke of Cornwall's Light Infantry 1702–1959* (Padstow: Tabb House, 2006), p. 236.
[54] E. Wyrall, *The History of the Duke of Cornwall's Light Infantry 1914-1919* (London: Methuen, 1932; repr. Uckfield, East Sussex: The Naval and Military Press, 2003), p. 396.
[55] 'To Marion Scott, September 1915' and 'To Herbert Howells, September/October 1915 (?)' in R. K. R. Thornton (ed.), *Ivor Gurney: War Letters* (Manchester: Carcanet, 1983), p. 36; 'My Dear Comtesse' in A. Boden (ed.), *Stars in a Dark Night: The Letters of Ivor Gurney to the Chapman Family* (Gloucester: Alan Sutton, 1986), p. 30.

50 British Army Music in the Interwar Years – Culture

Figure 2.5
The Band of the 2nd/5th Gloucestershire Regiment in 1915 with Ivor Gurney, fourth from right, back row (Soldiers of Gloucestershire Museum)

One of the consequences of so many local musicians joining up was that civilian military Bands suffered. For example, in Warrington, the 'T. J. Down's Military Band' was unable to continue performing, largely due to the lack of bass players.[56] But the real significance of these locally raised bands was that they kept regimental music alive throughout the war and demonstrated that there was an appetite for military bands to continue in the army at the regimental level. As a consequence, when the war ended, the regimental bands were re-established. But how did they fit back into the military establishment? And did they differ from their civilian counterparts?

The way we do things around here: the culture of soldier-musicians

It was unusual for soldiers to change regiments and for the military musician it was natural to be brought up in the culture of the regiment he joined. Bandsmen were identified in the military as a trade and they were unlikely to convert to another trade throughout

---

[56] A. Down, *History of T. J. Down's Bands: From February, 1905 to December, 1936* (Warrington: J. Walker, 1938), p.135.

their career, although there were exceptions to this, particularly during wartime when bandsmen could transfer to fighting roles in the regiment.[57] While many bandsmen would have liked to have been associated with their regiment, they were invariably identified as bandsmen by the other soldiers, and not 'proper' soldiers. Regarded with a mixture of disdain, respect, and envy by regimental soldiers, bandsmen were most of all seen as special and, while wearing the same uniform, considered different. Norman Wisdom neatly explains:

> The army would clothe me, feed me, keep me fit and educate me. As bandsmen, among four squadrons numbering eight hundred men, we were even known as "the Gentlemen of the Regiment"![58]

This passage from Norman Wisdom's memoirs shows his enthusiasm for his time in an army band, but it also exposes two aspects of bands that have shaped their function: bands were a part of the army and were bound by the same rules, regulations, and benefits of other soldiers; and bandsmen were somehow different to other soldiers, being treated in a distinct fashion.

This soldier-musician relationship was an uneasy one and Wilfred Bion's observations of bands during the First World War perhaps epitomises the soldiers' view of bandsmen and the difference in cultures. Bion, who was with the Tank Corps, noted:

> The troops in line with us were the 21st Division. This division used to be a good one, but it had been far too knocked about to be much good by this time. On our left we had the K.O.Y.L.I. [King's Own Yorkshire Light Infantry], and actually with us there was the Duke of Cornwall's Light Infantry Band, i.e., a small collection of young boys and unfit men with no knowledge of arms or anything else. Their officers were hopeless.[59]

He goes on to say that the bands seemed to fair better farther back at the 6th Corps Officers Club and Expeditionary Forces Club:

> We had a very pleasant evening. The food was very good and there was a band playing...It was solemn to think of what was coming, as we sat and

---

[57] See R. Napier, *From Horses to Chieftains: With the 8th Hussars 1934-1959*, 2nd edn (Bognor Regis, West Sussex: Woodfield, 2002); A. W. Brown, *A Memoir: from Music to Wars* (Aberdeen: A. W. Brown, 2001).
[58] N. Wisdom and W. Hall, *My Turn* (London: Arrow, 1992), p. 52.
[59] W. R. Bion, *War Memoirs: 1917-19*, ed. F. Bion (London: Karnac, 1997), p. 102.

listened to the band... I was told that whenever the band played, the enthusiasm was terrific.[60]

While Bion was almost certainly referring to one or two of the unofficial bands it highlights the view that soldiers considered bandsmen unsuitable for roles near the front line.

This 'musician first' position is furthered by senior (non-musician) army officers. Two examples, both written in forewords to books by former bandsmen, shows the slightly baffling view 'real' soldiers had of soldier-musicians. The first, penned by Colonel J. S. Cowley, the regimental secretary of the Light Infantry, describes ex-bandsman Bill Grainger's work on the Bands of the King's Own Yorkshire Light Infantry as 'of limited interest',[61] despite the unique contribution to regimental history. Similarly, Field-Marshal The Lord Harding of Petherton, Colonel of The Life Guards, wrote that another ex-bandsman's memoires had 'more to do with the anxieties and triumphs of a musical career than with life in the Army and the sterner business of War'.[62] This opinion comes from a lack of understanding of the bandsmen's culture and how far removed it was from other battalion soldiers. There is almost a sense of incredulity at the bandsman's way of life. What was it that made the 'gentlemen of the regiment' so different?

One significant difference was the privileges afforded bandsmen, which started from enlistment. 'Wilkie' Brown answered an advertisement in the local newspaper for musicians in 1933 for the Band of the 1st Battalion The Argyll and Sutherland Highlanders, at a time when 'only the unemployed or those running away from police or parents of girlfriends were joining the army'.[63] When going for a medical it was found that he had a potential heart problem but he was given a second chance as he was a 'special enlistment for the band'.[64] Once in recruit training, which lasted for five to six months, as a potential bandsman he was not allowed to undertake certain activities, such as boxing, with the Physical Training Sergeant Major making the point: 'if you get your lips damaged, I'll lose my job'.[65]

---

[60] *Ibid*, pp. 114 & 191.
[61] Grainger, *Life and Times*, Foreword.
[62] H. Sutherland, *They Blow Their Trumpets* (London: P. R. Macmillan, 1959), Foreword, p. 5.
[63] Brown, *Memoir*, pp. 14-16.
[64] *Ibid*.
[65] *Ibid*, p. 18.

The privileges continued in the day-to-day routines of bands. Hector Sutherland, when he joined the 2nd Life Guards as a band boy, revealed how a London-based band was indulged:

> I had not yet played with the Regimental Band, whose sole duties it seemed to me, were to arrive in Barracks at a casual 9.30 a.m. for practise from about 10 a.m. until 11 when the whole regiment took a break for refreshment. From 11.30 to 12.30 the band played, and afterwards promptly disappeared to London and elsewhere until the next day. If there was the slightest sign of rain they didn't play outside. Unlike the Foot Guards' musicians, they could either live in or out of Barracks, and apart from a very rare evening's mess playing, they did nothing else.
>
> Another surprising concession was that on Mondays they were not required at all. There had been a long standing privilege which enabled theatrical and music hall rehearsals to be attended by any Regimental musician who happened to have an engagement, which many of them did.[66]

This Monday off-duties was also enshrined in the Royal Horse Guards Standing Orders and would appear to have been an inspired instruction, enabling musicians to develop their musical skills outside of army duties: 'The Band may be granted leave for the day on Mondays by the Director of Music to attend private rehearsals. For this purpose no leave papers are required'.[67] It was undoubtedly seen by the musicians as being chiefly of financial benefit but the ability to develop their musical skills would have been of undeniable advantage to the band. This routine was quite different to that of a cavalry trooper who would have been on duty from the early hours to late evening, tending the horses and carrying out other duties, but the seemingly rogue attitude by bands was apparently tolerated, although not completely understood, by regimental officers, as long as the band favourably represented the regiment when performing.

---

[66] Sutherland, *They Blow Their Trumpets*, p. 24.
[67] 'Royal Horse Guards: Standing Orders', XIV. The Band, Leave (Aldershot: Gale & Polden, 1938), para. 107, p. 40.

Figure 2.6
The Band of the 2nd Life Guards, 1921, before amalgamation with the 1st Life Guards (Household Cavalry Band archive)

The continued compulsory band subscriptions of regimental officers was one reason why regimental bands were still considered the property of their regiments and while the public purse paid for bandsmen's salaries, officers continued to be responsible for all other expenses, giving up twenty days' pay each year for the privilege. This topic had been discussed by the War Office Council in 1900 and a decision was deferred, but although it did signal the start of the move away from regimental ownership of bands, it was by no means the end.[68] Part of the issue was competition between regiments, with an escalation of one-upmanship costing officers a significant amount. This competition even involved the bands creating sub-cultures within regiments. For example, Hector Sutherland was aware of the differences between the Bands of the 1st and 2nd Life Guards (Fig. 2.6), and when they merged in 1922 to form the Band of The Life Guards (1st and 2nd) 'the heartaches and disappointments of that merger

---

[68] TNA WO 32/8685, '103/Gen.No./826. War Office Council. 11th July, 1900. Compulsory Band.-Subscriptions of Regimental Officers'.

would suffice to fill a book…each regiment proud of its own customs and traditions, neither one giving way to the other'.[69] Each band had its own daily routine and even the slightest changes caused a considerable amount of angst:

> [I]nstead of rolling in casually about 10 a.m. our men of the 2nd Life Guards had to actually parade for inspection at 9.30 a.m. and were ticked off right and left if a boot wasn't sufficiently highly polished, or a spur lacked the gleam of the burnisher. Then at 10 a.m. sharp, the new musical Director would take the band at practise with the non stop don't waste a minute zeal of the conscientious fanatic.[70]

The loyalties to each regiment are surprising considering that the musicians deemed themselves separate to regimental soldiers, but bands still liked to have an identity, and that identity was the regiment. This had been demonstrated by the Band of the Welsh Guards which, as a comparatively new unit in 1915 (the same year as the regiment was created), soon took on the look and feel of the Household Brigade bands, but with its own distinct character, playing national airs and adopting all the trappings of a Welsh regiment.[71]

The officer-soldier relationship was not such a concern for most regimental bands as they were commanded by a Warrant Officer Bandmaster, with a Band President, usually the officer (Major) commanding Headquarters Company (or Squadron), responsible for overseeing band engagements, but with no day-to-day business with the band. Where bands did have an officer in charge (Guards, Royal Artillery, and a few others), the bandmaster (or Director of Music) held a quartermaster's commission from the ranks and so was not from the traditional officer class, recruited, on the whole, from privately funded schools (known as 'public' schools). Some of these differences in military culture are recounted in several extraordinary stories by former bandsmen. Bill Grainger relates an episode in Dover in the 1920s with 1KOYLI Band:

> Nobby, the long serving Percussionist, had obtained a job in the local Theatre Orchestra. Nobby, however, was the Band 'tippler', and prone to drinking his earnings. On the Saturday night, he had stayed out on 'the

---

[69] Sutherland, *They Blow Their Trumpets*, p. 83.
[70] *Ibid*.
[71] Cited in C. Dean, *The Band of the Welsh Guards – A Centenary* (London: Band of the Welsh Guards, 2016), p. 10.

town', and decided to return to barracks the next morning in a horse drawn carriage. As he arrived at the Guard Room, singing his head off, the Battalion was drawn up on parade, ready for Church. Nobby was duly doubled into a cell to recuperate. Unfortunately, he had borrowed the Bandmaster's civilian dress suit to do the job, and when Mr Raison [the bandmaster] eventually asked for it back; Nobby had pawned it.[72]

This short tale reveals several unique aspects of bandsmen's existence. 'Nobby' was clearly allowed to have time off to do another job with the local theatre orchestra which would not have been possible for a battalion soldier. While gambling was common with all soldiers, the fact that Nobby arrived in a horse-drawn carriage perpetuates the idea of bandsmen being the 'gentlemen' of the regiment. His apparent disrespect for the bandmaster, holding the most senior non-commissioned rank of Warrant Officer Class One (WO1) could only have been tolerated in the band; it would have been unthinkable for a battalion soldier to treat the Regimental Sergeant Major – also a WO1 – with the same disdain.

When bandmasters were given Warrant Officer rank, it elevated them to a high status within the regiment, but the relationship with military colleagues could be problematic,[73] particularly as bandmasters could be appointed at a very young age with, for example, Corporal George Smith of the Royal Fusiliers reported by *The Bandmaster* journal as being appointed Bandmaster of the 1st Battalion Sherwood Foresters at the age of twenty-five in 1925.[74] Regimental sergeant majors would have been at least ten years older.

Bands serving in the United Kingdom, and particularly in London, could remain aloof from their regiments for a great deal of the time, but retain regimental contacts for important occasions when it became useful to identify with the brand of the regiment. Bands serving overseas, however, tended to be more involved in military duties, such as guarding, but this depended on how the commanding officer wanted to use the band – as entertainment or extra manpower. Most commanding officers realised they could not have both and were content with the band performing music, preferring them to act as an ambassador for the regiment, rather than unwillingly undertake unfamiliar regimental tasks. The soldier-musician dilemma was

---

[72] Grainger, *Life and Times*, pp. 17-18.
[73] J. Mackenzie-Rogan, *Fifty Years of Army Music* (London: Methuen, 1926), p. 81.
[74] 'Interesting to Amateur Bandsmen', *The Bandmaster*, Vol. 1, No. 6, 15th August 1925, p. 81.

clearly evident with the Band of the 1st Battalion the King's Own Yorkshire Light Infantry:

> [M]usicians, as everyone knows, do not take kindly to adverse conditions...To them, purely military life was never a great attraction, but because of their early introduction to the rigours, and training of army life, and to many forms of sport, they always took pride in being able to fulfil any military duties, which were required of them.[75]

This 'early introduction' was due to the wholesale recruitment of boys from educational institutions (see chapter 3), and the military side of life could be put on when necessary. But bands had to strike a balance between doing what they wanted to do and serving the regiment, as resentment in the army could surface at any time. In many cases, however, it seems that bandmasters managed to overcome regimental demands and cultivated relations by the involvement of bandsmen in regimental sports. The high proportion of boys and bandsmen playing sports is evident from reports in regimental journals, with frequent inter-regiment competitions, such as the 'Enlisted Boys Football Cup' and the '1s XI Aldershot Command Football Shield', won by band boys of the 2nd Battalion the Royal Scots Fusiliers in 1937.[76] Sport was probably the only source of common interest between bandsmen and the rest of the regiment and helped alleviate the delicate balance between the two cultures.

As soldier-musicians the evidence so far has pointed towards army bandsmen identifying themselves as musicians first, but was there a sense of pride in being an army musician? Perhaps surprisingly, there is little indication to suggest that this was the case. Few of the sources have revealed if bandsmen were ever gratified by taking part in ceremonial parades, either at a regimental or national level, with the exception of those few Directors of Music who had reached the senior positions, such as Mackenzie-Rogan and Miller, who relished the occasions.[77] The army certainly saw a return to pre-war peacetime ceremonial activities as good for recruiting and public

---

[75] Grainger, *Life and Times*, pp. 2 & 129.
[76] J. C. Kemp, *The History of the Royal Scots Fusiliers: 1919-1959* (Glasgow: Robert MacLehose & Co/Glasgow University Press, 1963), p. 16.
[77] Mackenzie-Rogan, *Fifty Years of Army Music*; G. J. Miller, *The Piping Times in Peace and War: Being the Autobiography of a Royal Musician in Five Reigns*. Museum of Army Music. MS, n.d.

relations,[78] but the bandsmen seemed to be more interested in gaining extra pay with outside employment.

Hector Sutherland, who became a freelance trumpeter after leaving the Life Guards observed:

> [A] large number of the wind and string players in the London orchestras were from the Guards' Bands and Royal Artillery, whose full complement numbered over 500 musicians, approximately 60 each of Foot Guards, 36 each of Household Cavalry and 100 Royal Artillery.[79]

'Bunnie' Mason from the Royal Artillery Band explains how his outside engagements started in the pre-First World War years as a seventeen-year-old boy soldier, deputising as a cellist at the Collins Music Hall, Islington.[80] He later moved to the East Ham Palace for two years where the orchestra comprised fifteen musicians 'made up mainly of military men, Gunners and Guardsmen'.[81] In 1921 he became a member of the Queens Hall Orchestra under Sir Henry Wood, while still serving with the Royal Artillery Band, but eventually had to resign his position due to his commitments as principal cellist of the Royal Artillery Orchestra.[82]

In London, army musicians were present in the larger orchestras, but the majority of these engagements were small-scale, paid nonetheless, such as to augment the orchestras of amateur operatic societies:

> Salisbury's *Mikado* of 1923 relied on a lance-corporal for its oboe, a sergeant-trumpeter for the horn and an ordinary bandsman for the trombone; all were from the 12th Royal Hussars. Two years later the society borrowed three players from the Royal Artillery Band. In 1939 Cradley Heath, Birmingham, hired the string band of the Royal Artillery, for the quality of its playing. The conductor of the…Old Savilions [in 1920s Wakefield] was the bandmaster of the 4th King's Own Yorkshire Light Infantry.[83]

---

[78] R. Higham, *Armed Forces in Peacetime: Britain, 1918-1940, a case study* (London: G. T. Foulis & Co, 1962), p. 88.
[79] Sutherland, *They Blow Their Trumpets*, p. 24.
[80] Mason, *Memoirs*, p 7.
[81] *Ibid*, p 8.
[82] *Ibid*, pp. 18-19.
[83] J. Lowerson, *Amateur Operatics: A Social and Cultural History* (Manchester: Manchester University Press, 2005), pp. 194-5.

This snapshot reported by Lowerson is not untypical. Members of the Dance Band of the 1st Battalion The King's Own Yorkshire Light Infantry 'became quite wealthy' from payments for the weekly dances in the Assembly Rooms in Gibraltar, 1935-8.[84] In the early post-First World War years, Hector Sutherland was performing at the Slough roller skating rink three times a week and deputising at The Blue Halls Hammersmith.[85] He goes on to describe the system of deputising up until the time of sound films and how budding musicians made their way into the system. If a player had a 'regular shop', a regular engagement at a music hall, theatre, or cinema, but was asked to deputise for a colleague in a symphony orchestra, then a suitable deputy had to be found for his job. This seems to be where army musicians were particularly employed: 'There was nothing remarkable in some [army] musicians holding down regular engagements for many years. A trombone player in the Blues for instance, held the Chelsea Palace for over 20 years'.[86]

It was not only individuals that were able to hold down engagements as the Royal Artillery Orchestra had regular National Sunday League Concerts at the London Palladium up until 1932, with a second orchestra also performing at other London theatres and music halls. There was also an octet that appeared at various venues around London, including the Palladium.[87]

The influence of army bandsmen performing in orchestras is further discussed in chapter 5, but what the experiences have shown so far is that bandsmen, on the whole, identified with the music profession rather than as soldiers. One retired army bandmaster, A. E. Noble, writing in 1931 in the army musicians' journal, *The Leading Note*, remarked that promotion was very slow, often referring to 'dead man's shoes' as a term to describe this. He also bemoans the lack of aspiration of most bandsmen, suggesting that all they cared about is the next event.[88] This rather bleak description seems somewhat pessimistic but probably accounts for why so many bandsmen sought outside work. Noble also refers to the number of unemployed musicians waiting at Archer Street (the main place in London where

---

[84] Grainger, *Life and Times*, p. 20.
[85] Sutherland, *They Blow Their Trumpets*, pp. 66-68.
[86] *Ibid*, pp. 62-63.
[87] Mason, *Memoirs*, p. 20.
[88] A. E. Noble, 'Bandsmen.', *The Leading Note*, Vol. 1, No. 7, August, 1931, p. 11.

musicians were hired), 'the majority of whom were at one time the mainstay of an Army Band'.[89]

The music profession had always been precarious, with the composer Gordon Jacob describing the situation in pre-First World War Britain when 'music wasn't looked upon as a possible source of livelihood'.[90] Life outside of the army for bandsmen, without the cushion of an army salary, was not particularly comfortable, particularly when sound was introduced at cinema, eliminated the need for cinema musicians.[91] However much military bandsmen wanted to be recognised as professional musicians, they were very much part of a military culture which could be different from that experienced by civilian musicians. Whilst military musicians undoubtedly interacted with their civilian counterparts there were distinct symbols and rituals that made the experience different for bandsmen, characterised by their routines in barracks.[92]

Bandsmen may have become temporary civilians when they performed outside of the army, but two accounts of bands involved in the recording process reveal that they were still subject to military discipline. Recording manager, Joe Batten, described recording 'many military bands' while he was at post-war Edison Bell:

> [T]hese [recording] sessions were (and I believe still are) regarded by the Army as a regimental parade. A curious incident happened at one of these. During the recording I stopped the band to point out that one of the instrumentalists was playing a wrong note. The bandmaster first denied the obvious fault. I persisted. An argument then arose as to the identity of the culprit, the bandmaster blaming one innocent of the offence, who indignantly denied the "soft impeachment", whereupon: "Fall out two men," and he was placed under open arrest. This injustice urged me to speak plain words to the bandmaster, and I told him that if

---

[89] *Ibid.*
[90] Interviewed in 1977 and quoted in P. Liddle, *Captured Memories 1900-1918: Across the Threshold of War* (Barnsley: Pen & Sword, 2010), p. 202.
[91] McKibben, R. *Classes and Cultures: England, 1918-1951* (Oxford: Oxford University Press, 1998), p. 60. Ironically, it was sometimes army musicians who were hired to fanfare the opening of new cinemas. See for example, D. Inkster, *Union Cinemas Ritz: A Story of Theatre Organs and Cine-Variety* (Hove: Wick, 1999), p. 51
[92] A. H. Gregory, 'The roles of music in society: the ethnomusicological perspective', in D. J. Hargreaves & A. North (eds), *The Social Psychology of Music* (Oxford: Oxford University Press, 1997), p. 138 [pp. 107-140].

anyone should be on a charge it should be himself. And that, the serious crime of not knowing his job.

It was then discovered that the part had been wrongly scored and it was the score which the offender had followed, as he had done for years! And no doubt would have continued to do so had not my ear detected the inaccuracy.[93]

Another recording manager, Fred Gaisberg, described a session under Mackenzie Rogan when bandmaster of the Coldstream Guards:

Rogan was not a great musician, but he was the greatest bandmaster in the British Army. Brought up in the hard school of the army since his sixteenth year, he was, as can well be imagined, a strict martinet who never relaxed before his men. I can sense even now the solemn tension that reigned in the recording studio while Rogan, seated on high, transfixed in silence by forty pairs of eyes, indicated the start and finish of a record, never raising his voice above a whisper. During the entire three hours he was the only one permitted to speak. One felt that it would be a catastrophe involving nothing less than punishment by death for a player to sound the wrong note.[94]

The two accounts suggest that the regime to which army musicians were subjected was austere to say the least, but this approach was part of the military culture and ensured bandsmen were punctual and always smart – qualities that were noted by civilian colleagues (see chapter 5). This undoubtedly stemmed from the training of bandmasters at the Royal Military School of Music, Kneller Hall.

Training

The story of the establishment of the Military School of Music at Kneller Hall is well documented elsewhere,[95] and there is little to add to the account of the early years of its operation, suffice to say that

---

[93] J. Batten, *Joe Batten's Book: The Story of Sound Recording, Being the Memoirs of Joe Batten, Recording Manager* (London: Rockliff, 1956), p. 60.
[94] F. W. Gaisberg, *Music on Record* (London: Robert Hale, 1946), p. 79.
[95] P. L. Binns, *A Hundred Years of Military Music: being the story of the Royal Military School of Music Kneller Hall* (Gillingham, Dorset: The Blackmore Press, 1959); G. Turner and A. Turner, *The Trumpets Will Sound: The Story of the Royal Military School of Music Kneller Hall* (Tunbridge Wells: PARAPRESS, 1996); T. Herbert and H. Barlow, *Music and the British Military in the Long Nineteenth Century* (Oxford: Oxford University Press, 2013), chapter 6, pp. 126-153; C. Dean, *The Royal Military School of Music, Kneller Hall 1857-2017* (London: The Kneller Hall Club, 2017).

the RMSM – Royal was granted in 1887 – was responsible for training future bandmasters from the ranks of experienced military bandsmen. Historically, this had come about due to the preponderance of regiments in the early nineteenth-century employing foreign bandmasters, usually German or Italian, but in a bid to employ British bandmasters, and to standardise working practices, there was a need to train future bandmasters from within band ranks. The outcome was the setting up of the Military Music Class at Kneller Hall in 1857. In addition, younger bandsmen, having already served in bands for a few years, were instructed on a one-year 'Pupil's Course', ostensibly for those who might have potential to return as trainee bandmasters in the future (Fig. 2.7).

Figure 2.7.
Kneller Hall – The Band on Parade in 1920, including some very young 'pupils'. The variety of uniforms shows the different regiments. Student bandmasters instruct (MAM)

Initial musical training was undertaken in regimental bands after band boys, and a few adults, had been recruited directly to them. After a period of time in the band some would be sent to the RMSM for a year's instrumental training as a pupil. The training was taken very seriously but facilities were somewhat rudimentary. Boy Bunnie Mason, sent from the Royal Artillery Band to Kneller Hall for eighteen months to learn the clarinet and cello, explains that 'musicians from every regiment in the British Army practised every day (weather permitting) in the woods. The music stands were hooked on to trees'.[96] This rather comical picture belies the fact that by the late nineteenth century the RMSM was held in high esteem in the music industry and civilian music 'professor' appointments were considered important positions.[97] The clarinet position, for example, had been held by the well-known Henry Lazarus, also a teacher at the Royal Academy of Music, and later by George Clinton 'Professor at Kneller Hall, the Royal Academy of Music, and Trinity College, London'.[98]

Ehrlich has called the RMSM 'the most successful of nineteenth-century music colleges,[99] partly because the RMSM was a state-sponsored conservatoire that trained musicians for a specific job – whether as bandsman or bandmaster – a factor lacking in the civilian music colleges. Sir Dan Godfrey recognised the status of the RMSM, describing it in 1924 as 'our one real State School of Music...I commend the curriculum.'[100] But Kneller Hall's position in a leafy London suburb was away from the army's main hubs. This, coupled with its lack of facilities was the cause of debate after the First World War, with some proposing that it be relocated to Aldershot Camp, the army's main location, where it would have its own concert hall – there was no such facility at Kneller Hall – and also 'where its presence would be a valuable asset to the Army and a real centre of progress for the musical life of the soldiers' as it was 'completely detached from garrison life and surroundings' in its London suburb of Whitton.[101] Major General Sir George Evatt proposed the commissioning of all bandmasters and the creation of an Army Music Corps (pre-empting the Corps of Army Music by seventy-four years), but the proposal was too radical and the RMSM would stay in Whitton, with only a temporary move to Aldershot for the duration of the Second World War. With the RMSM's position confirmed in Whitton, the name Kneller Hall became synonymous with the RMSM and in most

---

[96] Mason, *Memoirs*, p. 7.
[97] The term 'professor' is used at the RMSM, and other music institutions, to refer to instrumental teachers and not an academic position.
[98] O. W. Street, 'The Clarinet and its Music', in *Proceedings of the Musical Association*, 42nd Session, 1915-1916, pp. 108 & 109 [pp. 89-115].
[99] Ehrlich, *The Music Profession in Britain*, p. 97.
[100] D. Godfrey, *Memories and Music: Thirty-five Years of Conducting* (London: Hutchinson, 1924), p. 26.
[101] G. J. H. Evatt, 'Royal Military School of Music. Proposed transfer of the Kneller Hall Army School of Music to Aldershot Camp', *Aldershot News*, August 6th, 1920.

records the term is interchangeable. It was important for the RMSM to remain at Kneller Hall, and maintain an identity, because Kneller Hall was not just home to the Royal Military School of Music, but also to a far-reaching control system that had great influence in the careers of bandmasters and directors of music.

Strategy was personality led with no coherent plan for future development, emerging from the private funding of bands to a loose network of affiliations between bands, held together by the link to Kneller Hall. Two individuals wielded the most power: the Commandant and the Director of Music. The Commandant, usually a full colonel near the end of his career, was always selected from a list of officers who had had no connection with military music, other than experiencing it in normal regimental duties. The Director of Music, however, was a bandsman, but while this position was one of the few commissioned posts for musicians, it was not a sought-after job, primarily because it did not come with the command of a band, and so did not attract the associated extra pay from private engagements. As a consequence, some of the incumbents in the position were not considered the best musicians in the army, having never commanded a senior band. One was Hector Adkins, who held the position of Director of Music from 1921-1942, but what he lacked in musical prowess he made up with personality. Adkins turned the Kneller Hall Band into a commercial venture, with little concern for the training of students, and by all accounts, he was a despot who bullied the student bandmasters. One former bandmaster, Charles Nalden, called his student days at Kneller Hall 'one of life's disillusionments',[102] due directly to Adkins' treatment of him, but despite Adkins' behaviour, trainee bandmasters were put through a thorough programme. This was overseen by the Commandant, whose position at Kneller Hall depended on the incumbent's willingness to engage in the training of army musicians, and as Kneller Hall was the *de facto* headquarters of army music, his involvement in the strategic direction of music in the military.

It is clear that some Commandants viewed an assignment to Kneller Hall as a chance to sit back and allow the Director of Music to lead, but others were keen to make a full contribution. Perhaps the most demanding was Colonel J. A. C. Somerville who became Commandant in January 1920 and was to stamp an instant impression upon the establishment. He was a keen amateur musician who wished, as he saw it, to raise standards, develop the repertoire,

---

[102] Nalden, *Half and Half*, p. 341.

and make army music respectable in the more highbrow music community. There is no doubt that he achieved this in some respects, but he also risked alienating the more conventional audiences who seemed contented, and probably had no need to be challenged when hearing a piece of music.

Somerville had highbrow intentions, in contrast to those of the Director of Music, Hector Adkins. Somerville was desperate for Kneller Hall to become a recognised part of the musical establishment, but Adkins wanted to focus on commercial music with his 'playing out band'. Somerville had tried to encourage composers to write more scholarly music for military band, but they were mostly not of the quality that he expected: 'Sir Charles Stanford, who was present [at an outdoor Kneller Hall concert], was seen to advance slowly but deliberately towards an adjacent duck pond' during a performance of Dr. Cuthbert Harris's *Egyptian Scenes*.[103] Adkins no doubt would have been content with the general failure of Somerville's plan, but the longing for respectability did not end with Somerville's retirement, as later Commandants toyed with the idea of direct entry for civilian bandmasters.

In 1936, the then Commandant, Colonel Parminster, put forward a scheme for the special enlistment of students from the civilian Royal College of Music and the Royal Academy of Music for fast-track attendance on the Bandmaster course. He claimed that current standards of bandmasters were generally not high enough (he states 40% are 'not good enough') and that there were insufficient applicants to the course.[104] He may have been inspired by the successful recruitment by the Royal Marines of Vivian Dunn as a direct entry officer in 1931,[105] but the scheme was rejected.[106] In a remarkable about-turn two years later Colonel Parminter stated that 'a very marked change has occurred in the number and standard of the

---

[103] 'Kneller Hall', *The Musical Times*, R. L., 62, 945, November 1921, p. 785. [pp. 784-785].
[104] TNA WO 32/4488, 'Army Bandmasters. Policy in connection with supply of'. Letter from Colonel Parminter to the Under-Secretary of State, the War Office, dated 20th February, 1936.
[105] D. Oakley, *Fiddler on the March: A Biography of Lieutenant Colonel Sir Vivian Dunn KCVO OBE FRAM Royal Marines* (London: Royal Marines Historical Society, 2000), p. 30.
[106] TNA WO 32/4488, 'Army Bandmasters. Policy in connection with supply of'. 43/K.H./165 (A.G.4.c.) Letter from Director of Personal Services, Colonel L. M. Gibbs to Colonel Parminter, dated 28th September, 1936.

students who are now entering for the bandmaster course here'.[107] It is not known if the standard had increased, or simply that Colonel Parminter needed to save face, but his rebuff ensured that the RMSM's original policy of training serving British army bandsmen to become bandmasters was to remain unchanged until the twenty-first century.

By considering Farmer's first and third research themes as cultural issues it has been possible to identify that regular army bandsmen comprised a distinct group of musicians within the music profession. This was whilst preserving links to industry practices through involvement in civilian engagements. Furthermore, bandsmen were identified by the rest of the army as being unusual and different, partly through their pursuit of fee-paying engagements, but also because of a lack of commitment in soldierly matters.

The soldier-musician balance was firmly on the side of the musician and this led to bands existing almost independently from their regiments, particularly in Britain. The relationship was mutually beneficial and was tolerated as long as associations with the regiment were preserved, resulting in the wholesale disregard for War Office regulations. With the reintroduction of pre-First World War customs, it was the War Office that reacted to the power structure of the regimental system and its bands, rather than the other way around.

The status of the RMSM as a control system was important, but it was personality based, and lacked strategic direction. Nevertheless, its strength and unique selling point was the maintenance of an enduring job-specific training system, in spite of the schemes of successive Commandants and Directors of Music.

---

[107] TNA WO 32/4488, 'Army Bandmasters. Policy in connection with supply of'. Letter from Colonel Parminter to the Under-Secretary of State, the War Office, dated 5th July, 1938.

CHAPTER 3

'BREAKING IN' THE YOUNG HANDS: THE DEPENDENCE ON BAND BOYS

Boys were recruited into the British army as musicians in such large numbers in the nineteenth and early twentieth centuries that they formed the basis of military bands and fundamentally fashioned their culture. First-hand accounts from regimental bands indicate that it is quite probable that band boys, known in army bands as 'young hands', and those who had originally joined as band boys, made up about two-thirds of the manpower of army bands in the 1920s and 30s.[1] The tradition of recruiting boys aged fourteen to sixteen (and younger) into the British army was long-standing,[2] but for boy bandsmen recruits the process began to take hold in the middle of the nineteenth century when boys were enlisted from the new orphanages, or similar institutions, and began to populate the regimental bands.[3] The peak era for numbers of pupils at the various institutions for boys was around the time of the First World War, with forty-four reformatories and 148 industrial schools in Great Britain, housing about 25,000 inmates (both boys and girls). By 1926 the figure had reduced to twenty-eight reformatories and fifty-six industrial schools with about 7,000 boys and girls,[4] and this was to have a significant impact on the flow of recruits into army bands.

A substantial number of boys joined the army as band boys from these institutions and for them music proved to be a lever for social mobility, with a significant number progressing to become bandmasters and directors of music, and several holding the highest

---

[1] See for example W. K. Grainger, *The Life and Times of a Regimental Band: A History of The Bands of The King's Own Yorkshire Light Infantry*. The Rifles Office, Pontefract, 1995, MS. Grainger provides lists of band members with a short description of their backgrounds.
[2] See A. W. Cockerill, *Sons of the Brave: The Story of Boy Soldiers* (London: Leo Cooper/Secker & Warburg, 1984).
[3] This is discussed in chapter 6 of T. Herbert and H. Barlow, *Music and the British Military in the Long Nineteenth Century* (Oxford: Oxford University Press, 2013).
[4] P. Higginbotham, *Approved Schools*, <http://www.childrenshomes.org.uk/AS/> [accessed 19th January 2015].

rank available to musicians – Lieutenant Colonel – including Lieutenant Colonels 'Jiggs' Jaeger and Duncan Beat. Others, such as Joseph Ricketts (known as Kenneth Alford) and his brother, Randolf (known as Leo Stanley), became interwar household names.[5] The only two bandsmen to receive the Victoria Cross had been educated at boys' institutions: John Shaul at the Duke of York's Royal Military School,[6] and Thomas Rendle at Kingswood Reformatory in Bristol.[7]

The institutions that cared for both boys and girls who were either orphaned or destitute were run by a variety of bodies including local authorities, charities, religious societies, philanthropists or philanthropic organisations, and also those administered by certain professions, including the police and military. Terminologies changed over time, depending upon legislation and fashion, and so the role of an institution could be quite different to its initial intended purpose. Industrial Schools, for example, were originally set up in early Victorian times for children whose parents were in the workhouse, but after 1857 they became schools for vagrant, destitute, and disorderly children who were considered likely to become criminals.[8] Likewise, Reformatories were for children who had actually committed criminal acts, but after 1933, as a result of the 1932 Children and Young Persons Act, the distinction between Industrial schools and Reformatories was abolished and they (mostly) became known as Approved schools.[9]

Another anomaly arises from the use of the term 'orphan', which would suggest a child with both parents deceased, but when boys from institutions are described as orphans, for many this was not

---

[5] J. Trendell, *Colonel Bogey to the Fore: A Biography of Kenneth J. Alford* (Dover: Blue Band, 1991), pp. 8-11.
[6] G. Shorter, *"Play Up Dukies": Duke of York's Royal Military School 1801-1986* (Leatherhead, Surrey: The Duke of York's Royal Military School, Old Boys Association, 1987), pp. 110-113; D. B. Hammond, 'Band Corporal John Shaul VC', *Fanfare: The Journal of the Corps of Army Music*, 2016, pp. 134-137.
[7] P. Oldfield, *Victoria Crosses on the Western Front August 1914-Apri 1915: Mons to Hill 60* (Barnsley: Pen & Sword Military, 2014), p. 274; 'Kingswood Reformatory, Kingswood, near Bristol, Gloucestershire', <http://www.childrenshomes.org.uk/BristolKingswoodRfy/> [accessed 17th January 2016].
[8] For a detailed discussion of the role of Industrial Schools, see N. Sheldon, 'Civilising the Delinquent and the Neglected: The Role of the Industrial School,' *History of Childhood Colloquium*, 21 June 2008, Oxford.
[9] P. Higginbotham, 'Education in the Workhouse', <http://www.workhouses.org.uk/education/workhouse.shtml#District> [accessed 20th January 2015].

strictly the case, with typical entries in registers from the late nineteenth century stating 'Father dead; Mother a charwoman; earnings very small; four children'.[10] The variation in circumstances for boys and the lack of a formal infrastructure for looking after destitute children probably explains the reason why there was a variety in the sort of institution available to children and so throughout this chapter, unless specified, each type of residential home, regardless of sponsor, shall be referred to as 'institution'.

This chapter is linked to two of Farmer's research themes: military music and its response to changes and developments in military regulation; and individual military bands as quasi-independent institutions. The first theme tracks the army's responses to changes in the far external environment related to sociological issues concerning children's education and how, in the near external environment, institutions as suppliers of recruits were critical stakeholders in the maintenance of army bands. The second theme relates to the internal environment and how the cultural artefacts of control systems, power structures, organisational structures, and rituals and routines, were particularly susceptible to the reliance on the high proportion of band boys recruited from institutions. But why did so many boys join the army as bandsmen?

Structural issues and motivations of institutions

There was no official army policy or strategy for the recruitment of band boys but it is not surprising that boys who had attended institutions were ready for military service as these establishments were generally run along military lines, with discipline and uniformity at the heart of their training. The whole arrangement of recruiting boys to the army seems to have come about by mutual benefit to both the army and the institutions, with the army being provided with prepared recruits and the institutions assured employment for their boys without the need to pay for apprenticeships. In the nineteenth century, boy soldiers were trained to go into several trades in the military, including as tailors, shoemakers, carpenters, and shirt makers,[11] but from the 1840s,

---

[10] LMA A/FWA/C/D1000/1 Newport Market Refuge. 'The Twenty-Eighth Annual Report of the Newport Market Refuge and Industrial School (Founded in 1863). Coburg Row, Westminster, S.W. 1892. London: T. Brettell & Co'.
[11] Cockerill, *Sons of the Brave*, p. 96.

band training and military drill (for fitness and possibly as a tool to maintain discipline) also became popular.[12]

PHYSICAL DRILL ON BOARD A TRAINING-SHIP.

Figure 3.1
Men and boys undergoing drill exercise on a ship, accompanied by the ship's band, in the late nineteenth century (RY Band archives)

Drill exercises to the accompaniment of music were instigated by the Royal Navy where, after the introduction of steam-powered ships, and the demise of sailing ships (and rigging), there was a need to keep sailors fit (see Fig. 3.1[13]). This relatively cheap but effective form of

---

[12] L. Murdoch, *Imagined Orphans – Poor Families, Child Welfare, and Contested Citizenship in London* (New Brunswick, New Jersey: Rutgers University Press, 2006), p. 122; A. Davin, *Growing Up Poor: Home, School and Street in London 1970-1914* (London: Rivers Oram Press, 1996) p. 125.
[13] The Band of The Royal Yeomanry (Inns of Court & City Yeomanry) archives. Untitled and undated picture book depicting photographs of Royal Navy and British army adult and boy training in the late nineteenth century. Handwritten

exercise then seems to have been taken up by the institutions as a tool to ensure boys were kept active.

For those boys who were to join army bands the environment would have been comparatively familiar and there would have been limited need for socialisation and training, with the burden of preliminary musical and drill training having already been absorbed by the institutions the boys attended.[14] It was soon reported that by far the most successful training for boys in institutions was for preparation for military bands, and 'by 1867 every metropolitan school had its band, taught by an efficient bandmaster'.[15] Thirty years later, one quarter (174) of all boys discharged from Metropolitan Poor Law Schools joined army or navy bands.[16] For boys joining an army band it seemed the natural progression from institutions, as described by one former pupil of the Foundling Hospital School from the interwar years, Harold Tarrant:

> Most of the boys who were fit to pass the army test were enlisted as band boys. This was very appropriate. We had been brought up like little militarists – we'd been members of an army-style band and a boy going into the army was no further cost to the hospital.[17]

Familiarity with the environment was important for the boys and they would always come across old boys from the various institutions. The Royal Dragoons Band, as a typical example, was full of boys from institutions and Boy Michael Kelly, when he was sent from the Royal Hibernian Military School, found that 'the Bandmaster and Band Serjeant both were ex-Hibernian boys while the Trumpet-Major and

---

inscription on inside cover 'George Hoult 14/4/[18]99' and 'John L. Taylor'. Viewed 13th July 2017. The caption reads: 'This illustration shows the boys at musical physical drill on board the "St. Vincent." This drill is an innovation of, comparatively speaking, recent years; its introduction into the Service generally being necessitated by the absence of masts and sails in modern ships-of-war. It was found necessary to find some substitute for the old sail-drill, which did so much to make the men active and develop their muscles, and physical drill is now carried out regularly on board all ships-of-war.'

[14] H. R. Clarke, *A New History of the Royal Hibernian Military School Phoenix Park, Dublin: 1765-1924* (Wynd Yarm, Cleveland: Howard R. Clarke, 2011), p. 458.

[15] W. Chance, *Children Under the Poor Law: Their Education Training and After-Care Together with a Criticism of the Report of the Departmental Committee on Metropolitan Poor Law Schools* (London: Swan Sonnenschein, 1897), p. 86.

[16] Chance, *Children Under the Poor Law*, pp. 284-5.

[17] Quoted in G. Pugh, *London's Forgotton Children: Thomas Coram and the Foundling Hospital* (Stroud: The History Press, 2007; repr. 2013), p. 125.

Corporal were ex-Duke of York Boys'.[18] Boy Castle, from the 2nd Battalion The Gloucestershire Regiment, emphasised this point: 'they'd all been boys, they'd been through the same procedure.'[19]

It was generally considered appropriate by both the army and the institutions to recruit fourteen-year-olds as non-combatant bandsmen because it was the usual age for leaving school, and there was no legal basis against it.[20] Moreover, it removed from society the potential for boys to be discarded on to the streets after leaving one of the institutions; so keen were the institutions to ensure that the boys stayed in employment that some of the institutions maintained partial responsibility for them until reaching adulthood, whilst serving in the army. The Foundling Hospital prescribed for boys' employers to report back to them, sending a small gratuity to the boy each Whitsun on receipt of a good report, with a final payment when reaching twenty-one.[21] Regardless of the institution, when boys reached the age of sixteen it became a necessity to join a band as, for Jack Troup, 'the nuns would not pay my National Insurance stamp'.[22]

Interwar accounts by former bandsmen are full of descriptions of boys from institutes in bands. Major 'Jimmy' Howe relates that in 1935 in the Band of the Royal Scots 'a lot of boys in the Services came from orphanages and boarding schools'.[23] Another account by 'Spike' Mays who joined up in 1924 at the age of sixteen and was sent to the band of the Royal Dragoons in Aldershot, describes that:

---

[18] 'Royal Hibernian Military School (1765-1924): Michael Kelly dwelling on the final era',
<http://www.richardgilbert.ca/achart/public_html/articles/hibernian/final_era.htm> [accessed 12 Mar 2015].
[19] E. Castle. Interviewed by Lindsay Baker for IWM, 10th September 2001. Catalogue number 22165.
<http://www.iwm.org.uk/collections/item/object/80021951> [accessed 19th February 2015].
[20] R. Holmes, *Soldiers: Army Lives and Loyalties from Redcoats to Dusty Warriors* (London: Harper, 2011), p. 278.
[21] J. Kelsey. 'Foundling Hospital Boys' Band'. Documentary evidence provided at lecture given at The Foundling Museum, London, 1st February 2015,
<http://www.foundlingmuseum.org.uk/events/view/sunday-feb-2015/> [accessed 1st February 2015]. See also G. Pugh, *London's Forgotton Children: Thomas Coram and the Foundling Hospital* (Stroud: The History Press, 2007; repr. 2013), p. 104.
[22] J. Troup, *The Life that Jack Lived: Experiences of a Norfolk soldier and policeman* (Dereham: Larks Press, 1997), p. 12.
[23] J. Howe, *A Conductor's Journey* (Eastbourne: J. H. Publishing, 2002), p. 17.

most of my new colleagues were orphans from schools like the Duke of York's where they had been taught music and to play instruments before their enlistment'.[24]

Furthermore, he notes that 'most of our bandsmen had been in the army from the age of fifteen and had only known the care of orphanages'.[25] To substantiate these accounts Charles Nalden writes that in 1921 'the majority of boys [from the London Foundling Hospital] were enlisted into army bands'.[26]

The relationship between the army and residential institutions for children

By the late nineteenth century boys from institutions were recognised as a significant source of manpower, with a Royal Military School of Music (RMSM) Commandant's report from 1892 listing twenty-nine 'Schools from which boys may generally be obtained' (Fig. 3.2).[27] The list also specifies in which instruments the schools specialise, such as 'Brass, reeds, flutes, and stringed instruments', or 'Brass instruments only'.[28] The explanation was as follows:

> As the Royal Military Asylum, Chelsea, and the Royal Hibernian School, Dublin, are only sufficient to meet the requirements of a very small proportion of boys required for bands, a list of such schools from which eligible boys can generally be obtained is herewith annexed.[29]

Despite the endorsement in the Commandant's report there was no official connection between the RMSM and these institutions. Perhaps there was some sort of unauthorised arrangement where bandmasters were welcomed to recruit boys, but there is no evidence to suggest that the understanding ever became fully sanctioned: it seems to have been run by an informal network of bandmasters and former army bandmasters who worked at the institutions. One of the consequences of this laissez-faire approach was that there was no

---

[24] S. Mays, Fall Out the Officers (London: Eyre & Spottiswoode, 1969), p.11.
[25] *Ibid*, p.14.
[26] C. Nalden, *Half and Half: The Memoirs of a Charity Brat 1908-1989* (Tauranga, New Zealand: Maona, 1989), p. 197.
[27] MAM archives, Kneller Hall Diary additional pages. 'Extracts from a Report by the Commandant, Royal Military School of Music, Kneller Hall, Hounslow.', 103: Kneller Hall: 586, April, 1892, p. 4.
[28] *Ibid*.
[29] *Ibid*, p. 3

standardised way of instructing boys to prepare them for army bands, and institutions' bandmasters were left to their own devices to prepare the boys.

School	Instruments
South Metropolitan District Schools, Sutton, Surrey	Brass, reeds, and flutes.
South Metropolitan District Schools, Witham, Essex	,, ,,
Central London District Schools, Hanwell, Middlesex	,, ,,
North Surrey District Schools, Anerley, Surrey	,, ,,
West London District Schools, Ashford, Staines, Middlesex	Brass instruments only.
Forest Gate District Schools, Forest Gate, Stratford, Essex	Brass, reeds, and flutes.
Kensington and Chelsea District Schools, Banstead, Surrey	,, ,,
Reading and Wokingham District Schools, Wargrave, Berkshire.	,, ,,
Training Ship, "Exmouth," Grays, Essex	Brass, reeds, flutes, and stringed instruments.
Hackney Industrial Schools, Brentwood, Essex	Brass, reeds, and flutes.
St. Pancras Industrial Schools, Leavesdon, Watford, Hertfordshire.	Brass instruments only.
St. Marylebone Industrial Schools, Southall, Middlesex	Brass, reeds, and flutes.
Bethnal Green Industrial Schools, Leytonstone, Essex	Brass instruments only.
Strand Industrial Schools, Edmonton, Middlesex	,, ,,
Westminster Industrial Schools, St. James's Road, Tooting, Surrey.	,, ,,
St. Georges-in-the-East Industrial Schools, Plasket, Plaistow, Essex.	,, ,,
Islington Industrial Schools, Hornsey Road, Holloway, Middlesex.	Brass, reeds, and flutes.
Holborn Industrial Schools, Mitcham, Surrey	,, ,,
Hendon Industrial Schools, Redhill, Edgware, Middlesex	Brass instruments only.
Mile End Old Town Industrial Schools, Bancroft Road, Mile End, Middlesex.	,, ,,
West Ham Industrial Schools, Leyton, Essex	,, ,,
Lambeth Industrial Schools, West Norwood, Surrey	,, ,,
St. Mary's Roman Catholic Orphanage, North Hyde, Hounslow, Middlesex.	Brass, reeds, and flutes.
Brighton Industrial Schools, Warren Farm, Brighton, Sussex.	,, ,,
Portsea Island Industrial Schools, Milton, Portsmouth, Hampshire.	,, ,,
Maidstone Industrial Schools, Coxheath, Maidstone, Kent.	,, ,,
Edmonton Industrial Schools, Enfield, Middlesex	Brass instruments only.
Brentford Industrial Schools, Isleworth, Middlesex	Brass, reeds, and flutes.
The Gordon Boys' Home, Chobham, Surrey	,, ,,

Figure 3.2
'Schools from which boys may generally be obtained' in 1892 (Museum of Army Music)

There were also several variances between regiments. Foot Guards bands (part of the Household Brigade) refused to accept boys for their bands, but they did recruit boys for other trades, including tailor boys, drummer boys, and specialist (clerks, motor transport, signallers, pioneers) boys.[30] The absence of band boys was almost certainly in order to maintain the culture of élite status at the Guards as they were able to internally recruit musicians from 'line' bands as well as adult civilian musicians. Other regiments did employ band boys alongside boy drummers and buglers, whilst the Royal Artillery and cavalry bands exclusively employed trumpeters. Even though these boys played musical instruments they were not recognised as bandsmen as a trade in the army and after a few years of boy service, up to the age of seventeen-and-a-half or eighteen, would normally transfer within their regiments, specialising in gunnery, signals, survey, administration, and fire control, with only a few specialising as trumpet sergeants and trumpet majors, continuing their trade as instrumentalists.[31] The exception to this were Household Cavalry trumpeters who were employed as bandsmen but followed a different career path up to the position of Trumpet Major and, as Hector Sutherland describes, would undertake 'Squadron and guard duties away from the band...whether we [the trumpeters] attended band practises was a matter of complete indifference to anyone'.[32] Some Royal Artillery trumpeters (who were not trained bandsmen), distinctively known as 'badgies' (derived from the Hindustani '*Baja Wallah* or 'music man'),[33] did become bandsmen but this was rare with only a few Royal Artillery boy trumpeters being reported as having joined the band full-time,[34] with others who became very proficient on the (natural) cavalry trumpet only occasionally invited to perform with the band.[35]

Notwithstanding the differences in regimental customs, the War Office did recognise the need for band boys and instructions for their recruitment remained relatively unchanged throughout the interwar period, with very few amendments to the King's Regulations for the Army regarding band boys from 1912 to 1940.[36] The 1923 King's

---

[30] See 'Boys' in *Regimental Standing Orders. Grenadier Guards* (London: Army & Navy Stores, 1939), pp. 85-89.
[31] B. Cloughley, *Trumpeters: The Story of the Royal Artillery Boy Trumpeters* (Bognor Regis: Woodfield, 2008), pp. 50-51.
[32] H. Sutherland, *They Blow Their Trumpets* (London: P. R. Macmillan, 1959), p. 31.
[33] J. W. Pennington, *Pick Up Your Parrots and Monkeys...and Fall in Facing the Boat: The Life of a Boy Soldier in India* (London: Cassell, 2003), p. 126.
[34] Cloughley, *Trumpeters*, pp. 19-21.
[35] *Ibid*, pp. 90-93.
[36] *The King's Regulations and Orders for the Army* (London: HMSO, 1912; 1923; 1928; 1935; 1940).

Regulations stated that 'Boys enlisted by special authority for training as musicians, but not included in the establishment, may be clothed like bandsmen, provided that expense to the public is not caused thereby'.[37] While this instruction seemingly allowed for an unlimited number of band boys, as long as they were maintained at regimental expense, it was not unknown for bands to employ at least sixteen.[38] In his account of the bands of the King's Own Yorkshire Light Infantry (KOYLI), Grainger provides biographies of all the band members serving in the late 1930s and discloses that thirty-three of the forty-two members of the 1st Battalion Band had been band boys when they enlisted, most of them coming from institutions with only a 'few Boys from civil life.'[39] This large proportion reveals that rather than just topping-up the numbers for military bands, boys from institutions undoubtedly formed the backbone of the military band system in the interwar years.

Both regular army and institutions' bandmasters would have certainly known one another with many of the institutions' bandmasters having themselves been trained at Kneller Hall and taken employment with the institutions after retirement. In London alone, by 1912 there were fifteen bandmasters employed by the Central London Schools District to instruct at boys' institutions and they were each responsible for upwards of thirty boys, with Bethnal Green having seventy and North Surrey 'a large number'.[40] At the Central London School District Workhouse Farm (Cuckoo School) at Hanwell 'many boys went to join army bands'[41]: between 1898 and 1901 fifty-one boys had joined army bands and fourteen old boys had become bandmasters from Hanwell.[42] One former band boy, Angus Macdonald, attended Hanwell from aged seven to fourteen after his

---

[37] *King's Regulations,1923*, para. 1434, p. 349.
[38] A. E. James, 'The Instruction of Boys', *"The Military Musician": The "Leading Note" of Military Music*, Vol. II, No. 4, April, 1934, p. 45.
[39] Grainger, *Life and Times*, pp. 20-32.
[40] LMA CLSD/252. '5th July 1912. Queries as to Salaries of Bandmasters in Metropolitan Schools: Particulars as to the Bandmasters' Appointments'.
[41] P. Higginbotham, 'Central London School District', <http://www.workhouses.org.uk/CentralLondonSD/#Homes> [accessed 14th December 2014]; Charlie Chaplin had attended the school in the late 1890s, see K. S. Lynn, *Charlie Chaplin and His Times* (New York: Simon & Schuster, 1997), p. 52.
[42] S. Stewart. *The Central London District Schools 1856-1933: A Short History* (Hanwell, London: Hanwell Community Association, 1980), pp. 16. WCA (Pamphlet 373.42 Central).

father died, and then joined the Band of the 1st Battalion Light Infantry in 1932. His recollection of his time at Hanwell is interesting in that it is unremarkable, and most certainly typical of the experiences of most boys at institutions. He described his experience at Hanwell as 'very happy' and 'everyone was nice to us', soon coming to the conclusion that there was nothing else to do except join the army. With no previous experience as a performer, Angus Macdonald swapped between the bugle platoon and band, playing cornet, then bugle, then French horn, but describing himself as 'never any good'.[43] This swapping of instruments was probably dependent upon the needs of the band as there are other examples of boys not having the choice of their first instrument at the institutions, as recounted by Peter Mawford from his time at Goldings William Baker Memorial Technical School for Boys in the late 1930s, who had wanted to play the drums but was given a trombone instead.[44]

Angus Macdonald also revealed that bandmasters would come to the school and offer the boys a shilling to join their regiment,[45] a process confirmed by Jimmy Howe who recounts that 'Bandmasters would visit these establishments and recruit boys from the age of 14'.[46] This unofficial recruiting method was very important to the institutions and bands, and ensured a steady trickle of boys fit to be sent into 'His Majesty's Regimental Bands', with about two boys being sent each quarter from Hanwell by 1927.[47] Undoubtedly favours were called between bandmasters at institutions and recommendations to take up appointments discussed before retirement, as these positions could be lucrative. In 1912 the non-residential bandmaster at Hanwell was responsible for forty-five boys and was earning £80 a year (plus a £5 allowance for uniforms) for

---

[43] Macdonald, A. J. Interviewed by Harry Moses for IWM on 27th January 2003. Catalogue number 24691.
<http://www.iwm.org.uk/collections/item/object/80022302> [accessed 4th March 2015].
[44] P. Mawford, 'Focus on Goldings,'
<http://www.goldonian.org/mem_sub_pages/peter_mawford_goldings.htm> [accessed 9th March 2015].
[45] Macdonald, A. J. Interviewed by Harry Moses for IWM on 27th January 2003. Catalogue number 24691.
<http://www.iwm.org.uk/collections/item/object/80022302> [accessed 4th March 2015].
[46] Howe, *A Conductor's Journey*, p. 17.
[47] LMA CLSD/31. 'Central London District School, Minute Book No. 31, Hanwell Ordinary Meeting 4th July 1927'.

eighteen-and-a-half hours per week,[48] but by 1925 the school clearly saw increased value in the band, with Mr John Alfred Perks, the new bandmaster, receiving £250 a year, including a residential allowance.[49]

One institution in London that was particularly noted for sending boys to army bands was the Foundling Hospital School, a large charity which had been set up in the eighteenth century and was famous for its donated art collection, and also where Handel, as a benefactor, had often performed his works. The school band had been started in 1847,[50] and was considered by some writers as 'the most important development of the activities of the children during the nineteenth century'[51] (see Fig. 3.3). The band soon became a major part of the institution and Charles Dickens heard it on several occasions when visiting. Membership of the band began at the age of eleven,[52] and it is claimed that by 1918, 80% of the boys leaving the institution enlisted into army bands.[53] This figure seems large but appears to tally with former pupil Charles Nalden's recollection that by the 1930s most of the boys who left the hospital joined army bands, with only a very small number not doing so.[54] The Foundling Hospital School's mark on some army bands was considerable as, for example, when Charles Nalden and two others from the school joined the Royal Artillery (Mounted) Band at the age of fourteen in 1922, there were ten ex-Foundling boys out of a band of about sixty (including boys).[55]

---

[48] LMA CLSD/252. 'Particulars as to the Bandmasters' Appointments'.
[49] LMA CLSD/31. 'Central London District School, Minute Book No. 31, Hanwell Ordinary Meeting 23rd November 1925'.
[50] 'A Letter to the Treasurer of the Foundling Hospital on the Expediency of Forming an Instrumental Band, From Amongst the Boys of the Hospital. Printed by Order of the Committee, 6th February, 1847.' John Brownlow. The Foundling Museum, Coram's Children Exhibition, Music, No. 9 (Visited 1st February 2015).
[51] R. H. Nichols and F. A. Wray, *The History of the Foundling Hospital* (London: Oxford University Press (Humphrey Milford), 1935), 321.
[52] 'Music at Foundling'
<http://foundlingvoices.foundlingmuseum.org.uk/themes/films/59.html> [accessed 31st January 2015].
[53] The Foundling Museum, 'Foundlings at War: Teachers Notes: December 2013-December 2015', p. 3, <http://foundlingmuseum.org.uk/wp-content/uploads/2016/12/Teachers-Notes-December-2013-December-2015.pdf> [accessed 7th July 2017].
[54] Nalden, *Half and Half*, p. 207.
[55] *Ibid*, p. 214.

Figure 3.3
London Foundling boys marching, early 1900s (MAM)

The Commandant's list at figure 3.2 only identifies institutions from the South of England, probably due to relative proximity to Kneller Hall, but it was not the only area of the United Kingdom that had boys who could be recruited into the army. Regimental bandmasters in the north of England also had a choice of institutions to visit for potential recruits, such as Manchester's Ardwick Industrial School which had many boys in its bands,[56] as did the Cumberland Industrial School, at Cockermouth, with about 150 boys and a band 'in demand for concerts and processions'.[57]

What is clear from the range of different institutions is that they all had a distinct focus on sending a large number of their boys to army bands as a relatively cheap and secure option for future employment. Some institutions were less overt in publicising their intentions but others, such as The Shaftesbury Homes and "Arethusa" Training Ship, explicitly promoted it as their unique selling point. In 1938, they reported that since 1843 they had given 34,169 children 'the chance of a good start in life', and of these 5,577 (approximately one third of the boys) had joined Service bands (Fig. 3.4),[58] making an average of approximately fifty-eight boys per year being sent to bands.

---

[56] 'Manchester and Stockport Certified Industrial Schools', *Manchester Family History Research* <http://www.manchester-family-history-research.co.uk/new_page_2.htm> [accessed 24th February 2015].
[57] M. Kohli, *The Golden Bridge: Young Immigrants to Canada, 1833-1939* (Toronto: Dundurn, 2003), p. 381.
[58] From the 'Newport Market Army Bands School Coronation Magazine and Report for 1937-8', Darrick Wood, Orpington, Kent, 1863-1935, No. 9, back cover. LMA/4647/D/03/01/011.

THE SHAFTESBURY HOMES and "ARETHUSA" TRAINING SHIP

(FOUNDED 1843).

WHAT the Society has done for the Nation and Empire.

Since 1843, 34,169 children have been given the chance of a good start in life.

5,577 boys have joined the Service Bands.

4,109 have joined the Royal Navy.

7,196 have joined the Mercantile Marine.

8,299 have been trained for civil employment.

1,046 have been helped to emigrate to the Dominions.

6,814 girls have been prepared for household duties.

There are now 1,200 boys and girls being accommodated in the Homes and Training Ship.

Donations and Legacies are urgently needed for their maintenance.

Headquarters:
164, SHAFTESBURY AVENUE, LONDON, W.C.2.

WILKINSON BROS., LTD., 37-42, Green Lanes, London. N.16

Figure 3.4
The back cover of the Newport Market Army Bands School (part of The Shaftesbury Homes and "Arethusa" Training Ship) Coronation Magazine and Report for 1937-8 displaying the number of boys sent to Service Bands (LMA)

Specialist band institutions

There were also a few institutions that specialised in training boys solely for the purpose of recruiting them into army bands. One was the St Augustine's Home for Boys, Sevenoaks, housing forty-two boys, and run by The Children's Society, which after its formation in 1921, changed its role to become a 'Special Training Home' for bands in 1932, with the age range to take boys raised from twelve to fifteen in order to accommodate the change in role.[59]

A larger institution, with about eighty boys, was the Newport Market Army Bands School (NMABS) which, from its inception in 1863, aimed to train poor boys aged between nine and fourteen for service in military bands (Figs 3.5, 3.6[60] & 3.7[61]). By the turn of the century it was reported that of the 1,000 boys who had passed through the school:

> 570 have become "Soldiers of the Queen," joining the bands of the Army straight from the school at the age of fourteen. About 150 more have entered the army later on.

In 1898, an officer commanding the 2nd Battalion The Wiltshire Regiment remarked that 'I can point to seven bandmasters from there [NMABS] in my time'.[62] At least one of the boys from the NMABS became both Senior Director of Music of the Household Division and Chief Instructor and Director of Music, The Royal Military School of Music, Kneller Hall: Boy Jaeger in 1923 to Lieutenant Colonel Jaeger in 1966.[63]

---

[59] 'St Augustine's Home For Boys, Sevenoaks', <http://www.hiddenlives.org.uk/cgi-bin/displayrec.pl?searchtext=band&record=/homes/SEVEN02.html> [accessed 22nd January 2015]; P. Higginbotham, 'St Augustine's Home for Boys, Sevenoaks, Kent', <http://www.childrenshomes.org.uk/SevenoaksStAugustineWS/> [accessed 22nd January 2015].
[60] LMA/4647/D/03/01/008. From 'Newport Market Army Bands School Magazine and Report for 1934-5', Darrick Wood, Orpington, Kent, 1863-1935, No. 6.
[61] LMA. LMA/4647/D/03/01/010. Newport Market Army Bands School Magazine and Report for 1936-7, Darrick Wood, Orpington, Kent, 1863-1937, No. 8, p. 33.
[62] LMA A/FWA/C/D1000/1 Newport Market Refuge. Lucy C. F. Cavendish, Letter to TheTimes 12 Dec 1900.
[63] C. Dean, *Jiggs: A Biography of Lieutenant Colonel C. H. Jaeger, OBE, Mus Bac, LRAM, ARCM, psm* (Tunbridge Wells: Parapress, 2013).

Figure 3.5
The Newport Market Army Training School Band, 1922 (LMA)

Figure 3.6
The Newport Market Army Bands School Cadet Corps, 22nd September, 1934 (LMA)

The Dependence on Band Boys 83

Figure 3.7
Old Boys of the Newport Market Army Bands School serving in the 2nd Battalion The Border Regiment in 1936: Boy E. Reilly, Bdsm. G. Froud, Boy D. Rielly, L/Cpl H. Russell (LMA)

One visiting officer to the NMABS in 1937 described the education as giving the boys 'a fine start towards quick advancement in the Service',[64] and there is no doubt that the musical and physical training received was considered an advantage for those who joined the army. One recruit, Boy Temple, noted that his time at the NMABS and in the army was very similar: 'comparing the life I had at the school and life in the army there was practically no

---

[64] KCL Archives, Kirke 5/1, Addresses to O.T.Cs., Cadets, Schools, etc, 'Address to Newport Market (Army Bands) School, Darrick Wood, Orpington, on July 2nd, by General Sir Walter Kirke', 1937.

difference.'⁶⁵ He had had no musical training beforehand as his family could not afford instruments or lessons and so he was fully taught at the NMABS.⁶⁶

The fact that the NMABS was purely dedicated to supplying boys for military bands, but had no official connection to the RMSM, is puzzling, considering the reliance on boys to populate the bands. This absence of connectivity with the boys' institutions by the authorities at Kneller Hall in general is inexplicable and it can only be assumed that the RMSM took for granted the supply of boys, seeing no need to extend its interest beyond an informal network. The lack of concern by the RMSM towards the NMABS is recognised by one writer in the RMSM's journal, *The Leading Note*, who commented that 'It is curious how little is known of this School when one realises that it lives, moves, and has its being entirely for the benefit of the Army'.⁶⁷ But this view does not seem to have been expressed elsewhere and, despite the singular role of the NMABS, the RMSM and army bandmasters were prepared to continue taking advantage of an ostensibly guaranteed flow of boy recruits.

The military boarding schools

In the nineteenth century they were schools based around the garrison towns at home as well as overseas, particularly in India. In addition to the garrison schools there were three military boarding schools in the United Kingdom, funded by the War Office, with the management and staff all serving military personnel: the Royal Hibernian Military School, Dublin (later moving to Kent); the Duke of York's Royal Military School, Dover; and the Queen Victoria School, Dunblane. There were also schools throughout the British Empire that followed similar curriculums and had military-style bands, such as the four Lawrence Military Schools in India, originally founded in 1847 for 'providing a home and refuge for children and

---

⁶⁵ O. W. Temple. Interviewed by Harry Moses, 4ᵗʰ August 1992 for IWM archives. Catalogue number 12713.
<http://www.iwm.org.uk/collections/item/object/80024469> [accessed 5ᵗʰ March 2015].
⁶⁶ LMA/4647/D/03/02/001. C. Blanchard, 'Newport Market Army Bands School', p. 7.
⁶⁷ *The Leading Note*, 'The Newport Market Training School', October, 1928, p. 33.

orphans of soldiers of the British Army.'[68] The military schools' role was principally to prepare boys for time in the army, but also a sign of a genuine care of the children of soldiers, a point expressed throughout Cockerill's study, *Sons of the Brave*.[69]

It has been suggested that in these schools, until at least the Second World War, army children's education was at the forefront of education reform, pre-empting the state by many years in issues such as compulsory education and curriculum.[70] This certainly appears to be the case concerning music education in the middle of the nineteenth century, with the *Report on the Regimental and Garrison Schools of the Army* advising on the benefits of learning music and that 'the musical instruction they [the boys] receive quickens their taste and intelligence'.[71] Furthermore, the schools employed bandmasters as well as sergeant drummers or pipers, with some of the bandmasters having been boys at the schools themselves who had gone on to have distinguished careers.[72] While these positions were sought after, and the schools did offer a music education not available to other children, the military boarding schools were not, as some have described, 'elite schools',[73] simply because the children attending them were the off-spring of rank-and-file soldiers who had never received a large salary or achieved high rank.

The accompanying text to the Commandant's report from 1892 (Fig. 3.2) names two of these military schools (the third was yet to be established) as providing band boys for the army. The Royal Hibernian Military School (RHMS) was the oldest of the three and had a permanent bandmaster on the staff, as recorded in both the 1901 and 1911 censuses.[74] A small marching band of fifes and drums

---

[68] B. E. Augwin, 'Music in a Famous Military School in India', *"The Military Musician": The "Leading Note" of Military Music*, Vol. III, No. 2, April, 1937, pp. 25-26.
[69] Cockerill, *Sons of the Brave*.
[70] See N. T. St J. Williams, *Tommy Atkins' Children: The Story of the Education of the Army's Children 1675-1970* (London: HMSO, 1971). Throughout his survey Williams continually emphasises this point.
[71] Quoted in Williams, *Tommy Atkins' Children*, p. 59.
[72] See for example, 'A Change of Bandmasters', *Hibernia: Quarterly Magazine of the Royal Hibernian Military School*, January, 1917, p. 11.
[73] N. Sheldon, 'The musical careers of the poor: the role of music as a vocational training for boys in British care institutions 1870-1918', *History of Education*, 38: 6, p. 750 [pp. 747-759].
[74] P. Callery, 'Part 2: 1901 Census (families and pupils)' and ' 'Part 3: 1911 Census (families and pupils)' in G. H. O'Reilly (ed), *History of the Royal Hibernian Military*

had been in existence at the school since at least 1825,[75] but a larger band was started in 1850 with the appointment of a 'Sergeant Instructor of Music'. From the earliest days boys were sent to army bands, with many becoming bandmasters, according to Boy E. Smith, who was enlisted into the 85th Foot as a cornet player and later (1908) wrote of the number of bandmasters.[76] The RHMS survived in Ireland until the forming of the Irish Free State in 1922 when it moved to Dover and was eventually subsumed into The Duke of York's Royal Military School in 1924 (see below).

The daily routine after World War One was the same as pre-war, as the Standing Orders of 1908 continued to be adhered to, with band practice an integral part of the curriculum.[77] Nevertheless, in 1919 it was decided that boys in the band and drums should be kept at the school until the age of 15, no doubt to fully utilise the skills of the musicians (Fig. 3.8[78]). It is not clear whether this hindered their general education or was a benefit, but it certainly pre-dated the leaving age for state education by several decades.

It is problematical to ascertain exactly which boys went to bands from the RHMS as the discharge register only specifies 'Band' for the Royal Artillery and Royal Garrison Artillery,[79] but over the years the school was to produce thirty-three army Bandmasters and Directors of Music. For example, Boy Patrick A. Purcell, who was to be appointed bandmaster of the Bedfordshire and Hertfordshire Regiment in 1929,[80] had been identified at RHMS as having great potential and after joining the army as a band boy won a year's

---

School Dublin (Dún Laoghaire, Co. Dublin: Genealogical Society of Ireland, 2001), pp. 37 & 55.
[75] M. Quane, 'The Royal Hibernian Military School Phoenix Park, Dublin: Part II', *Dublin Historical Record*, Vol. 18, No. 2, March, 1963, p. 48.
[76] Clarke, *New History*, p. 271.
[77] *Ibid*, p. 464.
[78] *Hibernia: Quarterly Magazine of the Royal Hibernian Military School*, October, 1919, front cover.
[79] TNA. WO 143/26. 'Royal Hibernian Military School, alphabetical index'.
[80] H. G. Farmer, 'Irish Bandsmen in the British Army', *The Irish Sword*, V: 18, Summer, 1961, p. 58.

scholarship to the Royal Academy of Music before he became a student bandmaster at Kneller Hall.[81]

Figure 3.8
The Royal Hibernian Military School Band, 1919

The acknowledgement by the military that many of the boys would eventually enter the regular army as band boys was evident by the inspection of the school band on several occasions by the Commandant and Senior Director of Music from the Royal Military School of Music. An inspection team of Colonel T. C. F. Somerville and Maj A. J. Stretton had visited in December 1916 and recommended more scale practice; a follow-up report in 1918 recognises that much good work had been done in trying to make performances more musical, and also that 'the knowledge of scales – the foundation of all music – would do credit to any band of men'.[82]

Another military school, originally known as the Royal Military Asylum (RMA), Chelsea, the Duke of York's Royal Military School (DoYRMS) already had a band of sorts in 1827 when it headed a procession for the lying in state of its founder, the Duke of York,[83] and

---

[81] 'Musical Honours for Patk. Purcell', *Hibernia: Quarterly Magazine of the Royal Hibernian Military School*, July, 1921, p. 4.
[82] 'Inspection – Bands and Drums', *Hibernia: Quarterly Magazine of the Royal Hibernian Military School*, April, 1918, p. 4.
[83] Williams, *Tommy Atkins' Children*, p.34.

it was evident that music was being taught in 1846 when an inspector came across 'the crash of many ill-tuned instruments'.[84] Documents from the Adjutant-General's office record that boys were recruited as musicians between 1819 and 1826,[85] and by 1842 there were 64 musicians in the Horse and Foot Guards in London who had been educated at the RMA, including one of the most famous clarinet players of the nineteenth century, Henry Lazarus, as well as the father of Sir Arthur Sullivan, Thomas Sullivan.[86] The school was inspected every year by the General Officer Commanding in Chief, Eastern Command, who invariably described the band, in this case in 1921, as 'a great feature of the school and has the advantage of starting boys early in this vocation'.[87] It is known that a considerable number of DoYRMS boys joined the army with many becoming bandsmen, but the exact number in bands is difficult to determine as the figures provided list 'Bandsmen, Boys, Warrant officers, and Non-Commissioned Officers', and these last two descriptions would have included musicians.[88] Even so, it has been suggested that the number serving as bandsmen at any one time must have been in the region of 300.[89]

The Queen Victoria School (QVS), Dunblane, founded in 1906, was the last of the three military schools to open in the United Kingdom. The standard of the school band seems to have depended greatly on the quality and enthusiasm of the bandmaster and the clash of curriculum time. After several Bandmasters in quick succession, the military band was given a boost with the arrival of Mr Felix Lax in 1931, a former Bandmaster of the King's Own Scottish Borderers.[90] He revised the timetable to de-conflict instrumental practice and classroom lessons,[91] and also implemented a system where more

---

[84] *Ibid*, p. 38.
[85] A. W. Cockerill, *The Charity of Mars: A History of the Royal Military Asylum (1803-1892)* (Cobourg, Ontario: Black Cat Press, 2002), pp. 193-4.
[86] *Ibid*, pp. 161 & 176-7.
[87] TNA. WO 143/73. 'Commandants Annual Report, 1921 June-1925 May'.
[88] TNA. WO 143/23. 'Discharges of male children, 1903-1923'.
[89] L. C. Rudd, *A Short Account of the Duke of York's Royal Military School, Dover (Founded 19th June, 1801)* (Dover: The Duke of York's Royal Military School, 1924), p. 25.
[90] Bandmaster Felix H. Lax, B.E.M., <http://www.mcdond.co.uk/qvs/1956/html/page_4_.html> [accessed 2nd February 2015].
[91] T. May, *Remembering the Past – Looking to the Future: 100 Years of Queen Victoria School* (Oxford: Gresham Books/Queen Victoria School, 2008), p. 70.

senior boys would coach youngsters. This produced rapid results: within a year the band was giving regular concerts, initially from the school theatre (relayed by loudspeakers throughout the school) and then at more public events.

The three military schools in the United Kingdom had a unique status amongst institutions for boys in that they were officially recognised by the War Office and were on occasion subject to musical inspections by the RMSM. Their ceremonial role was also established during the First World War when the drill staff at the schools were included in a request to the Treasury for the re-introduction of pre-war full-dress uniforms for bands.[92] Full dress for the army had been withdrawn during the First World War but the boys at the three military schools were allowed to retain it.

While the military schools were afforded a higher status by the War Office than other institutions for boys there does not appear to be a significantly larger proportion entering military bands. It is not even possible to say that they were better prepared for the military than boys from other institutions because all boys, regardless of institution, were brought up in a quasi-military environment. The enthusiasm and quality of the bandmaster and his relationship with the institution was probably the most important factor in deciding the preparedness of the boys. Nevertheless, palms were greased and deals struck with the bandmasters of the schools to recruit the best and reports in some regimental journals do suggest a hierarchy of boy recruits with, for example, *The Oxfordshire and Buckinghamshire Light Infantry Journal* reporting that boys from the DoYRMS, known for their '"Dukies" swagger', were particularly sought after.[93]

'Civilian' band boys

A minority of boys who had not been to institutions did gain employment in army bands and from the available first-hand accounts the experiences of these 'civilian' boys was quite varied. Most seem to have been treated with some curiosity and as outsiders, but others (although in the minority), such as Boy Edward Castle claimed that there was no real difference between those who had been

---

[92] TNA. T 161/105/7. 'Fighting Services. Clothing: Extension of Full Dress clothing to regimental bands and drill staff of the Queen Victoria, Duke of York's and the Royal Hibernian Military Schools'.
[93] 'Boys, 43rd', *The Oxfordshire and Buckinghamshire Light Infantry Journal*, Vol. X, No. 57, September, 1934, p. 189.

orphans and those who were not.[94] What they did have in common, though, was that they had not been institutionalised by a regime that mimicked military culture. They experienced a more complex application process and boys without musical knowledge or ability were usually sent to the tailor's or shoemaker's shop, but those who could already play an instrument could be admitted for audition, such as Hector Sutherland who joined the 6th Battalion The Durham Light Infantry, and later the 2nd Life Guards, as a band boy during the First World War. Sutherland reveals the extent to which boy soldiers were usually recruited from an established network:

> With very few exceptions, only boys of outstanding musical ability from the Royal Military Schools are considered, and to be entered at a military school meant having to be the son of a soldier. This perpetual evolution furnished the never ending need for boys of the right temperament and character. So to gate crash through that impregnable system was really something to be pleased about.[95]

The system certainly was hard for outsiders such as Hector Sutherland but, despite his experiences, boys who had not been to one of the institutions were not necessarily at a musical disadvantage as there were civilian organisations that encouraged music performance from a young age. For some, the transition from uniformed boys' groups to military bands was important, with Harold "Mick" Morris-Metcalf claiming that he would not have joined the 1st and 2nd Battalions The Gloucestershire Regiment as a boy drummer (and later as band boy) had he not played drums in the Bristol Boys' Brigade and sung in the local Salvation Army songsters.[96] Boys involved in these bands were generally able to supplement the lack of instrumental training in the typical school education system, but only as an additional activity, and it was hard for boys to devote as much time to musical performance and drill as those at the specialist military schools.

---

[94] Castle, E. Interviewed by Lindsay Baker for IWM, 10th September 2001. Catalogue number 22165.
<http://www.iwm.org.uk/collections/item/object/80021951> [accessed 19th February 2015].
[95] Sutherland, They Blow Their Trumpets, p. 18.
[96] H. F. Morris-Metcalf. Interviewed by Lyndsay Baker, no date for IWM archives. Catalogue number 22077.
<http://www.iwm.org.uk/collections/item/object/80021939> [accessed 5th March 2015].

It was normally possible for boys to be enlisted from civil life from the age of 15, but the army recognised that 'at 15 it is late to start a career as a musician',[97] and so for boy recruits to be successful who had not attended an institution, it was an advantage to have had a background of military music in the family, such as John Mackenzie-Rogan (who hailed from a long line of military men and had joined as a band boy in 1867, playing the flute before his enlistment).[98] In 1939, Boy Malcolm Morris and his four brothers joined the army as band boys as their father was a bandmaster and all five brothers played instruments to a reasonable standard before they joined.[99]

Individual reasons for joining the army were varied, ranging from personal drive to influence from those with connections. 'Bunnie' Mason, at the age of fifteen, joined the Royal Artillery Band as a boy against his father's wishes, but as a reasonably accomplished flautist (his father was a 'Professor of Music' – probably a teacher), he had been encouraged to play from the age of eight and pursued his desire to join.[100] Hector Sutherland suggested that his successful application to join the army as a bandsman, and subsequent transfer to the 2nd Life Guards, was through the influence of a local squire at Redworth, Co. Durham, a former Life Guard officer.[101]

There were also boys with no musical experience at all who still managed to get into the band, but for them there was the additional burden of having to learn an instrument and read music from scratch. It was assumed that Jack Troup, despite not playing an instrument, got let into the Band of the 2nd Battalion the Norfolk Regiment by someone who had 'dropped a bollock',[102] but he managed to stay. Perhaps unsurprisingly though, some, like Boy C. W. 'Spike' Mays, found it difficult to succeed with the demands of being a musician. Mays describes how on reaching his band, The Royal Dragoons, the Trumpet Major was concerned that Boy Mays had not come from an institution. Mays explains:

---

[97] A. E. Zealley, J. Ord Hume & J. A. C. Somerville, *Famous Bands of the British Empire* (London, J. P. Hull, 1926), p. 14.
[98] J. Mackenzie-Rogan, *Fifty Years of Army Music* (London: Methuen, 1926), pp. 4.
[99] R. M. Morris. Interviewed by Nigel de Lee, 25th July 2000 for IWM archives. Catalogue number 20468.
<http://www.iwm.org.uk/collections/item/object/80024469> [accessed 5th March 2015].
[100] H. B. Mason, *Memoirs of a Gunner Bandsman: 1907-1932* (Orpington: Mason, 1978), pp. 3-5.
[101] Sutherland, *They Blow Their Trumpets*, pp. 7 & 16-17.
[102] Troup, *The Life that Jack Lived*, p. 13.

[M]ost of my new colleagues were orphans from schools like the Duke of York's, where they had been taught music and to play instruments before they enlisted. Boy Rose, whose father was a captain Beefeater (the Yeoman of the Guard) at the tower of London, was the only one with a live father, and I appeared to be the one and only with two parents – and no music, apart from singing hymns in church, and on Ashdon Place Farm to scare off rooks. 'You can't play an instrument' asked Flutey Thomas. 'How the hell did you get into the band, then?'[103]

Like Boy Rose, Boy Mays had been accepted through the influence of family and friends, and for Mays it had been a local Scoutmaster in Essex who had the right connections.[104] But this was to prove too much for him and after some months Boy Mays was told that he was 'not likely to make progress as a musician and is recommended for return to duty [as a trooper]',[105] so that at the age of eighteen Boy Mays left the band and was sent to 3 Troop, C Sabre Squadron, as a trumpeter.

Another without any musical knowledge, Boy Harraway, joined the 2nd Battalion The Duke of Cornwall's Light Infantry aged 14 as a band boy in 1925, but he was luckier and managed to get through the training, explaining that once a boy was taught how to read music then he would go on to teach others.[106] Boy Edward Castle who joined in 1929 as a bandsman, aged fourteen, had had no formal musical training although he had sung in the local choir. He describes that, when he first joined, there were twenty band boys in one room and twenty drummer boys in the other room: 'a lot of them had come from the orphanages', mostly from London where they had played in the orphanage bands.[107]

---

[103] S. Mays, *Fall Out the Officers* (London: Eyre and Spottiswoode, 1969), p. 11; S. Mays, *The Band Rats* (London: Peter Davies, 1975), p. 25-26.
[104] S. Mays, *Reuben's Corner: An English Country Boyhood* (London: Eyre Methuen, 1969; repr. 1980), pp. 19-21; S. Mays, *The Band Rats* (London: Peter Davies, 1975); p. 7.
[105] Mays, *Fall Out the Officers*, p. 47.
[106] Harraway, Mr., Interviewed by Nigel de Lee for IWM, 6th January 2000. Catalogue number 19989.
<http://www.iwm.org.uk/collections/item/object/80021243> [accessed 2nd March 2015].
[107] Castle, E. Interviewed by Lindsay Baker for IWM, 10th September 2001. Catalogue number 22165.
<http://www.iwm.org.uk/collections/item/object/80021951> [accessed 19th February 2015].

Having a relative in the army also proved an incentive: Robert Hawksworth joined the Durham Light Infantry as a band boy in 1936, without any musical performance experience, after visiting his uncle who was an NCO in the regiment. Fortunately, he had 'the knack' on the clarinet and progressed well.[108] It seems that the successful progress of the non-musically trained boys depended on hard work and whether there was any latent musical talent that was recognised by the bandmaster. Norman Wisdom, a band boy with the 10th Hussars in the 1930s, and with no previous musical experience was told that he could 'bullshit them [the recruiters]' when he went to join as a bandsman.[109] He was not successful on the first attempt but, having been accepted and spending some weeks as boy drummer, then leaving the army and re-joining, he was recruited as a band boy with very rudimentary knowledge, but confidently delivered in his audition. Once accepted, Norman Wisdom described the process of deciding which instruments to play:

> We lined up in front of him [the bandmaster] as he consulted the list of new arrivals. 'Ah, Wisdom. Let's have a look at you.' He stepped up close, and examined my lips with his fingertips to judge the embouchure – the shape of my mouth and tongue – for the tautness with which I could grip a reed cap. 'Purse them...now smile...open wide'...Finally Mr Roberts stepped back. 'I'm putting you on clarinet, Wisdom'. Then he turned to the others, and an hour later we all knew our instrument: trumpet, trombone, oboe, bassoon euphonium...Simpson, who had somehow got through despite the drawback of a hairlip...drums![110]

This process of boys being assigned instruments is further embellished by Norman Wisdom in a comic style, but it concurs with other accounts available and shows how, in an audition of just a few minutes, boys were embarked on a career in music.

Band boy training

Once boys had reached their bands, training was given to take them up to the necessary standard to serve as adults. In 1926 Hector

---

[108] Hawksworth, R. W. Interviewed by Harry Moses for IWM, 4th August 1992. Catalogue number 12708.
<http://www.iwm.org.uk/collections/item/object/80012440> [accessed 4th March 2015].
[109] N. Wisdom and W. Hall, *My Turn* (London: Arrow, 1992), p. 42.
[110] *Ibid*, p. 53.

Adkins, the Director of Music at Kneller Hall, wrote an article that endeavoured to explain the process of training bandsmen, entitled *From Band-Boy to Band-Master*.[111] In one section, alarmingly called *Breaking In*, he appraises the system of recruiting and training band boys:

> "Breaking In."...Band-boys, who must be over fifteen years of age and possess certain educational qualifications, are drawn from various military schools, training ships, charitable institutes and the like. They need not possess musical knowledge, although this is highly desirable. Boys who are absolutely beginners are handed over to the band sergeant to be broken in, and to learn a little of the elements of music and harmony. But, at the same time, they do recruits' drill on the barracks square, and must obtain certain certificates of education laid down.[112]

The broad outline presented by Adkins suggests a systematic method of training band boys, but in the regimental band environment this was not always the case as it was dependent on the relationship the band had with its regiment, what resources were available, and the ability and enthusiasm of the bandmaster. Band NCOs responsible for training were often called away for regimental duties (Regimental Orderly Corporal, for instance) so that scheduled teaching rarely took place in the daytime, resulting in some bands having to resort to evening training as the best to instruct boys.[113] Boys were not allowed to associate with regular soldiers, except those in the band, and although no doubt a practical measure to keep boys together, the training process was further complicated by often having boy trumpeters, drummers, and band boys – who each needed separate training – placed under a single band NCO.[114]

Adkins' reference to 'breaking in' hints at a history of band boy training that was brutal and uncaring, and there are certainly examples of harsh treatment and severe punishment in Victorian and Edwardian times: John Mackenzie-Rogan describes the ruthless

---

[111] H. E. Adkins, 'From Band-Boy to Band-Master', *1st Battalion, The Duke of Cornwall's Light Infantry. "One and All." Gazette and Chronicle*, Vol. 1, New Series No. 7, January, 1926, pp. 10-12. First published in *The Radio Times* (National), Vol. 8, Issue 104, 18th September, 1925, p. 555.
[112] *Ibid.*, p. 11.
[113] A. E. James, 'The Instruction of Boys', *"The Military Musician": The "Leading Note" of Military Music*, Vol. II, No. 4, April, 1934, p. 45.
[114] Troup, *The Life that Jack Lived*, p. 13.

punishments dished out to soldiers,[115] and Arthur Pullinger recounts how, as a band boy with the Manchester Regiment, he witnessed the 'birching' of boys – he describes the process – for in-barracks offences up until 1907, when it was abolished.[116] Even though corporal punishment was officially over, band boys had to endure the lowest status in the band and regiment with Hector Sutherland reporting that in the 2nd Life Guards 'little or no personal interest did either [the band sergeant and director of music] take in the progress of our juvenile squad'.[117] 'Jiggs' Jaeger recollected that 'the band corporal's dog was a higher form of animal life [than band boys] in those days'.[118] In a professional army this is hardly unexpected and boys from institutions would have been used to a stern environment but, on the whole, conditions did improve and many describe the training given to boys from the bandmaster, musicians, as well as educationally, from both the Royal Army Education Corps and the Physical Training instructors, as being a very positive experience with bandmasters largely being especially attentive of their boy recruits.

Most personal accounts relate that boys underwent a strict routine of training, both musical and educational, with various approaches emerging from individual experiences. Boy Charles Nalden joined the Royal Artillery Mounted Band in 1922 and found himself sharing a room and training with fifteen other band boys who trained together.[119] Malcom Morris reports that there were about eight band boys in 1939 in the 7th Hussars Band in Egypt, trained by a Sergeant Instructor.[120] In the Royal Artillery Band, young hands were instructed at allotted times by the soloists of the band, with the NCOs receiving a teaching allowance from the band fund.[121] 'Bunnie' Mason recalled that for boys the day incorporated 'Reveille at 6 a.m., drill, marching, saluting, gymnasium, school and practice for the

---

[115] Mackenzie-Rogan, *Fifty Years of Army Music*, pp. 9-13.
[116] A. Pullinger, *Reminiscences* (Museum of Army Music, Kneller Hall: MS, 1939), p. 10.
[117] Sutherland, *They Blow Their Trumpets*, p. 28.
[118] *Desert Island Discs: Lieutenant Colonel C H Jaeger*. BBC Radio 4. Monday 18th November 1968. <http://www.bbc.co.uk/programmes/p009y1hw#p009y1hw> [accessed 16th February 2015].
[119] Nalden, *Half and Half*, p. 225.
[120] R. M. Morris. Interviewed by Nigel de Lee, 25th July 2000 for IWM archives. Catalogue number 20468. <http://www.iwm.org.uk/collections/item/object/80024469> [accessed 5th March 2015].
[121] Mason, *Memoirs*, p. 21.

remainder of the day – sometimes up to 8 p.m.'[122] Boy Castle remembered a typical routine in the 2nd Battalion The Gloucestershire Regiment band: PT and band practice in the morning. Everyday school in the afternoon. Two hours practice at night. Finish about 1930 then do kit.[123]

After a year or two in the band some boys (and also a few who had become adults) were sent to the Royal Military School of Music on the 'pupils' course 'in order to fit them to compete later for admission as students [bandmasters]'.[124] Even for those boys who stayed with the band, the system of musical training at regimental level in the army proved to be a major provider of education for the music profession, for all styles, and a key source of supply for wind and percussion instrumentalists. The implied curricula within regiments was both practical and focussed in comparison to conservatories.

Social changes and recruiting

The 1916 RMSM inspection of the RHS band, referred to above, had asked for the school to produce more bandsmen, over and above the fifty boys in training at the school. The school Commandant, Colonel J. McDonnell, replied that they could not give any more attention to music in the syllabus, remarking that he wished to see the status and prospects of army bandsmen being improved in order to entice more boys into band service.[125] Despite the comment being made in the middle of the First World War, at a time when bands had yet to be fully re-formed, it seems to contradict the view of other institutions on the worth of boys joining the army as band boys, and is the first sign of institutional dissatisfaction with the system of recruitment.

Other critical voices were to come later, such as Charles Nalden, who was disparaging of music education in the army:

> [T]he [Foundling] hospital's policy of sending most of its boys into army bands was for them no more than a temporary expedient; a postponement

---

[122] Mason, *Memoirs*, p. 7
[123] E. Castle. Interviewed by Lindsay Baker for IWM, 10th September 2001. Catalogue number 22165.
<http://www.iwm.org.uk/collections/item/object/80021951> [accessed 19th February 2015].
[124] *The King's Regulations for the Army and the Army Reserve*, 1928 (London: HMSO, 1928), para 836.(i), p. 247.
[125] 'Band and Drums Inspected.', *Hibernia: Quarterly Magazine of the Royal Hibernian Military School*, January, 1917, p. 10.

of the day when the majority of boys would find themselves faced with the unenviable task of carving out a new career at a time when the average man of like age had long since been settled in some trade or business. Far better had we all been taught trades, however lowly, which would have stood us in good stead throughout our lives.[126]

Nalden cites examples of good musicians who had become stokers or common labourers, but this might just have been a product of an era of unemployment in the late 1920s when large numbers of civilian musicians found themselves out of work. While Nalden undeniably did well out of a musical education – he became a professor of music in New Zealand – it is true that many other ex-bandsmen were not so lucky and would not have found employment as musicians. Colonel McDonnell did not have the foresight to predict the change in fortunes of professional musicians in the United Kingdom, but his and Nalden's dissatisfaction may not have been isolated cases as other institutions were becoming more aware of the need for greater welfare at a time of increasing involvement of parents and the state.

This was particularly so after the turn of the century when parents began to be consulted on the future trade of their children, with some requesting for their children to be removed from military programmes, particularly when it became public knowledge in 1919 that the War Office sent so many band boys to India.[127] Even at the specialist NMABS not all parents wanted their boys to join the army as band boys and sought specific undertakings that 'such schooling should in nowise pledge him to Army service'.[128] Other institutions became more wary about offering their boys to the army although it did produce a dilemma as the army guaranteed employment and bands raised funds for the institution. For example, over the forty years from 1870-1910, 15% of the boys who had left the Newcastle Ragged and Industrial School went into the army, with many of them

---

[126] Nalden, *Half and Half*, p. 207.
[127] L. Murdoch, *Imagined Orphans – Poor Families, Child Welfare, and Contested Citizenship in London* (New Brunswick, New Jersey: Rutgers University Press, 2006), pp. 138-139
[128] 'King's Royal Rifle Corps (Band Boy)', *House of Commons Debate*, 7th June 1917, Vol. 94, cc254-5W,
<http://hansard.millbanksystems.com/written_answers/1917/jun/07/kings-royal-rifle-corps-band-boy#S5CV0094P0_19170607_CWA_48> [accessed 25th February 2015].

becoming bandsmen,[129] and after the school moved to Axwell Park in 1922, the band flourished, practising many evenings,[130] with the boys' brass band 'earning money giving concerts and had added reed instruments'.[131] Nonetheless, a request from the War Office to add the school to a list 'from which boys are selected for service in the army or navy', was declined with no reason given.[132]

The issue raised by Colonel McDonnell appears to have stemmed from the time when boys who had enlisted at the start of the First World War were used to provide useful replacements for casualties of the Divisional Bands after they were created in 1915 to perform at the front line,[133] and there is evidence that during the First World War and after, training in institutions related to the military, including preparation for service as military musicians, increased.[134] Colonel McDonnell's comments seem to go against the trend at the time and they pre-empted more vocal protestations over the following twenty years, particularly when concern for boys being placed in harm's way became heightened by several high-profile cases in Ireland.

The Irish War of Independence of 1919-21 was essentially a guerrilla war and, as there was no front line, boys were exposed to the same dangers experienced by adult soldiers, and on 31st May 1921 the worst case occurred: three band boys of the band of the 2nd Battalion the Hampshire Regiment were killed in an attack on the band, with three other band boys being wounded.[135] This widely reported strike highlighted the dangers for band boys and, although they were not specifically targeted, they were in the band that was attacked.

---

[129] W. Prahms, *Newcastle Ragged and Industrial School* (Stroud, Gloucestershire: Tempus, 2006), p. 79. Prahms does not identify the number of boys who went to military bands but it is highly likely that the majority were bandsmen.
[130] *Ibid*, p. 85.
[131] *Ibid*, p. 63.
[132] *Ibid*, pp. 65 & 72.
[133] J. A. N. [initials only], 'Music Behind the Lines, 1915-1918.', *"The Military Musician": The "Leading Note" of Military Music*, Vol. I, No. 8, February, 1932, pp. 16-18.
[134] Murdoch, *Imagined Orphans*, pp. 150-151.
[135] 'Account of Outrage on Band 2nd Bn. At Youghal, perpetrated by the I.R.A.', *The Hampshire Regimental Journal*, June, 1921, pp.89-91; 'Hampshire Band Murders 31 May 1921'; <http://www.cairogang.com/soldiers-killed/youghal/youghal.html> [accessed 24 February 2015]. See Chapter 9 for a discussion of this attack.

A few days later, however, on 5th June, boys became the specific target with three band boys, Mathew Carson, Charles Chapman and John Cooper of the 1st Battalion the Manchester Regiment all murdered. They had left Ballincollig Barracks in Co. Cork, apparently stealing out to go exploring, but stumbled across a group of IRA men and, after being chased and surrendering, were executed.[136] The bodies were not found for some time and the incident triggered questions in Parliament, highlighting the risks of deploying boys with battalions.[137] Throughout the conflict in Ireland there were other band boys who died through firearms accidents or sickness,[138] but although death through sickness was not uncommon in India, when it occurred on home soil, and could be reported quicker, the profile was raised of the dangers boys in the army were exposed to.

India, on the other hand, was still a distant country with journeys from Britain taking weeks and boys being shipped to the sub-continent sometimes serving many years there. It is estimated that between 1925 and 1939 there would have been at least 1200 boys sent to India as trumpeters,[139] and sometimes ten new boys would be sent to join a band in India at one time.[140] These boys provided the continuity for the band when adult bandsmen retired and for this reason former Band Sergeant Major, W. K. Grainger, asserts that for those bands working abroad, 'the Band Boys were, perhaps the most important part of the band'.[141]

It is not surprising then that by 1920, despite the case that soldiers should only be sent overseas when they reached the age of 18, it was confirmed in the House of Commons by the Secretary of State for War, Winston Churchill, that there was an exception allowing

---

[136] R. Bonner, 'Ballincollig: Three Band Boys, Marie Lindsay and Others', *Military Historical Society Bulletin*, Vol. 59, Pt. 235, February, 2009, p. 129.
[137] 'Manchester Regiment (Band Boy Shot)', *House of Commons Debate*, 5th December 1922, vol 159, c1491,
<http://hansard.millbanksystems.com/commons/1922/dec/05/manchester-regiment-band-boy-shot#S5CV0159P0_19221205_HOC_145> [accessed 24th February 2015].
[138] 'Pettman, Boy John Frederick',
<http://archive.cloud.cwgc.org/archive/doc/doc5701043.JPG> (accessed 24th February 2015); 'Hunt, George Cockram', *Commonwealth War Graves Commission*, <http://www.cwgc.org/find-war-dead/casualty/350635/HUNT,%20GEORGE%20COCKRAM> [accessed 24th February 2015].
[139] Cloughley, *Trumpeters*, p. 133.
[140] Mays, *The Band Rats*, p. 81.
[141] Grainger, *Life and Time*, p.139.

'bandsmen or band boys who have attained the age of 15 years and have completed three months' service' to join their regiments abroad to ensure that bands maintained their numbers.[142] Up to twenty-five boys could be sent to India each year as 'drummers, bandsmen, buglers, trumpeters, etc…[and] must be physically fit for service in any part of the world',[143] and while the thought of being sent to India did not appeal to all band boys there was a loophole that allowed them to be liable for service in India from the age of fifteen, provided there was the consent of parents.[144] This consent would in most cases have been easy to gain for boys from institutions where parents were no longer alive, but some boys from institutions still had parents who had to be consulted. For example, in 1933 David Hook's mother, who was living on her own, objected to him joining the army because of the risk of being sent overseas, although he was in an institution.[145]

Where there were no parents, the institution made the decision for the boys but sometimes refused service overseas for their boys, presumably resulting from the objections of the head of the school who acted as legal guardian. For example, George Dennis Hart's mother died when he was ten and he was sent to a London County Council children's home. The home suggested that all the boys in the band join the army and most of the boys did this, but when he subsequently joined at fifteen the school would not consent to him serving overseas, so he joined the Devons who were based in the United Kingdom.[146]

By the late 1920s concerns about the recruitment of under-18s were again being aired in Parliament and there were attempts to amend the Army Act to stop the recruitment of boys. From the discussions it can be seen that there was an understanding that many boy recruits came from orphanages and industrial schools and that

---

[142] 'Troops in Palestine', House of Commons Debate 02 March 1920 vol 126 cc268-9W, <http://hansard.millbanksystems.com/written_answers/1920/mar/02/troops-in-palestine#S5CV0126P0_19200302_CWA_26> [accessed 10th March 2015].

[143] 'The Regulations for the Army in India, 1st July 1937, Chapter II', quoted in Cloughley, *Trumpeters*, pp. 190.

[144] 'Service Overseas (Boys)', *House of Commons Hansard*, Tuesday 14th February 1928, Fifth Series, Vol. 213, c31.

[145] Hook, D. E. J. Interviewed by Conrad Wood for IWM on 18th October 1976. Catalogue number 837. <http://www.iwm.org.uk/collections/item/object/80000831> [accessed 4th March 2015].

[146] Hart, G. D. Interviewed by Conrad Wood for IWM, 25th October 1988. Catalogue number 10454. <http://www.iwm.org.uk/collections/item/object/80010232> [accessed 2nd March 2015].

band boys, as well as boy drummers and buglers, were treated separately, with little understanding of their role and potential dangers of service, particularly overseas.[147] Some MPs did not show any sympathy for the requirement for trained boys to enter regimental bands, particularly those keen to rid the army of its boy soldiers, with one MP, Morgan Jones, arguing in 1933 that 'adults can be obtained quite easily, and I do not see why adults should not perform as well as boys in the band or as trumpeters,'[148] even though he appears to have not been able to support his argument, particularly as the state could not pay for, train, or supply, musicians from the state education system.

One other related area that provoked public disquiet was the alleged exploitation of boys for commercial use as musicians. The issue came to a head with a project started by an Australian, Mr A. E. Marie, to take the 'British Empire Boys' Band' on tour to South Africa and Rhodesia in 1936. The whole episode was halted after a test case in which a Magistrate refused to allow a child to perform overseas using Chapter 7 of the Children (Employment Abroad) Act, 1913, where it stated that children or young persons could not go out of the United Kingdom 'for the purpose of singing, playing, performing, or being exhibited, for profit'.[149] Parliament had confirmed that the definition of 'children' comprised those under fourteen years of age and 'young persons' were between fourteen and sixteen,[150] but the issue of using boys to perform for profit overseas whilst in the army was overlooked as band boys were regularly

---

[147] 'New Clause.–(Amendment of s. 76 of Army Act.)', House of Commons Debate 17 April 1928 vol 216 cc9-1137W,
<http://hansard.millbanksystems.com/commons/1928/apr/17/new-clause-amendment-of-s-76-of-army-act#S5CV0216P0_19280417_HOC_211> [accessed 10th March 2015].
[148] 'New Clause.–(Amendment of Section 76 of Army Act.)', House of Commons Debate 03 April 1933 vol 276 cc1501-43W,
<http://hansard.millbanksystems.com/commons/1933/apr/03/new-clause-amendment-of-section-76-of#S5CV0276P0_19330403_HOC_416> [accessed 10th March 2015].
[149] TNA. MEPO 2/4290. 'The British Empire Boys' Band: three months tour of South Africa and Rhodesia'.
[150] 'Children (Employment Abroad) Bill. [H.L.]', House of Lords Debate 06 February 1913 vol 13 cc867-75,
<http://hansard.millbanksystems.com/lords/1913/feb/06/children-employment-abroad-bill-hl> [accessed 16th March 2015].

involved in private engagements in India and other parts of the Empire.

It is surprising that campaigners against boys joining the army did not take the opportunity of this episode to argue against it as the debate in the 1930s in Parliament continued with opposition MPs arguing that the 3,111 boys in the army at the time could not be guaranteed to be kept away from 'difficult belligerent work'. The government's position was that band boys and buglers were only involved in the more peaceful side of the Army's activities'.[151] While this was largely the case it did again avoid the fact that band boys serving overseas, particularly in the middle- and far-east, were open to the same dangers as their adult counterparts. The recruiting age for boys in the army was discussed with an assurance from the War Office that band boys' recruiting age would be raised to fifteen in 1936,[152] but, incredibly, in the Royal Navy boy musicians could still be accepted at fourteen years old.[153]

While debates in Parliament were important, in the background there had been an underlying trend of the closure of boys' residential institutions which was eventually to severely limit the supply of boys to army bands. The number remaining was nonetheless significant, and there were institutions still being opened in the 1920s, such as the St Augustine's Home for Boys, Sevenoaks, run by The Children's Society, which was fielding a band by the 1930s,[154] but this tended to be the exception as other institutions struggled to maintain their bands, the Banstead School for instance, despite there being a large

---

[151] 'New Clause.–(Amendment of Section 76 of Army Act.)', House of Commons Debate 03 April 1933 vol 276 cc1501-43W,
<http://hansard.millbanksystems.com/commons/1933/apr/03/new-clause-amendment-of-section-76-of#S5CV0276P0_19330403_HOC_416> [accessed 10th March 2015].
[152] 'New Clause.–(Employment certificate).', House of Commons Debate 26 May 1936 vol 312 cc1872-9W,
<http://hansard.millbanksystems.com/commons/1936/may/26/new-clause-employment-certificate#S5CV0312P0_19360526_HOC_335>, [accessed 10th March 2015].
[153] 'Boys', House of Commons Debate 09 March 1939 vol 344 cc2376W,
<http://hansard.millbanksystems.com/written_answers/1939/mar/09/boys#S5CV0344P0_19390309_CWA_139> [accessed 10th March 2015].
[154] 'St Augustine's Home for Boys, Sevenoaks', *Hidden Lives Revealed*
<http://www.hiddenlives.org.uk/cgi-bin/displayrec.pl?searchtext=band&record=/homes/SEVEN02.html> [accessed 24th February 2015].

number of former pupils serving in army bands.[155] In many cases the problems were most likely financial with bands having to earn their keep in order to repair and replenish instruments as well as stocks of music, and with little money available embarked on performing engagements ranging from local societies to tattoos. For example, the boys' band at the 'Cuckoo' School at Hanwell tended to perform locally in order to raise funds, such as at an event for the London United Tramway Athletic Association for the 'usual terms: three guineas plus expenses', or for the Brentford Brotherhood for two guineas,[156] but engagements such as these could not solely maintain institutions' bands.

There are many reasons for the closure of the institutions. Part of the issue was the growing recognition that education for girls was important and that they should not just be prepared for domestic service, but have the opportunity to learn subjects such as music for intellectual development.[157] Even so, the decline was primarily due to changing views towards the treatment of destitute and orphaned children, with the focus moving towards family fostering. This was part of the piecemeal preliminary legislation from the turn of the century that recognised the rights of citizenship, equality, and security and was to develop into the more formalised post-Second World War welfare state.[158] The large Victorian buildings housing the various institutions were gradually shut down or rationalised, with the final demise of nearly all of the few remaining institutions being shortly after the Second World War. Correspondingly, the system of recruiting band boys remained until 1947 when it was re-assessed along with the amalgamation of regimental bands.[159]

There had been concern that boys recruited towards the end of the World War One, re-filling the regimental bands, would be prematurely out of work following the cuts in the army in 1922, particularly as 'in many cases they were trained for Army bands in

---

[155] A. E. Noble, '"Entre Naus."', *The Banstead Residential School Magazine*, No. 61, December 1935, pp. 10-11.

[156] LMA CLSD-2. 'Special Committee Minute Book Vol II', 18th May 1923 & 17th August 1923.

[157] J. Goodman and A. Jacobs, 'Musical literacies in the English inter-war secondary classroom', in *Paedagogica Historica*, Vol. 44, Nos. 1-2, February-April 2008, pp. 153-166.

[158] See A. Briggs, 'The Welfare State in Historical Perspective', *European Journal of Sociology*, Vol. 2, No. 2, 1961, pp. 221-258.

[159] TNA. WO 32/11071, 'Bands and Music: General (Code 62(A)): Boys for Regimental Bands'.

Poor Law and other similar institution', but the Under-Secretary of State for War, Lieutenant Colonel W. Guinness was content that band boys had been given the option of transferring to other units and that those who had declined the offer were given compensation.[160] This apparent glut of band boys probably explains the apathy that Kneller Hall showed towards recruiting and that they did not demonstration an overt interest in the institutions as some have suggested.[161] Despite several proclamations by the Royal Military School of Music on where to recruit boys to bands, for example in an article in 1926 by Colonel J. A. C. Somerville, former Commandant of the Royal Military School of Music,[162] there was no systematic joint recruiting policy in existence. One bandmaster, A. E. Noble, of the Banstead Residential School was particularly scornful of the whole system when writing in *The Leading Note*. As a former regular army bandmaster,[163] he made it clear that his job was 'to train boys for Service Bands and to encourage them to adopt music as a profession',[164] but was critical of the lack of interest by army bands of the work that institutions such as his were doing to provide recruits.

Bandmaster Noble was probably aware that by the 1930s there was also greater competition from other trades, as opportunities were advertised for boys aged fourteen or fifteen for places at the new technical training colleges such as at the Army Technical School for Boys, Chepstow.[165] Despite this, the military band establishment remained complacent about the flow of recruits from institutions even with their drastic reduction in number in the interwar years. There seems to have been no attempt to initiate other forms of recruiting for bands, undoubtedly due to the climate of demobilisation and cuts after the First World War, but beyond that, the rationalisation of the

---

[160] 'Band Boys', House of Commons Debate 11 December 1922 vol 159 cc2397W, <http://hansard.millbanksystems.com/written_answers/1922/dec/11/band-boys#S5CV0159P0_19221211_CWA_70> [accessed 10th March 2015].
[161] C. Gibson, *Army Childhood: British Army Children's Lives and Times* (Oxford: Shire, 2012), p. 37.
[162] Zealley, Ord Hume and Somerville, *Famous Bands*, p. 14.
[163] He had graduated from the RMSM in 1908. See G. Turner and A. W. Turner, *The Trumpets Will Sound: The Story of The Royal Military School of Music, Kneller Hall* (Tunbridge Wells: Parapress, 1996), p. 160.
[164] A. E. Noble, '"Band Boys."', *The Leading Note*, Vol. 1, No. 6, February, 1931, pp. 30-1.
[165] What Shall I Do With My Boy?', *The Oxfordshire and Buckinghamshire Light Infantry Journal*, Vol. X, No. 56, July, 1934, pp. 141-2.

system of institutions that supplied band boys went completely unnoticed. The significance for military bands was that the majority of recruits in the interwar years, and for about a hundred years before, had come from these institutions, and while two of the three Royal Military schools remained open, it was with the demise of the other boys' institutions that eventually resulted in the reduction in recruiting for service in army bands.

If Grainger's record of the KOYLI bands is typical – and it seems that it is – then the retention of band boys was particularly good.[166] Throughout the first-hand accounts there is an underlying feeling, particularly from those who had been to institutions, that they could not leave the army because they did not know what else to do. Boys from institutions expected to join the army. At no charge to the War Office there was a free supply of musicians to army bands and Bandmasters were always in touch with the schools, fully aware of the available resources. Experiences varied and there was rarely any choice for the boys at the Foundling Hospital School as 'you didn't speak to the bandmaster',[167] but at the NMABS, boys would be asked which regiments they would like to join. Regardless of experience, the culture of bands had been heavily influenced by the recruitment of young boys and, according to Hector Sutherland, the label stuck throughout their careers: 'through joining as a boy you were always regarded as a boy'.[168]

With the change in society's attitude towards the education and care of children, and the resultant closure of institutions, the burden of training boys for service in army bands shifted from the civilian sector to become the army's responsibility in the post-Second World War era. The recruitment of boys was not just an exercise to top up numbers, but essential to maintaining bands as a viable concern. Band boys were fundamental to the culture of army music and without them the military music scene would have been quite different.

---

[166] Grainger, *Life and Times*, pp. 20-32.
[167] 'Music at Foundling' <http://foundlingvoices.foundlingmuseum.org.uk/themes/films/59/> [accessed 31st January 2015].
[168] Sutherland, *They Blow Their Trumpets*, p. 74.

PART 2

PERFORMANCE

CHAPTER 4

SEASIDE, CEREMONIAL, AND AN UNHAPPY UNION: BANDS AND LIVE PERFORMANCE

Military bands were one of the main providers of professional live music in the interwar period, both in an official capacity for the army and state, and also on a commercial basis. The tradition of this dual role continued from pre-First World War practices, but while playing for major state events was very important for military bands, most performances were for regimental occasions or commercial public performances. The Victorian and Edwardian eras had seen a steady growth in military band performances of all kinds, but it was the interwar years that saw the peak of commercial activity, especially for seaside towns, with military bands finding themselves at the forefront of fashionable musical activity around the country. Furthermore, an eagerness for the army to promote itself amongst the British public with large-scale tattoos and pageants, coupled with the standardisation of the rituals for state ceremonial, provided military bands with areas of performance where they held monopolies.

The considerable role of military bands in public and commercial ventures ensured that state-sponsored military music remained integral to national music-making and while it is hard to ascertain what participating bandsmen thought about taking part in these large state events, the military ceremonies were their exclusive domain, unlike concerts or performing at seaside resorts where civilian bands also participated. This was not lost on organisations such as the Musicians' Union, who saw serving bandsmen working in the civilian sector as a threat to the profession and embarked on a concerted effort to reduce military band performances. While the Musicians' Union was unlikely to have influence over state ceremonial events, the more that military bands encroached on civilian areas of operations, the greater the likelihood of dispute.

Aspects of Farmer's second and fourth research themes, and also the fifth supplementary theme (the function of music in specific and routine military ceremonial; the associated relationship between military music and other musical traditions; the position of military music in the music industry) are addressed in this chapter, employing aspects of Porter's 'five forces', such as the bargaining power of customers and suppliers, and also artefacts from Johnson's 'cultural web', such as symbols, rituals and routines, and power structures.

Ceremonial

The Manual of Ceremonial 1935 stated that:

> The objects of ceremonial are to promote *esprit de corps*, and, by the attainment of a high standard of steadiness and cohesion on the parade ground, to assist in the development of the moral qualities which are essential to success in war.[1]

The link from ceremonial to success in war might seem rather tenuous but the army's emphasis was on cohesion and the deliberate use of out-dated drill was a tool for linking regimental tradition to cohesion. The ceremonial parades that had emerged by the interwar period had developed from a variety of functions, ranging from the real need for the military to provide protection to individuals and property in the eighteenth and nineteenth centuries, to the elaboration of a simple parade. As the nineteenth century progressed there was no requirement, with few exceptions, for the military to physically protect the royal family or to form-up in lines that had been appropriate for Wellington's army. Ceremonial events that developed from these functions were either a show of strength or a celebration and ceased to have an overt hard power military purpose. In this changing climate, the army delivered direct support to the state by providing military bands for ceremonial events, particularly in London, where most parades were held.

These public rituals were generally separated into two categories: 'public duties' and 'state ceremonial'. The origin of the term 'public duties' is obscure but it may have come from the mid-nineteenth-century practice of the Foot Guards regiments providing ceremonial guards for a number of prominent locations in London. Standing Orders of the Coldstream Guards from 1878 sometimes refer to 'Public Duties in the West End' when guards were stationed at Royal Palaces, the Bank of England (the Bank Piquet), Opera House, the Central London Recruiting Office, and the Magazine in Hyde Park, and so it is probable that the public nature of the buildings concerned

---

[1] *Manual of Ceremonial* (London: HMSO, 1935), p. 1.

gave rise to the term.² Public duties tended to be daily rituals that, by the interwar years, had mainly been reduced to guards at the Royal palaces, but also with the addition of the Bank Piquet. It is unclear when music became a consistent and regular feature of public duties but bands did march troops to and from these duties at least from the late nineteenth century: for Mackenzie-Rogan it was one of his first duties as bandmaster of the Coldstream Guards, in 1896.³ (The Bank Piquet was later led by a single drummer or piper and not supported by a full band.⁴)

State ceremonial was a much larger affair but was limited to important national events that were sponsored by parliament. It had developed during the Victorian period but had not been a particular feature of state affairs: Queen Victoria was not fond of public ceremony, especially after the death of her husband, Albert, when she became a recluse. Planned ritual of any sort in British society was not a constituent part of organisational culture at the time, with very little structured ceremony undertaken by either the church or state, including the military. This apathy for public ritual was probably further enhanced by suspicion of what were considered vulgar and flamboyant Ruritanian practices on continental Europe.⁵ Even so, after several ceremonial failings involving the British military, not least the musical shortcomings reported to have been experienced by the Duke of Cambridge at Scutari,⁶ it was seen that there was a need to stage-manage ritual with military bands being the primary stakeholders.

Queen Victoria's indifference did not endure with her son, Edward VII, who was keen to develop the spectacle of state ceremonial, particularly after witnessing grand state pageantry in Germany, and this enthusiasm was continued with his son, George V. George V was a traditionalist in all he did and music was not an exception. He took a keen interest in how *God Save the King* should be played; he liked it slow, like a hymn, whereas his father had urged conductors to

---

² C. Dean, 'Public Duties'. Private email message, 14th January 2016.
³ J. Mackenzie-Rogan, *Fifty Years of Army Music* (London: Methuen, 1926), p. 122.
⁴ T. J. Edwards, *Military Customs*. 5th edn (Aldershot: Gale and Polden, 1961), pp. 195-200.
⁵ Ruritania was a fictional country created by the author Anthony Hope and is used here a generic term for central and eastern European monarchies.
⁶ See Chapter 7 below.

'hurry it up'.[7] He also listened to the repertoire of the Guards' bands, and on at least one occasion let the Director of Music know his thoughts: when the Band of the Grenadier Guards performed extracts from Richard Strauss's opera *Salome* at the changing of the guard at Buckingham Palace he wrote a note: 'His Majesty does not know what the band has just played, but it is *never* to be played again'.[8] While this attitude by the monarch may not have facilitated the promotion of new music it did help re-establish the traditional role of ceremonial music.

The First World War brought a halt to state ceremonial, but for the two decades after the war a high point in state ceremonial in Britain was reached, for several reasons. Firstly, successive monarchs since Victoria, beginning with Edward VII, and developed by George V, had taken a direct interest in the conduct of state ceremonial which enabled the continuation of late-Victorian 'invented traditions'; secondly, in one fell swoop, grandiose royal ceremonies in Europe had ceased with the end of the monarchies in Germany, Austro-Hungary, and Russia, and replaced by modern ritual of 'hysterical novelty'.[9] By default, Britain found itself as the sole provider of increasingly lavish and well organised state ceremonial, with music essential to the production of these state events, and military bands at the heart of the performances (Fig. 4.1).

Furthermore, it was cost effective to use military musicians as they were already employed by the state, and being paid, whereas hiring civilians would have added extra costs. This was to cause problems in 1930s with the Musicians' Union when the government had tried to hire civilians at a reduced rate for the coronation of George VI in 1936, and the Musicians' Union had also reported that George V's Silver Jubilee celebrations had been 'of little financial benefit to musicians'.[10]

---

[7] Quoted in K. Rose, *King George V* (London: Weidenfeld and Nicolson, 1983), p. 319.
[8] *Ibid*.
[9] D. Cannadine, 'The Context, Performance and Meaning of Ritual: The British Monarchy and the 'Invention of Tradition', c.1820-1977', in E. Hobsbawm and T. Ranger (eds), *The Invention of Tradition* (Cambridge: Cambridge University Press (Canto)), 1992 [1983]), pp. 108, 145 & 148.
[10] *'The Musicians' Union: A Social History: 1931-1940*, <http://www.muhistory.com/contact-us/1931-1940/> [accessed 26th February 2016].

Figure 4.1
Army musicians performing at the coronation in 1937 (MAM)

By the 1920s ceremonial events in London had emerged as mass proclamations of state ritual, particularly the annual Trooping the Colour for the Sovereign's Birthday Parade, in what Giddings has called 'the finest public parade ever achieved'.[11] Although first celebrated in 1864, by the interwar years it had developed into a national event, with the massed Household Brigade bands providing the music. King Edward VII had taken a great interest in the parade (Queen Victoria had only been present to take the salute on one occasion), and while he made several changes it was George V who took a personal concern in the details, culminating in an updated format by 1914. The parade was halted for the duration of the First World War and it was the interwar years that saw the establishment of the modern parade format, peaking in 1938 with the nation able to share in the ritual with filming by the BBC for the first time.[12]

State events were generally limited to Royal participation, although there were exceptions: state funerals, for example, were decreed by order of the reigning monarch and by a vote by Parliament providing the fund.[13] But despite being almost exclusively confined to London, state ceremonial was not the sole provision of the London-based Household Brigade,[14] as regimental 'line' bands occasionally participated in state events due to their relationships with Royals: line regiments often had a Royal Colonel-in-Chief. For example, in 1936 the Band of 3rd Carabiniers (Prince of Wales's Dragoon Guards) preceded the Band of Household Cavalry on parade from Westminster Hall and Paddington Station in the funeral procession of King George V.[15] The king had had a special relationship with the 3rd Carabiniers, and its antecedent regiments, particularly when he

---

[11] R. Giddings, 'Delusive seduction: Pride, pomp, circumstance and military music', in J. M. MacKenzie (ed.), *Popular Imperialism and the Military, 1850-1950* (Manchester: Manchester University Press, 1992) p. 46 (pp. 25-49).
[12] J. Calder, M. Pigott & A. Bruce, *The Queen's Birthday Parade: Trooping the Colour* (n. p.: Julian Calder Publishing, 2015), p. 27.
[13] There are differences between state and ceremonial funerals. See P. Bowers, *State and ceremonial funerals*, United Kingdom, House of Commons Library, Parliamentary and Constitution Centre, SN/PC/06600, 31 July 2013; C. Pond, *Lyings in state*, United Kingdom, House of Commons Library, Parliamentary and Constitution Centre, SN/PC/1735, 12 April 2002.
[14] Comprising the Household Cavalry and Foot Guards.
[15] *Supplement to The London Gazette of Tuesday, the 28th of April, 1936*, 'Ceremonials Observed at the Funeral and Lying in State of His Late Majesty King George the Fifth of Blessed memory'. No. 34279, Wednesday 29th April, 1936, pp. 2763-2766.

had been the Prince of Wales,[16] and so it was not unusual for this more junior regiment, through its band, to be given a high profile. Performing at other Royal events, such as Buckingham Palace Garden Parties, was also open to selected 'line' bands where they were a perfect conduit for promoting the regiment, but these occasions were usually limited to special regimental events when, for example, the Band of the Royal Scots Fusiliers performed at the Buckingham Palace in July 1936 and was inspected by the king.[17]

Nevertheless, it was the Household Brigade bands in London that had continual frequent contact with royalty and it was typical for members of the royal family to be familiar with the names of the directors of music. The pre-war custom of playing for the royal family in the evenings was resumed in 1919 and when the Court was in residence at Windsor Castle, Household Brigade bands took it in turns to play for the royal dinner each evening, with an informal dance afterwards. A string band would play during dinner behind a grille in the dining room, in what the Prince of Wales described as

> a veritable Black Hole of Calcutta – a windowless, airless chamber in which the bandsmen in their tightly buttoned tunics sat drenched in sweat and half-fainting in their chairs.[18]

Despite the uncomfortable setting, the bands continued to perform and George Miller, when bandmaster of the 1st Life Guards, and later director of music of the Grenadier Guards, recalled several occasions when Queen Alexandra and Queen Mary asked for requests, and also when Queen Mary thanked him for performing suitable music for Princess Elizabeth's seventh birthday.[19] This regular, and almost informal, contact with royalty was unique to military musicians as while some of the established civilian music posts were linked to the royal family, such as the 'Master of the King's Music', there was no consistent contact, particularly after the demise of the Queen's Band

---

[16] S. Wood, *Those Terrible Grey Horses: An Illustrated History of the Royal Scots Dragoon Guards* (Oxford: Osprey, 2015), p. 152 & 170.
[17] J. C. Kemp, *The History of the Royal Scots Fusiliers: 1919-1959* (Glasgow: Robert MacLehose & Co/Glasgow University Press, 1963), p. 15.
[18] Edward Duke of Windsor, *A King's Story: The Memoirs of H.R.H. the Duke of Windsor K.G.* (New York: Putnam, 1951; repr. with an introduction by Philip Ziegler, London: Prion, 1998), pp. 185-186.
[19] G. Miller, *The Piping Times in Peace and War: Being the Autobiography of a Royal Musician in Five Reigns*. Museum of Army Music. MS, pp. 26-27.

under Edward VII, and finally George V, when the Household Brigade bands took over its functions.[20]

Remembrance and commemoration

Another ritual that became important after the First World War was that of remembrance, with formal commemoration services commencing within a year of the war ending. While the topic is dealt with in detail elsewhere, there is little assessment of the significance of the role of military bands.[21] Military bands might be considered the natural ensembles to be performing at the remembrance events but in the 1920s there was some considerable debate over the role of the military and established church in remembrance events and so their presence was by no means guaranteed.

The first annual national Armistice Day commemoration was only organised at a late stage after political wrangling between those who wanted a celebration and those who wanted a solemn affair. Eventually it was decided that there should be a solemn parade with festivities in the evening and for a few years civilian groups, such as the *Southern Syncopated Orchestra*, provided music for the costumed 'Victory Ball' at the Royal Albert Hall, along the lines of pre-war aristocratic parties.[22] The appropriateness of these functions was questioned by, among others, Canon Dick Sheppard,[23] and so the British Legion, an ex-service charitable organisation, became involved in the running of what many considered a more appropriate event. It initially featured John Foulds' *A World Requiem* with

---

[20] *The Royal Encyclopedia*, s. v. 'Master of The Queen's Music'. R. Allison and S. Riddell (eds) (London: Macmillan, 1991), p. 336. For a history of the Royal Private Band, see J. Harley, 'Music at the English Court in the Eighteenth and Nineteenth Centuries', *Music & Letters*, Vol. 50, No. 3, July, 1969, pp. 332-351.

[21] See for example, A. Gregory, *The Silence of Memory: Armistice Day 1919-1946* (Oxford: Berg, 1994).

[22] 'The Southern Syncopated Orchestra remembered', <http://jazzagefollies.blogspot.co.uk/2013/07/the-southern-syncopated-orchestra.html> [accessed 27th February 2016]; 'Motley & Morale - The Role of Fancy Dress in the First World War', <http://blog.maryevans.com/2015/12/motley-morale-the-role-of-fancy-dress-in-the-first-world-war.html> [accessed 27th February 2016].

[23] N. Saunders, *The Poppy: A Cultural History from Ancient Egypt to Flanders Fields to Afghanistan* (London: Oneworld, 2013), Chapter 7 (e-book).

civilian musicians,[24] a very popular work with both performers and audience, but disliked by critics, and last performed as part of Armistice commemorations in 1926. Foulds' biographer, Malcolm MacDonald, suggests that the demise of the work was largely due to the British musical establishment's distrust of large-scale works in the 1920s.[25] This may be the case but it is also most likely that it was a victim of the shift from civilian to military commemoration by the British Legion in 1929, as by 1927 this had transformed into a military event, featuring military bands, with a more immediate connection with the organising veterans' associations. This military connection was enhanced by the fact that the 'Remembrance Festival', as it had become, was broadcast on BBC radio around Britain, and also relayed across the Empire.[26]

By the 1930s the format and music programme of the evening event had been set, with the 'Massed Bands of the Brigade of Guards' performing shorter items, including marches, hymns, and rousing choruses of community singing led by the Choir of the Royal Military Chapel, Wellington Barracks. The 'Act of Remembrance' was now a regular feature that was bounded by the bugle calls *Last Post* and *Reveille* and the military ritual, organised by the British Legion, had replaced the civilian concert with a more focused event that was direct and prescriptive in its intentions. Indicative of the change in focus was that while Foulds' two hours and twenty minutes of *A World Requiem* was taken off the programme, in the 1933 'Festival of Remembrance' his four-and-a-half minutes of *A Lament (Keltic Suite)* was included in the programme.[27] In the late 1930s some at the BBC were concerned that the event was losing its quasi-religious aura and that 'the British Legion sing-song at the Albert Hall' had become a

---

[24] C. [alias for M.] MacDonald, liner note to *Foulds: A World Requiem*. 2008. Compact disc. Chandos. CHSA 5058(2). The work was temporarily revived in 2007 but not as part of Armistice commemorations.

[25] M. MacDonald, *John Foulds: his life in music* (Rickmansworth: Triad Press, 1975), pp. 26-31.

[26] 'A Remembrance Festival. Under the auspices of the Daily Express. Relayed from the Royal Albert Hall (Daventry only), Friday 11 November 1927, 20.00' <http://genome.ch.bbc.co.uk/schedules/2lo/1927-11-11> [accessed 8th November 2017].

[27] 'Festival of Empire and Remembrance. National Programme Daventry, 11 November 1933, 20.00'.
<http://genome.ch.bbc.co.uk/13e80c9268224ec4bbb4559f5cda1d3f> [accessed 27th April 2016].

'super-sentimental orgy',[28] but the popular format stayed, with military bands providing the bulk of the music.

While the Festival of Remembrance became standardised as a veterans' event there were still calls for the Armistice Day parade to be a civic affair without military connections. Nevertheless, Service personnel paraded each year in London on Armistice Day at what was a grand State occasion of public ritual. The military bands formed a large enough body to make a significant contribution to the uniformed presence and, considering the formalisation of other state rituals with music in the 1920s, it is quite possible that the chance to see the massed bands of the Brigade of Guards on parade, performing marches, folksongs, and laments, was one of the reasons for large numbers attending the ceremony.[29] Furthermore, as the London Cenotaph parade had become the focus for national broadcasting it exposed the London-based Guards bands to a national, and increasingly international audience.

By the late 1920s military bands had appropriated the major remembrance events from civilian musical involvement but also provided music for commemorative and charity events for the several First World War veterans' associations. Formed soon after the war, these associations commemorated fallen comrades and provided support and help for the wounded, and while most organised events were on a relatively small scale, some, such as that organised by the Imperial Institute, were sizeable, with musical support dominated by military bands (Fig. 4.2).

Another organisation, 'The Old Contemptibles' Association', founded in 1925, for veterans of the original 1914 British Expeditionary Force,[30] had military music as an integral feature of its commemoration process, such as at Woolwich in 1934 (Fig 4.3). The timing, 3 p.m., was deliberately chosen so that there would be no clash with the national commemorations at the Cenotaph at 11 a.m. and veterans could have time to attend both.

---

[28] Quoted in Gregory, *The Silence of Memory*, p. 84.
[29] Gregory, *The Silence of Memory*, pp. 128 & 131.
[30] 'Old Contemptibles, British Expeditionary Force', <http://www.westminster-abbey.org/our-history/people/old-contemptibles,-british-expeditionary-force> [accessed 1st February 2016].

Figure 4.2
Advertisement from the Illustrated London News for charity military band concerts at the Imperial Institute, in 1933 (Illustrated London News)

The choice of music by the Royal Artillery Band's director of music, Major Edward Stretton, is interesting in that he seems to be taking the opportunity to perform a concert with music unrelated to remembrance, particularly the Weber and Beethoven transcriptions. This may have been simply to allow the opportunity for the band to show off in performances of larger-scale repertoire as the number of Royal Artillery Band concerts had recently been reduced due to dwindling audiences in London and Woolwich.[31] Even though it was a peculiar choice, military bands were the first preference to perform for ex-service organisations and had the prerogative to impose repertoire.

---

[31] H. G. Farmer, *History of the Royal Artillery Band: 1762-1953* (London: Royal Artillery Institution, 1954), p. 358.

Founded 25th June, 1925.

The Old Contemptibles'  Association.

WOOLWICH & DISTRICT BRANCH.

Festival of Remembrance
to be held in
The Royal Garrison Church of S. George, Woolwich,
on
Sunday, November 11th, 1934, at 3 p.m.

Address by: The Rev. F. I. Anderson, C.M.G., Chaplain to the King,
Formerly Assistant Chaplain-General, Chaplain West London Branch O.C.A.

Officiants { The Senior Chaplain (C.E.) H.M. Forces, Woolwich.
{ The Rev. H. M. Webb-Peploe, O.B.E., M.A., C.F., (Ret.), Chaplain, Woolwich Branch.

THE BAND OF THE ROYAL REGIMENT OF ARTILLERY.
(By kind permission of the Officers, R.A.)

Conductor: Major E. C. Stretton, M.V.O., Director of Music, R.A.
Soloist: Miss Ella Pettitt—Soprano.
Organist: Mr. T. G. Eastop, F.R.C.O., &c.

2.45. p.m.   An Organ Recital
Mr. T. G. Eastop, F.R.C.O.

"Evensong"	Easthope Martin
"Requiem Aeternam"	Basil Harwood
"Prelude in C Minor"	Chopin

Order of Festival of Remembrance.

Processional Hymn .. "Soldiers of Christ, arise" .. A. & M. 270

PRAYERS.

(The Congregation will now stand.)

The Chairman of Woolwich Branch will place a wreath on the Memorial.

Relatives of Old Contemptibles will place their tokens.

(The Congregation will be seated.)

Overture	"Oberon"	Weber
	Band of the Royal Regiment of Artillery.	
Solo	"I know that my Redeemer liveth"	Handel
	Miss Ella Pettitt, with Orchestra.	
Anthem	"Crossing the Bar"	Barnby
	(Tennyson)	
	Royal Garrison Church Choir.	

Sunset and evening star,
And one clear call for me!
And may there be no moaning of the bar,
When I put out to sea,

But such a tide as moving seems asleep,
Too full for sound and foam,
When that which drew from out the boundless deep
Turns again home.

Twilight and evening bell,
and after that the dark!
And may there be no sadness of farewell,
When I embark.

For, though from out our bourne of Time and Place
The flood may bear me far,
I hope to see my Pilot face to face
When I have crost the bar. Amen.

Judex	"Mors et Vita"	Gounod
	Band of the Royal Regiment of Artillery.	

Address by the Rev. F. I. Anderson, C.M.G.

Symphony	"First Movement of the Fifth Symphony"	Beethoven
	Band of the Royal Regiment of Artillery."	

| HYMN | "The Supreme Sacrifice" | John S. Arkwright |

O VALIANT hearts, who to your glory came
Through dust of conflict and through battle-flame,
Tranquil you lie, your knightly virtue proved,
Your memory hallowed in the land you loved.

Proudly you gathered, rank on rank to war,
As who had heard God's message from afar;
All you had hoped for, all you had, you gave
To save mankind—yourselves you scorned to save.

Splendid you passed, the great surrender made,
Into the light that nevermore shall fade;
Deep your contentment in that blest abode,
Who wait the last clear trumpet-call of God.

Long years ago, as earth lay dark and still,
Rose a loud cry upon a lonely hill,
While in the frailty of our human clay
Christ, our Redeemer, passed the self-same way.

Still stands His Cross from that dread hour to this
Like some bright star above the dark abyss;
Still, through the veil, the Victor's pitying eyes
Look down to bless our lesser Calvaries.

These were His servants, in His steps they trod,
Following through death the martyred Son of God.
Victor He rose; victorious too shall rise
They who have drunk His cup of Sacrifice.

O risen Lord, O Shepherd of our Dead,
Whose Cross has bought them and whose staff has led
In glorious hope their proud and sorrowing land
Commits her children to Thy gracious hand.

OFFERTORY ON BEHALF OF
WOOLWICH OLD CONTEMPTIBLES' DISTRESS FUND.

| THE LAST POST | Trumpeters R.A. |

ONE MINUTE SILENCE OF REMEMBRANCE.

They gave what they had to give,
No matter—to die or live,
Life had no beacon, without death.
So, they fell; covering the world's breadth.
Heroes all—cowards none,
To die when Christ said "Come."

| REVEILLE | Trumpeters R.A. |
| HYMN | "Jerusalem" |

(1st verse by Choir only, 2nd verse by ALL.)

And did those feet in ancient time
Walk upon England's mountains green?
And was the Holy Lamb of God
On England's pleasant pastures seen?
And did the Countenance Divine
Shine forth upon our clouded hills?
And was Jerusalem builded here
Among those dark Satanic mills?

Bring me my bow of burning gold!
Bring me my arrows of desire!
Bring me my spear! O clouds unfold!
Bring me my Chariot of Fire!
I will not cease from mental fight;
Nor shall my sword sleep in my hand
Till we have built Jerusalem
In England's green and pleasant land.

The National Anthem.

The Blessing.

| RECESSIONAL HYMN | A. & M. 298 |

Organ Recital.

MR. T. G. EASTOP, F.R.C.O.

| Prelude in C Sharp Minor | Rachmaninoff |
| March in C Minor | Andrews |

God Save the King.

Figure 4.3
Programme for 'The Old Contemptibles' Association' commemoration service at Woolwich, 1934 (Countess of Wessex's String Orchestra Library)

Although the original Remembrance commemorations were supposed to be not religious in nature (the Cenotaph had no religious symbols on it in order to recognise the contributions of soldiers from all faiths), commemoration events in the army and for ex-service associations inevitably became linked to religion because of the relationship with the church – military church parades on Sundays were still compulsory until 1937. Hymns were sung and also the playing of *Last Post* and *Reveille* by buglers or trumpeters either side of a one (or two) minutes silence became standard practice during the period.[32]

Tattoos and pageants

Grand military tattoos were another form of display for the public but, while state funded, were organised along commercial lines. These impressive public displays were very large scale and supported by many different branches of the army. The music was provided by military bands and was the centre of the entertainment, but there were also other exhibits including army motorcycle and gymnastic displays, or 'bridging' competitions,[33] with the whole show culminating in a battle scene or grand pageant, depending upon the theme. For the 1926 Aldershot Tattoo this included a 'Vision' of the Battle of Hastings on the front cover of the programme.

The music at tattoos was subservient to the overall themes for each year but was by far the main component of the performances. For the 1926 Aldershot there were twenty-three regimental bands performing, fifteen corps of drums, seven pipe bands, three groups of cavalry trumpeters and one of buglers, which would have created a massed group of about 1,000 musicians[34] (Fig. 4.4). Surveys of the music performed at tattoos from the interwar period reveal little development, with only the occasional introduction of current popular tune arrangements,[35] but more importantly, the music was set to fit the theme of the event.

---

[32] See A. W. Turner, *The Last Post: Music, Remembrance and the Great War* (London: Aurum, 2014).

[33] H. A. Baker, 'Woolwich Tattoo, 1934', *The Royal Engineers Journal*, XLIX: June (1935), pp. 226-237.

[34] C. Dean, 'Tattoos and Pageants' in C. Dean and G. Turner (eds), *Sound the Trumpets Beat the Drums: Military Music through the 20th Century* (Tunbridge Wells: Parapress, 2002), pp. 136-137.

[35] See Dean, 'Tattoos and Pageants', pp. 135-166; J. Richards, *Imperialism and Music: Britain 1876-1953* (Manchester: Manchester University Press, 2001), pp. 211-247.

Massed Bands

1ST CAVALRY BRIGADE :—
1ST ROYAL DRAGOONS (Bandmaster S. S. SMITH).
10TH ROYAL HUSSARS (PRINCE OF WALES'S OWN) (Bandmaster M. ROBERTS).
17TH/21ST LANCERS (Bandmaster F. J. ALLSEBROOK, M.M.).
ROYAL ARTILLERY MOUNTED BAND (Bandmaster T. J. HILLIER).

1ST GUARDS BRIGADE :—
1ST BN. THE MIDDLESEX REGIMENT (DUKE OF CAMBRIDGE'S OWN) (Bandmaster J. W. CLARK).

2ND INFANTRY BRIGADE :—
2ND BN. THE ROYAL FUSILIERS (CITY OF LONDON REGIMENT) (Bandmaster R. TULIP).
1ST BN. THE KING'S REGIMENT (LIVERPOOL) (Bandmaster G. PASSLOW, M.M.).
1ST BN. THE LINCOLNSHIRE REGIMENT (Bandmaster C. S. TROWT).
1ST BN. SEAFORTH HIGHLANDERS (Bandmaster G. V. E. GRAYSON, L.R.A.M., A.R.C.M.).

3RD INFANTRY BRIGADE :—
2ND BN. THE EAST LANCASHIRE REGIMENT (Bandmaster W. M. FAYER).
1ST BN. ROYAL SUSSEX REGIMENT (Bandmaster S. A. GULMANT).
1ST BN. THE YORK AND LANCASTER REGIMENT (Bandmaster G. HART).
2ND BN. THE GORDON HIGHLANDERS (Bandmaster W. BARTLETT).

5TH INFANTRY BRIGADE :—
1ST BN. THE CAMERONIANS (SCOTTISH RIFLES) (Bandmaster H. E. DOWELL, L.R.A.M.).
1ST BN. THE GLOUCESTERSHIRE REGIMENT (Bandmaster S. YORKE, D.C.M.).
2ND BN. THE DORSETSHIRE REGIMENT (Bandmaster G. E. HUDSON).
2ND BN. THE RIFLE BRIGADE (PRINCE CONSORT'S OWN) (Bandmaster S. J. YOUNG).

6TH INFANTRY BRIGADE :—
1ST BN. THE DEVONSHIRE REGIMENT (Bandmaster H. CAROTT).
1ST BN. THE NORTHAMPTONSHIRE REGIMENT (Bandmaster W. CRESSWELL, L.R.A.M.).
2ND BN. THE QUEEN'S OWN ROYAL WEST KENT REGIMENT (Bandmaster A. D. W. HUNT).
2ND BN. THE KING'S ROYAL RIFLE CORPS (Bandmaster W. J. DUNN, M.C.).

ROYAL ARMY SERVICE CORPS (Bandmaster C. J. CROSBIE).
ROYAL ARMY MEDICAL CORPS (Bandmaster E. U. LANE).

Massed Drum and Fife Bands

2ND BN. GRENADIER GUARDS (Sgt.-Dmr. E. ALLWOOD).
2ND BN. COLDSTREAM GUARDS (Sgt.-Dmr. W. GOODEN).
1ST BN. IRISH GUARDS (Sgt.-Dmr. G. D. SMITH).
2ND BN. THE ROYAL FUSILIERS (CITY OF LONDON REGIMENT) (Sgt.-Dmr. C. HOBBS).
1ST BN. THE KING'S REGIMENT (LIVERPOOL) (Sgt.-Dmr. C. H. ANDREWS).
1ST BN. THE LINCOLNSHIRE REGIMENT (Cpl. B. A. KIME).
1ST BN. THE DEVONSHIRE REGIMENT (Sgt.-Dmr. A. S. SOUTH).
1ST BN. THE GLOUCESTERSHIRE REGIMENT (Sgt.-Dmr. R. H. MASON).
2ND BN. THE EAST LANCASHIRE REGIMENT (Sgt.-Dmr. R. H. NICKS).
1ST BN. ROYAL SUSSEX REGIMENT (Sgt.-Dmr. W. E. MARRISON).
2ND BN. THE DORSETSHIRE REGIMENT (Sgt.-Dmr. E. INKPEN).
1ST BN. THE NORTHAMPTONSHIRE REGIMENT (Sgt.-Dmr. F. HUNT).
2ND BN. THE QUEEN'S OWN ROYAL WEST KENT REGIMENT (Sgt.-Dmr. T. H. COUSINS).
1ST BN. THE MIDDLESEX REGIMENT (DUKE OF CAMBRIDGE'S OWN) (Sgt.-Dmr. G. W. GOODWIN).
1ST BN. THE YORK AND LANCASTER REGIMENT (Sgt.-Dmr. L. A. HEADLY).

Massed Pipe Bands

1ST BN. SCOTS GUARDS (Sgt.-Piper J. D. MCDONALD).
2ND BN. SCOTS GUARDS (Sgt.-Piper A. MCINTOSH).
1ST BN. IRISH GUARDS (Sgt.-Piper T. ATKINS).
1ST BN. SEAFORTH HIGHLANDERS (Sgt.-Piper D. MCLENNAN).
2ND BN. GORDON HIGHLANDERS (Sgt.-Piper C. TURNBULL).
1ST BN. ARGYLL AND SUTHERLAND HIGHLANDERS (Sgt.-Piper R. T. ANGELL).

Buglers

2ND BN. THE KING'S ROYAL RIFLE CORPS (Sgt.-Bugler R. B. BROOKES).

Massed Trumpeters

1ST ROYAL DRAGOONS.
10TH ROYAL HUSSARS (PRINCE OF WALES'S OWN).
17TH/21ST LANCERS.

Figure 4.4
Participating bands from the 1926 Aldershot Command Searchlight Tattoo (MAM)

Major General J. C. Harding-Newman, a producer of the Aldershot Tattoo in the late 1920s, provided an insider's account of how the event was staged, with the perhaps unsurprising revelation that the selection and organisation of the programme was not produced for soldiers 'but what will be most popular amongst the general public whom we are going to ask to pay for seeing the Tattoo'.[36] Through informal audience research (a kind of mass observation) Harding-Newman and his colleagues based the proportions of items for the programme and allocated a strict amount of timing to each:

> Historical pageantry, 75 per cent.; historical drill, 50 per cent.; modern drill, 80 per cent.; physical training, 80 per cent.; classical music, 10 per cent.; marching music, 90 per cent. (not more than ten minutes); modern military evolutions, 60 per cent.; modern battle, 25 per cent.[37]

With the tattoo starting at 9.30 p.m. it was scheduled to finish at two minutes after midnight and apparently did not deviate by more than two minutes from this time.

By the 1930s the tattoos had become an established part of the military calendar, but with the gradual move to mechanisation the army was showing some willingness to withdraw from the organisation of these events.[38] In 1934 Lieutenant Colonel H. H. Douglas-Withers, an acquaintance of the military strategist Basil Liddell Hart, was asked to take over production of the Aldershot Tattoo because it 'had become too big for the General Staff to run at the same time carry on with the necessary training of the army.'[39] Douglas-Withers had retired from the army eighteen months early to take over the appointment, which he considered to be part of a change in emphasis in the mind of the 'C-in-C [Commander-in-Chief] and is made in the interests of army training'.[40] This is not surprising as the various tattoos were a huge drain on resources, with the Aldershot Tattoo alone having grown from an audience of 25,000 in 1919 to

---

[36] J. C. Harding-Newman, 'The Making of a Tattoo', *The Army, Navy & Air Force Gazette*, July 7 (1932), pp. 538-540; J. C. Harding-Newman, 'The Making of a Tattoo–II', *The Army, Navy & Air Force Gazette*, July 14 (1932), pp. 558-559.
[37] Harding-Newman, 'The Making of a Tattoo–II', p. 558.
[38] Most horse-cavalry regiments were converted to motorised light reconnaissance regiments from 1928 to 1939. See, for example, M. Carver, *Britain's Army in the Twentieth Century* (London: Pan, 1999), pp. 153-162.
[39] LH15/3/13. KCL Basil Liddell Hart Archives, Letter from H. H. Douglas-Withers to B. Liddell Hart dated 4th September 1934.
[40] *Ibid.*

532,850 by 1938 and involving about 5,000 troops and 3,600 support staff.[41]

While the spectacle for those who attended would have been slick and professional, behind the scenes life for the regimental bandsmen was particularly arduous during performances. Spike Mays, who performed in the 1925 Aldershot Tattoo (and was in the audience in 1937), recalled how the military cast had to rehearse 'daily and nightly'.[42] Another participant, Charles Nalden, a harpist and clarinettist in the Royal Artillery (Mounted) Band, confirms this when performing with band in the late 1920s and early 1930s, talking of interminable rehearsals, and for mounted bandsmen, the prospect of five-and-a-half hours in the saddle, from 7 p.m. to 12.30 a.m., for ten to twelve consecutive nights.[43] Musicians had similar experiences at the Wembley Pageant of 1925, when performing a tattoo nightly from September until well into November: 'the rain and mud persevered to the end, and all performers were heartily glad to see the finish of that period in Wembley Stadium'.[44] These hardships that the musicians had to endure perhaps also further explain why the tattoos and pageants were exclusively military events, as civilian musicians would almost certainly not have been prepared to accept the working conditions.

Proceeds from the tattoos were channelled to army charities but the pull on military resources had led to criticism in parliament, with several members of the House of Commons questioning the utility of employing so many soldiers for charitable work rather than undertaking military training.[45] While the army was becoming concerned over the use of significant numbers of troops to produce the tattoos it could not be ignored that reasonably large amounts of

---

[41] Dean, 'Tattoos and Pageants', pp. 135-166.
[42] S. Mays, *The Band Rats* (London: Peter Davies, 1975), pp. 94-95.
[43] C. Nalden, *Half and Half: The Memoirs of a Charity Brat 1908-1989* (Tuaranga: Moana Press, 1989), pp. 266-267.
[44] Miller, *Piping Times*, p. 39.
[45] 'Aldershot Tattoo', HC Deb 02 July 1936 vol 314 cc632-3W, <http://hansard.millbanksystems.com/written_answers/1936/jul/02/aldershot-tattoo> [accessed 8th February 2016]; 'Aldershot Tattoo', HC Deb 15 December 1936 vol 318 cc2266-7, <http://hansard.millbanksystems.com/commons/1936/dec/15/aldershot-tattoo> [accessed 8th February 2016]; 'Aldershot Tattoo (Grants from Proceeds)', HC Deb 26 January 1937 vol 319 cc745-7, <http://hansard.millbanksystems.com/commons/1937/jan/26/aldershot-tattoo-grants-from-proceeds> [accessed 8th February 2016].

money were being given to military charities and so relieving the government of a welfare burden. For example, money distributed to charities in 1936 from the Royal Tournament, Aldershot Tattoo, Tidworth Tattoo and Northern Command Tattoo amounted to £65,402, which was almost all of the years' net profits.[46] In the same year, the Secretary of State for War, Duff Cooper, assured the House that the entertainment provided by the Aldershot Tattoo was of 'military importance',[47] but he did not qualify how this military importance manifested itself and so the link with funding for military charities, and relief for the Treasury, cannot be discounted. In any case, it would have been impossible for these grand events to have been staged by private companies as the expense of performers' pay alone would have been prohibitive. On one of the few occasions where it was attempted, the Wembley Empire Exhibition of 1925, George Miller, the director of music of the Grenadier Guards band, recounted how it had not been financially profitable and that:

> The Brigade of Guards' help was sought…there was an immediate success and I understand that the attendances amounted to a phenomenal figure of about ninety thousand each evening, and thus to some extent the guarantors were saved.[48]

It is unclear if the bands of the Brigade of Guards were financially reimbursed for their performances but it seems very unlikely that they received anything given the reasons they were approached in the first place. The Wembley Exhibition was an international event and to prevent its failure it is most probable that state sponsored music was provided to save any embarrassment for the government.

Regimental duties

Military rituals were part of the culture exclusive to the armed services, with variations in regimental customs and symbols acting to differentiate the various units in the army. There were more similarities than variances but distinct regimental ritual was at the core of soldierly behaviour and the music that supported these

---

[46] 'Royal Tournament and Tattoos (Profits)', HC Deb 27 July 1937 vol 326 cc2835-6, <http://hansard.millbanksystems.com/commons/1937/jul/27/royal-tournament-and-tattoos-profits> [accessed 8th February 2016].
[47] 'Aldershot Tattoo (Grants from Proceeds)', HC Deb 26 January 1937 vol 319 cc745-7, <http://hansard.millbanksystems.com/commons/1937/jan/26/aldershot-tattoo-grants-from-proceeds> [accessed 9th November 2017].
[48] Miller, *Piping Times*, p. 39.

behaviours was central to the perceived maintenance of discipline and tradition. This internal military market was not usually projected into public view, unless it was a deliberate act to promote the regiment, and so the various customs of regiments were a mixture of secretive practices and public ritual, and bands participated in both.

With the exception of the Foot Guards bands in London who carried out ceremonial duties on a rota system, usually independent of regimental affiliation, the day-to-day duties of army bands were inextricably linked to the workings of their regiments, and hence their cultures. On a weekly basis, line bands were required to perform for mess functions and church parades, with the emphasis on supporting the officers of the regiment. Even though the funding of bands had supposedly become a War Office matter in the nineteenth century, commanding officers still considered the band their own and bands were tasked as a regimental asset, particularly as officers in the regiment were expected to continue paying for military band materiel, as required.

Commanding officers were also keen to use their bands as advertisements to promote their regiments as a fashionable and attractive organisation, partly to entice officers and soldiers in the difficult interwar recruiting climate, but also to give kudos to a regiment that may be inactive on home service, and not least to gain some income for the band fund to relieve the officers' subscriptions. One way of doing this was by allowing the bandmaster to engage the band for a season touring popular seaside destinations, but while the army was content for its bands to be conspicuous in the wider community there is some evidence that not all commanding officers wished their bands to be away from the battalion. For example, the commanding officer of the 1st Battalion Royal Ulster Rifles wrote to his commander at Headquarters, 2nd Infantry Brigade, raising complaints about how the battalion hardly ever saw its band because it was touring seaside resorts.[49] It is unclear how widespread this view was but the temptation to release the band for a season away and earn some money for the band fund must have been great. Accordingly, throughout the summer, regiments were left with a reduced 'skeleton' band remaining at the battalion depot to maintain regimental duties made up of the 'young hands' and less skilled musicians, and there would be no bandmaster to conduct.

---

[49] TNA WO/32/3916. 1RUR/56/7 dated 1/8/1928.

Throughout the rest of the year engagements in the officers' mess were usually undertaken on a twice-weekly basis, depending upon demand and the location of the regiment. Charles Nalden calls these engagements 'one of the greatest farces musically speaking',[50] as bands were required to perform behind screens, or even in another room, with the officers' apparently taking no notice of the band until at the very end of the evening when requests were made. These mess engagements were far from trivial events, however, as etiquette demanded that a regiment would have its band in the officers' mess as a matter of course. Regimental bands would be expected to be fully aware of regimental customs and peculiarities, for example, when to play the National Anthem for the 'Loyal Toast', if at all, and whether it should be performed seated or stood up.[51] In many cases, senior members of the band would have been the experts in regimental customs, having performed them the most in the regiment and accrued the greatest experience.

Formal regimental parades every Sunday were eventually relaxed in 1937,[52] but until then regiments would be on show for church parades, and the band would lead the regiment in a march to the relevant Protestant church, performing for a part of the service, marching back to barracks, and then an informal concert on the parade square. These parades were big events, not so much for religious purposes, but as a display of pride where co-located regiments would compete to be the smartest and best turned-out.

Regimental bands of cavalry regiments had duties particular to their situation and were used to accompany the 'Musical Ride': a display of horsemanship by troopers from the regiment. Colonel Sir Mike Ansell recalled how the band of the 5th Inniskilling Dragoon Guards was integral to the display:

> The band took great care to find suitable music. As Corporal Samuels slid among the flowers on his surf-board they played *Life on the Ocean Wave*. As Corporal Samuels and Trooper Daly in their night-shirts pretended to sleep, naturally, it was *Let's put out the lights and go to sleep*…Trooper Knott drove Jerry [a horse] dragging a dray on which were mats; the four

---

[50] Nalden, *Half and Half*, p. 268.
[51] Edwards, *Military Customs*, pp. 43-44.
[52] *Morning Post*, 'Army Church Parade Concession: Order to Relax "Inspections": Guards Take the Lead', 2nd March 1937.

of us jumped aboard while the band played *Thanks for the Buggy Ride, I've had a Wonderful Time*.[53]

Before the mechanisation of cavalry regiments in the 1930s the cavalry regiment bands were regularly required to perform as mounted musicians and, like their infantry colleagues, were expected to lead the regiment on long marches, such as an occasion described by Colonel Ansell when the regiment marched into Madras with 'mounted band playing'.[54]

Nevertheless, the process of mechanisation forced changes to parade formats where horses had previously been used, and the *Manual of Ceremonial 1935* was updated from the 1912 edition to accommodate the changes required for mechanisation.[55] For celebrations of the King's Birthday Parade on Salisbury Plain the nature of cavalry bands' contributions to the parades was altered in June 1937, as reported by *The Times*:

> The [dismounted] massed bands of the cavalry turned about and retired from the middle of the arena. It was evident why as soon as one heard the tanks of the 5th Battalion, Royal Tanks Corps start up their engines and put their caterpillars in motion.[56]

Cavalry bands had played a significant role in regimental ceremonial parades but their relationship with other bands was appreciably altered by the mechanisation process. With their unique selling point as mounted musicians removed, they became the same as all other bands and were unable to sustain such an exclusive identity.

Most of the repertoire for regimental duties was uninspiring for the bandsmen, as alluded to by Charles Nalden above, and performed to largely unappreciative military masters and colleagues who would be more concerned about hearing the regimental march and a clear beat on the bass drum to keep in step. The summer season, however, offered bandsmen a different level of performance and was looked forward to as an opportunity for musicians to perform some challenging and varied repertoire, invariably sponsored by civilian organisations.

---

[53] M. Ansell, *Soldier On: An Autobiography by Colonel Sir Mike Ansell* (London: Peter Davies, 1973), p. 31-2.
[54] Ansell, *Soldier On*, p. 18.
[55] *Manual of Ceremonial 1935*.
[56] *The Times*, 'The King's Birthday Parade: Salisbury Plain Parade: Salute of Royal Standard', 10th June 1937.

Civilian funded engagements

The main income for band funds was through engagement by civilian organisations, particularly for performances on bandstands at seaside resorts. Concerts by military bands in parks and by the seaside had been a feature of Victorian and Edwardian Britain but peaked in the interwar years when many old bandstands were upgraded and their auditoria developed to accommodate more spectators. With the expansion of the railways, leisure excursions had become popular in the mid- to late-nineteenth century, particularly to the seaside. Furthermore, philanthropic interest in the welfare of the working population facilitated the endowment of public spaces within towns and cities for recreation. The main feature of the entertainment for these locations was the provision of music through the engagement of military bands and, while there were municipal orchestras, the outdoor environment was suited to wind and brass bands as their sound could project much farther (Fig 4.5).[57]

Figure 4.5
The bandstand at Folkestone, pre-1914 (MAM Archive)

---

[57] For an account of the resort orchestras see K. Young, *Music's Great Days in the Spas and Watering-Places* (London: Macmillan, 1968).

When orchestras were available they would tend to play out-of-season in closed pavilions and in the summer evenings for concerts,[58] but by the 1930s they had largely been replaced with jazz ensembles for dancing.[59] Military bands performed outdoors throughout the summer and generally remained popular with resorts for the whole interwar period, partly due to the prestige and uniforms of a fashionable regiment, but also because of bands' continued availability.

When bands were hired to perform at seaside resorts it was as a commercial venture largely because the business of entertainment had been increasingly taken into the hands of municipalities in the late Victorian period, as town councils realised that they could make large returns instead of profits going to private enterprise. By the post-war era many resort towns had made the change to municipal ownership to become what Roberts calls 'the Corporation as impresario',[60] where the town council had considerable influence over the hiring of military bands and the nature of their performance space.

Prior to the First World War, the working-class holiday meant a day trip to the seaside and this remained very popular in the interwar years but with the difference that holiday makers tended to stay longer, usually a week. This increase in working class people visiting the seaside for extended periods boosted the expansion of the seaside holiday resorts and with it the need for sustained entertainment.[61]

---

[58] There were exceptions, for example the Pump Room Orchestra in Bath which played throughout the year. See R. Hyman and N. Hyman, *The Pump Room Orchestra Bath: Three Centuries of Music and Social History* (Salisbury: Hobnob Press, 2011).
[59] J. K. Walton, *The British seaside: Holidays and resorts in the twentieth century* (Manchester: Manchester University Press, 2000), pp. 105-107.
[60] R. Roberts, 'The Corporation as impresario: the municipal provision of entertainment in Victorian and Edwardian Bournemouth', in J. K. Walton and J. Walvin (eds.) *Leisure in Britain: 1780-1939* (Manchester: Manchester University Press, 1983), pp. 137-157.
[61] Although legislation guaranteeing paid holidays, beyond the bank holidays, did not come in until the late 1930s, several industries had negotiated with unions separate deals to give workers a paid holiday of a week or more in the early 1920s. See, for example, S. Dawson, 'Working-Class Consumers and the Campaign for Holidays with Pay', *Twentieth Century British History*, Vol. 18, No. 3, 2007, pp. 277-305; 'Holidays with Pay Act 1938' <http://www.legislation.gov.uk/ukpga/Geo6/1-2/70/enacted> [accessed 11th June 2015].

The military band was at the forefront of this entertainment as recalled by 'Jimmy' Howe from the 1930s:

> During the summer months of 1935 the band [of the 1st Battalion, Royal Scots] would go around the seaside giving concerts to the holidaymakers. It was quite hard work, playing three programmes a day, each nearly two hours long, and seven days a week, never a day off in the summer. We certainly got through a vast amount of music, engagements starting at Dover, then Folkestone, Hastings, Eastbourne, the West Pier at Brighton, Worthing, Bognor Regis and finishing at Paignton. We wore full dress red ceremonial uniforms and it was a glamorous life playing in the Band which came to an abrupt end at the close of the season, when it was back to the barracks again in September.[62]

After the war, seaside towns continued to market themselves on the purported health-giving properties of sea air, sun and sea water, and this allowed for military bands to continue in this traditional setting, as described by Jimmy Howe, but by the 1930s there was a concurrent process of modernisation to attract more youthful customers with an up-to-date image. Military bands were challenged by the new entrants to the market but responded by including a larger proportion of modern popular pieces in their repertoire and also by introducing new jazz-styled ensembles in their programmes. Nevertheless, resorts did not neglect their old clientele as they still commanded a significant market segment,[63] which might explain the apparent success of the band tour witnessed by Jimmy Howe.

For most bandsmen seaside engagements were well-liked, as Charles Nalden explains:

> Seaside engagements were generally popular with the [Royal Artillery (Mounted)] band, for although we gave at least two, and sometimes three, performances on all seven days of the week, we had time still for sea bathing, playing on the local clock-golf course, and enjoying ourselves generally. Moreover, these engagements got us away from the barrack room for sometimes as many as eight weeks of the summer.[64]

Nalden's observations are interesting for various reasons: it confirms the large number of performances that bands were expected to carry out; it highlights the amount of time away from the regiment for paid

---

[62] J. Howe, *A Conductor's Journey* (Eastbourne: J. H. Publishing, 2002), pp. 16-17.
[63] J. Hassan, *The Seaside, Health and the Environment in England and Wales since 1800* (Aldershot: Ashgate, 2003), p. 105.
[64] Nalden, *Half and Half*, p. 269.

work; and it also hints at the notion that the bandsmen were, on the whole, not too keen on an overly military way of life.

Many resorts were keen to hold on to their bands and Torquay, despite the summer band programme making a loss, spent a fifth of its total resort improvement scheme budget in the late 1920s on a band enclosure project, presumably to maintain the appearance of elegance and refinement.[65] Even so, the style of many of the resorts changed in the interwar years, with less focus on class distinction, but a more relaxed feel promoted by the resorts, although some, like Scarborough, maintained clear demarcation lines between the classes. Other resorts, like Clacton-on-Sea in 1921, were keen to uphold the status of the band pavilion and bandstand by advocating a sense of exclusivity, seeing their use as a measure of the 'prestige of the town as a good class seaside resort',[66] with the presence of a band seemingly taken for granted.

Although favoured in pre-war Clacton-on-Sea, military bands were, however, having to make room for more novelty item performers as well as jazz and dance bands.[67] Walvin highlights that seaside resorts in the interwar years rapidly lost their Edwardian flavour with greater numbers of concert-parties and troupes performing, as well as an increase in the craze for ballroom dancing,[68] but the ensuing diversification of investment by resort towns perhaps explains the longevity of military bands at seaside venues throughout the interwar period because military bands were the catalyst to preserve links with the traditionalists, while acknowledging developing markets. Notwithstanding a certain move towards modernism it is likely that military band concerts remained well attended, as press reports from the 1920s noted that the popular periods at the sea front were 'when the band is playing',[69] a trend

---

[65] N. J. Morgan and A. Pritchard, *Power and Politics at the Seaside: The Development of Devon's Resorts in the Twentieth Century* (Exeter: University of Exeter Press, 1999), pp.166-170.

[66] Quoted in L. Chase, 'Modern Images and Social Tone in Clacton and Frinton in the Interwar Years', *International Journal of Maritime History*, 1997, Volume 9, Issue 1, p. 155 (pp. 149-170).

[67] H. Eiden, 'The Resorts Between the Wars' in Thornton, C. C. (ed.), *A History of the County of Essex: Clacton, Walton, and Frinton: North-East Essex Seaside Resorts*, The Victoria History of the Counties of England, Volume XI (Woodbridge: Institute of Historical Research/Boydell & Brewer, 2012), p. 160.

[68] J. Walvin, *Beside the Seaside: A Social History of the Popular Seaside Holiday* (London: Allen Lane Penguin, 1978), pp. 122-3.

[69] For example, Scarborough, 1926, quoted in Walton, *The British seaside*, p. 102.

which continued in the 1930s. It cannot be discounted that the bands played at the naturally popular times of day, but the crowds were there to see them and they continued to be engaged by the resorts, as one contemporary observer reported: 'Holiday resorts like crowds because they can have more bands, illuminations and sideshows'.[70]

By the mid-1930s millions of visitors were visiting the coast each summer,[71] and the sizeable investment in new bandstands as part of larger entertainment complexes suggests that they were a commercially viable part of the business case for resorts' money-making plans. Devon saw the greatest amount of seaside development in the interwar years, particularly at Plymouth and Torquay.[72]

Though some resorts did not make direct profits from military bands they were considered 'an integral component of the entertainment "package" at any British resort',[73] because of the income generated generally from visitors. This may have been partly because of an emphasis on maintaining the Britishness of the seaside encounter, as suggested by Charles Palmer in a debate in the House of Commons in 1920 regarding the advertising of resorts:

> I say good entertainment and good bands are essential; they are a great humanising influence, and if, instead of giving us imitations of foreign bands with a strong suspicion of German in their brass, they give us good bands, healthy entertainments, good roads, good bathing, and good Sunday games, I believe our English health resorts would soon be over-flowing with visitors.[74]

The issues in this debate over the 1920 Health and Watering Places Bill were focused around local councils using ratepayers' money to advertise their resorts mainly for British visitors and Palmer's comments further demonstrate how British bands were considered integral to the attraction of seaside towns.

---

[70] Quoted in Walvin, *Beside the Seaside*, p. 117
[71] Walvin cites the largest being Blackpool with 7 million visitors between June and September. Walvin, *Beside the Seaside*, pp. 124.
[72] Morgan and Pritchard, *Power and Politics at the Seaside*, pp.166-170.
[73] *Ibid*, p. 166.
[74] 'Health Resorts and Watering Places Bill' HC Deb 11 June 1920 vol 130 cc832-49, <http://hansard.millbanksystems.com/commons/1920/jun/11/health-resorts-and-watering-places-bill#S5CV0130P0_19200611_HOC_213>[accessed 13th May 2015].

Eastbourne's Grand Parade and Redoubt bandstands were both replaced at great expense in the 1930s to cater for larger numbers and an enhanced public experience (Fig 4.6).[75] What was to become known as the 'Nautical Moderne' style supplanted the more classical or Neo-Georgian styles of the mid-1920s, such as the new pier pavilion and bandstand at Worthing.[76] Gray has suggested that both architecture and music were important facets of seaside resort design,[77] and bandstands as structures featured in seaside town official guides,[78] but it was not just on the coast that this combination made an impact.

Figure 4.6
The new Redoubt Bandstand, Eastbourne, 1930s (MAM)

Up until World War Two bandstands were being advertised in the press as an ideal place to hear music with, for example, the *Daily*

---

[75] Hassan, *The Seaside*, p. 98. A British Pathé film from 1936 shows the capacity of the Grand Parade bandstand, see <http://www.britishpathe.com/video/new-bandstand-and-garden/query/Thorntons> [accessed 24th September 2015].
[76] S. Braggs and D. Harris, *Sun, Sea and Sand: The Great British Seaside Holiday* (Stroud: Tempus, 2006), p. 61.
[77] F. Gray, *Designing the Seaside: Architecture, Society and Nature* (London: Reaktion, 2006), p. 55.
[78] See for example Braggs and Harris, *Sun, Sea and Sand*, pp. 11-18, which provides a brief survey of official guides.

Express reporting in the summer of 1937 that there were 'sixty bands engaged to play at London parks with Sunday evening concerts from 7 to 9 o'clock'.[79] The acoustics of the covered bandstand were seen as a contributing factor for the success of the concerts with the audience able to hear 'every note from 300 yards away without difficulty'.[80] There were approximately 1,200 bandstands built in Britain from the mid-nineteenth century, with at least 167 built in the interwar years,[81] and occasionally army musicians were consulted on their design,[82] with some modern bandstands built for special events, such as the 1938 British Empire Exhibition in Glasgow (Fig 4.7).

Figure 4.7
Bandstand at the British Empire Exhibition, Glasgow, 1938 (MAM)

---

[79] Quoted in P. A. Rabbitts, *Bandstands* (Oxford: Shire, 2011), p. 15.
[80] *Ibid*.
[81] P. A. Rabbitts, 'Database of Bandstands – lost and existing', <http://www.paulrabbitts.co.uk/bandstands-database> [accessed 13th May 2015]; P. A. Rabbitts, 'Bandstands'. Private email message, 11th May 2015.
[82] TNA. Works/16/1105. 'Kensington Gardens New Bandstand'. Minute Sheet dated 8th October 1930 and Letter to First Commissioner, dated 10th October 1930.

While bandstands were not always used exclusively for band performances there seems to have been a clear expectation throughout the period that military bands were to provide the musical entertainment from these structures for the foreseeable future. Several brass bands were also on the bandstand performance circuit, as can be seen at the Glasgow listing (Fig 4.8), but they did not contribute the same number of performances. Civilian military-style bands were likewise involved, but it was army bands that overwhelmingly dominated the season. Even though the Glasgow British Empire Exhibition was a special event, the band listing is indicative of the proportion of bands performing around Britain (Figs 4.8 & 4.9).

```
The complete list of band engagements
up to date is as follows:—
H.M. Royal Horse Guards..  May  2-May  7
Highland Light Infantry .. May  2-May  7
Coldstream Guards ......   May  9-May 14
1st York. and Lanc Regt... May  9-May 14
1st Rifle Brigade .......  May 16-May 21
Corporation Gas Works ...  May 16-May 21
1st Black Watch .........  May 23-May 28
12th Royal Lancers ......  May 23-May 28
2nd Warwicks ............  May 30-June 4
Parkhead Forge ..........  May 30-June 4
1st Camerons ............  June 6-June 11
Royal Scots Fusiliers....  June 6-June 11
Royal Air Force .........  June 13-June 18
Clydebank Burgh .........  June 13-June 18
Royal Scots Greys .......  June 20-June 25
Scots Guards ............  June 20-June 25
Seaforth Highlanders ....  June 27-July 2
     Do. ................  June 27-July 2
K.R.R.C. ................  July 4-July 9
     Do. ................  July 4-July 9
A. and S. Highlanders ...  July 11-July 16
Govan Burgh .............  July 11-July 16
1st Royal Dragoons ......  July 18-July 23
West Calder .............  July 18-July 23
Kneller Hall ............  July 25-July 30
Oxfords and Bucks L.I. ..  July 25-July 30
Munn and Felton .........  Aug. 1-Aug. 6
Black Dyke Mills ........  Aug. 1-Aug. 6
Grenadier Guards ........  Aug. 8-Aug. 13
S.C.W.S. ................  Aug. 8-Aug. 13
2nd Bn. Glos. Regt. .....  Aug. 15-Aug. 20
King's Own Royal Regt ...  Aug. 15-Aug. 20
South Staffs ............  Aug. 22-Aug. 27
R.A. Lister .............  Aug. 22-Aug. 27
Royal Marines ...........  Aug. 29-Sep. 3
Welsh Guards ............  Aug. 29-Sep. 3
The Buffs ...............  Sep. 5-Sep. 10
Fodens ..................  Sep. 5-Sep. 10
R.A., Portsmouth ........  Sep. 12-Sep. 17
Irish Guards ............  Sep. 12-Sep. 17
2nd Lincolns ............  Sep. 19-Sep. 24
Wellesley Colliery ......  Sep. 19-Sep. 24
Q.R.R. ..................  Sep. 26-Oct. 1
Scottish Military Band ..  Sep. 26-Oct. 1
4th/7th Dragoons ........  Oct. 3-Oct. 8
Tank Corps ..............  Oct. 3-Oct. 8
R.A. Mounted Band .......  Oct. 10-Oct. 15
Callander Senior ........  Oct. 10-Oct. 15
```

Figure 4.8
The British Empire Exhibition, Glasgow, 1938, band list (MAM)

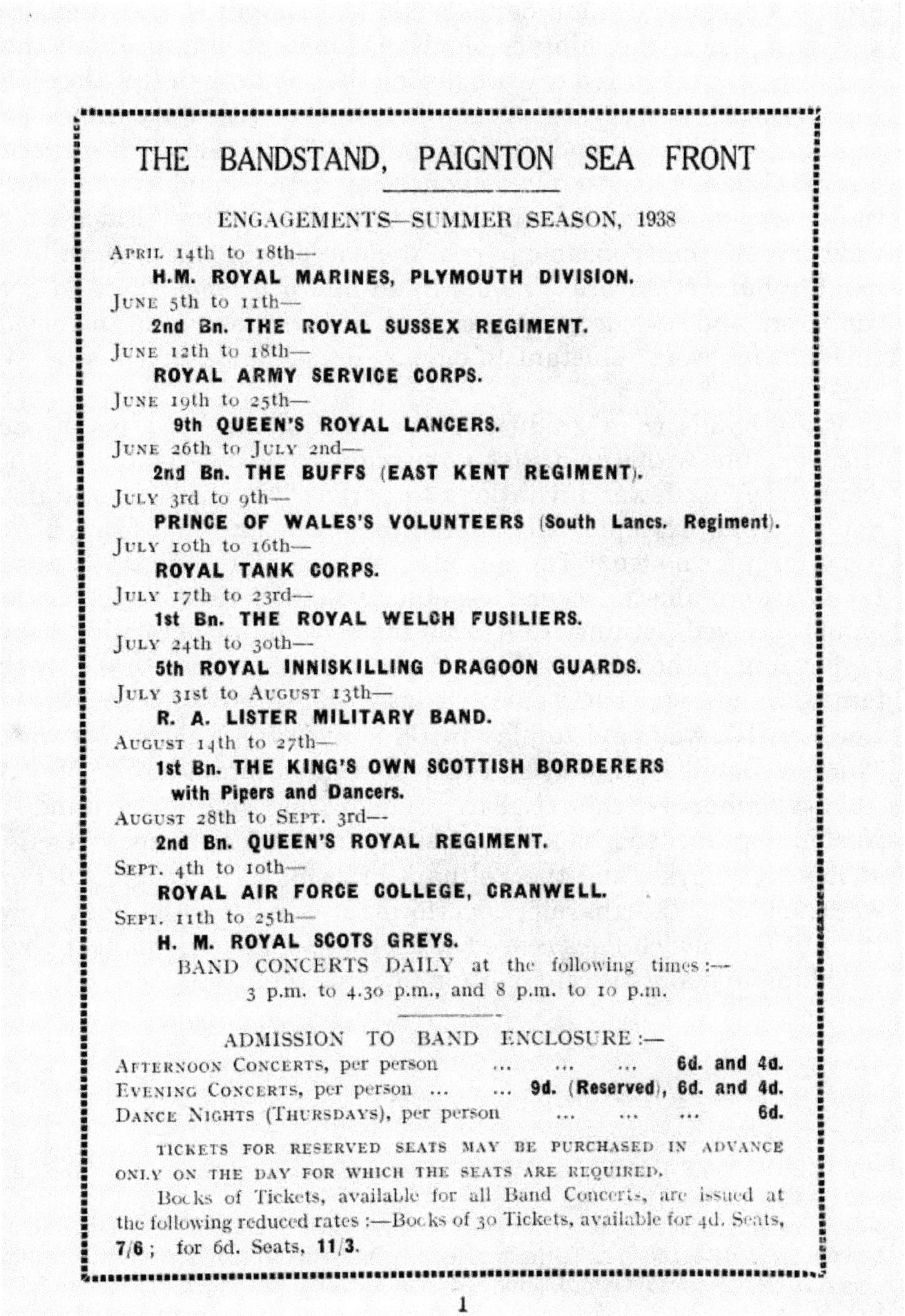

THE BANDSTAND, PAIGNTON SEA FRONT

ENGAGEMENTS—SUMMER SEASON, 1938

APRIL 14th to 18th—
H.M. ROYAL MARINES, PLYMOUTH DIVISION.
JUNE 5th to 11th—
2nd Bn. THE ROYAL SUSSEX REGIMENT.
JUNE 12th to 18th—
ROYAL ARMY SERVICE CORPS.
JUNE 19th to 25th—
9th QUEEN'S ROYAL LANCERS.
JUNE 26th to JULY 2nd—
2nd Bn. THE BUFFS (EAST KENT REGIMENT).
JULY 3rd to 9th—
PRINCE OF WALES'S VOLUNTEERS (South Lancs. Regiment).
JULY 10th to 16th—
ROYAL TANK CORPS.
JULY 17th to 23rd—
1st Bn. THE ROYAL WELCH FUSILIERS.
JULY 24th to 30th—
5th ROYAL INNISKILLING DRAGOON GUARDS.
JULY 31st to AUGUST 13th—
R. A. LISTER MILITARY BAND.
AUGUST 14th to 27th—
**1st Bn. THE KING'S OWN SCOTTISH BORDERERS
with Pipers and Dancers.**
AUGUST 28th to SEPT. 3rd—
2nd Bn. QUEEN'S ROYAL REGIMENT.
SEPT. 4th to 10th—
ROYAL AIR FORCE COLLEGE, CRANWELL.
SEPT. 11th to 25th—
H. M. ROYAL SCOTS GREYS.

BAND CONCERTS DAILY at the following times :—
3 p.m. to 4.30 p.m., and 8 p.m. to 10 p.m.

ADMISSION TO BAND ENCLOSURE :—
AFTERNOON CONCERTS, per person ... ... **6d. and 4d.**
EVENING CONCERTS, per person ... ... **9d. (Reserved), 6d. and 4d.**
DANCE NIGHTS (THURSDAYS), per person ... ... **6d.**

TICKETS FOR RESERVED SEATS MAY BE PURCHASED IN ADVANCE ONLY ON THE DAY FOR WHICH THE SEATS ARE REQUIRED.

Books of Tickets, available for all Band Concerts, are issued at the following reduced rates :—Books of 30 Tickets, available for 4d. Seats, **7/6**; for 6d. Seats, **11/3**.

1

Figure 4.9
The Bandstand, Paignton Sea Front, 1938, band list (MAM)

One reason why army bands overshadowed other types was probably because civilian bands could not commit to the number of performances as the military bands; as amateur organisations their members were required to work during the day in their full-time jobs. Furthermore, it was also most likely to do with appearance and repertoire. Military bands had regimental funds to pay for uniforms but brass bands had to rely on donations so the standard of uniform could vary quite considerably. In 1936 Russell and Elliot called uniforms 'an indispensable part of the equipment of a modern brass band',[83] but not all brass bands could afford to keep them in good condition, and seaside resorts, concerned with promoting the best of their towns, were reluctant to employ brass bands that had a poor appearance.[84]

Brass bands were gradually edged out of the lucrative seaside engagements, with *The British Bandsman* reporting that brass bands were receiving fewer invitations to perform at resort bandstands. Southend, for example, only offered the opportunity for brass bands to perform for no fee.[85] There is also evidence that military bands in London were able to secure fees and large donations while civilian bands received nothing. In a 1930 memorandum concerning bands performing in the London Royal Parks it is quite clear that only the famous bands were being paid: 'Godfrey's Band' (presumably Charles Godfrey III), was paid to play in Hyde and Green Parks, as was a 'Guards Band' that played every Sunday evening from May to August, whereas the civilian Kensington Volunteer Band at Kensington Gardens, bands provided by the National Sunday League at Regent's Parks, and the Feltham Prize Band at Richmond Park were not paid. Furthermore, performances by the Deptford Town Band at Greenwich Park ceased altogether as the park manager 'was unwilling to make his contribution towards their funds'.[86]

---

[83] J. F. Russell and J. H. Elliot, *The Brass Band Movement* (London: J. M. Dent and Sons, 1936), p. 165.

[84] D. Russell, ''What is Wrong with Brass Bands?': Cultural Change and the Band Movement, 1918-c.1964', in T. Herbert (ed.), *The British Brass Band: A Music and Social History* (Oxford: Oxford University Press, 2000), pp. 68-121 (p. 89).

[85] A. Hailstone, *The British Bandsman Centenary Book – a social history of Brass Bands* (Baldock: Egon, 1987), p. 203.

[86] TNA. Works/16/1105. 'Kensington Gardens New Bandstand'. Memoranda dated 4th November, 1930.

Instrumentation and repertoire

In 1895, Laubach, a former army bandmaster based in Edinburgh and later Canada, had contributed a chapter on *The Military Band* to Volume 5 of *The Musical Educator* which provides instrumentation lists for different size bands but cautions that 'it may not be possible to find two bands with quite the same instrumentation'.[87] Even after a conference at Kneller Hall in 1921 to standardise instrumentation, attended by 'Directors of Music of the Army, Royal Navy and Royal Air Force',[88] the Commandant of the Royal Military School of Music, Colonel J. A. C. Somerville, acknowledged that the agreement was 'completely ignored by army bands'.[89] Somerville reproduced the standard instrumentation list in a letter to *The Musical Times* in 1924 (Fig. 4.10),[90] but photographs of bands show that the numbers were never exactly adhered to (Figs 4.11 & 4.12).

Some writers at the time, such as Charles Hoby in his 1936 book *Military Band Instrumentation*, specify the variations of band size but are also pragmatic in the practicalities of regimental bands and discuss the size of the minimum possible band.[91] Forsyth in his book *Orchestration* discusses in several chapters the use of wind instruments in military bands.[92] But the normal size of the touring military band was twenty-five, the amount that would comfortably fit on a bandstand, and the number recommended for arrangers to work with when transcribing works for military band. This is the same number of performers (although different instruments) that had been authorised in 1873 for brass bands to compete at the Belle Vue contest,[93] and may have had some influence on the military band size,

---

[87] F. Laubach, 'The Military Band', in J. Greig (ed) *The Musical Educator: A Library of Instruction by Eminent Specialists: Volume The Fifth* (Edinburgh: T C & E C Jack, Grange Publishing, 1895), p 77 [pp. 77-100].

[88] TNA WO/32/3906. 'Employment of Military Bands in Civilian Engagements: Complaints by Musicians' Union on Breach of Regulations'. *Proceedings of a Conference Held at Kneller Hall on the 7th December, 1921, in Accordance with War Office Paper 103/K.H./915.*, dated 14th December 1921.

[89] A. Zealley, J. Hume and J. A. C. Somerville, *Famous Bands of the British Empire* (London: J. P. Hull, 1926), p.13.

[90] J. C. Somerville, 'Constitution of the Military Band', *The Musical Times*, Vol. 65, No. 978 (August 1, 1924), p. 738.

[91] C. Hoby, *Military Band Instrumentation: A Course for Composers and Students* (London: Oxford University Press, 1936).

[92] C. Forsyth, *Orchestration*. 2nd edn (London: Macmillan, 1935).

[93] J. L. Scott, 'The Evolution of the Brass Band and its Repertoire in Northern England' (PhD dissertation, Sheffield University, 1970), p. 155. The number was actually twenty-four with the addition of percussion allowed for concerts only.

but the instrumentation for military bands was not standardised until the 1921 conference.

While there were clear musical reasons for addressing this issue it is also very likely that one of the main drivers for standardisation was pressure from the civilian sector, particularly by Joseph Williams at the Amalgamated Musicians' Union, who wished to ensure that competition was fair. The minutes of a Kneller Hall meeting held a week later in December reveal that 'offers are frequently received from municipalities and others for bands of 15 or 16 performers in order to cut down expense' and that bandmasters were reluctant to turn down engagements in order not to lose them permanently.[94] The minutes go on to discuss the element of competition that this introduces and that, musically, it would be better to introduce a minimum number of twenty performers for indoors and twenty-five for outdoors. Perhaps most significant is that there was a concern about losing engagements to civilians, but this was dismissed in part due to non-musical reasons:

> The Conference was generally of opinion that this would not necessarily entail the loss of many engagements to civilian bands, as, besides the superiority of performance, the appearance and bearing of military bands, and their general popularity with the public would prevent this.[95]

An instruction was finally issued by the War Office in 1929 which caused difficulties in some bands, for example the Royal Artillery Band, who were concerned at the potential loss of engagements through increased costs.[96] Bands did inevitably transgress this edict but the number of twenty-five performers became embedded in the teaching at the Royal Military School of music with Hector Adkins, Director of Music at Kneller Hall, in his 1931 *Treatise on the Military Band*, written as a manual for students of orchestration, emphasising the point: 'Remember you are writing for a band of 25 performers'.[97]

---

[94] TNA WO/32/3906. 'Employment of Military Bands in Civilian Engagements: Complaints by Musicians' Union on Breach of Regulations'. *Minutes of a Conference Held at Kneller Hall*, dated 14th December 1921.
[95] *Ibid*.
[96] WO Letter, 103/General/5116 (A.G. 4c.) 3-12-1929. Cited in Farmer, *History of the Royal Artillery Band*, p. 354.
[97] H. E. Adkins, *Treatise on the Military Band* (London: Boosey & Co., 1931), p. 226.

CONSTITUTION OF THE MILITARY BAND

SIR,—With reference to a thoughtful and appreciative article in your July issue, entitled 'Music at the Wembley Exhibition,' the writer asks the questions: 'Is it anywhere laid down strictly what a military band consists of, and what it can do?'

To both of these the reply is in the affirmative; in proof whereof I have the pleasure to enclose an instrumentation table for bands of from twenty to fifty performers, determined at a conference of directors of music, bandmasters, and publishers held here in December, 1921. Also a pamphlet on 'The Military Band,' written about the same time at my request by 'A Service Bandsman' (now a director of music), which gives the compass, tonal characteristics, &c., of all the instruments in use, and some hints on scoring. I shall be glad to send copies of both to anyone interested. The table is subjoined:

INSTRUMENTATION OF MILITARY BANDS FOR TWENTY TO FIFTY PLAYERS

Number of performers	20	25	30	35	40	45	50
*Piccolo	1	1	1	1	1	1	1
*Flute					1	1	1
E♭ Clarinet	1	1	1	1	2	2	2
Oboe	1	1	1	1	2	2	2
Solo B♭ Clarinet	2	3	3	4	4	4	6
1st ,, ,,	1	1	2	2	2	3	4
2nd ,, ,,	1	2	2	2	3	3	3
3rd ,, ,,	1	1	1	2	2	3	3
Alto Saxophone		1	1	1	1	1	1
Tenor ,,		1	1	1	1	1	1
Bassoon	1	1	2	2	2	2	2
Horn (1st and 2nd)	2	2	2	2	2	2	2
,, (3rd and 4th)				2	2	2	2
1st B♭ Cornet	2	2	3	3	3	3	3
2nd ,, ,,	1	1	1	2	2	2	2
B♭ Trumpet						2	2
1st Tenor Trombone	1	1	1	1	1	1	1
2nd ,, ,,	1	1	1	1	1	1	1
Bass Trombone		1	1	1	1	1	1
Euphonium	1	1	1	1	1	2	2
E♭ Bombardon	1	1	2	2	2	2	3
B♭ ,,	1	1	1	1	2	2	2
Side Drum		1	1	1	1	1	1
Bass Drum and Cymbals	1	1	1	1	1	1	1
Bass Clarinet							1

JOHN C. SOMERVILLE
(Colonel-Commandant, Royal Military School of Music).

Kneller Hall.
July, 1924.

Figure 4.10
Constitution of the military bands (The Musical Times)

144 *British Army Music in the Interwar Years – Performance*

Figure 4.11
The Royal Artillery Band at Woolwich in 1933, with sixty-eight bandsmen, six boys, and Director of Music (MAM)

Figure 4.12
The Band of the 2nd Battalion The Queen's Royal Regiment at Felixstowe, 1934, with twenty-seven bandsmen and Bandmaster (MAM)

Repertoire continued to be based on classical music transcriptions and bandmasters were trained at Kneller Hall to orchestrate in this manner which can account for the tendency for often overly thick orchestrations and multiple doublings in military band transcriptions. This approach to orchestral transcription had been at the heart of Kneller Hall's instruction in the nineteenth century with Charles (or Carl) Mandel, an instrumental teacher at Kneller Hall and civilian Director of Music from 1859-1874, clear in his view of the purpose of military band instrumentation when he wrote in his 1860 *Treatise* that '[m]usic for reed bands can, therefore, consist merely of arrangements of universally known and popular operas, songs, and other compositions'.[98] Although Mandel was accused of having 'narrow views',[99] his work remained influential to a generation of bandmasters instructed by him. This approach continued in the latter part of the nineteenth century with Jacob Kappey, a Royal Marines bandmaster, who saw the military band as the primary medium for presenting orchestral music to the public.[100]

Arrangements could be played with bands larger than twenty-five but, essential for outdoor performances, there was extensive cueing of parts, such as cornet for oboe, and euphonium for bassoon. Gordon Jacob, a contemporary composer and arranger for military bands, noted the practicalities of this issue in his book *The Composer and his Art*:

> Since the military band usually plays out of doors there is a danger of light scored passages being lost, especially on a windy day. Therefore much more doubling of the parts than the orchestral composer is accustomed to. Out-of-door combinations are like post-art, which gets its effect broadly and in which subtlety of design and colour is wasted. This does not mean that the band should be considered a dull monochromatic medium with everything playing all the time, but it does demand a larger proportion of brass writing than is usual in the orchestra.[101]

---

[98] C. Mandel, *A Treatise on the Instrumentation of Military Bands; Describing the Character and Proper Employment of Every Musical Instrument Used in Reed Bands* (London: Boosey and Sons, 1859), p. 3.
[99] Quoted from *The British Musician* (1894) in Turner and Turner, *The Trumpets Will Sound*, p. 36.
[100] J. A. Kappey, *Military Music: A history of Wind-Instrumental Bands* (London: Boosey & Co, 1894), p. 94.
[101] G. Jacob, *The Composer and his Art* (London: Greenwood, 1955), pp. 66-67.

Jacob's approach to orchestration is eminently realistic and reflects his experience as a practitioner who had encountered the issues first-hand.[102] This style of arranging had already been taken on by the main publishers in the late nineteenth century, with Chappell, Novello, and Boosey and Hawkes,[103] producing large numbers of transcriptions in 'Journals': collections of arrangements published on a regular basis. It was common to have house arrangers, usually serving or retired bandmasters, such as Frank Winterbottom and James William Duthoit (successive instrumentation professors at Kneller Hall), sometimes writing under a *nom de plume* (Duthoit can frequently be seen as W. J. Dawson, for example). Occasionally arrangers were uncredited, such as Royal Military School of Music Student Bandmaster George Smith, who transcribed *Mars* from Gustav Holst's *The Planets*, published by Boosey & Co in 1924.[104]

One of the features of the 'Journal' pieces was that there were no full scores. This was for a number of reasons, including cost, but also because it would have been useless for the conductor to have a full score, with many page turns, in only the slightest of breeze when performing outdoors. Moreover, through necessity (sickness, for example) instrumentation changed due to the availability of players and bandmasters often acted as arrangers to enable a credible performance for the ensemble at hand. The usual format was a double or triple stave with instrumental cues, as in the 1919 Dan Godfrey transcription of Wagner's *Good Friday Music from Parsifal* (Fig 4.13).

George Miller, whose son, also called George Miller, was to become Director of Music of the Band of the Grenadier Guards in the 1930s, had recommended in 1912 that even original compositions should be produced in short score given the 'fearful and wonderful dimensions' of a military band full score.[105] But sometimes very little cueing is evident, as in the short score of Ansell's *Three Irish Dances*, again a 1919 Dan Godfrey transcription (Fig 4.14).

---

[102] Jacob started to develop his orchestration skills for a small group of mixed instrumentalist while a prisoner of war at at Bad Colberg in the First World War. See E. Wetherell, *Gordon Jacob: A Centenary Biography* (London: Thames Publishing, 1995), pp. 22-33; P. Liddle, *Captured Memories 1900-1918: Across the Threshold of War* (Barnsley: Pen & Sword, 2010), pp. 208-209.
[103] Boosey and Hawkes was created in 1930 with the merger of Boosey & Company and Hawkes & Son, both music publishers.
[104] J. C. Mitchell, *From Kneller Hall to Hammersmith: The Band Works of Gustav Holst* (Tutzing, Germany: Hans Schneider, 1990), p. 178.
[105] G. Miller, *The Military Band* (London: Novello and Company, 1912), p. 101.

Figure 4.13
Dan Godfrey's transcription for military band of Wagner's *Good Friday Music from Parsifal* (Household Cavalry Band Music Library)

Figure 4.14
Dan Godfrey's transcription for military band of Ansell's *Three Irish Dances* (Household Cavalry Band Music Library)

Occasionally, there was only a 'lead sheet' of either solo cornet or solo clarinet, or piano part, both assuredly labelled 'conductor', with limited or no cueing, but by the 1920s a more complete short score was more usual with reasonably comprehensive markings.

Typically, programmes would start with a 'march', such as Eric Coates' *Knightsbridge*, as in the Royal Horse Guards' afternoon performance at Southend in 1936 (Fig 4.15). Classical transcriptions are particularly evident in bands' programmes, such as Herold's *Overture to Zampa*, performed by the Royal Irish Fusiliers at an afternoon concert at Southend in 1919 (Fig. 4.16). They also feature in the example of the Shrewsbury Flower Festival programme which contains a wide variety of pieces, including an original work for band (Vaughan Williams), selections by Noel Coward and Leslie Stuart, and light music such as John Foulds' *A Keltic Suite* (Fig 4.17).[106]

Bands usually kept meticulous records of the music they performed which can be seen in the Band of the Grenadier Guards band sergeants' notebook from 1929 (Fig. 4.18). The variety of repertoire is again evident which included a work by Gustav Holst at the Westminster Central Hall concert, *Fugue a la Gigue*, written as a transcription exercise for the BBC Wireless Military Band. In their Northampton concert is a Winterbottom transcription of the Eva Dell'Acqua popular soprano song, *La Villanelle – With the Swallow* from 1893, still popular in 1930 when the band recorded it.[107]

While the main repertoire remained classical transcriptions in the style of Mendel and Kappey, the pinnacle of transcriptions had been reached by the early 1930s when arrangements of light music that could be played by jazz-style bands were introduced. Popular tunes had been prominent in the repertoire in the nineteenth century, but there was a distinct move in the interwar years to perform more contemporary popular music in tandem with the modernisation that was prevalent in seaside resorts.

---

[106] 'Shrewsbury Flower Show: A Record of the Bands and their Conductors which have appeared on the Bandstand 1875-1993'. MAM Archive. No date.
[107] *The Band of the Grenadier Guards*, 'La Villanelle – With the Swallow' (Eva Dell'Acqua, arr. Winterbottom). Clarinet and Oboe duet by Sergt. Matthews and Musician Harrington. Matrix no. AX 4587, 1930. Re-issued on vinyl record IMMS 03 (n. d.).

PROGRAMME

OF MUSIC TO BE PERFORMED BY BAND OF H.M.

ROYAL HORSE GUARDS
(THE BLUES)

(By kind permission of Lieut.-Col. F. B. de Klee)
Director of Music :- Lieut. J. A. THORNBURROW,
L.R.A.M., A.R.C.M., p.s.m.

SATURDAY, AUGUST 22nd, 1936

Ideal for Health and Happiness

SOUTHEND-ON-SEA
COUNTY BOROUGH OF
CLIFFS BANDSTAND PROGRAMME 1d

BANDSTAND ON THE CLIFFS.

The Following
H.M. ARMY BANDS AND CIVILIAN BANDS
have been engaged to perform in the above Band-stand daily.
MORNINGS 11 a.m. to 12.30 p.m. (Fridays and Sundays excepted)
AFTERNOONS 3 to 4.45 } (Fridays and Sundays included)
EVENINGS 8 to 10

Weather and other circumstances permitting) by permission of the respective Officers commanding.

EASTER HOLIDAYS.	
ROYAL ARTILLERY	10th to 17th April
WEEK-ENDS.	
2nd Battn. THE BUFFS (Royal East Kent Regiment).	18th and 19th April
2nd Battn. NORTH STAFFORDSHIRE REGIMENT	25th and 26th April
QUEEN'S BAYS (2nd Dragoon Guards)	2nd and 3rd May
2nd Battn. DEVONSHIRE REGIMENT	9th and 10th May
METROPOLITAN POLICE CENTRAL	16th and 17th May
2nd Battn. EAST SURREY REGIMENT	23rd and 24th May
SEASON.	
2nd Battn. KING'S SHROPSHIRE LIGHT INFANTRY	30th May to 6th June
(Including Dance Orchestra and Vocalist).	
IRISH GUARDS	7th to 13th June
1st Battn. SUFFOLK REGIMENT	14th to 20th June
(Including Male Voice Choir and Vocalist).	
ARCHIE ANDRE AND HIS FAMOUS CARLTON	21st to 27th June
ROYAL MARINES (Portsmouth)	28th June to 4th July
(Including Vocalists, Dance Band and String Orchestra).	
ROYAL IRISH FUSILIERS (Princess Victoria's)	5th to 11th July
(The Faugh-a-Ballaghs). (Including Irish Pipers and Dancers Vocalist and Male Voice Choir).	
ROYAL NORTHUMBERLAND FUSILIERS	12th to 18th July
PETULENGRO AND HIS NINETEEN GIPSY HUSSARES	19th to 25th July
4th QUEEN'S OWN HUSSARS	26th July to 1st August
(Including Massed Trumpeters and Male Voice Choir).	
ROYAL SIGNALS	2nd to 8th August
(Including Male Voice Choir).	
AL. DAVISON AND HIS CLARIBEL	9th to 15th August
(Including Vocalist).	
ROYAL HORSE GUARDS (The Blues)	16th to 22nd August
1st Battn. BORDER REGIMENT	23rd to 29th August
(Including Dance Orchestra, Male Voice Choir and Vocalist).	
YOUNGMAN AND HIS FAMOUS CZARDAS	30th Aug. to 5th Sept.
2nd Battn. CAMERONIANS (Scottish Rifles)	6th to 12th September
(Including Pipers and Dancers, Dance Band and Male Voice Choir).	
1st Battn. OXFORDSHIRE AND BUCKINGHAMSHIRE LIGHT INFANTRY	13th to 19th September
(Including Vocalist and Male Voice Choir).	
BOBBY HOWELL'S	20th to 26th September
9th QUEEN'S ROYAL LANCERS	27th Sept. to 3rd Oct.
(Including Massed Trumpeters, Male Voice Choir, Symphonic Dance Orchestra, Piano Accordeon Soloist, etc).	

BANDSTAND IN CHALKWELL PARK

CONCERTS by the FERNAND KRISH ORCHESTRA and VOCALIST will be given on WHIT SUNDAY 31st May and on each Sunday to 13th SEPTEMBER, from 3 to 5 and 8 to 9.45

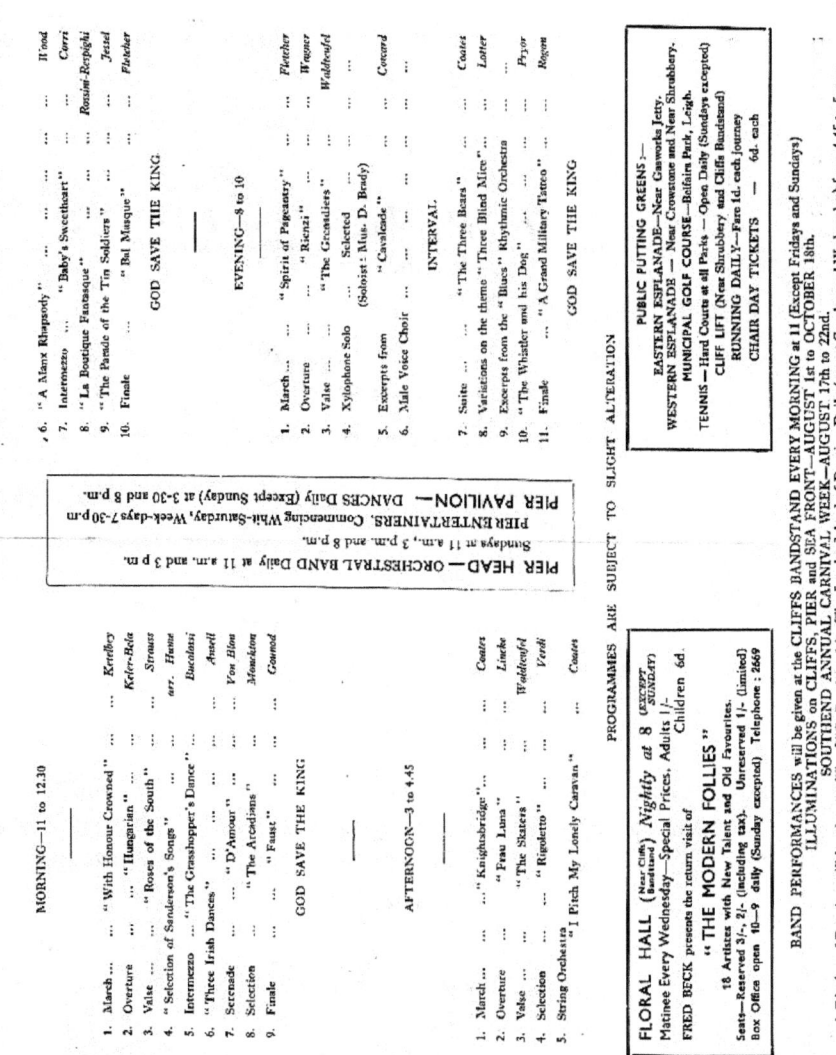

Figure 4.15
Royal Horse Guards Band, Southend, 1936, music programme (MAM)

Sunday, June 29th 1919.

PROGRAMME.

Band of

H.M. 2nd Battalion
ROYAL IRISH FUSILIERS,
(FAUGH-A-BALLAGH).

By kind permission of Lieut. Col. P. W. Cross & Officers.

Bandmaster — **L. P. BRADLEY, L.R.A.M.**

Places and Times of Performance.

WEEKDAYS—From 11 a.m. to 12-30 p.m. ; Pier Head (except Fridays From 3.0 to 5.0 p.m. and from 7.45 p.m. : Bandstand on the Cliffs.

SUNDAYS— From 11 a.m. to 12.30 p.m. ; Pier Head. From 3.0 to 5.0 p.m. and from 8 p.m. · Bandstand on the Cliffs.

MORNING, 11 to 12.30.

1	March	...	"Bride Elect" ...	Sousa
2	Overture	...	"Festival" ...	Leutner
3	Selection	...	"The Gondoliers" ...	Sullivan
4	Valse	...	"Thrills" ...	Ancliffe

Interval

5	Rhapsody	...	"Slavonic" ...	Friedman
6	Melodie	...	"Un peu D'Amour" ...	
7	Selection	...	"Chu Chin Chow" ...	Norton
8	Patrol	...	"U.S.A." ...	Coxmoore

REGIMENTAL MARCH.
St. Patrick's Day. Garryowen. Norah Creina.

GOD SAVE THE KING.

AFTERNOON 3 to 5.

1	March	"New Colours"	Williams
2	Overture	"Zampa"	Herold
3	Song	"Friend O'Mine"	Sanderson
4	...	"Nell Gwyn Dances"	Ed. German
	(a) Country Dance (b) Merrymakers Dance		
5	Valse	"Thoughts"	Alford

Interval.

6	...	"Caprice Italiene"	Tschaikowsky
7	...	"Liebeslied"	Dora Coombs
8	Four Indian Love Lyrics	Amy Woodforde-Finden	
	"The Temple Bells" "Less than the Dust"		
	"Kashmiri Song" "Till I wake"		
9	Polonaise	"Masken"	Faust

REGIMENTAL MARCH.

St. Patrick's Day. Garryowen. Norah Creina.

GOD SAVE THE KING

EVENING 8 to 10.

1	Hymn	"Abide with Me"	...
2	March	"El Abanico"	Gounod
3	Overture	"Mirella"	Frank Lambert
	(a) Menuet (b) Valse	"D'Anian" "Caressante"	
		Conducted by the Composer	
4	Suite	"Casse Noisette"	Tschaikowsky
	(a) Miniature Overture (b) Danse de la Fee Dragee (c) Valse de Fleurs		
5	...	"Three Light Pieces"	Fletcher

Interval.

6	Overture Solennelle	"1812" (By request)	Tschaikowsky
7	Bell Gavotte	"Les Cloches de St. Malo"	Rimmer
8	Song	"She is far from the Land"	Frank Lambert
		Lieut. W. BENTLEY, R.A.F. Conducted by the Composer	
9	Naval Patrol	"Britain's First Line"	Williams

REGIMENTAL MARCH.

St. Patrick's Day. Garryowen. Norah Creina.

GOD SAVE THE KING

List of His Majesty's Army Bands.

Engaged to perform at Southend-on-Sea, during the Season of 1919, by permission of the respective Colonels commanding.

PERIOD (both days included)	BAND	PERIOD (both days included)	BAND
19th May to 6th June (except Sundays)	2nd Batt. ROYAL IRISH FUSILIERS. (Bandm'r Ballagh.) Conductor—Mr. J. P. Bradley, L.R.A.M.	19 July to 1st August	B.M. ROYAL ARTILLERY MOUNTED BAND Conductor—Mr. A. J. LUKIN.
7th to 20th June	2nd Batt. SUFFOLK REGIMENT. Conductor—Mr. H. E. ADKINS, Mus. Bac.	2nd to 15th August	1st Batt. BLACK WATCH ROYAL HIGHLANDERS Conductor—Mr. F. T. TRUSSELY.
21st June to 4th July	2nd Batt. ROYAL IRISH FUSILIERS (Bandm'r Ballagh) Conductor—Mr. L. P. BRADLEY, L.R.A.M	16h. to 29th. August	B.M. IRISH GUARDS Conductor—Mr. C. HASSELL
5th to 18th. July	B.M. ROYAL MARINES, DEAL. Conductor—Lieut. J. S. NICHOLSON	30h. August to 12th September	1st. LIFE GUARDS Conductor—Mr. G. MILLER
		13th September to 6th October	1st Batt. RIFLE BRIG. DE Conductor—Mr. C. H. BARRY

Figure 4.16. Royal Irish Fusiliers Band, Southend, 1919, music programme (MAM)

Programme. 6 Wednesday.
Combined Regimental Bands
of H.M. ROYAL MARINES and H.M. WELSH GUARDS.

1.—OVERTURE... "Die Meistersinger" ... Wagner
    The Overture contains some of the chief thematic material of the Opera. It opens (1) with the massive theme of the Mastersingers. This is followed by (2) the impetuous march which portrays the lovers and is taken from Walter's Prize Song. After this impassioned exposition into (3) the motive of the Artistic Brotherhood and given place in its turn to a theme (4) with dignified motive of counterpoint. Couplet as the music is, the genius of comedy presides over the Overture.

2.—SELECTION ... "I Pagliacci" ... Leoncavallo
    (Opera in two acts; music and text by Leoncavallo, first performance at the Dal Verme, Milan, May 21st, 1892. First performance in London, May 19th, 1893).

3.—SELECTION ... "Merrie England" ... Ed. German
    Including:—Introducing; Hornpipe—"The English Rose." "The Yeomen of England" and "Graceful Dawn," "My Irish is Pigtails," "When Cupid First"; and "Robin Hood's Wedding."

4.—THREE BAVARIAN DANCES ... ... Elgar
    (Nos. 1, 3 and 5 of the Choral Suite "From the Bavarian Highlands.")
    1—Sommernacht.   3—Bei Meran.   5—(The Marksmen).

Conducted by Capt. R. P. O'Donnell, M.V.O., H.M. Royal Marines.

5.—GRAND MARCH ... "Szabadi" ... Massenet (1842-1912)
    He Jules Emile Frederic Massenet was one of the best-known of modern French composers. Born at Montaud, near St. Etienne, in a musical family, he studied at the Paris Conservatoire and achieved great success with his operas. On attaining the lyric stage, he was celebrated for his opera "Manon." One of his most popular operas is "Manon." He died in 1912.
    This march is so popular both in the repertoire of most military orchestras on the Continent. [long biographical paragraph]

6.—EXCERPTS from ... "Rienzi" ... Wagner (1813-1883)
    Wagner's third opera "Rienzi" was composed between 1837 and 1839, and was first produced at Dresden, October 20th, 1842. The composer has been important part of that of Capellmeister at the Dresden Opera. Founded on Bulwer Lytton's novel, "Rienzi" was written by Wagner himself. The opera has very little in common with that of the other author, and if possible to rival, the French style as exhibited in the works of Spontini and Meyerbeer. The selection to be played was arranged by the late French Winter-bank, Chief Musician of La Garde (Act II) — Chorus; New Scene (Act II) — Song, "O Noble and Citizens of Rome" (Act II) — Chorus; "Now come, O stars and skies"; (Act L) — Prayer (Act IV) ... Finale to the Overture.

7.—FROM THE "FOLK SONG SUITE." ... Vaughan-Williams (1872 —)
    1. March—Seventeen come Sunday.
    2. Folk Songs from Somerset.
    3. March—Folk Songs, which perhaps is the most important in his opera, shows Dr. Vaughan-Williams has displayed great skill in collecting and preserving English Folk Music.

8.—MELODIES FROM THE MUSICAL PLAY.
    "Bitter Sweet." ... Noel Coward
    Introducing:— "Zigeuner"— "The Call of Life"—"Tokay"—"I Kiss your"—"If love were all"—"Zigeuner"— "The Call of Life"—and "I'll see — you again."

Conducted by Capt. Andrew Harris, L.R.A.M., H.M. Welsh Guards.

Programme. 7 Wednesday.
Band of H.M. Irish Guards
5 to 7.

1.—OVERTURE ... "Fingal's Cave" ... Mendelssohn

2.—SELECTION from the favourite Operas of Offenbach (arr.) Aoudi
    Introducing:—Chorus Act I. (La Grande Duchesse) Song—"Oh, I dote on the Military" (La Grande Duchesse) Song, La Princesse Trebizonde—"Dites Lui," (La Grande Duchesse) "Saber Song" (La Brigande), Song, "La Perichole" (La Perichole), Duet, "Gendarme Duet" (Genevieve de Brabant), Song—"Rat-a-plan" (La Fille du Tambour Major); The Sabre Song, "La Grande Duchesse), Finale Galop (Orphee and Enter).

3.—EXCERPTS FROM THE BALLET "Sylvia" ... Delibes
    Leo Delibes, French composer and pianist, born at St. Germain de Val, on 21st February, 1836, will always be known for his sparkling music. In his always proved agreeable and never wearisome. His operatic works, introduced into Paris, where he died on 16th January, 1891.

4.—A KELTIC SUITE ... ... Foulds
    (1)—On the Cairn. (2)—A Lament. (3)—The Gift.

5.—PICCOLO SOLO ... "Silver Birds" ... Le Thiere
    (SOLOIST—MUSICIAN R. COLSTON.)

6.—SELECTION ... "The Belle of New York" ... Kerker
    Introducing:—"She is the Belle of New York,"—"The Anti-Cigarette Society"— "The Purity Brigade"—"La Belle Parisienne,"—"They all follow me,"—"When we are Married," "On the Beach at Narragansett,"—"Teach me how to Kiss, Dear,"—"They call me the Belle of New York."

7.—VALSE ... "Wein, Weib und Gesang" ... Strauss

8.—POTPOURRI ... "A Musical Jigsaw" ... (arr.) Alston
    [further text]

9.—FINALE FROM THE "Fourth Symphony." ... Tschaikowsky
    The Fourth Symphony stands quite on a level with any of the composer's other symphonies. The Finale is based on a Russian Folk Song, but before this appears there comes a very brilliant scale passage, followed by phrases of the song theme. These are followed by a theme of a march-like character, and the the full band. It is a resilient movement, and will rank with anything ever written by Tschaikowsky.

Conducted by Lieut. J. L. T. Hurd, L.R.A.M.

7-15 to 9-15.
Combined Regimental Bands
of H.M. ROYAL MARINES, H.M. IRISH GUARDS and H.M. WELSH GUARDS.

1.—PASO DOBLE ... "Mayo Florida" ... Leo

2.—DRAMATIC OVERTURE ... "Patrie" ... Bizet (1838-1875)
    The "Patrie" Overture was produced at a Pasdeloup concert in 1874, and made an instant hit; the composer being credited with having given expression to the feelings of a patriotic Frenchman.
    George Bizet, born Paris 1838, died Bougival 1875, was one of the most promising of modern French composers. He was a student of the Paris Conservatoire under Halevy (whose daughter he married); and won the Prix de Rome at the age of 19. His setting of the great military victory of back for the best music composed—there were 78 competitors—and in the same year won the coveted Prix de Rome. His "Les Pecheurs de Perles" (1867) and his "La Jolie Fille de Perth (1867)" Djamileh (1872), however, are great impression. "Carmen" in 1875, which made his name world famous, The opera has been performed in less than 1,000 times at the theatre of its production, the Opera Comique.

Programme.   8   Wednesday.

3.—FOURTH MOVEMENT from SYMPHONY No. 5 in E. Minor ... *Dvorak*
("From the New World.")   (1841-1904)

Anton Dvorak, born 1841, died 1904, was a Bohemian composer. He composed several operas on national Bohemian subjects. When, years ago, he settled in New York as Director of the National Conservatory of Music, several of his compositions, notably the beautiful Symphony (from which this movement to be played is an excerpt) were based on themes in which he has imitated the "Plantation" melodies, peculiar of the American negro, and the songs of the Indian tribes. His view, though not naturally universally endorsed, was that these tunes should form the basis of American national music.

Conducted by Capt. Andrew Harris, L.R.A.M., H.M. Welsh Guards.

4.—"VALSE DES FLEURS" ... ... *Tschaikowsky*

Peter Iljitsch Tschaikowsky, the Russian Beethoven, was born at Wotkinsk, in Russia, in 1840, and died in 1893. The large interest taken in the Russian School of Composers in this country at the present time is entirely owing to the influence of his compositions, which are very numerous, the most popular being the "Pathetic" Symphony, the "Casse-Noisette" (Nutcracker) Suite, and the Overture "1812."

5.—FINALE from ... "The Rhinegold" ... ... *Wagner*

This wonderful scene depicts the finale to the "Rhine gold." The mountain regions are enveloped in cloudy mists. Donner, the God of thunder, whose "motive" is heard first, ascends the heights, and there swings his mighty hammer, and lo! in a flash of lightning and a thunderous crash, the clouds vanish and Valhalla is revealed.

6.—SELECTION of LESLIE STUART'S POPULAR SONGS ... *(arr.) Hume*

INTRODUCING :—"The Coon Drum Major"; "I may be crazy, but I love you," "Is your mammy always with ye?" "Sweetheart May," "The Shade of the Palm," "I want to be a military man," "Little Dolly Daydream," "The Lily of Laguna," Finale "The Soldiers of the King."

Conducted by Lieut. J. L. T. Hurd, L.R.A.M., H.M. Irish Guards.

7.—OVERTURE... ... "Semiramide" ... ... *Rossini*

The opera of "Semiramide" was produced at Venice in 1823. It was at one time very popular, but now only one or two of its songs alone survive, with this overture, in this country. The overture is specially noted for the very beautiful quartett of horns at its commencement. This is taken from the oath scene in the opera. Other subjects from the acts are utilised, and the overture concludes in a brilliant and effective climax.

8.—SELECTION ... "Samson and Delilah" ... *Saint-Saens*

Saint-Saens in his early days wrote chiefly music of a light order, but after a sad catastrophe in his life, the great composer turned to the creation of more noble works. The above is a fine specimen of his genius.

9.—NORWEGIAN RHAPSODY ... ... *Lalo*

By birth a Frenchman (b. Lille 1823, d. Paris 1892), but of Spanish descent, Edouard Lalo was never guilty of the flippancy so common in many of his musical compatriots. His sympathies were far reaching, and although he could be as piquant as Bizet, he could equally enter into the spirit of the Spanish folk-song on which is based his "Symphonic Espagnole," so dear to the hearts of the lamented Sarasate.

The Rhapsody which now concerns us, exemplifies his use of Norwegian melodies, which he has introduced so winsomely, that some fairy must surely have turned him into a Scandinavian for the purpose.

Conducted by Capt. R. P. O'Donnell, M.V.O., H.M. Royal Marines.

N.B.—*The Irish Guards will combine at 7-45 p.m.*

"GOD SAVE THE KING."

Figure 4.17
Shrewsbury Flower Show programme, 1929 (MAM)

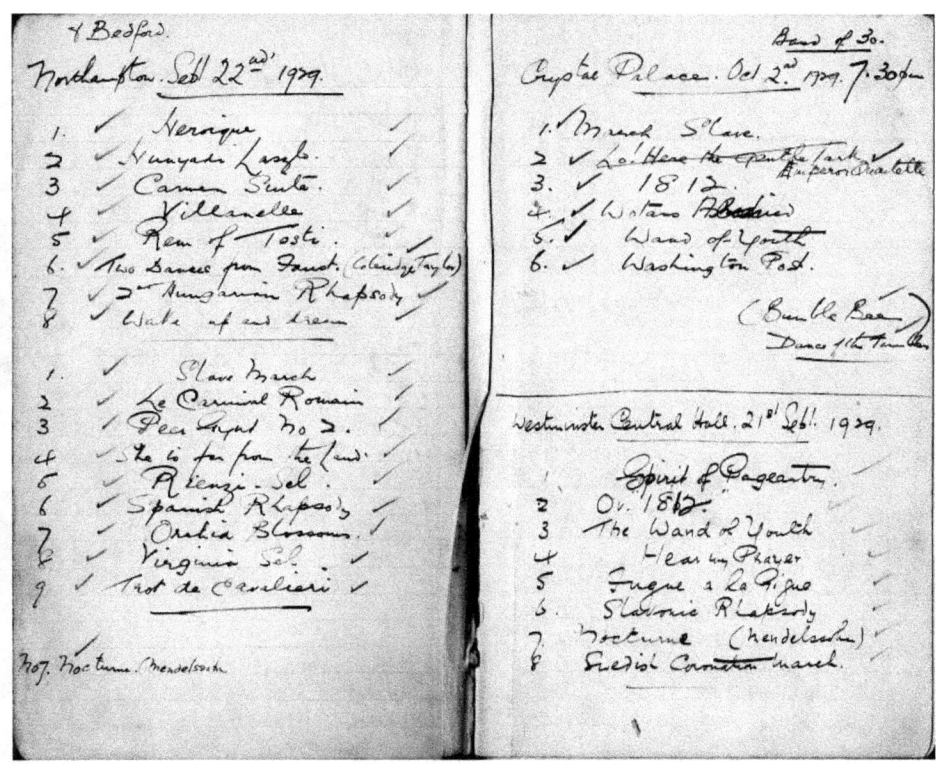

Figure 4.18
Band of the Grenadier Guards programme notebook, 1929 (Grenadier Guards Band archive)

By the 1930s, dance band and popular song music became more evident with the inclusion in programmes of 'Dance Orchestras' and 'Rhythm Orchestras', performed by military band musicians. These 'Rhythm Bands', like that of the Royal Dragoons (Fig 4.19), were also making appearances overseas in the 1930s in a development that reflected customer demands and changes in market dynamics. Some bands, like the Duke of Cornwall's Light Infantry (DCLI), created fully-fledged dance orchestras (Fig. 4.20).

The Band of the 1st Battalion Royal Fusiliers called their modern music group 'The Symphonic Rhythmic Combination' which allowed for broadening of the repertoire, and by 1939 single performances could include a large scope of music, encompassing the older classics, contemporary light music, and the more jazz-influenced dance music (Fig 4.21).

158 British Army Music in the Interwar Years – Performance

Figure 4.19
The 'Rhythm Band' from the Band of the Royal Dragoons, Meerut, India, 1932 (MAM)

Figure 4.20
The DCLI Dance Orchestra, Blackdown, 1938 (Cornwall's Regimental Museum)

As a consequence of this shift in musical style the competition from brass bands started to wane further in the 1930s as they were reluctant to embrace various jazz styles of performance within programmes, and less able, due to their rigid instrumentation requirements. Jones, in his study of Brighouse and Rastrick Brass Band, suggests that by the mid-1930s even the best brass bands were moving away from outdoor performances and focussing on indoor concerts.[108] As military bands were more able to adapt to the demands of the market they increased their market share ensuring they were the dominant presence in professional outdoor performances.

Orchestras

While the main musical output of military bands was for wind and percussion instruments, as well as the diversification into jazz instruments in the 1930s, a smaller but continuous part of military music making was for stringed instruments. The term 'orchestra' tended to refer to any group that included strings, from a small salon ensemble to a full-sized symphony orchestra, and so it is difficult to estimate the numbers involved. While the band with the largest orchestra was the Royal Artillery (Woolwich) Band, which had a history of orchestral playing from at least 1811,[109] there was a continuous presence of string performance in many army bands throughout the nineteenth century.[110] The penchant for strings in the military was confirmed by the fact that the Royal Military School of Music, Kneller Hall, had employed a violin and viola 'professor' continuously since 1857, and later for double bass (1910), harp (1911), and violincello (since at least 1912).

Most of the orchestral work was functional, with Charles Nalden recalling that the strings usually performed at church fetes and garden parties.[111] There were other outlets, however, such as banquets at the Mansion House, and string bands were maintained by the bands of the Household Brigade (Fig. 4.22).

---

[108] R. A. Jones, '"Banding Together": Power, Identity and Interaction within the Concert and Contest Performance Contexts of the Brighouse and Rastrick Brass Band' (PhD thesis, Sheffield University, 2007), pp. 58 & 257.
[109] Farmer, *Royal Artillery Band*, pp. 97-98.
[110] T. Herbert and H. Barlow, *Music and the British Military in the Long Nineteenth Century* (Oxford: Oxford University Press, 2013), p. 151.
[111] Nalden, *Half and Half*, p. 261.

PROGR

1.	Fanfare	"For a Ceremonial Occasion"	A. W. KETELBY.
2.	Overture	"The Wanderer's Goal"	SUPPE.
3.	Entr'acte	"The Drummer's Birthday"	H. ELLIOTT-SMITH.
4.	Excerpts from the Ballet	"Coppelia"	LEO DELIBES.

Valse Des Heures (Valse of the Hours)
Noce Villageoise (Village Wedding)
Czardas (Hungarian Dance)

Leo Delibes first produced the Ballet Coppelia in 1870.
His music is distinguished for its melodiousness, vivacity,
and elegance of instrumentation.

5.	Selection	"Irving Berlin Cavalcade"	IRVING BERLIN.

Including the New Numbers from the Film
"Alexander's Ragtime Band"

6.	Duet for Trombone and Cornet	"Stay but a little Longer" From "Romeo and Juliet"	GOUNOD.

Soloists:—L/Cpl. E. Claxton.
L/Cpl. R. Orchard.

7.	Humorous Descriptive	"A Southern Wedding"	ADOLPH LOTTER.

Parson	Bassoon	Fus. Stiles.
Bride	Clarinet	Bdsn. Parker.
Bridegroom	Trombone	L/c. Claxton.

8.	Excerpts from the Opera	"Iolanthe"	SULLIVAN.

INTERVAL.

RAMME

9. Modern "Music" By

"*The Symphonic Rythmic Combination*"

1. "A Review of 1938"

2. Accordion Solo Selected

Soloist :—Bdsn. T. Parkes

3. An Impression of "*Flat Foot Floogee*"

4. Saxophone Solos Selected by

Bdsn. R. Addison.

INTERVAL

10. Part Songs by   "*The Male Voice Choir*"

11. Grand Scena   "*La Benediction des Poignards*"   MEYERBEER.

In the days of the 16th century it was the custom in France for all gallant knights to gather for a religious ceremony at which the church's blessing was bestowed upon their swords.

This scena from the opera "Les Huguenots" depicts that ceremony with all its pomp and grandeur, and gives life and reality to the splendours and chivalry of the middle ages.

REGIMENTAL MARCH   RULE BRITANNIA
GOD SAVE THE KING.

Figure 4.21
The 'Symphonic Rhythm Combination' from the Band of the 1st Battalion Royal Fusiliers, Jhansi, India, 1939 (MAM)

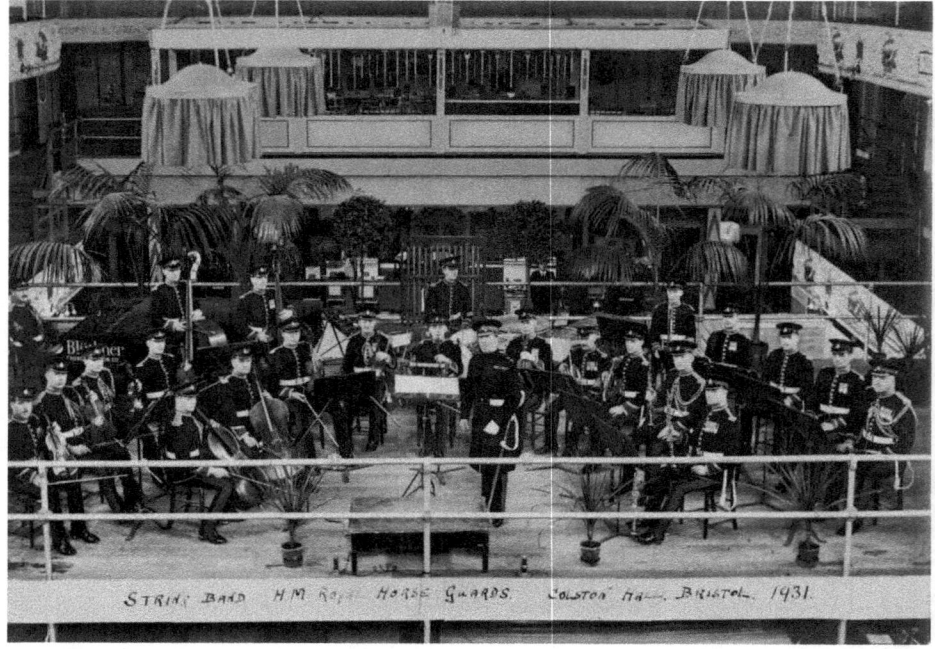

Figure 4.22
The 'String Band' (salon orchestra) of H.M. Royal Horse Guards, Colston Hall, Bristol, 1931 (Household Cavalry Band archive)

As has already been noted, the Household Brigade string bands took over the duties of the Royal orchestra at Windsor Castle and Buckingham Palace in the 1920s, performing during dinner. Unfortunately, though, they were not able to develop their repertoire enough for the younger royals and on one occasion, the Prince of Wales, in an attempt to liven up the after-dinner proceedings asked the musicians to play jazz, but while 'the musicians, more familiar with classical music and martial airs, made an earnest attempt to cope with outmoded fox-trots, which were as close as they could come to jazz', they did not manage to provide suitable entertainment and the experiment was not tried again.[112] By the 1930s the saxophone replaced the cello at the Buckingham Palace State Balls, with Captain Stretton, the Royal Artillery Band Director of Music, explaining that 'American jazz had arrived and that saxophones were now taking the place of the cello and we must move with the times!'.[113]

---

[112] Windsor, *Memoirs*, p. 186; H. Sutherland, *They Blow Their Trumpets* (London: P. R. Macmillan, 1959), p. 71.
[113] H. B. Mason, *Memoirs of a Gunner Bandsman: 1907-1932* (Orpington: Mason, 1978), p. 21.

Regimental officers had to pay to book their regimental band to perform at private functions, but the regimental 'String Band' would cost more, as described in the Grenadier Guards Regimental Standing Orders:

> The normal charge for the Band at an Officer's wedding is £10, but should an Officer require the String Band to play at his wedding, the charge will be increased to £20 to cover the extra work and expenses entailed.[114]

Even for the well-established string ensembles at the Household Cavalry, Royal Artillery and Foot Guards, regimental groups were more likely to have been largely for show, as regimental officers would indulge in social one-upmanship with rival regiments.

Repertoire for the smaller salon orchestras was based around popular and light music of the day, but the more established orchestras were able to perform some of the larger nineteenth-century symphonic music. While there was no appetite to seek out challenging contemporary classical music, evidence from the former Royal Artillery Band music library suggests that there was a continual purchase of newly available music, such as Parry's *An English Suite for String Orchestra*, acquired by the Royal Artillery Band in 1922, the year of its publication (Fig. 4.23).

It is unclear how much of this new music was performed as there is evidence that the Royal Artillery Band orchestral repertoire for dinner engagements was probably not rotated that often. Band Sergeant 'Bunnie' Mason recounts how, at a Lord Mayor's Banquet at the Mansion House, all the orchestra's music slid into a large vat of soup. The Director of Music, Captain Stretton, addressed the musicians: 'Gentlemen, by reason beyond our control, we appear to have lost all our programme of music. We will, therefore, play every note from memory and it had better be good!'. The ensemble apparently still managed to perform successfully,[115] suggesting that the repertoire for this sort of engagement had been in the 'pads' for some time.

---

[114] *Regimental Standing Orders. Grenadier Guards* (London: Army and Navy Stores, 1939), para. 62, p. 14.
[115] Mason, *Memoirs*, pp. 19-20.

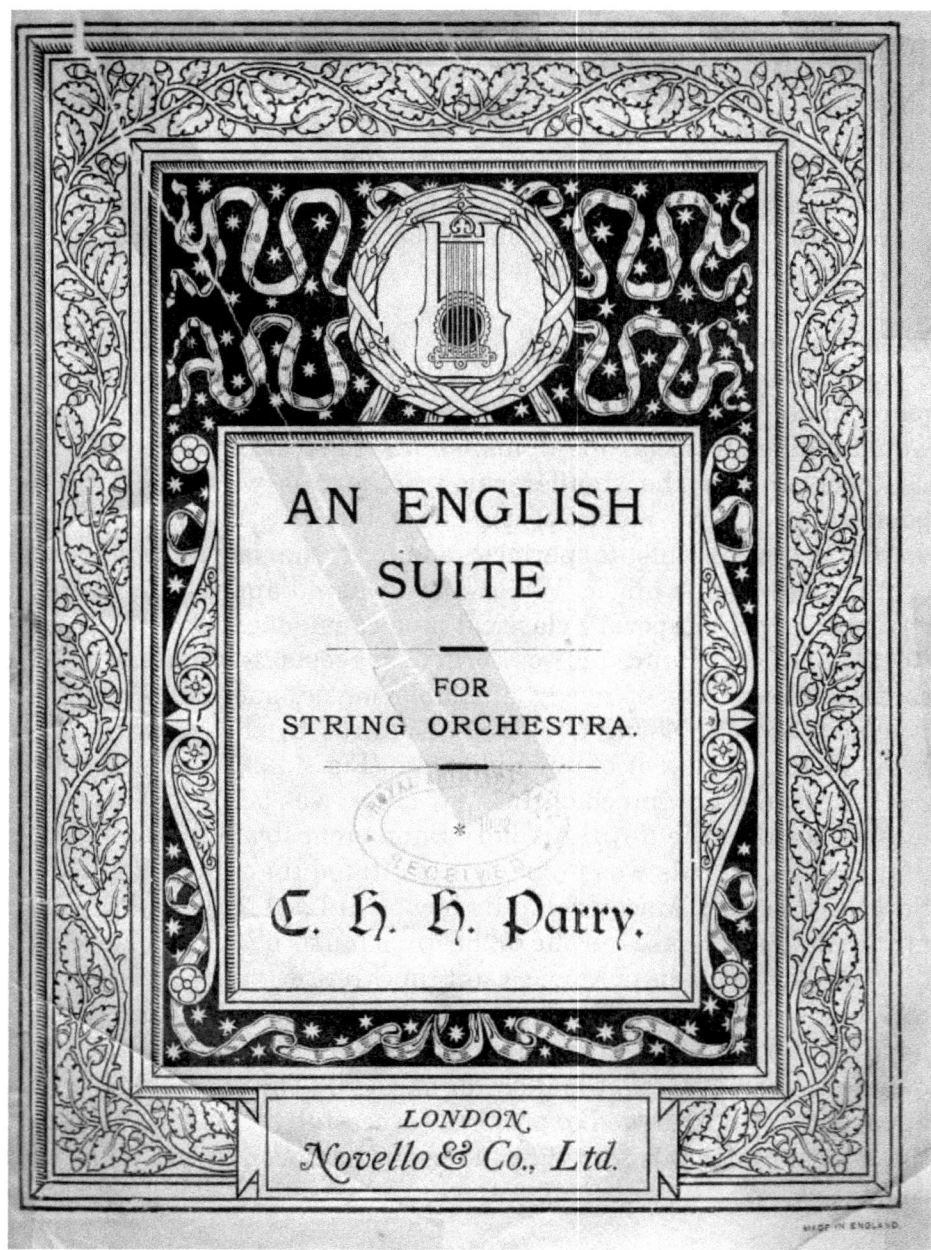

Figure 4.23
Score for Parry's *An English Suite for String Orchestra* (Countess of Wessex's String Orchestra Library)

Controversy and competition

Political issues rarely caused problems for bands but there were some incidences that were sufficient to attract attention. The militaristic nature of tattoos aroused some political opposition, particularly after Britain accepted the 'Kellogg Note' of 1928, where nations stated that war be no part of their national policy.[116] Tattoo producers were also required to change some of the battle scenes to appease overseas political sensitivities, such as with the theme of 'Loyalty' at the 1933 Aldershot Tattoo, where the organisers were forced to alter the main historical episode away from that of the storming of the Kashmir Gate (from the Indian Mutiny) to Gordon at Khartoum.[117] Presumably sensibilities towards India were greater than those towards the Sudan.

Instructions in *King's Regulations for the Army* forbade soldiers from taking part in political events, particularly in uniform, but while it did not specify political band engagements – it did for displays of horsemanship or gymnastics at local fetes – the orders were obvious enough.[118] Remarkably, as a result of a misinterpretation, a transgression at a garden fete by the Band of the Depot of the Buffs in 1928 brought the issue to the attention of the highest military authorities. The band had been advertised to perform at a garden fete on the Isle of Thanet, run by the local Conservative Association (Fig. 4.24),[119] which invoked a complaint from a Member of Parliament and triggered dialogue between the Secretary of State for War and the Adjutant General, particularly about the application of wording from *King's Regulations*. While there was some sympathy for the officer commanding the Buffs depot who had authorised the performance, the bandmaster would have been familiar with the delicacy of the issue and should have advised the officer commanding against participation, even though the band had apparently performed at the same event for some years previous.

---

[116] 'Military Tattoo', HC Deb 26 June 1928 vol 219 c215, <http://hansard.millbanksystems.com/commons/1928/jun/26/military-tattoo> [accessed 8th February 2016].
[117] CHAR 2/192/95-96. Churchill Papers, Churchill College Cambridge. 'Telegram from the Belfast Telegraph to Winston Churchill', dated 20th March 1933.
[118] *King's Regulations for the Army*, 1912, paras 451-452, p. 105.
[119] TNA WO/32/3913. 'Prohibition of Military Bands at political meetings, demonstrations and entertainments', 1928.

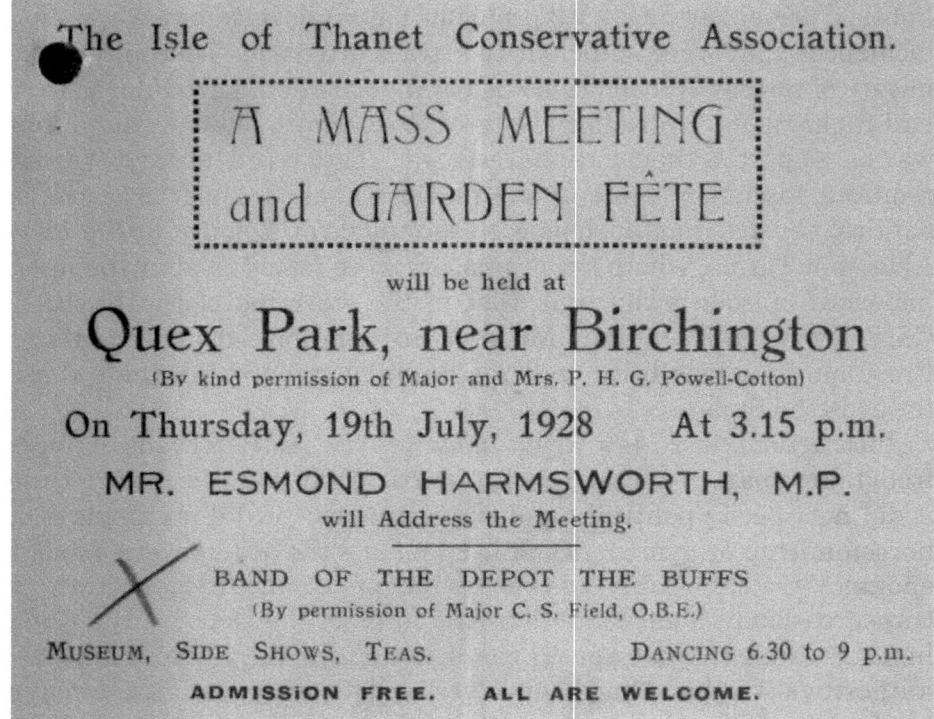

Figure 4.24
Flyer for the Isle of Thanet Conservative Association Mass Meeting and Garden Fête in 1928 which became the subject of a political controversy (TNA)

Had this been a civilian band involved then this seemingly superficial occurrence would not have mattered, but with a military band there was considerable fallout, prompting the inclusion of specific instructions for bands in the 1935 up-date of *Kings Regulations*.[120]

Within the music industry, one major area of tension was between army bands and the Performing Rights Society (PRS), with the dispute extending to India.[121] In the late 1920s there were protracted arguments over the licencing of performance of music by bands inside barracks with the PRS claiming that when music was performed at station mess functions a licence was required, but the army asserted

---

[120] *King's Regulations for the Army*, 1935, para 1403(c), p. 425.
[121] TNA WO/32/14914. 'Performing Rights Society – Purchase of Licence From – For Dance in Regimental Institutes – Necessity of: Span 1928-1931'; WO/32/3904. 'Performing Rights Society – Purchase of Licence from – for Dances – necessity of'.

that it was a military duty and so the Crown was exempt. The arguments continued with the PRS focusing on engagements where guests were invited, which apparently included military bands performing to the public after Sunday church parade.

There was more prolonged controversy with the army's relationship with the Musicians' Union. While military band participation in state ceremonial and public duties were uncontested, the involvement of military bands in commercial activities such as bandstand performances proved to be contentious.

The core issue was that when military bands performed on bandstands at resorts they were paid over and above their army pay, and the same occurred when individual musicians worked in theatre and cinema orchestras. As bandsmen were already receiving an army salary, and associated benefits, such as pension rights, military musicians could afford to undercut their civilian counterparts by a considerable amount. The quarrel had not been a new one – Ehrlich reports that it was initiated in the 1890s by Joseph Williams, the General Secretary of the Amalgamated Musicians' Union (one of the antecedents of the Musicians' Union)[122] – but as the Musicians' Union was an organisation that had politically left-leaning sympathies, with direct links to the Labour Party and Trades Union Congress, there were potential fundamental differences with the military. For example, a resolution adopted at the London Labour Party conference in 1927 specifically called for the ending of military bands as 'superfluous establishments subsidised at the expense of the ratepayer' by competing with civilian bands, and also condemned the practice of the 'engagers of these Bands to undercut the terms and conditions of employment, which the Musicians' Union had established'.[123] This long-running battle was to peak in the interwar years.

Part of the problem was the legacy of performances during the First World War. Military bands had continued to play at seaside resorts during the war even though there were calls in parliament for them to serve at the front,[124] particularly as civilian musicians had

---

[122] C. Ehrlich, *The Music Profession in Britain since the Eighteenth Century: A Social History* (Oxford: Clarendon, 1985), p. 151.

[123] TNA WO/32/3906. 'Letter form Herbert Morrison to the Secretary of State for War' dated 2 December 1927.

[124] 'Military Bands with Expeditionary Force', HC Deb 27 April 1915 vol 71 c552, <http://hansard.millbanksystems.com/commons/1915/apr/27/military-bands-with-expeditionary-force#S5CV0071P0_19150427_HOC_78> [accessed 13th May 2015].

been called up to serve overseas while military bandsmen performed for extra pay. In 1915 in Warrington, the civilian 'T. J. Down's Military Band' was unable to undertake its usual season of performances at the town park due to many of its musicians serving away in the armed forces.[125] Whereas at Firth Park Bandstand, in Sheffield, locals recalled that during the First World War 'there would be a [military] band in the park on Sunday nights and everybody would dance around it, they'd have a lovely time'.[126]

For some civilian musicians who had joined the army and were serving overseas they found this particularly irksome. This was a widespread view and there were cartoons during the war in the Musicians' Union magazine, the *Musicians' Report and Journal*, lambasting military musicians who stayed at home while their civilian colleagues served overseas.[127] Another difficult situation arose where civilian musicians who had joined the army were confined to barracks while the military bandsmen were standing in for them at public performances.[128] For one musician serving in France, J. S. 'Jack' Ratcliffe, the situation was hard to accept:

> I am pretty well satisfied myself with conditions out here, but I do think it's a bit empty when we see pictures in the Mirror, etc, out here of the Guards' massed bands, 250 strong, mostly younger men than myself, many of them single, still at home, serving towards a pension. But, looking ahead, how are all the hundreds of men going to stand on returning, especially Londoners, finding these chaps of the Guards still in their shops while *they* come home, out of practice for 12 months or more, and have to compete with Guardsmen who have been in touch with their instruments all along? The pictures and accounts of the visit of the Garde Republicaine and our Guards marching about London made some of us feel sick out here.[129]

---

[125] A. Down, *History of T. J. Down's Bands: From February, 1905 to December, 1936* (Warrington: J. Walker, 1938), pp. 134-137.
[126] *From Bandstand to Monkey Run* (Sheffield: Sheffield City Library, 1989), pp. 12-13.
[127] 'Dispatches from the front, 1916', *The Musicians' Union: A Social History*, <http://www.muhistory.com/dispatches-from-the-front-1916/> [accessed 23rd February 2016].
[128] M. Jempson, 'History of the British Musicians' Union', p. 8, <https://www.yumpu.com/en/document/view/39707293/musicians-union-history-the-first-100-years> [accessed 26th February 2016].
[129] 'Dispatches from the front, 1916'

After the war Ratcliffe was a very active Musicians' Union activist, becoming Scottish organiser in 1931 and his experiences will have been influential in the union's relationship with military bands. Dissatisfaction with army bands peddling for work had evoked the ire of union men like Ratcliffe, and a systematic process for complaining about army musicians undercutting civilian musicians was started. There were petitions to parliament, with the Secretary of State for War in the early 1920s, Sir Laming Worthington Evans, and his successors fielding questions in the House of Commons.[130] The arguments became particularly caustic in the 1920s and continued up until the Second World War with the Musicians' Union's new General Secretary, Fred Dambman, in 1937 attempting to reinvigorate the policy of 'the abolition of service band competition'.[131] Most of the questions were based on the dispute that military musicians were undercutting civilian musicians on two counts, as ensembles and as individual musicians.

Contracts were usually negotiated with military bandmasters who were keen to get the best engagements and without having the concern of paying bandsmen a wage from the fee it was inevitable that there would be an attempt to undercut the Musicians' Union rates, and this seems to have been widespread practice. In the immediate post-war era resorts were advertising for military bands in *The Stage*, with the magazine also acting as a medium for bands to advertise: 'Famous Military Band Vacant' was typical of the sort of advertisement that was placed by bandmasters seeking lucrative employment,[132] even though this was contradictory to *King's Regulations* which did not allow bands to advertise in the press.

---

[130] See for example: 'Army Bandsmen'. HC Deb 24 February 1920 vol 125 cc1460-1.
<http://hansard.millbanksystems.com/commons/1920/feb/24/army-bandsmen#S5CV0125P0_19200224_HOC_27> [accessed 24th February 2016];
'Bands (Civilian Engagements). HC Deb 08 November 1921 vol 148 cc189-91.
<http://hansard.millbanksystems.com/commons/1921/nov/08/bands-civilian-engagements#S5CV0148P0_19211108_HOC_69> [accessed 24th February 2016];
'Bands (Private Engagements). HC Deb 05 August 1924 vol 176 cc2767-8W.
<http://hansard.millbanksystems.com/written_answers/1924/aug/05/bands-private-engagements#S5CV0176P0_19240805_CWA_10> [accessed 24th February 2016].
[131] 'The Musicians' Union: A social History: 1931-1940',
<http://www.muhistory.com/contact-us/1931-1940/> [accessed 26th February 2016].
[132] See, for example advertisements in *The Stage*, Thu 6th February 1919 for bands to be engaged in Harrogate and Torquay; *The Stage* Thursday 29th January 1931, p.19.

There was also concern over whether military bandsmen where taking the place of striking Musicians' Union members in a dispute with the Pavilion Cinema in Tooting, again forbidden in *King's Regulations*:

> An engagement is not to be accepted on terms which are lower than those which would, in the same circumstances, be offered to a civilian band, or in order to replace a civilian band which is on strike.[133]

But the Secretary of State for War simply replied in parliament that while two Irish Guards musicians played in the cinema orchestra, they were 'not receiving less than the Musicians' Union rates of pay, nor were they taking the place of men on strike'.[134] The Musicians' Union increased its activities though with front page news of *The Musicians' Journal* of October 1927 dedicated to the matter of 'Service Bands' (army, navy, air force, and police bands) and how they were not observing *King's Regulations*.[135] There was concern about platitudes in parliament and that military bands were using agents to book engagements, another prohibited activity in *King's Regulations*: 'Engagements are not to be sought through the public press, nor will they be arranged for or accepted through musical or other agents'.[136] The Musicians' Union seems to have gone to extraordinary lengths to attain information on bands, even deploying its own 'Secret Service', presumably activists who were logging when military bands were playing, or ex-Service musicians in the Musicians' Union who knew what was going on.

To ensure equal terms in the 1920s the Musicians' Union published booklets to establish rates for military bands, for example the *Schedule of Minimum Rates for Military Band Engagements 1925* which specified 'For all Areas outside London where M.U. Terms are not already fixed. In no case shall this Schedule be used to reduce rates already established.' There was also a clause stating '1st Class

---

[133] *King's Regulations for the Army*, 1912, para 1119A, p. 234.
[134] 'Bandsmen, Irish Guards (Trade Dispute, Tooting)'. HC Deb 18 February 1926 vol 191 cc2130-1W. <http://hansard.millbanksystems.com/written_answers/1926/feb/18/bandsmen-irish-guards-trade-dispute#S5CV0191P0_19260218_CWA_32> [accessed 23rd February 2016].
[135] TNA WO/32/3906. 'Employment of Military Bands in Civilian Engagements: Complaints by Musicians' Union on Breach of Regulations'.
[136] *King's Regulations for the Army*, 1912, para 1119A p. 234.

Military Bands – 10 per cent. extra above these rates' which, although not explicit, could only have meant professional Service bands. Furthermore, a surcharge for bands in uniform implied that civilian bands with military band instrumentation could undercut service bands.[137]

The subject of service bands had become a 'hardy annual' topic at the Trades Union Congress,[138] but they became weary of the arguments, with Musicians' Union delegates being jeered at the 1929 Trades Union Congress conference in Belfast for persevering with the topic.[139] Nevertheless, allthough the government was also overtly dismissive of the Musicians' Union claims, internally there was a great deal of investigation, with the War Office deciding to issue new instructions to bands and even asking the Colonial Office to apply the rules to bands under their jurisdiction (locally raised bands in the Empire under British or Dominion control) when visiting Britain.[140]

King's Regulations were eventually updated in 1935 but only to allow military bands to book engagements through agents: recognising a practice that had been going on for years. But the stock answer from the government to the Musicians' Union was merely to state that military musicians were not allowed to undercut civilians and that rules were in place to ensure that did not happen. As far as individual musicians were concerned, the government's view was that what soldiers did in their spare time was up to them. Government policy was that of attrition, hoping that the problem would simply go away and the changes they did make did not fundamentally address the concerns of the Musicians' Union.

The research themes have identified that British army bands responded to the threat of new entrants to the market by establishing their own dance bands and created a new relationship with their audiences through other musical traditions, as well maintaining a link with their established markets. Bands' position in the music industry was constantly under challenge from the Musicians' Union and PRS, but the situation was circumvented by events in the far external environment with the momentous consequences of the Second World War. The relationship of army bands with the military and state was augmented through the increasingly active interest in

---

[137] TNA WO/32/3906.
[138] Quoted in Ehrlich, *The Music Profession in Britain*, p. 214.
[139] M. Jempson, 'History of the British Musicians' Union', p. 34, <https://www.yumpu.com/en/document/view/39707293/musicians-union-history-the-first-100-years> [accessed 26th February 2016].
[140] TNA CO/15885. 'Acceptance of Civilian Engagements by Army Bands: 3 Apr 24'.

ceremonial by the monarch and also the desire by the army to keep itself in the public eye through large-scale events. On the other hand, while regimental bands were more evident performing for public engagements, there were few opportunities for rank and file soldiers to hear their bands as part of their routines.

CHAPTER 5

A CLEAR AND HOMOGENOUS SOUND: PERFORMANCE PRACTICE AND RECORDING

When referring to military bands in his research on British clarinet playing Pitfield maintained that a certain amount of inflexibility in clarinet performance in the late nineteenth and early twentieth centuries was probably due to an unartistic disciplined military style,[1] and that military ensembles lacked 'orchestra-like dynamics and expressive qualities'.[2] Likewise, Worthington in her work on wind playing in London orchestras describes this period of performance as 'an inartistic, unexpressive [sic], military-band-style wind-playing tradition.'[3] These statements raise several questions about what military band playing was like in the early years of the twentieth century but, unfortunately, both authors offer no explanation or indeed provide any examples of 'military-style' playing, if there were such a thing.

The terminology used implies that a military band style was inferior to orchestral performance style, but the criticism may be based upon the notion that the military sound was just distinctive in some way, and that the issue is essentially about performance idiom rather than quality. One of the ways to approach the matter is to consider the position of military bands in the interwar recording industry. While a full comparative analysis of early twentieth-century performance styles would be too large a project to undertake for this book there are recordings available of military bands and orchestras from the late nineteenth century onwards that make it feasible to evaluate the role of military band performances as a contribution to the recording industry, using what Cook describes as

---

[1] S. S. Pitfield, 'British Music for Clarinet and Piano 1880 to 1945: Repertory and Performance Practice' (PhD thesis, Sheffield University, 2000), p. 153.
[2] *Ibid*, p. 9.
[3] E. C. Worthington, 'The modernisation of wind playing in London orchestras, 1909-1939: A study of playing style in early orchestral recordings' (PhD thesis, York University, 2013), p. 27.

the 'close listening' approach.⁴ At the same time, it is possible to explain the reasons for the boom in military band record sales, followed by their swift decline during the interwar period, by examining the potential influence of the military band idiom on general performance practice in the music industry.

Ehrlich, the economic historian, has partitioned the development of the recording industry into five phases, the first three of which are relevant to this study: the recording horn and the cylinder (1877-c1907); the acoustic disc (c1907-c1925); and microphone and electrical recording (c1925-c1948).⁵ In the first two phases, one of the most prevalent styles was light music performed by military and brass bands (the other being popular songs by music hall artists), but having gained a swift entrance to the market, and becoming a primary stakeholder in the recording industry, military bands saw a rapid decline in record sales by the mid-1920s, and almost disappeared from recording studios by the middle of the third period. Notwithstanding this rise and fall of market share in the recording industry, for a forty year period military bands had a significant impact on the nature of repertoire available, and how it sounded, for public consumption through the mass distribution of their records. Furthermore, as a source of performance style, the record buying public often came to know military band arrangements and interpretations of light music years before they were available in their original orchestral versions. But why were military bands initially so important to the recording industry only to fall out of favour after a few decades? And was their playing different to that of orchestras?

There are several components, based around technological, social, and economic factors, which provide answers to these questions but they have tended to be obscured by researchers focusing on the rise of orchestral and dance band recordings in the 1930s, sometimes resulting in the type of speculative statements on military band performance style by Pitfield and Worthington noted above. Some researchers, such as Patmore, have recognised that military bands

---

[4] N. Cook, 'Methods for analysing recordings', in N. Cook, E. Clarke, D. Leech-Wilkinson and J. Rink (eds.), *The Cambridge Companion to Recorded Music* (Cambridge: Cambridge University Press, 2009), p. 221-222 [pp. 221-245].

[5] Cited in D. N. C. Patmore, 'Selling sounds: Recordings and the record business', in N. Cook, E. Clarke, D. Leech-Wilkinson and J. Rink (eds.), *The Cambridge Companion to Recorded Music* (Cambridge: Cambridge University Press, 2009), p. 120 [pp. 120-139].

dominated the first two of Ehrlich's phases, but do not assess the reasons or consider the longevity (or otherwise) of the military band recording catalogue.[6] To address these issues, this chapter utilises Farmer's fourth research theme as well as the fifth supplementary theme (the associated relationship between military music and other musical traditions; the position of military music in the music industry). Technological innovations in the far external environment as well as several of Porter's forces concerning the bargaining power of customers and suppliers, and the threat of new entrants to the market, are particularly relevant to the discussion.

The suitability of military bands for recording

The recording industry in Britain expanded considerably in the Edwardian years, with growing markets in Britain, the USA, Europe, and Japan by the outbreak of the First World War.[7] After initial scepticism by musicians to involve themselves in a process that was originally envisaged as an aid to office dictating, by the early 1900s it was clear that the production of records as a new device for listening to music was gaining momentum in the music industry. Even with the distorted sounds produced by the embryonic technology of wax discs, the medium proved successful as it brought the presentation of music away from a mass experience into what Eisenberg has called 'Ceremonies of a solitary'.[8]

As early as 1904 competition in the cylinder record market allowed lower wage earners to purchase machines, establishing the opportunity for middle and working class people to hear performances in the privacy of their own space.[9] The disc market was initially aimed at higher wage earners, but by the end of 1903 at least one label was selling discs at a price comparable to cylinders,[10] and by 1909 discs were in the ascendancy, with complete dominance after the First World War: the resultant growing competition amongst disc

---

[6] Patmore, 'Selling sounds', pp. 121-122.
[7] See P. Martland, *Recording History: The British Record Industry, 1888-1931* (Lanham: Scarecrow, 2013) for a detailed analysis of the industry.
[8] E. Eisenberg, *The Recording Angel: Music, Records and Culture from Aristotle to Zappa* (London: Picador, 1988), p. 35.
[9] F. Andrews, *A History of the Marketing of Sound Recordings in Britain: 1890-1903*, The City of London Phonograph and Gramophone Society Reference Series No. 16 (London: CLPGS, 2012), p.25.
[10] Andrews, *Sound Recordings in Britain*, pp. 26-27.

recording companies allowed prices to drop, with discs becoming available in the interwar years for as little as 6d.[11]

It is possible to ascertain that the main reason for the early success of military bands was primarily due to the balanced sound and limited frequency bandwidth of military bands which suited the technological limitations of wax recording. For instance, in 1908 Edison Bell deemed the clear and homogenous sound of the military band suitable for use as demonstration discs, with the *Royal Military Band* recording of Suppé's *Morning, Noon and Night in Vienna* overture (probably a transfer from an Edison Bell cylinder recording of an army band) presented as a model.[12] But once the wax technology was superseded by electrical recording in the 1920s, and the introduction of a greater clarity of sound reproduction, increased dynamic range, and the presence of bass notes, it became possible for other ensembles, such as orchestras, to record more successfully. Secondly, changes in taste, partly influenced by the greater freedom provided by electrical recording, but also by general musical trends favouring dance music, moved the military band recording catalogues into the cultural fringes. Thirdly, substitute devices in the form of other media, such as radio broadcasting, challenged the role of records. Lastly, the Great Depression in the 1930s resulted in an economic squeeze on the whole industry.

Martland, in his study of the early years of recording, recognised that there is a paucity of information regarding record sales, particularly from the pre-First World War era, and so it is difficult to be precise about the scale of military band sales.[13] Furthermore, Nott in his work on interwar popular music comments that although military band music was part of the huge provision of established light music, its popularity was not necessarily recognised by the use of record sales statistics: as a measurement tool, sales statistics measured the 'moment of exchange' rather than the 'moment of use' through listening at live performances or as background music and may not have been an accurate gauge.[14]

---

[11] W. Dean-Myatt, 'Scottish vernacular discography: 1888-1960', Introduction, p. 3, <http://www.nls.uk/catalogues/scottish-discography> [accessed 10th January 2017]; F. Andrews, *The British Record Industry during the Reign of Edward VII: 1901-1910*, The City of London Phonograph and Gramophone Society Reference Series No. 3 (London: CLPGS, 2010), p. 34.
[12] Andrews, *The British Record Industry*, p. 27.
[13] Martland, *Recording History*, p. 308.
[14] J. J. Nott, *Music for the People: Popular Music and Dance in Interwar Britain* (Oxford: Oxford University Press, 2002), p. 4.

Another consideration is that researchers rarely differentiate between military and brass bands in their analysis, which compounds the problems of determining exactly how many military band records were made, and how many of these were sold. There are other inconsistencies in accounting that exacerbate the problem, including the identification of bands through the use of generic names by recording companies. In the case of the Zonophone label house band, the *Black Diamonds Band* was the name used not only for military bands, but also brass bands and other ensembles performing popular songs of the day.[15] The complexity of identifying recording artists is highlighted by recording manager, Joe Batten, who revealed that some bands with generic titles were

> in name only…Actually there never was a Denza Dance Band. It was a generic term given at this time by Columbia to any electrical recording made by one of their many American dance bands.[16]

This leads to questions about who the players in these bands were and whether they produced a distinctive sound.

The military band sound

It is very likely that musical performances were affected by the recording process: four-and-a-half minutes of music was all that could fit on a twelve-inch disc and two-and-a-half minutes on a ten-inch disc, and so the early acoustic recordings necessitated a compromise in the performance, such as number of performers, type of instruments, technique (because of cramped conditions), tempo (in order to fit the music on one side of a record), or cutting (again to fit on a record).[17] How much this influenced military bands in particular is unclear, but for all musicians, regardless of ensemble, the conditions would have made performances for recordings different than for the concert hall, bandstand, or parade square.

Andrews, a recording historian, suggests that the repertoire from early recordings would have simply mimicked the music already

---

[15] Martland, *Recording History*, p. 289.
[16] J. Batten, *Joe Batten's Book: The Story of Sound Recording, Being the Memoirs of Joe Batten, Recording Manager* (London: Rockliff, 1956), p. 66.
[17] See S. Trezise, 'The recorded document: Interpretation and discography', in N. Cook, E. Clarke, D. Leech-Wilkinson and J. Rink (eds.), *The Cambridge Companion to Recorded Music* (Cambridge: Cambridge University Press, 2009), pp. 193-196 [pp. 186-209].

familiar with the public accustomed to outdoor music performed on bandstands around the country.[18] While this seems plausible, some recorded works appear to be performed at unusually fast tempos, and although it was common practice to speed up pieces in order to fit them onto one side of a record, to make them commercially viable, cutting sections of music out was normal practice for orchestras, even in live performances.[19]

Since the late twentieth century there has been growing interest in the analysis of the sound of recorded music but it does tend to focus on pianists, violinists, and singers on an individual basis.[20] Analysis of wind (woodwind and brass) and percussion playing, as well as ensemble sound, is virtually ignored in studies by Philip, Day, and Leech-Wilkinson,[21] which is curious considering the large number of military band recordings in the first and second phases of recording history, when compared to the scarcity of orchestral recordings. There is, however, evidence to suggest that a military style of wind playing in Britain was the standard many strived to achieve. In the 1930s some commentators were suggesting that Kneller Hall-trained musicians were superior to others, for example, a piece in *The Musical Times* in 1931, quoting British conductor Basil Cameron's admiration for German military band wind players, declares that the standard of wind playing was very high and that it would also be in England if Kneller Hall could be the source of wind players.[22] John Borland, writing an educational article in *The Musical Times* in 1935 recommends students to listen to the brass in the

---

[18] Andrews, *Sound Recordings in Britain*, pp. 18-19.
[19] R. Philip, *Performing Music in the Age of Recording* (New Haven: Yale University Press, 2004), pp. 29 & 34-38.
[20] For example, 'The Arts and Humanities Research Council (AHRC) Research Centre for the History and Analysis of Recorded Music (CHARM)', <http://charm.rhul.ac.uk/index.html> [accessed 18th November 2017].
[21] R. Philip, *Early Recordings and Musical Style: Changing Tastes in Instrumental Performance* (Cambridge: Cambridge University Press, 1992); R. Philip, *Performing Music*; T. Day, *A Century of Recorded Music: Listening to Musical History* (New Haven: Yale University Press, 2000); R. Philip, 'Brass Playing Before Globalization', in *Brass Scholarship in Review: Proceedings of the Historic Brass Society Conference, Cité de la Musique, Paris*, Bucina, No. 6, 2006, pp. 275-288; D. Leech-Wilkinson, 'Recordings and histories of performance style', in N. Cook, E. Clarke, D. Leech-Wilkinson and J. Rink (eds.), *The Cambridge Companion to Recorded Music* (Cambridge: Cambridge University Press, 2009), pp. 246-262.
[22] 'Mr. Basil Cameron', *The Musical Times*, Vol. 72, No. 1060 (Jun. 1, 1931), p. 497.

band of a good line regiment to grasp the possibilities of the instruments in tone qualities and in agility...He may then go a step further and listen to one of the Guards' bands or to the full band at Kneller Hall. No monotony of tone is found here even in the tone of a single group of the brass.[23]

While these examples are not conclusive, and not all military band recordings are of the finest quality, military bands had the advantage of enjoying ample time to rehearse, allowing bands to maintain a very tight ensemble and demonstrate homogeneity of sound. Whereas orchestras, blighted by the deputy system, had little time to rehearse as an ensemble; even though Henry Wood brought an end to the practice at the Queen's Hall Orchestra, it was rife in other orchestras in the 1920s.[24] If anything, the military band musicians, through their culture and musical performances, brought professionalism and thoroughness to ensemble playing, distributed through the medium of records, that was a feature lacking in the impromptu orchestras in the first half of the early twentieth century. The technical agility, dynamic range, and style in a 1931 recording of the Grenadier Guards Band performing Herold's *Zampa*,[25] does not give the impression that military band musicians were the poor relation in the interwar music industry, and perhaps explains the body of opinion that held the military band tradition of wind playing in high esteem.

In addition to the issues of ensemble, the limitations of the orchestra for recording were clear to recording engineers. When orchestras did record, the tuba usually doubled the bass line and continued as a practice even into the electrical recording era with, for example, the Royal Albert Hall Orchestra using a tuba on the double bass part for a 1926 recording of *A Midsummer Night's Dream*.[26] To overcome the limitations, the advantages of military bands were duly recognised, most notably by two pioneering and successful recording managers, Joe Batten and Fred Gaisberg.

The influence of recording managers

The responsibility of finding artists to record rested with recording managers such as Gaisberg and Batten (a role to become known as

---

[23] J. E. Borland, 'Brass Bands for Elementary Schools (Concluded)', *The Musical Times*, Vol. 76, No. 1113 (Nov., 1935), p. 993.
[24] There would often be different players in the rehearsals to the performances.
[25] *The Band of the Grenadier Guards*. Long playing record. IMMS 103. Side A, Track 2 'Zampa Overture' [1931].
[26] Philip, *Performing Music*, p. 65.

'record producer' in the second half of the twentieth century) and, if successful, they wielded considerable power within the recording company, not only selecting artists, but accompanying singers, making arrangements for whatever ensemble was available, and even conducting bands and full symphony orchestras. Joe Batten and Fred Gaisberg both documented their experiences, with Gaisberg's book published in Britain in 1946 and Batten's memoirs published posthumously in 1956.[27] Although they write with a certain amount of self-aggrandisement, they do corroborate on some versions of events, providing detailed insights into the industry throughout Ehrlich's first three phases.

From their writings there is a broad consensus that military bands were straightforward to record: bands required limited acoustic bandwidth and suited the technological limitations of wax recording. They also agreed that before the introduction of electrical recording, orchestras were less suitable as more sensitive equipment was needed to pick up stringed instruments effectively. Gaisberg noted the popularity of recordings of the Sousa band in the early days while '[w]omen's voices and stringed instruments such as violins did not record well',[28] although he does concede that the human voice was practical for recording, as long as it was full and even with sustained power 'and all nuances, such as *pianissimo* effects, were omitted.'[29] Next in order came military bands with their brass, wind and percussion instruments. 'Therefore' he says, 'in pre-1914 catalogues you will find that vocal and military band records predominate.'[30]

Gaisberg reveals that 'there was no pretence of using the composer's score, we had to arrange it for wind instruments entirely',[31] further explaining that for vocalists 'if there was an orchestral accompaniment, then half a dozen wind instrumentalists...would be crowded close to the singer.'[32] The only string instrument present might be a hardly audible Stroh violin – a violin with a protruding sound horn. One of the most revealing insights on this issue, and why military bands were preferred for

---

[27] F. W. Gaisberg, *Music on Record* (London: Robert Hale, 1946). It was initially published in the United States as *The Music Goes Round* (New York: Macmillan, 1942); Batten, *Joe Batten's Book*.
[28] Gaisberg, *Music on Record*, p. 14.
[29] *Ibid*, p. 80.
[30] *Ibid*, p. 78.
[31] *Ibid*, p. 80.
[32] *Ibid*, p. 43.

recording, is divulged by Batten, who maintained that early recordings of orchestras actually sounded like military bands:

> [T[he recorded effect suggesting muted strings against blatant brass. The average listener would have hazarded that he was listening to a military band and not to an orchestra.[33]

There is abundant evidence verifying that this was the sound produced. For example, in a recording of Violet Essex singing Arditti's *Il Bacio* in 1915 it is apparent that the accompanying winds dominate the sound, with the strings almost impossible to hear.[34] On the other hand, the clarity of the winds in a 1906 Coldstream Guards recording of a *Gilbert and Sullivan Selection* shows why the strings would be superfluous.[35] The resultant simplistic, yet pragmatic, approach was to use military bands to record classical repertoire rather than orchestras, and so in all probability military bands were the reference point for performance practice before electrical recording and broadcasting, and the only sources of classical repertoire for the public to hear.

Percussion could mask other instruments to such an extent that they were often not heard at all, but it depended on which percussion instrument, as Batten recollects:

> The side-drum recorded well, but the timpani were reluctant, the big drum sounded as if the needle had passed over a small hole in the record.[36]

Batten seems to dislike the bass drum, and can do without timpani, but would use the side drum if necessary, which would account for military band recordings sounding as a wind ensemble with very little percussion. For example, a recording of the Band of the Welsh Guards playing *Punjaub* in 1916 omits the bass drum, cymbals, and side drum parts that would have been used on parade.[37] Batten goes

---

[33] Batten, *Joe Batten's Book*, p. 35.
[34] Available at <http://www.charm.rhul.ac.uk/sound/sound_search.html> [accessed 10th December 2012].
[35] *The Band of the Coldstream Guards: Steps of Glory*. 2016. Compact disc. BMMACG1601. Track 4 'Yeoman of the Guard' [1908].
[36] Batten, *Joe Batten's Book*, p. 36.
[37] *A Tribute: The Band of the Welsh Guards*. 2015. Compact disc. BMMAWG1502. CD1, Track 7 'Punjaub' [1916].

on to say that percussion solos were good for recording, which might explain the popularity of xylophone solos in the repertoire at the time.[38] In a 1920s recording by the Band of the Grenadier Guards of Kenneth Alford's *Sparks*, the xylophone can be clearly heard above the rest of the ensemble.[39]

Even within the wind band, sound projection was a key issue when recording, with some instruments being more suitable than others: Batten recalled that for early recordings 'the brass bore the brunt of the work and a three-hour session was more than enough'.[40] But the main advantage of the military band over the orchestra was that it was easier for recording engineers to balance bands due to the smaller difference in frequency range and amplitude within the ensemble, allowing the engineers to record at generally higher levels to enable a greater play-back volume. In 2015 this was put to the test with a comparison of recording levels of orchestral and military band acoustic wax recordings of Tchaikovsky's *Waltz of the Flowers* from *The Nutcracker Suite*, one by the Band of the Coldstream Guards, from 1912, and the other by the Royal Albert Hall Orchestra, from 1922. The results show that, using the same acoustic process, the military band recording is at a much higher level, justifying recording managers' early preference for military bands.[41]

Gaisberg and Batten had considerable influence over who would be chosen to record, with personal relationships a key factor in the decision making. Batten's relationship with Mackenzie-Rogan, Bandmaster of the Coldstream Guards, proved particularly fruitful, especially as both men were high profile members of the influential *Savage Club*. It was, however, Gaisberg who takes credit for Mackenzie-Rogan's fame, reporting his scoop in his diaries:

> The Band of the Coldstream Guards appeared to me to answer the requirements for gramophone records completely, so I hunted out the leader, Lieutenant Rogan, in his Streatham home, and started him on his

---

[38] Batten, *Joe Batten's Book*, p. 37.
[39] *Historic Grenadiers*. 2008. Compact disc. Beulah 1PD19. Track 2 'Sparks' [c1920s].
[40] Batten, *Joe Batten's Book*, p. 36.
[41] A. Kolkowski, D. Miller and A. Blier-Carruthers, 'The Art and Science of Acoustic Recording: Re-enacting Arthur Nikisch and the Berlin Philharmonic Orchestra's landmark 1913 recording of Beethoven's Fifth Symphony', *Communications (Science Museum Group Journal)*, Spring 2015 (10.15180; 150302 Research), pp. 24 &. 41, n. 72. [e-Journal].

career of recording which spread the fame of the Coldstreams to the ends of the world...At one time our catalogue contained over one hundred titles of records by the Coldstream Guards' Band, so great was their vogue.[42]

Gaisberg had had early experience of military bands (as a youngster in the 1880s he had turned pages for Sousa on windy days),[43] and he admitted to 'still being carried away by military band music', even in later years.[44] Unsurprisingly, it was with the United States Marine Band that Gaisberg made his first band recordings and it was no coincidence that, once he knew what military bands could do in the recording studio, he sought out the most renowned conductor and band in Britain with Mackenzie-Rogan and the Band of the Coldstream Guards.[45]

The naming of military bands

Gaisberg and Batten would not only choose the bands, but as recording managers, they frequently orchestrated for, and conducted, military bands on recordings,[46] many of which were made by generic military-style bands engaged on an *ad hoc* basis by the record companies. While Batten catalogues several War Office military bands in his list of 'Recording Artistes' First Engagements' (the Bands of the Grenadier Guards, Coldstream Guards and Irish Guards, in 1904, the 1st Life Guards in 1909-10, and the Royal Horse Guards (Blues), in 1911-12), also notable are non-War Office sponsored bands, such as the Empire Military Band.[47] This practice exposes one of the more complicated aspects of the military band recordings, where a number of assorted names may have been used for the same band, or at least the same pool of musicians.

This system of employing non-War Office named bands was to become more prevalent by the mid-1920s, with most military-style recording bands being of this type. A typical record company catalogue of the time, the 1924 Zonophone catalogue,[48] contains about 10% military and brass band recordings, with the main contributing band employed as the Zonophone house band, the *Black Diamonds*

---

[42] Gaisberg, *Music on Record*, pp. 78 & 79.
[43] *Ibid*, p. 136.
[44] *Ibid*, p. 79.
[45] *Ibid*, p. 136.
[46] Batten, *Joe Batten's Book*, p. xiv.
[47] *Ibid*, Appendix C, pp. 183-188.
[48] *Complete Catalogue of Zonophone Records Including Supplement No. 7, September 1924.*

Band, which recorded as either a brass or military band. Other military-style bands listed include the *Home Guards Band, Imperial Band, Imperial Festival Band, Imperial Guards Band, London Municipal Band, London Regimental Band,* and the *Zonophone Military Band*. The only specifically brass bands itemised are the *Besses o' th' Barn Band, Horwich R.M.I. Band,* and *St. Hilda Colliery Band*, and of the approximately 400 brass and military band recordings listed, the only army bands featured are four recordings by *The Band of H.M. 1st Life Guards* and thirteen by the *Band of H.M. Royal Irish Fusiliers*. In any case, as the 1st Life Guards had ceased to exist by 1924 these would have been back-catalogue pre-war recordings. Although this is from just the Zonophone catalogue, the trend can be seen across the record labels.[49]

There is very little documentary evidence as to why so many non-War Office military style bands were employed but it was most likely that it was cheaper to re-issue army band recordings under fictitious names, both for licensing and practical reasons. Despite the post-First World War decline in military band recordings, Zonophone and several other labels seemed keen to exploit not only the popularity, albeit reduced, of the military band sound, but also to give a sense of authenticity to the specially assembled bands, with additional names such as the *Royal Guards Band, British Imperial Guards,* and *King's Military Band*. Similarly, the 1924 Regal Catalogue contains eight pages (of thirty-two) of military band recordings by the *Scots Guards* and *Welsh Guards* Bands, but also *The Silver Stars Band, Palace Guards Band, Royal Military Band,* and *King's Military Band*.[50]

The names were all very similar and it appears that there was a desire by the record labels, and the bands, to be afforded recognition with royal and military establishments with the hope of increasing sales. It is unclear if the sought-after link was in order to establish a sense of authenticity, with a suggested association to the royal and military brand, or to be associated with the sound of established military bands, but it did imply that War Office military bands had some credibility.

Many of these military-styled bands did not exist as separate entities but were pseudonyms for re-issues of army band recordings,

---

[49] See, for example, the 'Label Discographies' published by The City of London Phonographic & Gramophone Society, <http://www.clpgs.org.uk/label-discographies.html> [accessed 19th November 2017]; also other work by F. Andrews listed in his obituary, <http://blogs.bl.uk/sound-and-vision/2015/07/frank-andrews-1920-2015-.html> [accessed 19th November 2017].
[50] *General Catalogue of Records (Regal Records)*, September 1924.

usually re-named for copyright reasons. This can be established by looking at the serial number on the disc which provides the code for the date of the recording session. For example, Royal Artillery Band recordings were also issued under the names of *Albion Military Band*, *Scala Military Band*, *Caledonian Military Band*, and *Beltona Military Band*.[51] This practice continued from pre-First World War years when different record labels changed the name for convenience: all the May 1910 *Band of H. M. Scots Guards* recordings for Rena were issued on Regal as *Palace Guards Band*, and 1917 recordings as *Neptune Military Band*.[52]

It is very probable that serving and ex-army bandsmen comprised the majority of personnel of these additional bands recording, with the likelihood of this being an accurate assessment supported by a curious set of correspondence from 1911. The case involved the bandmaster of a quasi-military band, 'The London Philharmonic Military Band', who asked the Home Office for permission to add 'Royal' to the band's title. The request was denied but in a further letter to the Under Secretary of State, the ex-army bandmaster, Mr Robinson ('B.M. Late H.M. Coldstream Guards'), pleads that his players 'are all pensioned members of His Majesty's Guards Bands…[who need]…to compete for a living.'[53] Two further cases were also referred to by the Home Office in 1911, that of the 'King's (or 'Royal') ex-British Guards' and the 'Imperial Guards Band, Ltd', and so it would be reasonable to infer that typical membership of civilian military-style bands would have been ex-service musicians.

Mr Robinson's clamour to attain the royal title, undoubtedly for marketing purposes, by claiming the dominance of ex-Guards musicians suggests he thought that Guards bands were of superior quality and that the sound of his band would also have that quality. It is not documented what were the consequences of his failure to attain the royal title but it does reveal the practice of civilian military-style bands employing large numbers of ex-service personnel. Regardless of the branding issues, these civilian military-style bands spent time recording, in addition to official War Office bands, continuing well into the post-war period, revealing a hitherto

---

[51] Dean-Myatt, 'Scottish vernacular', Discography section 18: R, pp. 26-27, <http://www.nls.uk/catalogues/scottish-discography> [accessed 10th January 2017].
[52] Dean-Myatt, 'Scottish vernacular', Discography section 19: Sa-Shand, pp. 7-8, <http://www.nls.uk/catalogues/scottish-discography> [accessed 10th January 2017].
[53] TNA HO 144/1173/215639, 'Title, Royal. London Philharmonic Military Band', 'Letter from P. S. Robinson to Under Secretary of State, Home Office', dated Dec 2nd 1911.

unidentified group of musicians, trained by the army, producing a sound that was available to be heard on a global scale. Did this mean that there was a military style of playing?

While it is clear that the technological, social, and economic factors were responsible for the reduction in military band recordings, there is no indication that inferior playing quality was responsible. This should not be surprising because the impression gained is that, at least until the 1960s, it seems irrefutable that ex-military band musicians comprised a sizeable proportion of the rank-and-file brass and woodwind positions in British orchestras. Colin Casson, an ex-Irish Guards bandsman, recalled that Brian Altham, second trombone of the BBC Welsh Symphony orchestra had also been in the Irish Guards, Bill Maney, bass clarinet player with the BBC Northern Symphony Orchestra, had been in the band of the Cheshire Regiment, and Ernest Hall, principal trumpet of the London Symphony and BBC Symphony Orchestras, 'seemed to spend more time regaling me with his tales of life in the Army'.[54]

At least four members of the Band of the Coldstream Guards who survived the 18th June 1944 V1 attack on the Guards' Chapel were to have careers as civilian musicians: Jack Ellory (flute) played with the Philharmonia Orchestra from 1945 as well as being a session musician. Ernest Dalwood (solo clarinet) performed with the BBC Symphony Orchestra in 1948 and was principal clarinettist with the Edmonton Symphony Orchestra in Canada for twenty-three years. Lionel Goring (bassoon) joined the BBC Scottish Orchestra and later the BBC Symphony Orchestra. Don Stutely (string bass) was a well-known session player.[55] While this list is only from a small sample it is likely to be a representative section from all the Guards' bands.

Furthermore, prominent orchestral musicians such as Jack Brymer, Denis Wick, and Danny Hannaby were schooled in military bands and took with them to orchestras the emphasis on accuracy and precision. Working in orchestras in the 1950s, they were aware of the legacy of military musicians, with the trombonist, Denis Wick, speaking of brass players in the Bournemouth Symphony Orchestra and later at the City of Birmingham Symphony Orchestra referring to one as 'an old soldier, of course, as they all were'.[56] He goes on to

---

[54] C. Casson, *Blowing My Own Trumpet: Memoirs of a Yorkshire Bandsman* (Stroud: The History Press, 2008), pp. 75, 72 & 63
[55] J. Gore, *Send More Shrouds: The V1 Attack on the Guards' Chapel, 1944* (Barnsley: Pen & Sword Military, 2017), pp. 117-121 & 150-153.
[56] D. Wick, Interviewed by T. Herbert 21st February 2008. British Brass Musicians interviews, British Library SoundServer, C1395.

say that he did not meet anyone who had been to music college and that the ex-military men were totally reliable as they turned up on time and were properly dressed. He does, however, caveat that they were not particularly imaginative and most were chain smokers. Danny Hannaby, another player active in the 1950s speaks of how military band players were good at sight reading and knew how to turn up on time.[57]

Accordingly, while Philip describes early twentieth-century performances as 'under-rehearsed laissez-faire,'[58] this could not be said of the best military bands who performed together as a single unit on a regular basis and had time to rehearse, producing, on the whole, a more homogenous sound. Orchestras, even though they used ex-military men – and it was only men at this stage – were blighted by the system of deputising, and did not have this luxury.

The demise of military band recordings

Despite the initial success, the third of Ehrlich's phases, from c1925, saw the gradual demise of military band recordings. This was a time of turbulence for the recording industry which by the late 1920s was suffering from the influence of external environmental factors, such as the challenge from broadcasting. Furthermore, by the height of the Great Depression in 1931 there was the biggest rationalisation of the recording industry in Britain, with mergers of the big companies and many smaller ones going out of business.[59]

Gaisberg reminds us that at the turn of the nineteenth and twentieth centuries the recorded repertoire comprised 'only popular and comic songs, valses, and marches in their simplest settings…with a playing time of 1½ to 2 minutes', and that military band records occupied one-third of early issues, but in the late 1930s 'seldom does more than one record of a military band appear'.[60] Technical innovation was a large factor, as electrical production, using microphones, had a better sound and, according to Gaisberg, 'with the introduction of the new electrical recording process the symphony orchestra and their conductors became of paramount importance'.[61]

Changing social preferences also made their mark with the dance band idiom becoming more popular. Greater access to highbrow

---

[57] D. Hannaby, Interviewed by T. Herbert 2nd March 2008. British Brass Musicians interviews, British Library SoundServer, C1395.
[58] Philip, *Performing Music*, p. 89.
[59] Martland, *Recording History*, pp. 328-329.
[60] Gaisberg, *Music on Record*, pp. 23 & 78.
[61] *Ibid*, p. 134.

orchestral music, although not quite as large a market share as Gaisberg suggests, was linked to a change in public taste in recordings after the First World War. Nevertheless, the scramble to record famous conductors and orchestras was not for commercial reasons, as Batten openly admits, but as a crusade to increase the popularity of 'good music' (he was referring to classical music).[62] Even though Batten and Gaisberg both had a developing penchant for orchestral music above military bands, it was popular music that remained the cash cow for the industry. Herbert Ridout, head of advertising for Columbia in Britain recounted that

> always and ever it was the popular music, the topical song, the revue hit, the newest musical comedy waltz, and the comic song that carried the business on its back and made classical adventure possible.[63]

Ironically, the first ever electrical recording made was of a military band performing hymns at a service at Westminster Abbey for the Unknown Soldier on 11th November 1920,[64] but once the technology was fully harnessed it opened up opportunities for other ensembles, and orchestras began to feature more in the catalogues of the two main labels, Columbia and HMV. This conforms with Martland's analysis of sales figures and popularity surveys which show that by 1930 sales of military band records, by consumer preference, made up only 0.3% of the market share, and that 'the strong pre-1914 sales of brass and military band music records had, by the 1920s, been largely replaced by dance band and other kinds of popular music'.[65] While consumer preferences for orchestral music (sometimes labelled 'serious music') were also not highly rated they became preferable to military band music. (It should be noted that these figures are for consumer preference surveys and not actually sales, but they do give a broad impression of the inclinations of the record-buying public.)

The military band repertoire of light music and marches had conveniently fitted onto one side of a wax record and while this did not change until after the Second World War, with the introduction

---

[62] Batten, *Joe Batten's Book*, p. 63.
[63] Quoted in D. N. C. Patmore, 'Commerce, Competition and Culture: The Classical Music Recording Industry, 1923-1932', *ARSC Journal*, vol. 46, no. 1, 2015, p. 48. [pp. 43-65]
[64] See P. Copeland, *Sound Recordings* (London: The British Library, 1991), pp. 15-16.
[65] Martland, *Recording History*, p. 309.

of long-playing records, the growing popularity of dance music in the 1920s and 30s supplanted the military band repertoire. Increasing sales by other categories of music through the 1920s and 30s drove military band recordings to the mid-price labels that were marketed for a more lowbrow audience, such as the HMV Plum Label.[66] There was, however, one notable spike in the market for military bands: recording companies continuing to issue live records of the Aldershot Tattoo throughout the 1930s as 'one of the exceptions where recordings of actual performances have been a continued success.'[67]

Competition from substitute devices, such as radio broadcasting, was also a challenge to the recording industry. Coupled with the effects of the Great Depression in the 1930s, which made a reduction in artists and contracts 'an imperative,'[68] all record sales were considerably reduced, with military bands a significantly smaller part of a shrinking market share: total record sales having been 150 million discs in the USA in 1929, but only 10 million in 1933; a situation also reflected in Europe.[69]

Examination of Farmer's research theme concerning the associated relationship between military music and other musical traditions has shown that with recordings, military bands enjoyed a heyday of popularity in the early twentieth century but dwindled as consumer taste moved towards the new entrants to the market with dance band music. Suppliers continued to re-issue recordings of military bands as a cheaper alternative to employing bands to make new recordings, and classical recordings, although not much more popular than those by military bands, were given a boost with the application of new technology. These factors from the far and near external environments reduced the position of military bands in the recording industry as a primary stakeholder. Even so, there is no evidence to suggest that military band playing was inferior to that of orchestras, or even that it was a different style, as many of the orchestral wind players had been military musicians themselves.

---

[66] *Ibid*, p. 293.
[67] Gaisberg, *Music on Record*, p. 172.
[68] *Ibid*, p. 80.
[69] Quoted in Patmore, 'Selling sounds', p. 126.

CHAPTER 6

'TONIC' MUSIC AND DISCORD WITH THE BBC: REPERTOIRE AND BROADCASTING

Throughout the interwar years, the focus of music industry stakeholder engagement by the authorities at Kneller Hall depended to a large extent on the personal ambitions and interests of the presiding Commandant at the Royal Military School of Music. There were certain relationships, however, that could not be ignored and engagement with the British Broadcasting Corporation (BBC) was to challenge all interwar Commandants. While there were initial constructive signs of mutual benefit in the early 1920s, and a brief collaboration between Kneller Hall and the BBC in the late 1930s regarding the issue of pitch, the relationship between the two institutions was tense throughout the interwar years.

Army bands had first been broadcast by the BBC in 1923 but until the eve of the Second World War, with increased militarisation, the amount of airtime given to them was inconsistent. The marginalisation of army bands can largely be attributed to political wrangling between the authorities at Kneller Hall and the BBC, based around cultural differences regarding programming and quality appraisal, as well as variations in broadcasting policy in the BBC regions. The disagreements also highlighted internal friction in the organisation of military music, with Kneller Hall asserting power over bands through a system of band quality gradings. Furthermore, army bands faced considerable competition from Royal Marines (RM) and Royal Air Force (RAF) Bands, as well as civilian bands, including the BBC Wireless Military Band.

The historian, Asa Briggs, has recounted the story of the BBC in detail and much of its early history is well known,[1] but discussions of music policy have tended to focus on the role of classical orchestral

---

[1] For the interwar years see A. Briggs, *The History of Broadcasting in the United Kingdom: Volume I: The Birth of Broadcasting* (Oxford: Oxford University Press, 1995); A. Briggs, *The History of Broadcasting in the United Kingdom: Volume II: The Golden Age of Wireless* (Oxford: Oxford University Press, 1995).

music, and dance and jazz band music,[2] overlooking the position of military bands. Identifying the role of military music in BBC entertainment policy, and uncovering the cultural differences between the BBC and the Royal Military School of Music (RMSM), is central to assessing the impact and reception of the repertoire and performance of military bands at a time of increased competition from the broadcasting of dance bands and orchestras.

The repertoire and broadcasting chapter correlates to Farmer's fourth research theme as well as the fifth supplementary theme (the associated relationship between military music and other musical traditions; the position of military music in the music industry). Based around models from the near external environment, it considers the threat of new entrants to the market (for example the BBC Wireless Military Band) and the industry structure relationships resulting from the bargaining power of the BBC as a customer. From the internal environment, power structures as cultural artefacts are prevalent in the tussle between Kneller Hall and the BBC.

Appendices 1 to 5 and the end of the book provide some supporting material to this chapter.

Repertoire

The British Broadcasting Company had been set up in 1922 as a consortium with a single broadcast licence and in 1927 it became the British Broadcasting Corporation as a non-commercial, Crown-chartered, organisation. Much of the BBC's early policy was shaped by its director, John Reith, the first General-Manager and Director-General, who had significant influence over the nature of broadcast music material through oversight of the Musical Advisory Committee (MAC). Formed in July 1925, the MAC comprised Sir Hugh Allen of the Royal College of Music (as chairman), Professor Tovey, Sir Walford Davies, J. B. (later Sir John) McEwen of the Royal Academy of Music, Sir Landon Ronald, Dr Whittaker, and Colonel J. A. C. Somerville, the recently retired Commandant of the Royal Military School of Music, Kneller Hall.[3] Somerville remained an active

---

[2] See for example J. Doctor, *The BBC and Ultra-Modern Music, 1922-1936* (Cambridge: Cambridge University Press, 2000); J. J. Nott, *Music for the People: Popular Music and Dance in Interwar Britain* (Oxford: Oxford University Press, 2002), chapter 3.

[3] Briggs, *Broadcasting: Volume I*, p. 223.

member until the Second World War,[4] but from his correspondence with the BBC it can be seen that his opinion became less influential, being criticised for 'poor suggestions' when, for example, he advocated military band broadcasts be used as a recruiting tool.[5] Nevertheless, his position on the MAC was an important one for the army as the authorities at Kneller Hall could have direct access to him as a person of influence, even though his views were not always in concordance with the administration at Kneller Hall.

Despite the prominent personalities on the MAC, Reith still had considerable influence on the type of music that was to become familiar to the growing radio audiences around the country. He had already shown his resolve with religious broadcasting where, despite marked criticism of some policies, his opinion as a strict Presbyterian shaped decisions made by the 'Sunday Committee' (later the Central Religious Advisory Committee), the first advisory committee to the BBC.[6] The BBC's general policy towards music tended to be less austere than its religious policy, but the religious requirements of 'Reith Sundays' required the broadcasting of only earnest music on the Sabbath, including a complete series of Bach Cantatas every Sunday during 1928.[7]

Reith's overarching influence was considered by some to place repertoire too much towards the highbrow, with critics, such as the public administration academic, W. A. Robson, complaining as late as 1937 that the BBC had 'only the vaguest and most remote contact with the world of listeners',[8] claiming that the broadcast material was very austere, with an emphasis on education rather than entertainment which did not account for a large proportion of the public. This view was substantiated with the rise and success of commercial radio stations, such as Radio Luxembourg, Poste Parisien, and Radio Normandie, which directed their appeal to the lower-middle and working classes, much to the annoyance of the

---

[4] See for example, 'Musicians on the B. B. C. Staff', *The B. B. C. Year-Book 1932* (London: BBC, 1932), p. 139.
[5] BBC WAC R27/209/2 Music General Military Bands File 1B 1935. Handwritten comment by Mr. Wellington on 'BBC Internal Circulating Memo: Military Bands', from D. E. to P. D. and M.D. dated 5th March 1935.
[6] See M. Bailey, ''He Who Has Ears to Hear, Let Him Hear': Christian Pedagogy and Religious Broadcasting During the Inter-War Period', *Westminster Papers in Communication and Culture*, Vol. 4(1), pp. 7-8.
[7] *Ibid*, p. 16.
[8] Quoted in A. Briggs, *Governing the BBC* (London: BBC, 1979), p. 172.

BBC.[9] Broadcasting almost exclusively from gramophone records, commercial radio stations from mainland Europe were providing significant competition to the BBC by the mid-1930s and while popular songs and dance music was the main output, 3-4% of their broadcasts were of military bands, above that of classical music, but a similar proportion to that of the BBC.[10]

Although there is evidence in 1937 of military band gramophone records being substituted for live performance,[11] most BBC performances for radio were broadcast live. In addition, the BBC's regular location broadcasts were a significant substitute in the music industry, competing against attendance at live concerts. Few in the recording industry recognised broadcasting's impact,[12] with recording manager, Joe Batten, disdainful of the BBC's choice of music, deriding what he saw as 'the pundits of the B.B.C. infected with the queer delusion that they know better the type of entertainment the public enjoys than do the listeners themselves.'[13] The conductor, composer, and critic, Constant Lambert, summed up the initial scepticism when he scorned that 'the more people use the wireless the less they listen to it',[14] hinting that it merely added to the clutter of background noise.

Despite the critics, and Reith's sanctimonious stance, broadcasting increased audience exposure to a greater variety of music.[15] There was a deliberate policy by the BBC to reject a distinction between highbrow and lowbrow programming and emphasis was placed upon the choice between programmes that required concentrated listening and those more suited to casual hearing. Briggs quotes the BBC

---

[9] For a discussion of the issues see J. J. Nott, *Music for the People: Popular Music and Dance in Interwar Britain* (Oxford: Oxford University Press, 2002), pp. 82-85.
[10] Quoted in Nott, *Music for the People*, pp. 74-75.
[11] BBC WAC R27/209/3 Music General Military Bands File 2A 1936-1937. 'BBC Internal Circulating Memo: Military Bands'. From Mr. Denis Wright to D.D.M. through Mr P.S.G. O'Donnell, dated 3rd November, 1937.
[12] D. Patmore, 'Selling sounds: Recordings and the record business', in N. Cook, E. Clarke, D. Leech-Wilkinson and J. Rink (eds.), *The Cambridge Companion to Recorded Music* (Cambridge: Cambridge University Press, 2009), p. 125.
[13] J. Batten, *Joe Batten's Book: The Story of Sound Recording, Being the Memoirs of Joe Batten, Recording Manager* (London: Rockliff, 1956), p. 17.
[14] C. Lambert, *Music Ho! A Study of Music in Decline* (London: Hogarth, 1985 [1934]) p. 200.
[15] Hargreaves and North call this 'acculturation'. See D. J. Hargreaves and A. North, 'Experimental aesthetics and everyday music listening', in Hargreaves, D. J. & North, A. (eds.), *The Social Psychology of Music* (Oxford: Oxford UP, 1997), p. 89.

Handbook from 1929 where, in a matter of fact way, the writer assumes that an individual who may prefer concentrated listening to chamber music might also like the chance to relax with 'a military band or musical comedy programme which would normally leave them uninterested.'[16] This point is noteworthy because it places military bands at the lower end of a musical hierarchy, where, for example, it was considered appropriate for the BBC to use military band music as 'tonic music' to be broadcast early on weekday mornings, presumably to help wake listeners up.[17] Other views came from letters to the BBC, with one writer in the 1930s placing military bands as a bridge between listening to jazz and full symphonies, suggesting a more middlebrow position.[18] The placing of military band music in a musical hierarchy was not unique to broadcasting but the issue highlighted divisions that were to develop between the BBC and the military band authorities at Kneller Hall, as well as within the BBC itself.

The Band of the Irish Guards was the first military band to broadcast at 7.30-9.30 p.m. on Tuesday 23rd January 1923 from Marconi House on The Strand, for 'The London Station "2LO" of the British Broadcasting Co. Ltd', conducted by Lieutenant C. H. Hassell, in a programme that included light classical transcriptions, selections, and marches, interpolated with vocal numbers (see Fig. 6.1).[19] There was some competition from other bands, but although it has been claimed that the RAF Central Band was the first military band to be broadcast, the date, 22nd April 1923, is two months later than that of the Band of the Irish Guards.[20] The Bands of the Grenadier Guards and Royal Air Force soon began to feature more often,[21] and by the early 1930s a handful of bands maintained a monopoly in London that the authorities at Kneller Hall were determined to see undone.

---

[16] Quoted in Briggs, *Broadcasting: Volume II*, p. 28
[17] *Ibid.*, p. 44.
[18] *Ibid.*, p. 66.
[19] A. Briggs, *The BBC: The First Fifty Years* (Oxford: Oxford University Press), pp. 46-47 & 364.
[20] I. Kendrick, *More Music in the Air: The Story Of Music In The Royal Air Force* (Ruislip: RAF Music Services, 2011), p. 19. In the *Foreword*, by Air Chief Marshal Sir Stephen Dalton, 1922 is given as the year, but there is no evidence provided and this must be assumed to be an error.
[21] Briggs, *The Birth of Broadcasting*, p. 254.

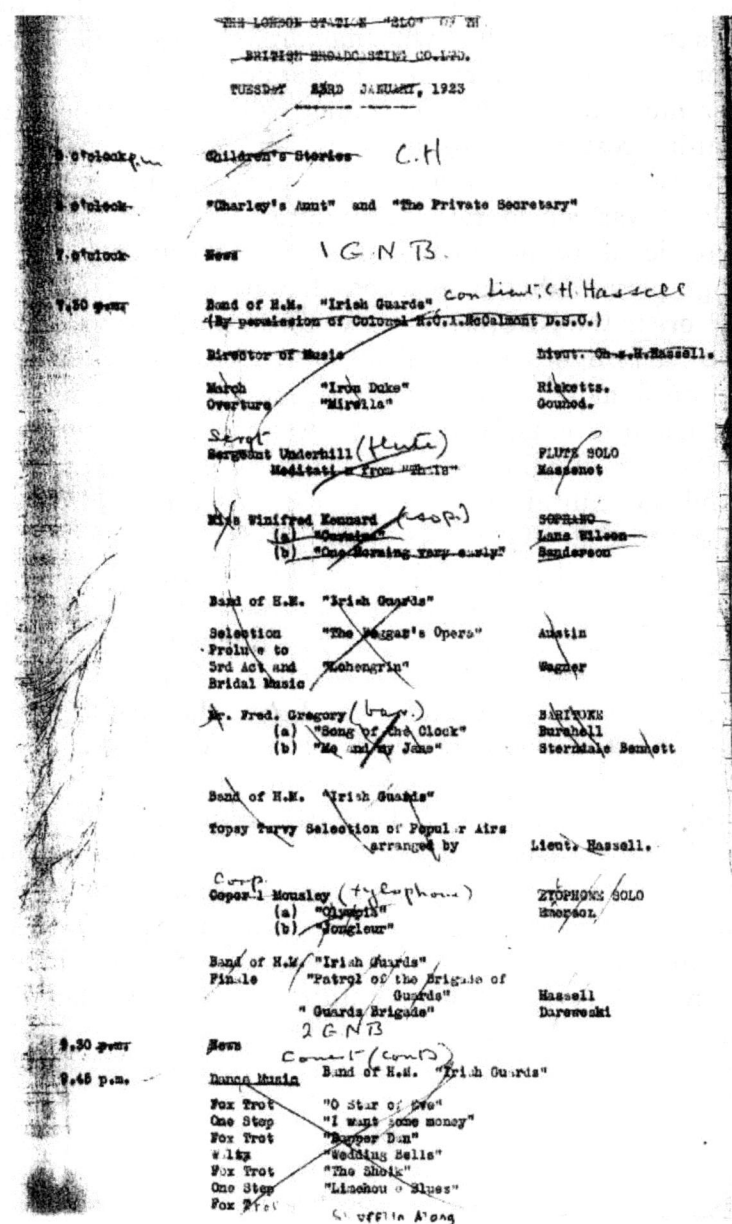

Figure 6.1
Programme of the first military band broadcast by the Band of the Irish Guards (BBC WAC)

The Irish Guards band programme (Fig. 6.1)[22] was essentially a broadcast version of what the public would have recognised at a live concert, but in the early days the process of broadcasting bands was very similar to that of recording for gramophones, with the same cramped conditions for the musicians.

The Grenadier Guards Director of Music, George Miller, recalled that for broadcasting, the band played 'into a receiving trumpet-shaped recording instrument with the solo players standing up and directing their solo excerpt as occasion demanded from the body of the band'.[23] Despite the Grenadier Guards band being one of the most popular broadcast groups, Miller was critical of the BBC's 'perfunctory' attention to balance of tone, particularly the lack of sound boards for French horns and, even after the onset of electrical microphones, when 'one rarely catches the string-bass tone'.[24]

One particular complainant, Colonel Sir Francis N. Elphinstone-Dalrymple, Commandant at Kneller Hall from 1925-1929, claimed that for radio broadcasts it was the wind band that particularly suffered in sound quality, in contrast to the experience of listening to gramophone records, where the strings were masked. He wrote in an article in the *The Leading Note* in 1929 that when broadcast:

> [T]he woodwind section of the Orchestra or Military Band is, to my mind, almost unrecognisable...[and]...in the case of the brass section...the Cornet sticks out like an elephant on the dining room sideboard...while the Bass and the Tympani are more often than not entirely absent.[25]

There is no evidence to suggest that broadcast engineers were particularly careless with military bands but these views reflect a frustration with the BBC that was to erupt in the 1930s.

---

[22] Programme provided by email from C. Dean, 30th April 2017, from correspondence between C. Dean and J. Walden, BBC archives researcher, dated 14th June 2007. Ref JW/505/D.
[23] G. J. Miller, *The Piping Times in Peace and War: Being the Autobiography of a Royal Musician in Five Reigns*. Museum of Army Music. MS, n.d., p. 189.
[24] *Ibid*, pp. 189-190.
[25] F. N. Elphinstone-Dalrymple, 'Wireless Music', *The Leading Note*, V1, 3, August 1929, p. 18.

More positive were the experiences with relays of outside broadcasts where the expectations of sound quality would have been lower and emphasis placed upon the novelty of sharing the experience of the occasion. Outside broadcasts from Kneller Hall summer concerts were initially popular, finding favour in *The Musical Times*,[26] as well as the broadcasting of several national events. A special broadcast made on Armistice Day in 1923 encompassed performances by the massed bands of the Coldstream Guards and City of London Regiment,[27] and BBC broadcasts of the ceremony held at the Cenotaph in London on Armistice Day and the 'Festival of Remembrance' at the Albert Hall put military bands on the radio as a matter of course, helping to set the standard for commemorations around Britain.[28] The Cenotaph service itself was first broadcast in 1928, complete with two minutes' silence, which allowed the country to hear military bands performing direct from London.

It is difficult to tell if this greater exposure had an overall positive or negative effect upon military music. On the one hand, military music could be broadcast to a wider audience, but on the other there was not so much need for military bands to play orchestral transcriptions to audiences who would have increasing access to the orchestral originals on the radio.

Colonel Elphinstone-Dalrymple's article would have had no real influence beyond the military band fraternity, and it is surprising that the image chosen to accompany the article emphasised the distortion to string instruments (see Fig. 6.2),[29] but the views would have been important at Kneller Hall where there was irritation with the BBC's influence on repertoire, with the suspicion that MAC member and former Commandant, Colonel Somerville, had undue influence.

---

[26] 'Wireless Notes', *The Musical Times*, Vol. 65, No. 979 (1 Sep), 1924, p. 829.
[27] A. Gregory, *The Silence of Memory: Armistice Day 1919-1946* (Oxford: Berg, 1994), p. 133.
[28] A. W. Turner, *The Last Post: Music, Remembrance and the Great War* (London: Aurum, 2014), pp. 143-146.
[29] *The Leading Note*, August, 1929, p. 19.

Figure 6.2
Image from Colonel Elphinstone-Dalrymple's article complaining of the distortion of music when broadcast

The Director of Music at the RMSM, Captain Hector Adkins, had been no fan of Colonel Somerville when he had been Commandant, but continued to perform transcriptions of more highbrow music for the BBC until at least 1925, including works by Wagner, Leoncavallo, Verdi, and Tchaikovsky (Fig. 6.3). His popularity with the BBC authorities was such that he was invited to write three articles for the *Radio Times* on successive weeks.[30] In one of the articles he complains about the broadcasting experience:

> I have always found that the heavily-draped walls of the broadcasting studio have a very depressing effect, not only on the players, but on the conductor also. Pieces which sound *forte* outside, seem to be dead with those hangings all round. I venture to say that most of the military bandsmen who have broadcast would sooner do an hour and a half's work outside, than half an hour before that terrible microphone.[31]

---

[30] H. E. Adkins, 'The Making of Military Bands', *Radio Times*, Vol. 8, No. 102, Friday, September 4th, 1925, pp. 453-454.; H. E. Adkins, 'Soldiers at the Microphone', *Radio Times*, Vol. 8, No. 103, Friday, September 11th, 1925, p. 503; H. E. Adkins, 'From Band-Boy to Band-Master.', *Radio Times*, Vol. 8, No. 104, Friday, September 18th, 1925, p. 555
[31] Adkins, 'Soldiers at the Microphone', p. 503.

200   British Army Music in the Interwar Years – Performance

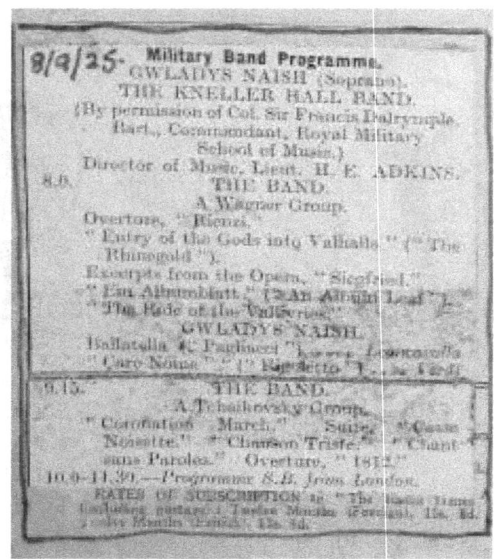

Figure 6.3
Adkins art music programme with the Kneller Hall Band for BBC broadcast in 1925 (*The Radio Times*, MAM)

It is not known if this had a direct effect on Adkins' subsequent move towards the lowbrow, but he was partially influenced by Colonel Elphinstone-Dalrymple's opinion that anything too intricate was lost when broadcast. It was also because he was more concerned with showmanship rather than musical substance (see Fig. 6.4). Although this photograph is from the late 1930s it is typical of Adkins' move to focus on the popular image of the band and quite different to Somerville's highbrow expectations.

Even though military band music had been flippantly, and unofficially, given the status of 'tonic music', the MAC, including Somerville, was consistent in its desire for military band repertoire to be placed towards the higher end of middlebrow. When the BBC first broadcast its new Wireless Military Band on Sunday 2nd January 1927,[32] conducted by former Royal Marines director of music, B. Walton O'Donnell,[33] the BBC made a clear statement that there was an expectation for repertoire to be aimed at the high-end middlebrow,

---

[32] Briggs, *The Golden Age of Wireless*, p. 9.
[33] For biographical notes on Walton O'Donnell see P. L. Scowcroft, *British Light Music: A personal gallery of 20th-century composers* (Binsted, Dance Books, 2013 [1997]), pp. 74-76.

and Somerville was at the forefront of compliments.[34] Acclaim by Somerville was based upon his assertion that the band had transcended the 'military' role of army bands and was now free to explore more grandiose repertoire in a civilian environment[35] – Somerville was probably unaware of the irony that most of these 'civilian' musicians were ex-military bandsmen.[36]

Figure 6.4
Adkins and the Kneller Hall No. 1 Band in 1938 with an emphasis on showmanship (MAM)

The BBC took its own military band very seriously and the new Broadcasting House in London, ready in 1932, had a specially built 'Military Band Studio' on the eighth floor, designed by Chermayeff, the decorator of the elaborate Cambridge Theatre. According to the 1932 BBC Year Book, it was the only studio in the entire building to

---

[34] J. C. Somerville, 'Military Band Music', in *The BBC Year Book 1931* (London: BBC, 1931), pp. 181-183.
[35] Somerville, 'Military Band Music', p. 183.
[36] BBC WAC R29/148 ORCH GEN BBC Wireless Military Band. Miss Rainbow's Correspondence 1932-1947.

be served by natural as well as artificial light, showing the BBC's commitment to its military band:

> The studio is a large one and, as in all the orchestral studios, great care has been taken to arrange the lighting in such a way that no shadow will be cast anywhere on the music-stands which normally occupy the floor space.[37]

Already having made its mark, the BBC's band flourished in its new surroundings, with Joe Batten considering that it 'produced the finest performances of this class of music that have been heard in this country'.[38] This was despite being plagued by the system of deputies as the BBC military band often had five players sending in deputies most weeks, usually for outside engagements, but also for sickness.[39]

While there is no specific evidence that the BBC Wireless Military Band was formed as a direct result of the divergence in doctrine between the BBC and Kneller Hall, the BBC had greater control over repertoire with its own ensemble and was able to keep it performing what it considered appropriate music at the higher end of middlebrow. This was in contrast to Adkins and the Kneller Hall band when, in 1932, Adkins' pursuit of lowbrow repertoire sparked an incident resulting from the broadcast of a piece called *A visit to the dentist*. Charles Nalden, a student bandmaster at the RMSM at the time, witnessed the episode as a member of Adkins' band:

> It was the nature of this, the BBC programme, which led to a first-class row between Adkins and the BBC. It resulted in a rupture which was to remain unhealed during Adkin's remaining 10 years as director of music.
>
> The BBC objected to the style of our programme. The corporation complained, very rightly I felt, that this was not the sort of offering they would have expected from the 'crack' Kneller Hall No.1 Band, which after all comprised some of the most talented musicians of the British Army[...
>
> The] piece, which probably sparked off the row, was a sketch entitled *A Visit to the Dentist*. Here is the sketch's opening:
>
> Narrator: Ladies and gentlemen – It was a typical English summer's morning.

---

[37] *The B. B. C. Year-Book 1932* (London: BBC, 1932), p. 74.
[38] Batten, *Joe Batten's Book*, p. 82.
[39] BBC WAC R29/146/1 ORCH GEN BBC Wireless Military Band. Contracts File 1. 1936-1938. 'BBC Internal Circulating Memo: B.B.C. Military Band. Deputies.' From P. C. Ex. to Mr. P.S.G. O'Donnell Orchestral Manager, dated 23th November 1937.

Band: Opening of *Morning* form Grieg's *Peer Gynt Suite*.
N: The rain was beating against the windows!
B: The 'Storm' episode from *William Tell Overture*.
N: I awoke – my tooth was throbbing.
B: Slow semitone trill on xylophone.
N: So, I jumped out of bed!
B: Loud thump on bass drum.
N: But it was cold.
B: Brrr...
N: So I jumped back in again.
B: Louder thump on bass drum.
N: But the tooth throbbed more violently than ever, etc.

Here was a military band, with the potential greater probably than any other band in all the three services, being reduced to putting across this sort of drivel.[40]

The occurrence was to strain relations between Kneller Hall and the BBC, which later reported in a memo in 1936 that the Kneller Hall Band had not been broadcast since 1932 because, according to a BBC official, the performance:

> had not been satisfactory. Even I would have some misgivings about the band of the Royal Military School of Music playing a piece called "A Visit to the Dentist".[41]

After a meeting between Adrian Boult, the BBC Director of Music, and Colonel Parminter, the Commandant at Kneller Hall, the Kneller Hall Band claimed to put itself in a self-imposed broadcasting exile,[42] but this seems an unlikely outcome considering the BBC's view on programming. Even so, with the Kneller Hall band off the airwaves it was up to the other Service bands to continue to be broadcast alongside the BBC Wireless Military Band.

The feeling within the BBC among its executives was beginning to change in 1933, however, and the MAC's insistence on more highbrow music was not immune to challenges from within the BBC, with

---

[40] C. Nalden, *Half and Half: the memoirs of a charity brat 1908-1989* (Tauranga, New Zealand: Moana Press, 1989), p. 312.
[41] BBC WAC R27/209/3 Music General Military Bands File 2A 1936-1937. 'BBC Internal Circulating Memo: Military Bands'. From Mr. Johnstone to A.D.M. Dated 18.2.36.
[42] BBC WAC R27/209/3 Music General Military Bands File 2A 1936-1937. 'BBC Internal Circulating Memo: Military Bands'. From Adrian Boult (D.M.) to A.D.M. Dated 4th May 1936.

Walton O'Donnell facing a dilemma on repertoire due to instructions from the BBC music executive for the Wireless Military Band to begin 'lightening' its programmes.[43] Whether or not as a result of Adkins' programming, this directive came as a surprise to O'Donnell who vigorously defended his choice of repertoire, quite clearly fearing a descent to the lower end of the middlebrow, and dismissing that 'Musical comedy and similar selections should be left to the light and restaurant orchestras and bands', while 'Marches, Strauss and other valses, National and Sullivan selections, and pieces of this kind', to be the remit of 'Service and other military bands'.[44] O'Donnell's response did not go down well with the BBC's Director of Entertainments and Music Director who considered it a defence of the current position 'without altering it in the slightest', rather than showing a willingness to adapt, despite the instruction.[45] O'Donnell did eventually concede, reluctantly, but saw the move as a lowering of standards:

> Recently, on your instruction I have lowered the standard and aim of our work. I have done this against my judgment and with much misgiving, since I consider it is definitely a retrograde step in policy and the effect it will undoubtedly have on the quality of the band.[46]

The perceived descent towards the lowbrow was exactly what O'Donnell and Somerville had wished would not happen, but while the 'Visit to the Dentist' incident caused the BBC to reject the lowbrow out of hand, it may have instigated a rethink towards the softening of the other extreme that O'Donnell and Somerville were espousing.

Alongside the programming issues were difficulties of resentment about the balance of broadcasting time between the Services. Somerville, still on the MAC, prompted by one of his successors at

---

[43] BBC WAC R27/209/1 Music General Military Bands File 1A 1933-1934. 'BBC Internal Memo: Military Band Programmes.' Dated 15th November, 1933.

[44] BBC WAC R27/209/1 Music General Military Bands File 1A 1933-1934. 'BBC Internal Memo: Military Band Programmes.' From Mr. O'Donnell to Ent. Ex. [?]. Dated 22.11.33.

[45] BBC WAC R27/209/1 Music General Military Bands File 1A 1933-1934. 'BBC Internal Memo: Military Band Programmes.' From Music Director to Music Executive. Dated 9/12/33.

[46] BBC WAC R27/209/1 Music General Military Bands File 1A 1933-1934. 'BBC Internal Memo: Military Band Programmes.' From B Walton O'Donnell to Music Director. Dated 9.3.34.

Kneller Hall, Colonel Parminter,[47] complained that the RAF and Royal Marines were getting more broadcasts than the army, which was true, but his claim that it was because of an O'Donnell conspiracy – O'Donnell had connections with both the Royal Marines and RAF – was denied by the BBC.[48] Although there is a hint from the BBC that they considered the RAF and Royal Marine bands to be of a very high standard, it appears that the real reason was due to cost. The RAF and RM broadcasts were considered outside broadcasts (OBs) which attracted a considerably lower fee (from £10 to £12), rather than £40 for an 'A' band in the studio. The RAF and Royal Marines had managed this by putting on free public concerts in Uxbridge and Plymouth, in venues with good acoustics for broadcast, in or near barracks and without the need to travel, during the daytime 'pool' broadcasting period.[49] No army band could match this 'special arrangement', if indeed they knew about it,[50] and as these broadcasts were considered outside broadcasts by the BBC they were not included in the same statistics for the number of military band studio broadcasts.

Apart from the RAF and Royal Marines putting on weekly outside broadcast performances, the main season for outside broadcasts was the summer and these were generally a success as the rules for the vetting of bands were not applied so rigorously. One problem, though, was that the bands received the full outside broadcast fee and local councils were not prepared to accept this – they wanted their cut. For example, in 1936 Derby Arboretum Superintendent's Office claimed an additional fee and as a consequence the BBC raised the outside broadcasts fee from £10 to £12.[51] The following year Derby refused

---

[47] BBC WAC R27/209/3 Music General Military Bands File 2A 1936-1937. Private letter from Col Parminter to Col Somerville, dated 20-1-36.
[48] BBC WAC R27/209/3 Music General Military Bands File 2A 1936-1937. 'BBC Internal Circulating Memo: Military Bands'. From Mr. Johnstone to A.D.M., dated 18.2.36.
[49] BBC WAC R27/209/3 Music General Military Bands File 2A 1936-1937. 'BBC Internal Circulating Memo: Military Bands'. From D.M. (Adrian Boult) to Controller (P), dated 17th March, 1936.
[50] BBC WAC R27/209/3 Music General Military Bands File 2A 1936-1937. 'BBC Internal Circulating Memo: Military Bands'. From Mr. Johnstone to A.D.M., dated 18.2.36.
[51] BBC WAC R27/209/3 Music General Military Bands File 2A 1936-1937. 'BBC Internal Memo – Midland Region: Military Band O.B.S.' From Midland Regional Director to Outside Broadcasts Executive, dated 10th March, 1936; 'Military Band

broadcast of the Coldstream Guards at the Arboretum, and also Nottingham of the Grenadier Guards at the Castle, on the grounds of insufficient cost, which was frustrating for the BBC who wanted to broadcast these well-known and popular bands.[52]

The BBC was also concerned about the issue of contracts with bands and in particular a problem in Northern Ireland over the question of fees. The Belfast BBC station had refused to employ any of the local regimental bands in mid-1934 due to demands by the bands for 'exorbitant' fees,[53] with the Bandmaster of the 1st Battalion The Border Regiment, Mr Owen W. Geary, causing the BBC some considerable angst, being described as 'a prime pet of the head of the music at Kneller Hall.'[54] Geary was side-lined by the BBC, despite the BBC reluctantly acknowledging that he was popular with the public, which might suggest that Geary was one of Adkins' lowbrow protégés; but he was a serious musician who had broadcast for the BBC in 1928 a programme that included works by Friedemann, Tchaikovsky, Delibes, and Wagner.[55] According to Henry Farmer, who later knew Geary as the Director of Music of the Royal Artillery Band at Woolwich, Geary was responsible for making the Border Regiment band 'the most sought-after Line band in the Service' and was duly awarded the M.B.E. in 1934.[56]

There is little acknowledgement in BBC correspondence that Geary was so admired and so it is possible that other bandmasters worked against him because they were envious of his success.[57] The

---

O.B.S.' From Outside Broadcasts Executive to Midland Regional Director, dated 11th March, 1936.
[52] BBC WAC R27/209/3 Music General Military Bands File 2A 1936-1937. 'BBC Internal Memo – Midland Region: Outside Broadcasts of Military Bands:.' From M.R.D. to P.C. Ex., dated 11th June, 1937.
[53] BBC WAC R27/209/1 Music General Military Bands File 1A 1933-1934. 'B.B.C. from Music Director Belfast Offices to Programme Finance Head Office: Military and Brass Band Engagements'. Dated 22nd May, 1934.
[54] BBC WAC R27/209/1 Music General Military Bands File 1A 1933-1934. 'B.B.C. From Music Director Northern Ireland Regional Offices to Music Executive Head Office. Military Band. Private'. Dated 10th December, 1934.
[55] *Radio Times*, 'A Concert: Band of the 1st Battalion The Border Regiment, Conductor Mr. O. W. Geary, 2LS Leeds, 9.5, 20 May 1928', Vol. 19, No. 242, Southern Edition, 18 May 1928, p. 296.
[56] H. G. Farmer, *History of the Royal Artillery Band: 1762-1953* (London: Royal Artillery Institution, 1954), p. 369.
[57] See R. Stanley, 'A formative force: the BBC's role in the development of music and its audiences in Northern Ireland, 1924-39' (PhD thesis, Queen's University, Belfast, 2012), p. 303-304.

situation was only resolved through the arrival of new regimental bands in Northern Ireland on standard regimental rotation, but the general state of affairs throughout the United Kingdom was deemed 'so delicate' that there was a proposal to re-engage with the Kneller Hall band, but with caveats:

> [I]t seems to me that the present position would be eased by the simple expedient of offering Kneller Hall another engagement as soon as we can ascertain that their programme and playing will not demean either that world famous institution or ourselves.[58]

While the Kneller Hall band was to remain primarily involved in commercial performance ventures, and generally staying off the airwaves, the few professional civilian military bands available were having to turn down broadcasting offers due to Musicians' Union (MU) disagreements over pay with, for example, The Merseyside Professional Military Band advised by the MU General Secretary, Mr. Dambman to turn down offers of contract to broadcast.[59]

Kneller Hall and BBC grading systems

With the loss of the high-quality Kneller Hall band for broadcasting there was still a gap for service bands to be broadcast on national and regional programmes, but the BBC was worried about the quality of army line bands and by 1935 it was suggested that military band broadcasts be reduced to 45 minutes from one or 1¼ hours, with the unlikely excuse that it 'seems to be more attractive in a shortened form, thus leaving the public wanting a bit more'.[60] Part of the problem was that the assessment of the standards of army bands by Kneller Hall was not trusted by the BBC. Kneller Hall's gradings were given to bands after they had been inspected by the Commandant and Director of Music, but these inspections could be controversial as they were subject to Adkins' personal preferences,

---

[58] BBC WAC R27/209/3 Music General Military Bands File 2A 1936-1937. 'BBC Internal Circulating Memo: Military Bands'. From Mr. Johnstone to A.D.M. , dated 18.2.36.
[59] BBC WAC R27/209/4 Music General Military Bands File 2B 1938-1940. 'BBC Internal Memo – North Region: Merseyside Professional Military Band.' From Programme Ex. to Mr Langham, Copy to Mr. Denis Wright, Mr. Arthur Wynn, dated 23rd June, 1939.
[60] BBC WAC R27/209/2 Music General Military Bands File 1B 1935. 'Short Military Band Concerts' internal memo from Mr. Wright to Mr. O'Donnell, 1/2[1?]/35.

with the London-based Guards bands being particularly resentful of interference from Kneller Hall.

In the early 1930s there was a great deal of internal correspondence within the BBC to try and assess which bands were suitable for broadcasting, especially as some bands considered 'outstanding' by Kneller Hall were not deemed so by O'Donnell at the BBC. They were also concerned about a further suggestion by the Commandant, Colonel Jervis, asserting that 'half a dozen regimental bands are equal or superior to the B.B.C. Military band.'[61] Colonel Jervis had been in contact with Colonel Somerville and was keen to promote the opportunities for line bands. Somerville was persuaded and wrote to the music executive asking for more line bands to be aired, but Walton O'Donnell was advised by the music executive that that this should be done only after the staff bands had been 'vetted', apparently with the subsequent sanction of Somerville.[62]

In August, Colonel Jervis provided a confidential list of bands graded 'Outstanding', Very Good', and 'Other fine Bands', but the list did not include staff bands, revealing Colonel Jervis's infatuation with the notion of promoting line bands:

> [It is] somewhat invidious to compare them [staff bands] with the "Line" Bands...It must not be supposed that the Staff Bands are in every case superior to those shown on the list. In many cases quite the reverse.[63]

Unfortunately, Colonel Jervis's singlemindedness had a negative effect on the BBC who furtively expressed that it did not trust the list:

> I am afraid these recommendations are quite unreliable, but it would naturally be impolitic to say so. One wonders when, in all the history of the Army, it possessed 32 bands that could be considered by any person with knowledge "very good" or better![64]

---

[61] BBC WAC R27/209/1 Music General Military Bands File 1A 1933-1934. Letter from Colonel H.S. Jervis, Kneller Hall. Dated 5.9.34.
[62] BBC WAC R27/209/1 Music General Military Bands File 1A 1933-1934. Letter from Colonel John C. Somerville. Dated 25th June 1934.
[63] BBC WAC R27/209/1 Music General Military Bands File 1A 1933-1934. Letter from Colonel H.S. Jervis, Kneller Hall, to Mr Eckersley. Dated 5. Aug. 34.
[64] BBC WAC R27/209/1 Music General Military Bands File 1A 1933-1934. 'BBC Internal Circulating Memo: Army Bands'. From Music Executive to Ent. Ex. Dated 14.11.34.

Had Colonel Jervis included staff bands on his list then the BBC may have had more sympathy and treated the list with less suspicion. The previous year Colonel Somerville had supplied a similar list of 'outstanding' bands to the BBC but it did not filter out the staff bands and was welcomed by the BBC, in contrast to Colonel Jervis's offering. The consequence of the omission of staff bands was further mistrust by the BBC and so in 1935 the BBC Music Executive introduced a grading system for military bands of its own. The grading system ('A', 'B', or 'C') was based upon studio auditions undertaken by Walton O'Donnell, or a suitable local representative, who wrote reports on the bands. Grade A was the minimum for broadcast and a Grade C (not suitable) would automatically be given to a band that had not been auditioned.[65] It was independent of Kneller Hall's own system of ranking bands but the BBC did rely upon Kneller Hall's sift of 'outstanding' and 'very good' bands.

The first task was to audition all the 'outstanding' bands and this was completed by February 1935, but the BBC was concerned that, other than the Irish Guards, there were no other 'Staff Bands' on the list provided by the War Office.[66] In the next eighteen months there were a number of lists promulgated, but the Kneller Hall gradings were disregarded by the BBC and in a list of eight Kneller Hall rated 'outstanding' bands in 1935, none were given an 'A' by the BBC, with the only staff band, the Irish Guards, not yet given a classification (although it would be given an 'A' the following year).[67] Walton O'Donnell, writing to the BBC music executive was perplexed by the choice of outstanding bands: 'Does that mean that we should not broadcast any of the Staff Bands? I think that this is a thoroughly bad proposition, yet it seems to be the intention of Kneller Hall'.[68] O'Donnell suggested that there was some sort of rift between the

---

[65] BBC WAC R27/209/3 Music General Military Bands File 2A 1936-1937. 'BBC Internal Circulating Memo: Army Bands'. From Mr. A. Wynn Programme Contracts (Music) to P.C. Ex. Dated 8.7.36.

[66] BBC WAC R27/209/1 Music General Military Bands File 1A 1933-1934. Letter from L.M Gibbs to Colonel A.G.C. Dawnay, Broadcasting House. Dated 7th November, 1934.

[67] BBC WAC R27/209/2 Music General Military Bands File 1B 1935. 'BBC Internal Circulating Memo: Army Bands'. From Ent. Ex to Mr. Cruttwell, dated 7th May, 1935.; BBC WAC R27/209/2 Music General Military Bands File 1B 1935. From Mr. A. Wynn Programme Contracts (Music) to P.C. Ex. Dated 8.7.36.

[68] BBC WAC R27/209/2 Music General Military Bands File 1B 1935. 'BBC Internal Circulating Memo: Letter from Colonel Somerville – Military Bands', from Mr. O'Donnell to M.D. dated 28th February 1935.

Royal Military School of Music and the staff bands and, although not publicly discussed, Colonel Parminter (Jervis's successor) at Kneller Hall revealed in 1937 that he thought there were too many broadcasts by RAF bands, but also, astonishingly, also of Guards bands, revealing that the preoccupation with line band broadcasts had continued.[69]

A significant problem with the audition system was that O'Donnell could not get to hear all applicable bands before their report period lapsed, usually two years, after which they were taken off Kneller Hall's list and required a new inspection from the army. This caused confusion in the BBC regions who wanted to broadcast bands that were waiting to be graded and so technically could not be broadcast. There were further complications in Northern Ireland where there was access to only three army bands, and initially none of them were on the list, so assumed 'C' grade and not eligible for broadcast. O'Donnell did get to hear the bands in Belfast and found a range in the quality that he outlined in his reports. The reports reveal how O'Donnell approached his assessments, with particular emphasis on tuning, tone quality, and technique. The three bands he auditioned in 1935, the bands of the 2nd Battalion the North Staffordshire Regiment, 2nd Battalion The King's Royal Rifle Corps, and the 2nd Battalion The Leicestershire Regiment, received different recommendations, scoring respectively: 'this band comes into category B', 'I would place this band among leaders of category B', and 'I would place this band not very high in category C + cannot really recommend it for broadcasting on its musical merits'.[70]

O'Donnell's emphasis on musicianship was in sharp contrast to what the BBC's Denis Wright later viewed Kneller Hall's approach to inspections in that the Kneller Hall's gradings were

> to some extent, ruled by the "spit and polish" aspect of the band, its instruments and its library – not a very effective way of judging a band's fitness to broadcast'.[71]

---

[69] BBC WAC R27/209/3 Music General Military Bands File 2A 1936-1937. 'Record of Interview with C(P), Colonel Parminter and self [R. S. Thatcher, BBC Deputy Director of Music]', dated 15th June, 1937.
[70] BBC WAC R27/209/1 Music General Military Bands File 1B 1935. Attached documents to 'B.B.C. Mr. B. Walton O'Donnell Northern Ireland Regional Offices to Music Executive. Head Office. Private & Confidential.' Dated 13th June, 1935.
[71] BBC WAC R27/209/5 Music General Military Bands File 2C 1941-1942. 'BBC Internal Memo – Glasgow: Service Band Auditions, Routine.' From Mr. Denis

To complicate matters, a grading system was proposed for light orchestras, but for some reason civilian military bands were excluded.[72] There were relatively few professional military bands in the United Kingdom – the BBC and MU could not agree on the number, with the BBC listing two and the MU five (although this might not be a comprehensive list).[73] Nevertheless, civilian military bands were soon incorporated into the grading scheme and the BBC regions agreed gradings for their bands. For example, the BBC Northern Region suggested that the Merseyside Military Band (as the 'only wholly professional' band) should be classed as an 'A' band, whereas Staveley, Belle Vue, Adamson, and Salford City Police should be graded as 'B' bands.[74] The MU, however, was reluctant to differentiate between amateur and professional musicians and there were also problems over the definition of 'Light Orchestra', with the BBC recommending the broadcasting strength to be six to eight players, but conceding that it could also be up to thirty-one players.[75]

Significantly, brass bands were taken out of the equation because they did not include MU members and were not seen to present competition because they did not include professional players.[76] This was true as far as fees were concerned, but they did compete for airtime, particularly in the BBC Northern region. Over a protracted period and after a stalling of negotiations, the civilian military band aspect was removed, only to return to the table in 1938 when questions of competition between brass and military band fees arose, but the situation was still unresolved by the outbreak of the Second World War.

Wright to Mus. Ex. (Bristol), Copy to: Mr. P.S.G. O'Donnell, dated 21st January 1941.
[72] BBC WAC R8/119/2 Artists Policy Musicians Union Light Orchestras and Military Bands File 2 1937-1946. 'BBC Internal Circulating Memo: Studio Engagements of Light Orchestras and Military Bands', from Mr. Crutwell to Music Executive, dated 9th April 1935.
[73] BBC WAC R8/119/1 Artists Policy Musicians Union Light Orchestras and Military Bands File 1 1934-1936; BBC WAC R8/119/2 Artists Policy Musicians Union Light Orchestras and Military Bands File 2 1937-1946.
[74] BBC WAC R8/119/2 Artists Policy Musicians Union Light Orchestras and Military Bands File 2 1937-1946. 'B.B.C. Northern Regional Offices to Head Office: Light Orchestras and Military Bands Employed in B.B.C. Studios.', from North Regional Director to Head Office (Mr. Cruttwell, Programme Finance), dated July 26th, 1935.
[75] *The B. B. C. Handbook 1929* (London: 1929), pp. 157 & 160-161.
[76] The single exception being St Hilda's Band.

By the late 1930s the army band grading system was abandoned in the rush to militarise the airwaves and bands were approached directly by the BBC as potential for broadcasting. Former bandsman, Spike Mays, recounted that the bandmaster of The Royal Dragoons (1st Dragoons), Mr. Alfred Singer, was approached by Dennis Wright of the BBC to audition for broadcast. The test programme included the selection *Fire over England* and after the band passed the audition, and was broadcast, 'their programme was so well received that Singer had to engage a minor brigade of ink-spillers to answer the listeners' letters of appreciation'.[77] Mays is notably biased towards the popularity of his regimental band but there was a resurgence in military music broadcast on the eve of the Second World War, and in 1938, and again in 1939, there were internal requests for more popular works to be performed by bands, prompting a complaint of trivialising the music from Walton O'Donnell.[78]

The demand for lower-end middlebrow repertoire increased with the frantic militarisation process on the eve of the Second World War, and especially at the beginning of hostilities in September 1939. The BBC saw the opportunity to take full control of band programming away from the Kneller Hall authorities at a time of disruption for army music when the RMSM was moved from Kneller Hall to Aldershot in December 1939. In doing so, the BBC temporarily rejected its own grading system to accommodate political wishes when, for example, New Zealand and Australian Army Bands, were broadcasting by the BBC after arriving at Aldershot, despite no verified knowledge of their standards.[79] The final blow to the military band authorities came in 1941 when Denis Wright wrote to another BBC official rejecting the Kneller Hall band grading system altogether,[80] and the BBC eventually took over complete control of which bands were fit for broadcast, issuing its own 'Instructions' for military bands, demanding specific performance requirements, for the *Music While You Work* series in the Second World War.[81]

---

[77] S. Mays, *The Band Rats* (London: Peter Davies, 1975), pp. 106-107.
[78] BBC WAC R27/209/4 Music General Military Bands File 2B 1938-1940.
[79] *Ibid.*
[80] BBC WAC R27/209/5 Music General Military Bands File 2C 1941-1942. 'BBC Internal Memo – Glasgow: Service Band Auditions, Routine.' From Mr. Denis Wright to Mus. Ex. (Bristol), Copy to: Mr. P.S.G. O'Donnell, dated 21st January 1941.
[81] Quoted in B. Reynolds, *Music While You Work: An Era in Broadcasting* (Lewes, East Sussex: Book Guild, 2006), p. 8.

Analysis of the position of military music in the music industry, as a subject of the supplemental research theme, has revealed that the BBC had considerable power as a customer and was able to introduce its own new entrant to the market, in the form of the BBC Wireless Military Band, to challenge the army's position in supplying bands for broadcast. The associated relationship (Farmer's fourth theme) with army music changed during the interwar years as the personalities within both power structures tried to influence and dominate the type of music to be broadcast, and who was to perform it.

Within a few years, in the middle of the Second World War, Adkins was court martialled for fraud, the RMSM had moved from Kneller Hall, and the BBC Military Band disbanded. Thus ended the cultural impasse between Kneller Hall and the BBC, and missed opportunities by both organisations. Had there been a more constructive relationship the broadcasting landscape might have been quite different, with military bands being more prominent in middlebrow broadcast repertoire.

PART 3

INFLUENCE

CHAPTER 7

KNELLER HALL AND THE PITCH BATTLE WITH THE WAR OFFICE

The question of musical pitch had been an on-going matter in Britain during the nineteenth century after pitch had risen steadily until the 1840s, when sharp pitch at A=453 – known as 'Old Philharmonic pitch' – prevailed.[1] A similar situation was evident in Europe where bands and orchestras increased pitch height because of the supposed more brilliant tone for the winds, with bands in particular becoming notorious for their 'sharp and penetrating sound'.[2] In Austria, sharp-pitched instruments made for military bands by Stephan Koch in Vienna soon permeated Viennese theatres as military musicians were de-mobilised after the Napoleonic Wars, and this contributed to the overall rise in pitch.[3]

The issue of differing pitches in the many British military bands would no doubt have contributed to the 'Scutari incident' of 1854, when it is reported that massed bands performed *God Save the Queen* in different keys and arrangements. This tipping-point for British military music has been often quoted,[4] but the story has been complicated by some writers' confusion over the location of the Grand Review. For example, Colonel Somerville, the post-First World War Commandant at Kneller Hall, suggests that the incident took place at Varna in Bulgaria, but although the town hosted a British military supply camp, there is no evidence that this is where the parade took place.[5] Others have confused the Italian name for Shköder – Scutari – in Albania, where there was never a British Crimean War-era base,

---

[1] See T. Herbert and H. Barlow, *Music and the British Military in the Long Nineteenth Century* (Oxford: Oxford Uuniversity Press, 2013), pp. 210-14.
[2] Quoted in B. Haynes, *A History of Performing Pitch: The Story of "A"* (Lanham, Maryland: Scarecrow Press, 2002) p. 361.
[3] M. W. Jackson, *Harmonious Triads: Physicists. Musicians, and Instrument Makers in Nineteenth-Century Germany* (Cambridge, Massachusetts: MIT, 2006), p. 198.
[4] For an account of the 'Scutari incident' see Herbert and Barlow, *Music and the British Military*, pp. 140-1.
[5] A. Zealley, J. Hume and J. A. C. Somerville, *Famous Bands of the British Empire* (London: J. P. Hull, 1926), p. 12.

for that of Scutari in Turkey.[6] Despite these inaccuracies, a Grand Review provoked a desire for standardisation and the realisation of the Kneller Hall project, establishing a central military music training school. Subsequently, the British army officially adopted A=452.4 in 1878, and this became the industry standard until the turn of the century.[7]

The effect of the sound of bands performing at high pitch became a topic of discussion as to whether it would be advantageous to keep it high. Part of this required an understanding of psychoacoustics and so David Blaikley, acoustician at the instrument manufacturers, Boosey & Co, was invited to lecture on the subject at Kneller Hall on several occasions in 1887.[8] In 1910, Blaikley produced a pamphlet that was circulated to all army bands confirming the regulation standard pitch, known as 'Kneller Hall pitch', as '479.3 vibrations at 60° Fahrenheit for B flat, corresponding with 452.4 for A and 538 for C at the same temperature'.[9]

By the 1920s the national standardisation of pitch had become a subject of paramount importance, but full standardisation could not be achieved without the acquiescence of the military because of the large number of military musicians. The main catalyst for civilian musicians had been in 1896 when Henry Wood's Queen's Hall Orchestra performed with newly purchased low-pitched instruments.[10] This was to come in line with low French 'diapason normal' pitch that had been established on the continent – and followed by most of the rest of Europe – as an aid to singers to prevent them from having to strain their voices.

Professional civilian musicians in London fairly rapidly followed suit, which prompted the Philharmonic Society to convert to the

---

[6] J. Mitchell, 'J. A. C. Sommerville [sic] and the British Band in the Era of Holst and Vaughan Williams', in F. J. Cipolla and D. Hunsberger (eds.) *The Wind Ensemble and its Repertoire: Essays on the Fortieth Anniversary of the Eastman Wind Ensemble* (New York: University of Rochester press, 1994), p. 112 [pp. 111-120].

[7] Haynes, *Performing Pitch*, p. 356.

[8] These lectures were later published by Boosey & Co: D. J. Blaikley, *Acoustics in Relation to Wind Instruments. A Course of Three Lectures Delivered at The Royal Military School of Music, Kneller Hall, by D. J. Blaikley. With an Appendix on Musical Pitch* (London: Boosey & Co, 1890).

[9] Quoted in *The Musical Times*, 'Memorandum on the pitch of Army Bands. By D. J. Blaikley. Boosey & Co.', January 1, 1910, p. 23.

[10] For a description of the episode see M. Pearton, *The LSO at 70: A History of the Orchestra*. London: Victor Gollancz, 1974), p. 22.

flatter 'New Philharmonic Pitch' (A=439), with London piano makers adopting it only a few years later in 1899,[11] but there remained military bands, brass bands, and many civilian musicians in the provinces at the high, 'Old Philharmonic', pitch, by now known as 'Kneller Hall Pitch'.

The issue of pitch discussed in this chapter relates to the supplementary fifth theme (the position of military music in the music industry). It analyses the process of the adoption of 'New Philharmonic' pitch by British army bands in the 1920s and 30s and reveals how the army was a primary stakeholder in the music industry, particularly when influencing the bargaining power of musical instrument manufacturers in the supplier markets. The implications for joint performances by army and civilian musicians, and also British army band collaborations with foreign bands, are considered in the context of the music industry environment in Britain and overseas. Furthermore, the discussion exposes the power relationships between the War Office and the authorities at Kneller Hall.

Appendices 6 and 7 at the end of the book provides some supporting material to this chapter.

The impetus to change

The retention of high pitch by British army bands had been endorsed in *The Queen's Regulations and Orders for the Army* in 1868,[12] and was confirmed in *The King's Regulations and Orders for the Army* in 1912, 1923, and 1928, as follows:

> In order to ensure uniformity throughout the service, band instruments will be of the pitch known as the "Kneller Hall" pitch, which is 479.3 vibrations at 60° Fahrenheit for B flat, corresponding to 452.4 for A, and 538 for C at the same temperature. Arrangements have been made whereby first class instruments for regimental bands may be obtained through the Royal Military School of Music at 25 per cent. less than the published prices. Forms for this purpose can be obtained from the Commandant, Royal Military School of Music.[13]

---

[11] Haynes, *Performing Pitch*, p. 359.
[12] *The Queen's Regulations and Orders for the Army: Revised Army Regulations, Vol 2* (London: Her Majesty's Stationery Office, 1868), p. 90, para 385.
[13] *The King's Regulations and Orders for the Army 2* (London: His Majesty's Stationery Office): 1912, p. 235, para 1129; 1923, p. 352, para 1450; 1928, p. 375, para 1376.

Specific tuning forks were cast so that Kneller Hall pitch could be maintained throughout the army and bands were each required to possess one of these tuning forks (Fig 7.1).[14] This meant that with the military still at high pitch, army musicians wishing to perform with most professional civilian ensembles, or study at civilian establishments, needed to acquire low pitched instruments. Hector Sutherland, a trumpeter with the 2nd Life Guards band, who had won a scholarship to the Royal Academy of Music in 1917, recalled that while most of his colleagues needed to buy new instruments, 'the horn player luckily only had to get a low pitched slide to put him in tune'.[15]

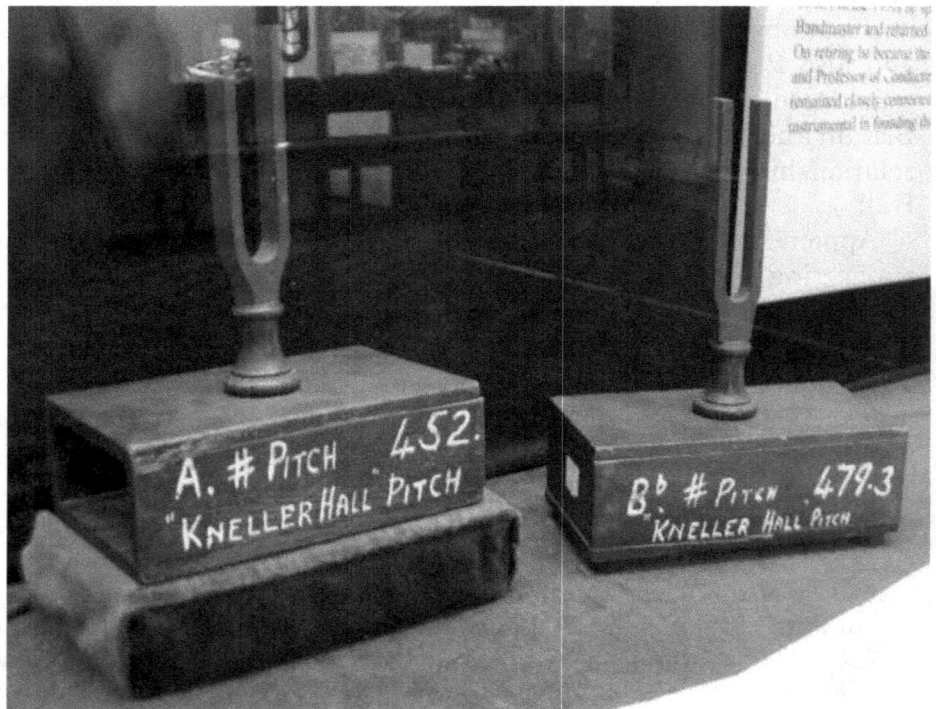

Figure 7.1
'Kneller Hall' pitch tuning forks, which by 1876 every regiment was required to possess (MAM)

---

[14] Circular memorandum to General Officers Commanding, General Number 103.-109., Horse Guards, 20 December 1876, reproduced in Herbert and Barlow (2013, 283).
[15] H. Sutherland, *They Blow Their Trumpets* (London: P. R. Macmillan, 1959), p. 36.

This need for musicians to acquire new instruments at low pitch was a change for the supplier market of instrument manufacturers as they were now obliged to produce instruments at both high and low pitch, causing major firms, such as Hawkes & Son and Boosey & Co, Ltd, to advertise in their instrument catalogues in the late 1920s for instruments at both 'low' and 'high' pitch[16] (Fig. 7.2). In the *Foreword* to Boosey's catalogue the company takes great pains to explain standards of pitch, highlighting the difference between 'Military Regulation,' 'New Philharmonic or Flat Pitch,' and 'American Pitch,' cautioning that 'Orchestral players when ordering instruments should therefore be careful to define the pitch required, either as "Military Regulation" or "New Philharmonic".'[17] Besson, another significant instrument manufacturer in London, had largely adopted Boosey's designs by the early 1930s.[18]

For the manufacturers there were both advantages and disadvantages to this dual pitch system. The main advantage was that while a significant proportion of the customer market continued to perform at high pitch (military bands, brass bands, and some regional orchestral musicians) the British instrument manufacturers would have an oligopoly over the supply to these musicians, as those manufacturers from the European continent and North America did not tend to produce instruments at high pitch. The main disadvantage was that economies of scale could not be achieved within the British customer market because of the need to produce different standards of instruments, although this was not a concern for Salvation Army instrument manufacturers who continued to produce exclusively high-pitched instruments – they had claimed to produce 1,000 instruments a year by 1904.[19]

---

[16] *Military Band Instruments* (London: Hawkes & Son, 1927) and *Military and Orchestral Band Instruments* (London: Boosey & Co, 1929).
[17] Military and Orchestral Band Instrument, p. 4.
[18] A. Myers. 'Brasswind Manufacturing at Boosey & Hawkes, 1930-59', *Historic Brass Society Journal*, 1, 3, 2003, p. 56.
[19] Cited by T. Herbert, 'God's Perfect Minstrels', in *The British Brass Band: A Musical and Social History* (Oxford: Oxford University Press, 2000), p. 200.

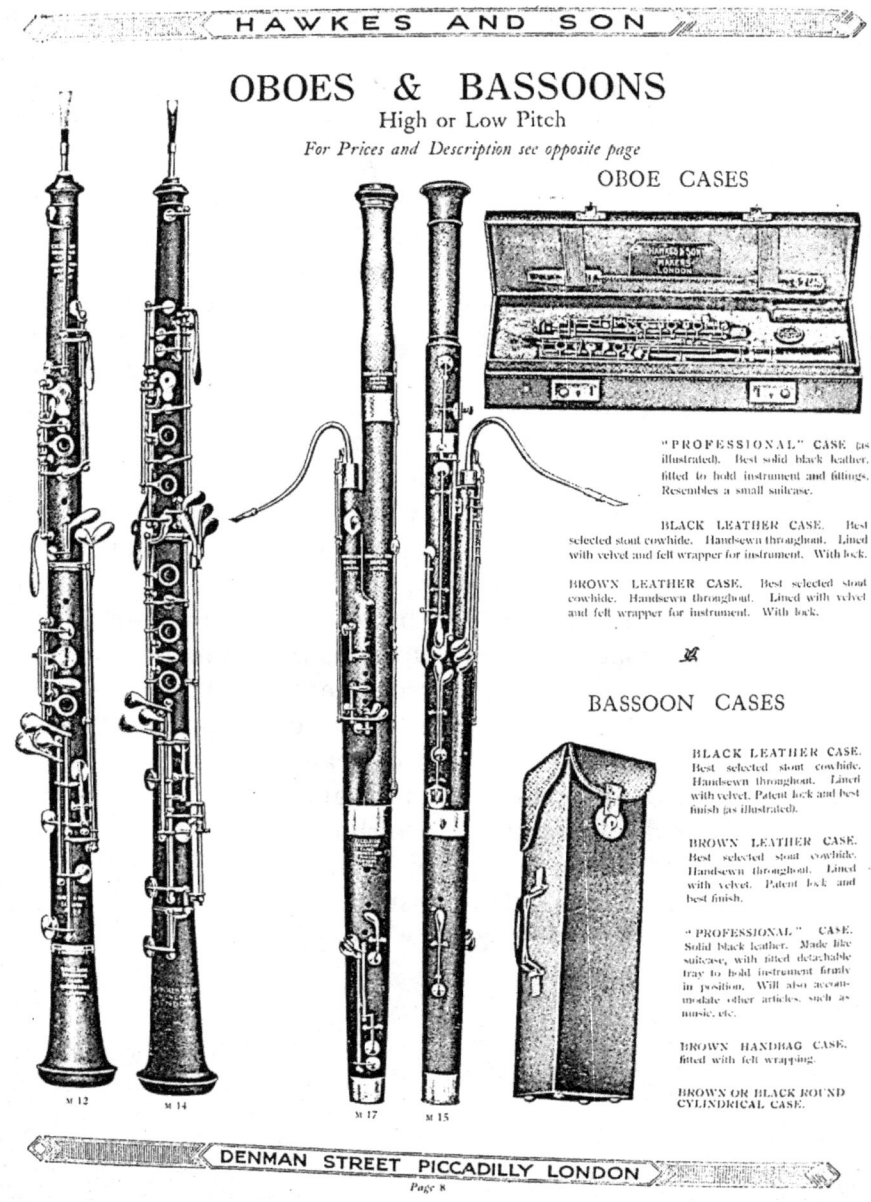

Figure 7.2
Hawkes and Son's advertisement for high and low pitch oboes and bassoons in their instrumental catalogue of 1927

Developing interest and pressure on the War Office

With the arrival of a new Commandant at the Royal Military School of Music, Kneller Hall, in 1920, there was a move to reinvestigate the issue of pitch in the army. Colonel John Arthur Coghill Somerville, a keen amateur musician, had every intention that military musicians should perform at the same pitch as civilians, but the cost of a complete re-issue of instruments was not palatable to the War Office.

The issue of pitch for Colonel Somerville was part of a broader concern he had that was based around his wish for military bands to have more formal links with the art music side of the industry. Military band repertoire relied primarily on transcriptions of classical standards and renditions of the popular music of the day, and this was what was taught at the Royal Military School of Music at Kneller Hall, but Colonel Somerville had ideas of grandeur, wanting military musicians to play original music, explaining:

> We in the army have been content to continue in the old rut, croaking to one another like frogs in a pond – damned impenetrable from the main stream of progress – and continuing to regard the overture to "William Tell", "Zampa" and other such rococo claptrap as the summit of ambition for the band to play or the soldier to appreciate.[20]

Part of his plan was to move military music towards the highbrow and ensure compatibility with orchestras by standardising pitch, progressing army bands to 'New Philharmonic' low pitch. Although he did not achieve this in his five-year tenure at the RMSM, Colonel Somerville was largely responsible for the change a few years later when he had left the army.

Colonel Somerville had attended the British Music Societies' first congress in May 1920 (after being nominated *ex officio* to take the chair),[21] which discussed 'The Possibilities of a World Standard Pitch'. *The Times* reported Colonel Somerville as remarking that the War Office had told him that 'he had chosen a strangely inopportune moment and that there was not a ghost of a chance of anything being

---

[20] J. A. C. Somerville, (n.d.) 'Military Music, Past and Present'. Draft submission for *The Army Quarterly* (n. d.), p. 2. MAM.
[21] TNA WO/32/3920. Letter from Col Somerville to the Secretary, War Office, dated 22nd April 1920.

done which involved expense',[22] despite the implications when musicians performed together, as *The Times* further related:

> Lord Shaftesbury narrated an experience which existed when he assisted to organize the Festival of Empire at the Crystal Palace some years ago. There was a choir of 4,000 and an orchestra and they wanted to bring in the organ and band of the Coldstream Guards. They all had a different pitch and he left the result to their imagination.[23]

The Conference agreed that Kneller Hall (representing army bands) was the '*anathema marantha*',[24] with delegates declaring:

> once Kneller Hall admitted it was wrong it was only a question of money and that could easily be settled...Kneller hall was the source of the trouble because from there issued most of the military band instrument players who went to all parts of the Colonies.[25]

There was clearly an interest by primary stakeholders in the industry to get military bands to come down in pitch, and even though Colonel Somerville did not achieve his ambition at the time, after he retired he kept the issue alive.

In March 1925 he saw an opportunity when he forwarded a letter from a Mr Midgley to his successor at Kneller Hall, Colonel Dalrymple, which offered to fund a complete conversion of military bands to low pitch.[26] The letter was from what seemed to be an unlikely source – Mr Midgley was the Chairman of the Committee of the Bradford Permanent Orchestra – but he had picked up on Colonel Somerville's earlier discussion in the press from 1920 and 1921 about the case for lowering the pitch of army bands and claimed that 'we have various kinds of enthusiasts in the Bradford district' who could be found to cover the costs of £50,000 (he cites an example of a recent donation of £40,000 to a local cause) 'if he could improve the outlook for army band players in the Kingdom and Empire'.[27] Colonel Dalrymple wrote to the Assistant Adjutant General (AAG) at the War

---

[22] 'A Standard Pitch', *The Times* (London, England), Wednesday, May 05, 1920; p. 14; Issue 42402.
[23] *Ibid*.
[24] Literally translated as 'accursed Lord is coming!'.
[25] 'A Standard Pitch', *The Times*.
[26] TNA WO/32/3915. Letter dated 10th March 1925.
[27] *Ibid*.

Office, Colonel Nation, clearly considering this to be a serious proposition.[28] Colonel Nation noted that a catalogue of requests to change the pitch of military bands had been refused since 1885 'mainly for reasons of expense' and was aware of the implications for Territorial, Indian, Dominion, and Colonial troops, but his main reasons were as follows:

> I do not think the W.O. [War Office] can be under an obligation to a private individual who volunteers to finance the cost of the changes. It might also be a further grievance to the M.U. [Musicians' Union]. Let sleeping dogs lie?[29]

This view hints of a staff officer who does not want to get involved in the wrangle because of the potential for too much work. He would have considered that military bands were earning extra money from private engagements which went into the battalion band fund, and used for purchasing instruments. Furthermore, while the reference to the Musicians' Union may have been accurate, Colonel Nation would almost certainly have not done any serious analysis of the impact of the funding on other stakeholders in the industry.

If Colonel Nation had thought he had heard the last of the matter, he was mistaken, as Colonel Dalrymple attended the Music Industries Convention at Llandudno in May of the same year, and explained to the delegates the issues of cost but also announced, probably unintentionally, that there was a private individual who was prepared to pay for the change and that the War Office was aware of this.[30]

In 1925 the Federation of British Music Industries became involved, with a letter to the Secretary of State for War requesting a meeting with a delegation headed up by Sir Edward Elgar (Fig 7.3).[31] The request was turned down, despite the stature of the delegates, on the grounds that the exercise would be too expensive and would have to include the bands of the Indian Army, Dominions, and Colonies.

The issue continued in the background, however, with questions from the War Office about why Kneller Hall needed to keep a set of low pitched instruments, the suspicion being that the low-pitched instruments were purely for the musicians to make money with extra work.

---

[28] TNA WO/32/3915. Letter dated 23rd March 1925.
[29] TNA WO/32/3915. Hand written note dated 25th March 1925.
[30] *The Stage*, 4th June 1925.
[31] TNA WO/32/3915. Letter dated 10th December 1925.

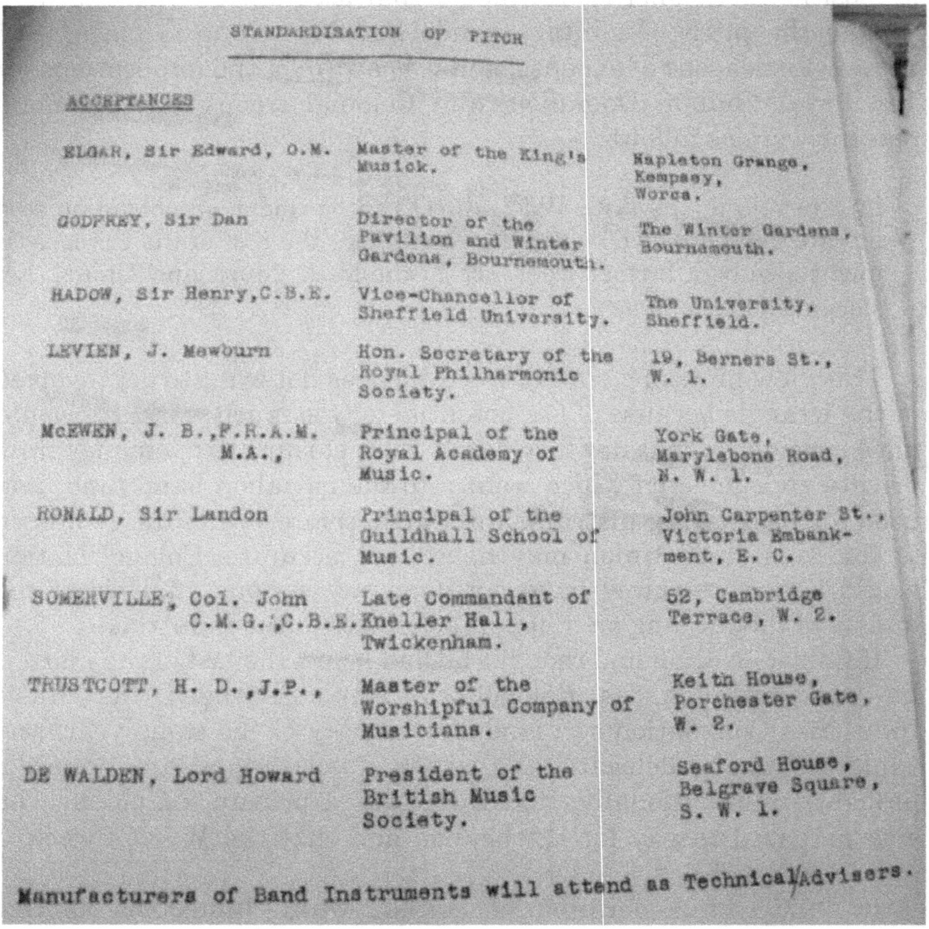

STANDARDISATION OF PITCH

ACCEPTANCES

ELGAR, Sir Edward, O.M.	Master of the King's Musick.	Napleton Grange, Kempsey, Worcs.
GODFREY, Sir Dan	Director of the Pavilion and Winter Gardens, Bournemouth.	The Winter Gardens, Bournemouth.
HADOW, Sir Henry, C.B.E.	Vice-Chancellor of Sheffield University.	The University, Sheffield.
LEVIEN, J. Mewburn	Hon. Secretary of the Royal Philharmonic Society.	19, Berners St., W. 1.
McEWEN, J. B., F.R.A.M. M.A.,	Principal of the Royal Academy of Music.	York Gate, Marylebone Road, N. W. 1.
RONALD, Sir Landon	Principal of the Guildhall School of Music.	John Carpenter St., Victoria Embankment, E. C.
SOMERVILLE, Col. John C.M.G., C.B.E.	Late Commandant of Kneller Hall, Twickenham.	52, Cambridge Terrace, W. 2.
TRUSTCOTT, H. D., J.P.,	Master of the Worshipful Company of Musicians.	Keith House, Porchester Gate, W. 2.
DE WALDEN, Lord Howard	President of the British Music Society.	Seaford House, Belgrave Square, S. W. 1.

Manufacturers of Band Instruments will attend as Technical Advisers.

Figure 7.3
The list of delegates who agreed to represent The Federation of British Music Industries (FBMI) in a proposed meeting with the Secretary of State for War in 1925. Sir Hugh Allen, Director of the Royal College of Music and Heather Professor of Oxford University, did not reply to the invitation to represent the FBMI. Gustav Holst was the only person to refuse (TNA)

The commandant responded that the low pitched instruments were for orchestral work as this was more suitable with stringed instruments,[32] but this was not the only use as they were lent out to bands when touring overseas to perform with low-pitched foreign bands, most likely those used by Mackenzie-Rogan and the Coldstream Guards for their visit to France in 1907 when performing with the Garde Républicaine band as 'we used the Continental pitch for this *entente*'.[33] The War Office had struck a nerve, though, as the Kneller Hall band and orchestra under Adkins were out performing most nights on commercial engagements.

Nevertheless, Somerville did not give up and in retirement he wrote a letter to *The Times* on 6th November 1926,[34] which sparked off a chain of events effecting the eventual change in pitch for the military: the king, George V, had noticed the letter in *The Times* and the next day wrote, via his Private Secretary, Lieutenant Colonel The Rt Hon The Lord Stamfordham, to the Adjutant-General to the Forces at the War Office asking for the issue to be taken up as it was 'a matter in which His Majesty has always been interested'.[35] The reply came two days later stating that there was a problem with cost, but undeterred, the King suggested in a letter on 1st December to the Secretary of State for War, The Right Honourable Sir Worthington-Evans, that 'His Majesty trusts that it may be possible to insert into next year's estimates a sum sufficient at all events to make a start in the alteration of the instruments'.[36]

This seems the language of Royal command and cannot have been far off the boundaries of acceptability from a constitutional monarch. It also appears unusual that the king had seemingly taken an interest in what many at the War Office considered a trivial issue, but there is no doubt that the letters are from the king's office. Even though the king did not have much interest in cultural matters, and was particularly conservative in his musical tastes, he did pay attention to the repertoire of the Household Brigade bands.[37]

---

[32] TNA WO/32/3915. Minute sheet (R5/794) note 8 from Col Dalrymple dated 8th January 1926.
[33] J. Mackenzie-Rogan, *Fifty Years of Army Music* (London: Methuen, 1926), p. 164.
[34] Somerville, J. C. (1926). 'Pitch of Military Bands', *The Times* (London, England), Nov 6. Letters to the Editor.
[35] TNA WO/32/3914. Letter to the Adjutant-General, dated 7th November 1926.
[36] TNA WO/32/3914. Letter to the Secretary of State for War, dated 1st December 1926.
[37] See chapter 4.

Whatever the reasons for the king's intervention, it did, understandably, cause quite a stir behind the scenes at the War Office where frantic staff work was undertaken, with several propositions for funding being put forward. Proposals included: reducing initial appointment pay for Bandmasters; replacing woodwind instruments, but converting the brass (by tube extension); funding only the 'playing out' bands of twenty-five instrumentalists; spreading the costs over twenty-seven years.[38] There were also follow-up letters to the army's adjutant general, where the commandant at Kneller Hall assessed that for the 163 established regular bands listed,[39] the cost of conversion to low pitch (the replacement of woodwind but adaption only of brass) was estimated to be £66,107.[40]

The plan was put to the War Office Estimates Committee where the bands of the Household Cavalry, Brigade of Guards, Royal Artillery, Royal Engineers, and Kneller Hall would all be furnished with new instruments at public expense at a cost of £6,500 – a tenth of the overall cost of £66,000. But this would have meant a commitment to see that all other bands convert over the next ten years and, after a warning from the War Office Director of Personal Services,[41] it proved too much for the Estimates Committee at a meeting in January 1927, who declared that 'Provision for this Service was struck out of the estimates. Saving £6,500'.[42] The shock for the War Office was probably that it had not had to pay for instruments before, except fifes and drums, as band instruments had been built up by the proceeds of bands' own engagement fees or were presentation instruments, and thus the property of individual regiments.

The king's request had had an impact and although the funds were not granted in the 1927-28 Estimates, the Secretary of State for War affirmed that he was optimistic that the project would succeed when

---

[38] TNA WO/32/3914. Letter from Col Dalrymple, Commandant Royal Military School of Music to the Under Secretary of State, War Office, dated 23rd November 1926.
[39] The list includes bands grouped under fourteen different headings which suggests that there were bands with fourteen different instrumentation requirements.
[40] TNA WO/32/3914. Letter from Col Dalrymple to the Adjutant General, Lt Gen Sir R. Whighan, dated 26th November 1926.
[41] TNA WO/32/3914. Letter from the DPS, dated 21st December 1926.
[42] TNA WO/32/3914. Estimates Committee Minute, dated 13th January 1927.

considered in the 1928-29 Estimates.[43] The king wrote once again to the Secretary of State for War on 27th January 1927 acknowledging 'the necessity for economy in every direction',[44] but the momentum was still there for a change, with clear and open backing from the very top of the establishment. Furthermore, the problem had not gone away for the War Office with mounting pressure in the Press: *The Times* had run a piece in December 1926 discussing the virtues of Colonel Somerville's letter of the previous month, including a summary of the issues.[45] In the article there was a focus on the supplier market of instrumental manufacturers with a discussion of the cost of new instruments and making the point that immediate action should be taken rather than wait until instruments became even more expensive over time. It had also noted the potential of new entrants to the instrument supply market with an inflow of instruments from continental manufacturers.

David Blaikley, Boosey & Co's acoustician, had observed that in the 1890s some manufacturers 'either from inattention, or through yielding to outside pressure, habitually send out instruments which are considerably above the pitch laid down to be observed in Queen's Regulations'.[46] While it is not known if the release of instruments had been deliberate or through defects in the manufacturing process, like Blaikley, some manufacturers would have been in favour of a standardisation of pitch, but were concerned about the commercial implications of lowering the pitch to that of the continent and would have seen the advantages of artificially maintaining a high-pitched instrument market. Overseas producers had gradually been reducing construction of high-pitched instruments and by the time Boosey and Hawkes became a single company in 1930 it had a large share of the manufacturing oligopoly in the market for high-pitched instruments. While the majority of British wind instruments were still being produced at high pitch, this oligopoly would remain,[47] but there was a serious threat from overseas imports with a move to low pitch.

By 1928 the matter was back in the public domain, with newspapers around the country still discussing the issue. The

---

[43] TNA WO/32/3914. Letter to the Private Secretary to the King, Lt Col The Rt Hon The Lord Stamfordham, dated 25th January 1927.
[44] TNA WO/32/3914. Letter to the Secretary of State for War, dated 27th January 1927.
[45] 'The Pitch of Army Bands. A Reform Overdue.' *The Times*, December 4, 1926.
[46] Blaikley, *Acoustics in Relation to Wind Instruments*, p. 37
[47] Myers, 'Brasswind Manufacturing at Boosey & Hawkes, 1930-59', pp. 57-58.

Bradford Telegraph & Argus, for example, wrote a piece called 'The Brass Band's Predicament: Handicapped by a Too High a Pitch [*sic*]' which, prompted by a concert by the Band of the Grenadier Guards, stated that the lack of a change to low pitch 'has precluded co-operation with the orchestras, and has restricted the repertoire'.[48] As important as this argument was for musicians it was not considered relevant to many in the stakeholder group that had the most legitimacy: those in the military who were responsible for the command and control of the bands, usually the commanding officers of regiments. This was made clear in many of the replies to a War Office sanctioned circular consultation document to 'Officers Commanding all Units at Home' sent out by the Commandant at Kneller Hall, Colonel Dalrymple, on 23rd October 1928.[49]

The consultation had begun with letters written by Colonel Dalrymple to various home units in July 1928 to canvass opinion. One of the main objections to the change was financial, with commanders concerned that many band funds did not have the assets to cover the expense, and some indignation that the War Office was not prepared to pay the bill.[50] Not all units were covered in the distribution and in a remarkable omission it would appear that Colonel Dalrymple did not ask for the opinion of London District, which included responsibility for the five Foot Guards' bands. The chain of command had been circumvented, though, with the Director of Music of the Grenadier Guards, George Miller, being consulted early on in the process. He was very much in favour of the change but recounts how it was difficult to convince the military hierarchy:

> You may imagine the impact of a subject like 'pitch' upon the minds of a fox-hunting Colonel commanding, and a 'blimpish' General sitting in the seats of the mighty at command headquarters?...One morning the Grenadier and Coldstream bands were ordered to parade on Chelsea Barracks Square, the one in low and the other in high pitch, the General wished to satisfy himself and a committee of officers as to their relative qualities of sound, the bands to play marches in turn. The wise ones listened profoundly, but in the end could come to no decision, as no-one could detect any difference, and concluded that we musicians were

---

[48] 'The Brass Band's Predicament: Handicapped by a Too High a Pitch.' *Bradford Telegraph & Argus*, 8th June 1928.
[49] TNA WO/32/3916. 'To Officers Commanding all Units at Home'. Circular 17A, dated 23rd October 1928.
[50] TNA WO/32/3916. 1RUR/56/7 dated 1/8/1928.

making a lot of fuss about nothing: finally the General thought the two bands might play together, perhaps to discover which could 'do the other in?' This might have been a joke, but it put 'the cap on' the general futility of the morning, so the bands were dismissed.[51]

With the general and colonels unconvinced, the focus on cost remained paramount: if no-one could hear any difference and the public purse was not going to pay then why should commanding officers authorise band funds to cover the costs?

The order to change

Pressure was mounting and the continued press activity and high-powered engagement on the subject in London [Military] District led to a House of Commons debate on 19 December 1928, where Sir Grattan-Doyle MP asked the Secretary of State for War 'whether it has been decided to lower the pitch for military bands; and, if so, whether there will be in consequence any charge on public funds?' Mr Duff Cooper (the Financial Secretary to the War Office) replied that 'the answer to the first part of the question is in the affirmative, and to the second in the negative. An Army Council Instruction will be published shortly.'[52] Eventually, after much canvassing and deliberation, Army Council Instruction 544, published the same day, decreed that bands would reduce their pitch, at regimental expense, as opposed to War Office expense, in the following financial year 1929-30 'after massed band performances had been completed'.[53] The 1935 edition of *The King's Regulations and Orders for the Army* was the first to recognise the adoption of 'New Philharmonic' pitch for military bands in Britain:

> In order to ensure musical uniformity, band instruments will be of the pitch known as "The New Philharmonic Pitch", which is 465 vibrations a second at 60° Fahrenheit for B flat, corresponding to 439 for A and 522 for C at the same temperature.[54]

---

[51] G. J. Miller, *The Piping Times in Peace and War: Being the Autobiography of a Royal Musician in Five Reigns*. Museum of Army Music. MS, n.d., pp. 88-90.
[52] 'Bands', House of Commons Debate 19 December 1928 vol 223 cc3031-2W <http://hansard.millbanksystems.com/written_answers/1928/dec/19/bands> [accessed 25th November 2017].
[53] *Ibid.*
[54] *The King's Regulations and Orders for the Army (1935)*, p. 428, para 1415.

George Miller was ahead of the game, however, as he had a sympathetic and supportive commanding officer who had already given permission to spend £2000 of the Grenadier Guards band fund's money on low-pitched instruments, but the band had to keep the high-pitched instruments in reserve for massed band performances, as the other Foot Guards' bands' commanding officers had initially refused to support their Directors of Music. The first outing of the Grenadier Guards Band with their low-pitched instruments, advertised as a 'Concert of special interest', took place at the Queen's Hall on Wednesday 4 December 1929.[55]

The high-profile nature of the military band pitch issue continued with further questions in the House of Commons in 1929 asking about the potential costs of the change, and again in 1931 about the repercussions for civilian bands.[56] It was also a challenge for part-time army bands, but some responded quickly to the change with the Band of The Duke of Lancaster's Own Yeomanry converted to low pitch, at regimental expense, by the 1930s, having been urged by their Bandmaster, Mr Henry Mortimer, a professional orchestral musician.[57]

Implications for farther afield were also important as both the British Music Societies' Congress and the War Office had been right about the spread of the change of pitch to the Empire. For example, in Australia, the Grenadier Guards Band tour in 1934 probably prompted the change to low pitch in the Dominion with the Service bands there starting the conversion to stay in line with the 'mother country' in 1936.[58] In India, bandmasters found novel ways to perform with low-pitched pianos at the Hill Stations where dance bands were required for the summer season, as Bandmaster Campbell of the 1st Battalion The Gordon Highlanders reports:

---

[55] Concert advertisement in *The Household Brigade Magazine*, Autumn, 1929, p. 248.

[56] 'Army Estimates', House of Commons Debate 21 July 1929 vol 225 cc2209-69 <http://hansard.millbanksystems.com/commons/1929/feb/28/army-estimates-1929#S5CV0225P0_19290228_HOC_369> [accessed 25th November 2017]; 'Bands', House of Commons Debate 21 July 1931 vol 255 cc1216-7 <http://hansard.millbanksystems.com/commons/1931/jul/21/bands#S5CV0255P0_19310721_HOC_16> [accessed 25th November 2017].

[57] J. Brereton, *Chain Mail: The History of The Duke of Lancaster's Own Yeomanry* (Chippenham: Picton, 1992), p. 196.

[58] S. A. Purtell, S. A. (2011). "In tune with the times': The history of performing pitch in Melbourne' (PhD Thesis, University of Melbourne, 2011), p. 183.

Pitch is difficult where dance bands are concerned, especially if one's instruments are of sharp pitch...On one occasion we met with one [piano] just over half a tone down, but as the mechanism permitted, we removed the top key and pushed all the others up a step, thus raising the instrument a semi-tone and making it suit us.[59]

The military bands of the Irish Free State were not hampered by the same issues as they had converted to low pitch with the purchase of new German instruments shortly after the arrival of their German bandmaster, Fritz Brase, in 1923. From the outset they were able to work with orchestras on a regular basis with the *Irish Times* reporting in 1927 that the (military) wind playing was particularly good.[60] The Free State military bands also provided all brass players for the Radio Éireann Orchestra until the employment of the first civilian horn player in 1943.[61]

For British army bands, performances with bands from other countries now became more possible with the change to low pitch. For example, in India a joint concert in Calcutta in December 1933 with two British Military Bands, the 1st Battalion the Norfolk Regiment and the 1st Battalion the Royal Rifle Corps, together with the Naval Band of the visiting German Cruiser, The Karlsruhe, highlighted the need for a standard pitch (Fig. 7.4).[62] It was a very important political statement, but a British army musician present reported on the more compelling issue for those in the bands:

We couldn't bother very much about the political soundness because we wanted to find out if the proposition was musically sound. Social overtures were cordially met; we were joyed to find no variation in pitch, and from then events moved rapidly.[63]

---

[59] W. N. Campbell, 'A Few Serious and Humorous Impressions during a Ten Years' Foreign Service Tour', *The Leading Note*, V1, No 7, August 1931, p. 27 [pp. 25-27].
[60] Cited in R. Pine, *Music and Broadcasting in Ireland* (Dublin: Four Courts Press, 2005), p. 53. Pine is surprised by this comment in the *Irish Times* as he incorrectly assumes that the pitch of the military band instruments would have been high pitch, and different to the strings.
[61] Pine, *Music and Broadcasting in Ireland* (Dublin: Four Courts Press, 2005), p. 34.
[62] *The Military Musician*, April, 1934 (II, 4), p. 28.
[63] *Ibid*, p. 29.

Figure 7.4
Massed Bands of the 1st Bn. The Norfolk Regiment; 1st Bn. K.R.R.C.; German Kreuzer "Karlsruhe." Calcutta, 12th December, 1933. All three bands were able to perform together at the same pitch

Although musicians were more concerned with creating the right sound, it is quite probable that the senior officer in charge in Calcutta would have insisted upon the bands playing together even if the pitches were not compatible, as it has already been noted that most military officers could not necessarily hear the difference. The ability for bands from different nations to play together at low pitch had real political significance as it could now be approached in a positive manner. George Miller emphasised this when referring to European bands:

> We were now enabled to combine with continental bands, and on our annual visits to France, L'Entente was cemented over and over again by 'massed' demonstrations in our national anthem and 'La Marseillaise.'[64]

As soon as Army Council Instruction (ACI) 544 was published, instrument manufacturers and agents started to advertise low-pitched instruments for sale (Figs 7.5[65] & 7.6[66]). But the change process was not immediate: Ernie Waites was still being issued with a high-pitch simple-system B♭ clarinet when he joined the Band of the 1st Battalion Green Howards (Alexandra's Princess of Wales Own Yorkshire Regiment) in 1943 as a band boy, aged fifteen, and

---

[64] Miller, *The Piping Times*, p. 90.
[65] *The Leading Note*, February, 1929, inside cover.
[66] *The Military Musician*, February, 1932, inside cover.

continued to play it when he started the 'Pupils Course' at Kneller Hall in 1947.[67]

Figure 7.5
Keith Prowse & Co, Ltd started to advertise for low-pitched instruments only a few months after ACI 544 was published

Importantly, the change in pitch allowed new entrants to the market, particularly overseas instrument manufacturers – continental woodwind instruments could now be bought and eventually wide-bore American brass instruments would be imported. The newly amalgamated Boosey and Hawkes advertised in military band journals for instruments both in low and high pitch and encouraged Bandmasters to purchase new brass instruments rather than adding the (cheaper) extensions to existing ones (Fig. 7.6).

Judging from the correspondence and articles in Kneller Hall's journal, *The Leading Note*, the response of military musicians was broadly in favour of the change not least because of the chance of brand new instruments, but there were also some cynics (Fig. 7.7, for example[68]). Nevertheless, they were fully aware of the advantages of the change when performing together with civilian musicians,

---

[67] W. A. Lindsay, *And the Band Plays On: The Biography of Ernie Waites M.B.E. as told to Wally Lindsay* (Sale: Wilshere, 1994), pp. 65 & 80.
[68] *The Leading Note*, Vol. 1, 6, p. 47 February, 1931.

perhaps most apparent at the weekly church parade when regimental bands performed alongside organists. The flat-pitched organ competing with the high-pitched band had caused huge problems with one military bandsman reporting that 'the woeful effect of this [combination] cannot be imagined'.[69]

The change to low pitch ultimately altered the sound of military bands – they reportedly lost their high pitch sparkle and the imported wider bore instruments had a different timbre – but this was not necessarily seen as a bad thing as some musicians argued that the high-pitched sound was only suited to music on the march, whereas 'the "new" pitch is far more suitable where anything in serious vein, anything impressive, is to be performed'.[70] When British brass bands finally made the shift to low pitch in the 1960s the alteration in sound was stark for some: Roy Newsome recalled that the difference was 'enormous' and the Black Dyke Band sounded like a 'band of flugal horns' with a loss of brightness.[71] This may have been the result of larger bore instruments but the change also had an influence on the sound.

The whole issue of pitch standardisation was always going to be problematic because it is a subjective measurement and does not necessarily correspond directly with the objective nature of frequency. In the 1930s, music psychologist, Carl Seashore, defined pitch as 'a qualitative attribute of auditory sensation which denotes highness or lowness in the musical scale',[72] and so it is not surprising that, as a subjective measure of musical height, the international standardisation of pitch – where A=440 cycles per second – was not agreed upon until May 1939.[73]

---

[69] A. Lemoine, 'Musings on the Change to "Low Pitch"', *The Leading Note*, vol. 1, no. 7, August, 1931, p. 31.
[70] *Ibid*, p. 28.
[71] R. Newsome, interviewed by T. Herbert 30th May 2007. British Brass Musicians interviews, British Library SoundServer, C1395.
[72] C. E. Seashore, *The Psychology of Music*. New York: Dover, 1967 [1938]), p. 53. A more modern definition by Moore states that 'pitch is that attribute of auditory sensation in terms of which sounds may be ordered on a musical scale'. B. C. J. Moore, *An Introduction to the Psychology of Hearing*, 3rd edn (London: Academic Press, 1989), p. 336.
[73] The pitch standard was not internationally ratified until 1953 due to the outbreak of war, but was made official in the United Kingdom in 1939. See British Standards Institution, *British Standard Specification: Musical Pitch*. B.S. 880:, 1950, p. 7; International Organization for Standardization, *Acoustics – Standard tuning frequency (standard musical pitch)*. First edition – 1975-01-15. ISO 16-1975 (E).

Figure 7.6
Boosey and Hawkes, Ltd were keen to emphasise the need for new brass instruments and not extensions to those of high pitch

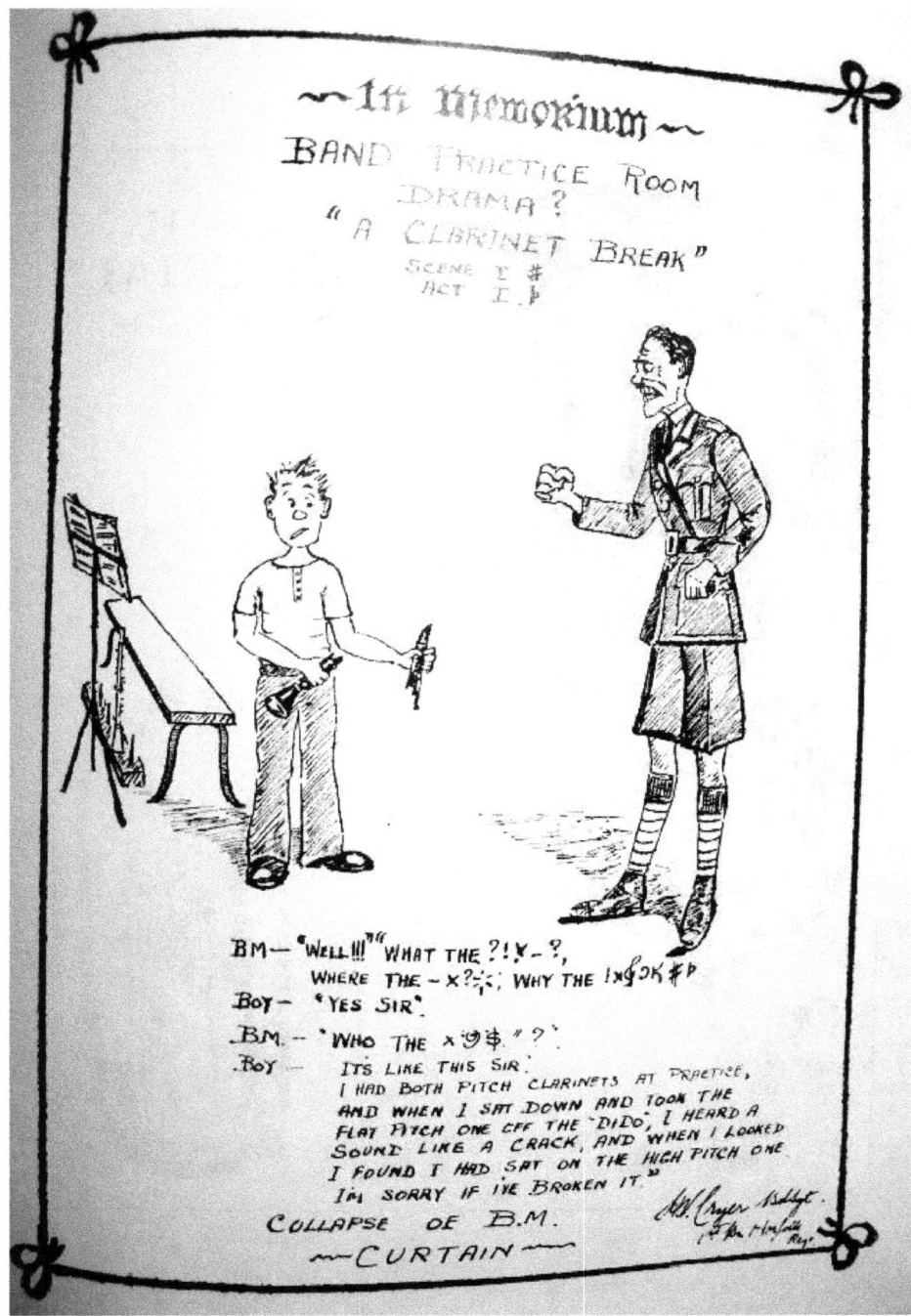

Figure 7.7
A cartoon showing a boy soldier having broken a high-pitched clarinet, to the anger of the Bandmaster. The implication is that the Bandmaster favoured instruments at high pitch

One of the main reasons why there was a push to standardise pitch in the 1930s was not because of uniformity for instrumentalists, but due to the need for parity in international broadcasting for test tones and transmission frequencies. Kneller Hall's position at the negotiating table in the late 1930s was perhaps due to the high profile public debate on the military band conversion, with the BBC duly noting at Broadcasting House that 'reference may be made…to the lowering in 1927 [sic] of the pitch of the British Army bands from 455 to 439'.[74] It is not clear how much the army had been a contributing factor, as in 1932 the BBC had claimed that it was the success of the BBC Wireless Military Band performing at low pitch that was largely responsible for 'giving a lead to…the lowering of army bands to symphonic pitch'.[75]

Even so, in May 1938 a meeting was called by the British Standards Institute at Broadcasting House with the Royal Military School of Music sending a representation,[76] and while both the 1938 and 1939 meetings were reported in the press,[77] with mention of the army's adoption of A=439, not all were happy with the outcome. Ironically, it was Henry Wood, responsible for generating the change to low pitch in 1896 with his Queen's Hall Orchestra, who argued that A=440 was not a standard pitch:

> It is only a pitch for piano and organ tuners to tune their instruments to for a heated concert hall. The French diapason normal pitch is A 435.5 at a temperature of 59deg., and this should be the standard pitch at which all wind instruments are made (as in France).[78]

Nevertheless, the change to low pitch by the army was reported in the press as a very positive move and it continued to be a topic for popular discussion up until the Second World War. It helped the United Kingdom have a significant influence on the international standardisation of musical pitch and, without Army Council Instruction 544, the meeting at Broadcasting House in 1938 may not

---

[74] G. W. C. Kaye, 'International Standard of Concert Pitch', *Nature*, no. 3630, May 27, 1939, p. 905.

[75] *The B. B. C. Year-Book 1932* (London: BBC, 1932), p. 130.

[76] G. W. C. Kaye, 'International Standard of Musical Pitch', *Nature*, vol. 142, November 5, 1938, p. 820 [pp. 820-21].

[77] 'Concert Pitch', *The Times* (London, England), Monday, Aug 22, 1938, p. 7, Issue 48079; 'Concert Pitch' *The Times* (London, England), Wednesday, Jan 31, 1940, p. 6, Issue 48527.

[78] H. J. Wood, 'To Stabilize Concert Pitch', *The Times* (London, England), Wednesday, May 17, 1939, p. 10, Issue 48307, Letters to the Editor.

have been successful, and the subsequent meeting in 1939 would probably never have happened.

This investigation of the army's transition from low to high pitch in the 1920s has exposed the nature of relationships both between the War Office and the authorities at Kneller Hall, and also the interaction of army music with those in the supplier markets of the music industry. The antipathy of the War Office, personal drive of Somerville, and intervention of the king, all contributed to the ebb and flow of the journey towards low pitch. Most important of all though, was the position army music was placed in the music industry structure and how its decision to change influenced the overall outcome of the final adoption of low pitch as the international standard.

CHAPTER 8

PUNCHING ABOVE THEIR WEIGHT: SOFT POWER INFLUENCE OF BRITISH ARMY BANDS OVERSEAS

Despite being considerably reduced after the 'Geddes Axe', the British army was given the enormous task of protecting Britain's possessions and communication systems throughout the Empire. Colonial administrations in particular were keen to maintain their hold over indigenous populations by preserving the cultural ideologies and brand (and thereby associated power) of the mother country. It was also important for Britain to preserve friendly relations and influence wherever there was a British interest, predominantly to retain competitive advantage in markets at a time of austerity. But there were limited resources to achieve this and the policy of relying on the British army to police these issues was optimistic at best.

'Imperial Policing' as a concept was first scrutinised in 1934 by Major-General Sir Charles Gwynn, and the title of his book that analysed the British army's role around the Empire.[1] Gwynn acknowledges that one of the problems for the British army was that its numbers fell far below those recommended to carry out policing duties.[2] This was especially difficult when the needs of British imperial defence in the interwar period probably reached their peak in 1930, and when the British army was at its most stretched.[3] Continuous conflict in the North-West Frontier, problems in Palestine and the threat of Japan in the Far East, coupled with the need to retain a home commitment force capable of deployment to continental Europe, meant that tangible resources were extended to their limits. The defence of the Empire was reliant on colonial troops (principally those from India and the dominions), but Britain had not been able to muster much support after the First World War, and there was no system of integrated imperial defence with the

---

[1] C. W. Gwynn, *Imperial Policing*, 2nd edn (London: Macmillan, 1939).
[2] *Ibid*, p. 8.
[3] B. Bond, *British Military Policy between the Two World Wars* (Oxford: Clarendon, 1980), p. 93.

dominions until the late 1930s.[4] Should Britain need help, allies would have to be enticed and attracted, with particular opportunities for the nations of the Empire whose subjects could identify with 'Britishness'; states that needed to be co-opted, rather than coerced, into desiring the same political outcomes as Britain.

The concept of Britishness is a complex issue,[5] but Marshall considers that Britishness fostered an imperial identity in the early twentieth century which could generally be thought of as being based upon a collective, paternalistic attitude towards freedom, through the humane trusteeship of overseas possessions, even when this freedom was withheld from some populations. The Empire contributed to a sense of Britishness as the population of Britain reaped the rewards and developed a sense of pride, especially when working within the Empire's institutions, at home and overseas.[6]

In the early twentieth century it was considered in the population's interests to maintain the Empire, and also in the interests of British subjects around the globe (both those of British descent and the indigenous privileged classes), to share in the wealth it generated through mutual protection and trade. The brand of Britishness could also be used as a symbol of associated power, with small colonial outposts able to call upon this identity to enforce the status of cultural institutions, often based around finance or commodity markets, such as in the Malay States where the British

---

[4] B. Bond and W. Murray, 'The British Armed Forces, 1918–39', in A. R. Millett and W. Murray (eds), *Military Effectiveness Volume 2: The Inter-war Period* (New York, NY: Cambridge University Press, 2010), p. 109.

[5] This has been the subject of several interdisciplinary conferences: 'Expressions of Britishness: Music and the Arts in the Twentieth Century' at the Institute of Musical Research, London, 11 January 2013,
<http://music.sas.ac.uk/sites/default/files/files/Expressions%20of%20Britishness%20programme%20v5.pdf> [accessed 10th September 2013; 'Britishness in the 21st Century', Keele University, 19 June 2013,
<http://globalfaultlines.files.wordpress.com/2013/06/britishness21century.pdf> [accessed 10th September 2013].

[6] P. J. Marshall, 'Imperial Britain', in P. J. Marshall (ed.), *The Cambridge Illustrated History of the British Empire* (Cambridge: Cambridge University Press, 1996), pp. 318–22. A more recent review of the meaning of Britishness can be found in D. Grube, 'How can 'Britishness' be Re-made?' *The Political Quarterly* (Vol. 82, No. 4, October-December 2011), pp. 628–35.

controlled the essential functions of government, or Buenos Aires where the British community enjoyed an elite status.[7]

As a form of 'cultural imperialism', Britishness could be used as a positive symbol for British subjects by embracing or antagonising foes, encouraging them either to be associated with the culture or be wary of its power. While the term cultural imperialism is almost exclusively used in the literature to refer to post-World War Two American influence,[8] it can be used in other discourses and does not necessarily have to imply the comprehensive imposition of a culture, nor cultural domination.[9] For example, research into the cultural impact of American music in the early Cold War period has shown that rather than being a mere addition to hard power politics:

> [T]he presence of musicians brought into being personal connections that opened the possibility of many kinds of further engagement, including more direct political action.[10]

Engagement through cultural imperialism can manifest itself as a form of soft power influence where, as bloom explains:

> [I]nfluence techniques comprise any act or inaction intentionally taken to affect the perceptions and behaviours of a chosen target for the benefit of the initiator.[11]

---

[7] A. Stockwell, 'Power, Authority, and Freedom', in Marshall (ed.), *Cambridge British Empire*, p. 163; P. J. Marshall, 'Introduction: The World Shaped by Empire', in Marshall (ed.), *Cambridge British Empire*, pp. 11-12.

[8] See for example: R. Bayazitova and A. K. Bangura, 'Cultural Integration: Effect of Music on Cultures', in *Journal of International Diversity* (Vol. 2012, No. 3, September 2012); J. Galeota, 'Cultural Imperialism: An American Tradition', *The Humanist* (May/June 2004), pp. 22–4, 46; P. H. Kim and H. Shin, 'The Birth of "Rok": Cultural Imperialism, Nationalism, and the Glocalization of Rock Music in South Korea, 1964–1975', *positions* (Vol. 18, No. 1, Spring 2010), pp. 199–230. Occasionally, British pop music is included in the discussion, as in M. Stokes, 'Globalization and the Politics of World Music', in M. Clayton, T. Herbert and R. Middleton (eds), *The Cultural Study of Music: A Critical Introduction*, second edition (Abingdon: Routledge, 2012), pp. 107–116.

[9] J. Tomlinson, *Cultural Imperialism: A Critical Introduction* (London: Continuum, 2002), pp. 1–33 & 94.

[10] D. Fosler-Lussier, 'Music Pushed, Music Pulled: Cultural Diplomacy, Globalization, and Imperialism', *Diplomatic History* (Vol. 36, No. 1, January 2012), p. 64.

[11] R. W. Bloom, 'Propaganda and active measures', in R. Gal & A. D. Mangelsdorff (eds.) *Handbook of Military Psychology* (San Francisco, CA: John Wiley, 1991), p. 694.

The two classes of influence can be described as propaganda (soft power) and active (hard power) measures. The use of soft power as an influence tool can achieve desired outcomes through attraction, rather than coercion, as it uses cultural and ideological means by encouraging emulation.[12] Soft power is not only less violent than kinetic or brute force but much less costly and is more appropriate in many instances for both short and long-term influence. These different types of power have been described by Fraser as 'Hard power threatens; soft power seduces. Hard power dissuades; soft power persuades'.[13]

The soft power 'Britishness' brand had to be treated carefully, however, as certain associations could cause problems. The American poet Henry Wadsworth Longfellow once famously described music as the 'universal language of mankind',[14] yet music carries the baggage of the culture that it is representing; rather than being an international language, it is more of an international communication system with many different languages. As such, the type of music played will have implications depending on the context in which it is performed due to the cultural symbols that it represents, and this significance can be amplified when performed by a military band whose uniform already symbolises a particular brand.[15]

In the 1920s and 1930s, British military bands could be found performing around the world, promoting the brand of Britishness and, albeit mostly unwittingly, reducing the need for overt political means or physical coercion. Bands were a particularly effective and economic resource: through the expression of British symbols, routines and rituals, they epitomised the British control systems and power structures, complementing the resources needed for 'hard power' engagement or totally replacing them, allowing Britain to be 'punching above its weight'[16] at a time when it 'faced defense [sic]

---

[12] For a discussion of the uses of soft power see J. S. Nye, Jr, and J. Wang, 'Hard Decisions on Soft Power: Opportunities and Difficulties for Chinese Soft Power', *Harvard International Review* (Vol. 31, No. 2, Summer 2009), pp. 18–22.

[13] M. Fraser, *Weapons of Mass Distraction: Soft Power and American Empire* (Toronto: Key Porter, 2003), p. 10.

[14] Quoted in D. Watson (ed.), *The Wordsworth Dictionary of Musical Quotations* (Ware: Wordsworth, 1994), p. 7.

[15] J. Richards, *Imperialism and Music: Britain 1876–1953* (Manchester: Manchester University Press, 2001), p. 17.

[16] D. Hurd, 'Making the World a Safer Place: Our Five Priorities', *Daily Telegraph*, 1 January 1992.

problems arguably beyond its resources, no matter how well managed'.[17]

Through a series of case studies that primarily correspond to the supplementary sixth theme (military music in marketing, propaganda, and diplomacy, at home and abroad), and relevant to political and sociological factors from the far external environment, this chapter considers the influence and soft power role of British army bands in three separate areas of overseas activity. The function of bands in shoring up the establishment in British India is assessed, where they were very much part of the trappings of the upper echelons of British society, performing at clubs, race meetings, tattoos, and ceremonial occasions, to bolster the image of the British as rulers. In a different context, bands' support to military operations in Shanghai is analysed, where several high profile events led by military bands assisted in allowing the British to exercise authority over the International Settlement. The final case study examines the Band of the Grenadier Guards tour to Southern Africa that was responsible, in part at least, for a reinvigoration of ties between Britain, a politically volatile South Africa, and the new colony of Southern Rhodesia.

Military band soft power influencing activities

The British Empire had increased in size after the First World War, comprising many different sorts of administrations (dominions, colonies, mandates, and protectorates) and, as a result, the utilisation of hard power engagement in all situations that required British influence for resolution was not a real prospect. Soft power influencing to reinforce loyalty to the mother country, on the other hand, was relatively cheap to achieve: a platoon-strength group of musicians on parade could deceive and distract a foe with a high-profile musical performance while other agencies concurrently carried out counter-insurgency intelligence gathering. Bands could also have an impact on local and international relations at a level disproportionate to the size of the unit. Whilst this was not unique to the period in question it was made more important in the interwar years due to the sheer size of the expanding Empire and the increased

---

[17] J. P. Harris, 'Obstacles to Innovation and Readiness: The British Army's Experience 1918–1939', in W. Murray and R. H. Sinnreich (eds), *The Past as Prologue: The Importance of History to the Military Profession* (New York, NY: Cambridge University Press, 2006), p. 211.

responsibilities of imperial policing which created, what Boycott called in 1931 'a strategic problem of the first importance.'[18]

For colonial administrations it was important to preserve the cultural ideologies and brand (and thereby associated power) of the mother country in order to maintain their hold over indigenous populations, and music was one way of doing this. Brass and wind bands were particularly useful in this role and were prevalent at the far reaches of the Empire, with Gramit pointing out that in Canada in the late nineteenth and early twentieth centuries bands were a prominent part of musical life in 'virtually every pioneer town'.[19] This was even the case in what is referred to as the 'informal Empire',[20] territories under the influence of Britain either for the defence of vital strategic points – such as Egypt – or for guaranteed access to natural resources or trade – such as parts of Persia and Shanghai in China, respectively.

Britain was not the only country to use its military bands in support of operations beyond its borders. Pre-First World War Austro-Hungarian military bands in Bosnia-Herzegovina were 'utilised as a symbol of Austro-Hungarian power',[21] and were also used to try to win over the population by performing in local musical styles,[22] in what Pennanen calls 'acoustic symbolism'.[23] Bands in Sarajevo performed music appropriate to Orthodox Serbs, Roman Catholics, and Muslims, respectively, in support of the administration's attempts to win the hearts and minds of the various ethnic populations, but the *Kaiserhymne* was always played as an integral part of any public event that had a connection with the

---

[18] A. G. Boycott, *The Elements of Imperial Defence: A Study of the Geographical Features, Material Resources, Communications, and Organization of the British Empire* (Aldershot: Gale & Polden, 1931), p. 50.
[19] D. Gramit, 'The Business of Music on the Peripheries of Empire: A Turn-of-the-Century Case Study', in C. Bashford and R. Montemorra Marvin (eds) *The Idea of Art Music in a Commercial World, 1800-1930* (Woodbridge: Boydell, 2016), p. 283.
[20] M. Banton, *Administering the Empire, 1801–1968: A Guide to the Records of the Colonial Office in The National Archives of the UK* (London: Institute of Historical Research/The National Archives, 2008), p. 5.
[21] R. P. Pennanen, 'Tattoos, Neo-Traditions and Entertainment – The Roles of Military Bands in Habsburg Bosnia and Herzegovina (1878-1918)', in M. Schramm (ed.) *Militärmusik zwischen Nutzen und Mißbrauch* (Bonn: Militärmusikdienst der Bundeswehr, 2011), p. 17.
[22] J. Talam, 'Meterhane and their influence on Bosnian folk music', in M. Schramm (ed.) *Militärmusik zwischen Nutzen und Mißbrauch* (Bonn: Militärmusikdienst der Bundeswehr, 2011), p. 10.
[23] Pennanen, 'Tattoos, Neo-Traditions and Entertainment', p. 18.

emperor or state.²⁴ Through involvement in all spheres of music making in Bosnia-Herzogovina – state and religious ceremonies, classical concerts, educational and pastime concerts, and dance music – military bands were symbols of power and legitimacy. They formed part of the political machinery and, according to Pennanen:

> served as an important instrument of colonial policies and imperialist propaganda which initially sought to keep the colonised populations satisfied with the occupation.²⁵

The Austro-Hungarian example hints at a systematic integration of military music in the governing of Bosnia-Herzegovina by the imperial power, and this may have been the case, but it was more likely to have been more informal and spontaneous than that. Undoubtedly, the military bands were a symbol of the colonial authority but they were probably increasingly employed in the towns as they were the only musicians available to provide up-to-date entertainment. By doing this they were, perhaps coincidentally, increasing the aural and visual dominance of the occupying power.

There were comparable situations in central and South America. In mid-nineteenth century Mexico, where bands were very popular, the numerous military bands were under the control of the clergy and conservative regular army, but the opposition liberal leaders were 'determined to appropriate the popular appeal' as they had realised that 'music sheets and instruments were as important a part of electoral or military preparations as rifles, ammunition, food rations, and ballot cards.'²⁶ When French and Austrian military musicians arrived in Mexico, they were conscious of the power of the local traditions and were careful not to impose their methods but rather absorb the Mexican musical traditions.²⁷ Similarly, in Brazil in the second half of the nineteenth century, the popular military-styled 'Bandas de Música' were being appropriated by the Roman Catholic church in order to replace local traditional religions by putting on

---

²⁴ *Ibid.*
²⁵ *Ibid.*, p. 25.
²⁶ G. P. C. Thomson, 'The Ceremonial and Political Roles of Village Bands, 1846-1974', in W. H. Beezley, C. E. Martin, and W. E. French (eds) *Rituals of Rule, Rituals of Resistance: Public Celebrations and Popular Culture in Mexico* (Lanham, Maryland: Rowman & Littlefield Publishers, 1994), pp. 315-316.
²⁷ *Ibid.*, p. 317.

military-style parades and processions in military formations to gain favour.[28]

Although there had been overseas tours by British army bands in the late nineteenth and first decade of the twentieth centuries it was during the First World War that British army bands were initially actively employed to support British influencing activities. For example, the Royal Artillery Band carried out several tours to the British front, completing 209 engagements, including joint concerts with the French, on their first tour from 20 December 1915 to 25 April 1916.[29] Similarly, from 1915, the bands of the Brigade of Guards rotated through three-monthly tours of duty on the continent,[30] with 'political propaganda' tours undertaken to Paris and Italy. This deliberate use of military bands to project the brand of Britishness as part of promoting collective security and British interests abroad continued in the interwar years with some musicians fully aware of their role. Bandmaster Campbell relates how, with the Band of the 1st Battalion The Gordon Highlanders in Turkey in 1921:

> The band was sent to Ismidt 'on a few days' propaganda work. The idea being to show the local inhabitants what a fine race the British were, as represented by a British Military Band.[31]

The local Brigadier who used Campbell's band appears to have done so intentionally, and the tactic reportedly had the desired positive effect with the assembled Turks, Greeks, and Armenians.[32] As such, through its expression of British symbols, routines and rituals – which epitomises the British control systems and power structures without the need for hard-power engagement – the military band represented a particularly economic, effective, efficient and ethical resource for the promotion of Britishness as part of information activities overseas.

Like the Austro-Hungarians, the British took their bands with them when their armies were deployed abroad, but unlike the Austro-

---

[28] S. A. Reily, 'The Localization of the Civic Wind and Brass Band in Minas Gerais, Brazil', in M. Schramm (ed.) *Militärmusik zwischen Nutzen und Mißbrauch* (Bonn: Militärmusikdienst der Bundeswehr, 2011), p. 126.
[29] H. G. Farmer, *History of the Royal Artillery Band: 1762–1953* (London: Royal Artillery Institution, 1954), p. 335.
[30] J. Mackenzie-Rogan, *Fifty Years of Army Music* (London: Methuen, 1926), p. 188.
[31] W. N. Campbell, 'A Few Serious and Humorous Impressions during a Ten Years' Foreign Service Tour', *The Leading Note*, V1, No 7, August 1931, p. 26.
[32] *Ibid.*

Hungarian Empire, the British Empire was a vast sprawling entity spanning the globe and so the bands had the potential for influence in many more places and much farther afield.

British army band service overseas

Whilst the interwar period by its very name suggests a period of peace, there were conflicts overseas that required British military intervention, further to the normal imperial policing, including Russia, Turkey, and Palestine. These deployments were in addition to the garrisoned troops in all parts of the Empire with some parts in a continual state of conflict, such as India's North-West frontier.[33]

Most British army infantry regiments were arranged into two regular battalions, one territorial battalion, and a regimental depot, and it was usual for one of these regular battalions to serve overseas, in Germany, India, Egypt, the Far East or other parts of the Empire. Bands went with their batallions and are evident where ever there was trouble, for example throughout the 1922 Chanak affair in Turkey.[34] With the Treaties of Locarno in 1925 that settled, albeit temporarily, the peace for central and eastern Europe, Britain's focus for the army developed into maintaining lines of communication through the Mediterranean to Singapore and the Far East, and so Britain's home defence front became the Rhine.[35]

Bands were stationed in Germany, with their battalions, for the whole occupation period, usually as part of a series of postings. The 2nd Battalion, The Duke of Cornwall's Light Infantry (2DCLI) was fairly typical of a battalion serving much of its time overseas in the interwar period, working hard and undertaking a great deal of travelling. In 1918 they were in Salonika, Serbia, Bulgaria, and Transcaucasia, returning to England for a short spell in 1919 before moving to India the same year. The rebellion in Iraq meant a move there in 1920, followed by a brief interlude in Malta in 1921, which was cut short to assist in potential disturbances from the miners' strike in Britain. A quick move to assist with the troubles in Ireland in 1921 followed, before being sent to Cologne as part of the British Army of Occupation of the Rhine (BAOR) in 1922. This lasted for two

---

[33] P. Docherty, *The Khyber Pass: A History of Empire & Invasion* (New York: Sterling, 2008), p. 216.
[34] See, for example, D. Walder, *The Chanak Affair* (London: Hutchinson, 1969), pp. 208 & 311.
[35] Bond, *British Military Policy*, p. 81.

years, with two companies being dispatched to plebiscite duties in Silesia. In 1924 they spent three years in Guernsey and Alderney, and then moved to Aldershot for five years. In 1932 the battalion was sent to Gibraltar for three years, finally returning to England in 1935, where they remained until the outbreak of war in 1939.[36] This arduous series of assignments highlights the role of Imperial police for 2DCLI with the band accompanying the battalion for much of its time.

Whilst in Germany the 2DCLI Band was involved in many of the parades that continued to be held as a mark of authority (Fig. 8.1) as the Rhineland had become a de-militarised zone (of German troops) as part of the Treaty of Versailles, which made centres like Münster assume the function of a military border town.[37]

Figure 8.1
Unidentified bands (possibly Cornwalls and Leicesters) in a parade in Cologne, Germany, in 1919. Parades continued throughout the occupation by the BAOR (Cornwall's Regimental Museum)

---

[36] H. White, *One & All: A History of The Duke of Cornwall's Light Infantry* (Padstow: Tabb House, 2006), pp. 286-95.
[37] G. Dethlefs and M. Schadewitz, *Messenger of Peace and Send Sword: Citizens and Soldiers* (Münster, Germany: Stadtmuseum Münster, 1995), p. 71.

India

Foreign service was fixed at five years in India and shorter periods in countries 'where the climate of a small island would lead to a reduction in military efficiency'.[38] But when a soldier did find himself in India, he usually had to serve an extra year abroad, known as the King's Year or 'buckshee year'.[39] The first real awareness of being sent overseas would most likely have been on board the troopship ready to embark on the long sea voyage. An account by ex-bandsman Spike Mays who had travelled east on HMT (His Majesty's Troopship) Neuralia in 1927, describes the experience.[40] It is corroborated by William 'Penny' Pennington, who provides us with first-hand accounts of the role that bands played in both sending troops off to the Empire and receiving them in-theatre. His descriptions provide a feeling of the sense of occasion as experienced by a boy soldier. Whilst Penny was not a bandsman, he had an understanding of music in his role as trumpeter and had been on parade with the Royal Artillery Band at Woolwich.

In the first account, the fifteen-year-old Penny observed life on board the HMT Neuralia as it was waiting to depart from Liverpool on its way to Bombay in December 1935:

> His Majesty's bands were already present on the quay, resplendent in scarlet and gold-trimmed jackets and black trousers with the plume-tipped Busby helmets, in sharp contrast with the drab khaki uniforms of those of us who were about to board. Playing martial tunes proclaiming the might and glory of the British Empire, with instruments gleaming in the now-risen sun, they marched the length of the quay adjacent to the troopship with all the pomp and circumstance that the British Army does so well. It was a stirring spectacle…And as the hawsers were cast off, severing the ship from the dock, the hundreds who still lined the shore broke into rousing cheers to the sound of the band as it played 'Rule Britannia'…with the band now playing 'Auld Lang Syne', those on the ship became more emotional.[41]

On arrival in Bombay the following month there was a military band waiting:

---

[38] W. A. Vaughan, *Regimental History Flash* (Leeds: E. J. Arnold, 1943), p. 44.
[39] C. Allen (ed.), *Plain Tales From the Raj: Images of British India in the Twentieth Century* (London: Deutsch, 1975), p. 38.
[40] S. Mays, *Fall Out the Officers* (London: Eyre & Spottiswoode, 1969), pp. 106-120.
[41] J. W. Pennington, *Pick Up Your Parrots and Monkeys…and Fall in Facing the Boat: The Life of a Boy Soldier in India* (London: Cassell, 2003), p. 85-86.

> The stentorian voices of those in command, both aboard and ashore, were clearly heard above the bedlam of noises, as were the martial tune of the Royal Artillery Band as it marched the length of the docks with its measured tread. Beyond the activities alongside the ship stood the troop train, black smoke rising from the funnel. Its drabness was punctuated only by the flashes of colourful headwear and the dress of the bandsmen.[42]

Six years later, in January 1942, as an officer about to go in to battle with the Japanese, Penny puts the context of military bands in a rather more cynical light:

> The bands were there to meet us [at Bombay] of course, for England always rolled out the pomp and circumstance when her troops arrived overseas, not so much to welcome the soldiers, more to impress upon the locals how mighty was their army.[43]

The bands at the quayside accordingly served a two-fold purpose: to bolster the morale of the troops and their families as they left Britain for foreign lands by persuading them that what they were doing was for a noble cause, and to seduce the foreign indigenous populations into thinking that their rulers were worthy masters of a large Empire.

Once in India, however, it was an arduous and generally unpopular assignment for British soldiers, and yet it was experienced by a large part of the army at any one time in the interwar years – 68,000 serving alongside 164,000 Indian army troops by the 1930s.[44] There was no leave back to Britain for those in the ranks and a significant number of soldiers, including bandsmen, died of disease and illness:

> ...how sorry we are in losing Bdsmn. Westall who died from lobar pneumonia on December 4th, 1938. He was a very popular member of the Band, and we offer our sincerest condolences to his parents for their great loss.[45]

---

[42] *Ibid*, p. 77.
[43] *Ibid*, p. 254.
[44] Boycott, *Elements of Imperial Defence*, p. 224.
[45] 'Band, 52nd.', *Journal of the Oxfordshire and Buckinghamshire Light Infantry*, XV: 84, March (1939), p. 74.

For the rank and file the conditions were quite miserable and it is not surprising that soldiers' songs of the interwar period were dominated by the theme of leaving India and returning home to Britain.[46]

Bandsmen lived and operated in this environment, participating in regimental sports and events and also undertaking military duties and training. Bandmaster Pullinger, with the Band of The 1st Battalion The Border Regiment recounts how the military, string, and dance bands were kept busy in Peshawar, in 1922. He was also involved with training Indian Army bands to ensure they could perform to (British) acceptable standards.[47] Penny describes how they led the Church Parades on Sundays in Meerut:

> The troops marched down to the Church to the sounds of the massed bands, parading along the Mall [most British settled towns had a road called the Mall] in all the pomp and splendour the British Army does so well. Dressed immaculately in khaki drill uniforms, with buttons and bayonets flashing, it made both British civilians and off-duty soldiers lining the route feel pride in their country.[48]

The repertoire in India was no different to that played in any part of the Empire, with the programme book of the Band of the 2nd Battalion the West Yorkshire Regiment (Prince of Wales's Own) from India in 1922 containing music that would have been equally as familiar in any British garrison town (Fig. 8.2).

Military bands were also a fundamental part of the big ceremonial events that took place, including at the 1936 Delhi Durbar (ceremonial gathering), as well as performing as an essential part of the socialising afterwards.[49] Tattoos were normal happenings around the Empire and not limited to the famous events held in the United Kingdom, but were also exported to parts of the Empire as a statement of Britishness.

---

[46] See 'Between the Wars' in R. Palmer, *"What a Lovely War!": British Soldiers' Songs from the Boer War to the Present Day* (London: Michael Joseph, 1990), pp. 128-144.
[47] Pullinger, *Reminiscences*, pp. 88-9.
[48] Pennington, *Pick Up Your Parrots and Monkeys*, p. 117.
[49] *Ibid*, pp. 152 & 155.

Officers Mess.   20-9-22.

1. Fest March from "Tannhäuser."   Wagner.
2. Overture.   "A Midsummer Night's Dream." Mendelssohn.
3. Selection.   "The Golden Moth."   Novello.
4. Valse.   "Sleeping Water."   Joyce.
5. Morceau.   "J'en ai Marre."   Yvain.
6. Suite.   "Hiawatha."   Coleridge-Taylor.
7. One Step.   "Swanee Rose."   Gershwin.
8. Descriptive. "A Hunting Scene."   Bucalossi.

———

Boxing Ring.   22-9-22.

1. Fest March from "Tannhäuser."   Wagner.
2. Selection.   "The Golden Moth."   Novello.
3. Valse.   "Sleeping Water."   Joyce.
4. Fox Trot.   "April Showers."   Silvers.
5. Descriptive. "A Hunting Scene."   Bucalossi.
6. Morceau.   "Tell her at Twilight." Monquin.

———

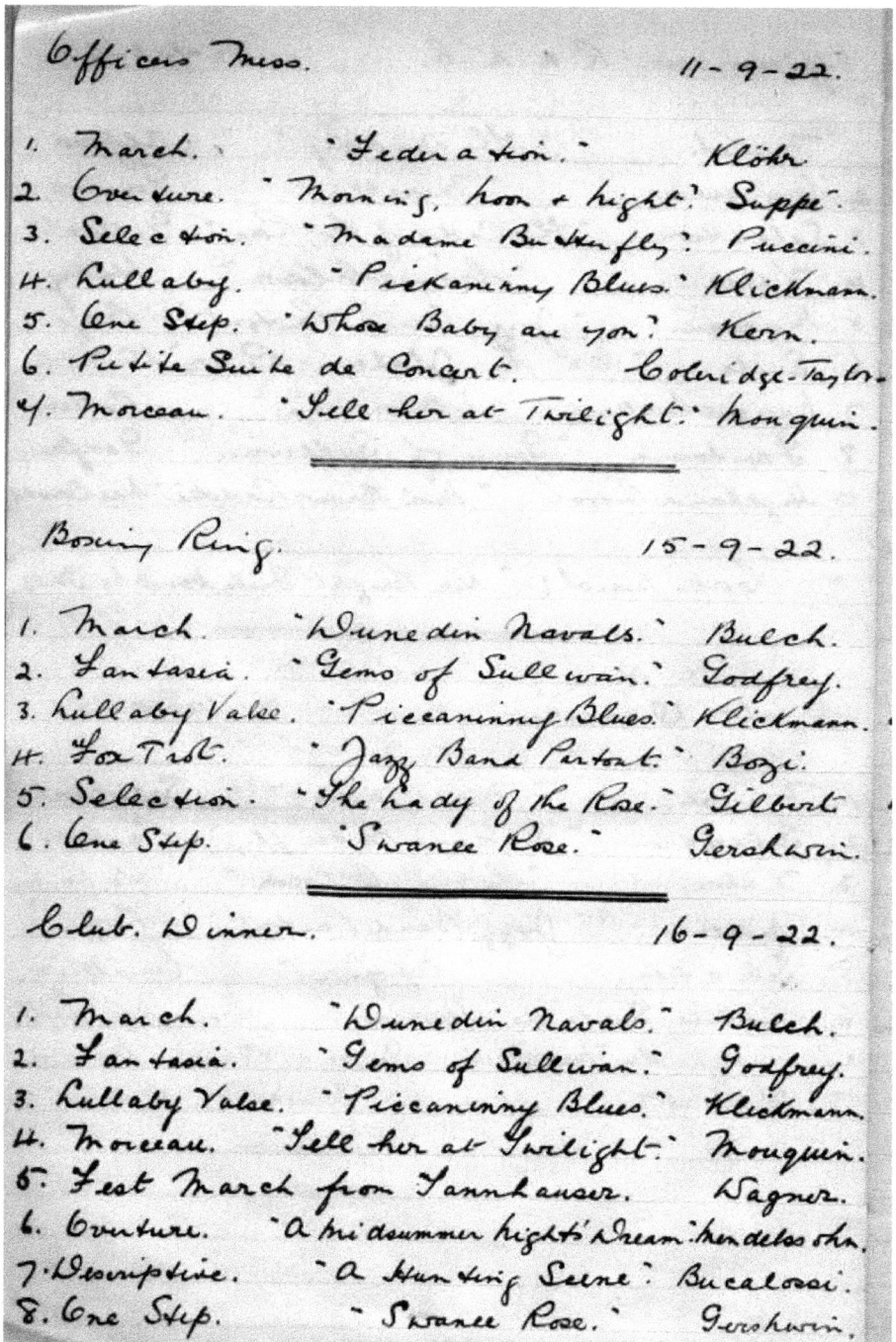

Figure 8.2
The Band of the 2nd Battalion the West Yorkshire Regiment (Prince of Wales's Own) programme book, India, 1922 (MAM)

The India cantonments hosted several tattoos, such as the annual Calcutta Searchlight Tattoo, with the Band of the 1st Battalion the Duke of Cornwall's Light Infantry (1DCLI) announcing in their regimental journal: 'with our fellow conspirators, the "Linnets," [The Dorsetshire Regiment] we help to supply the musical side of the programme' (Fig. 8.3).[50]

Figure 8.3
The Band of the 1st Battalion Duke of Cornwall's Light Infantry, Lucknow, India, 1925 (Cornwall's Regimental Museum)

These tattoos were modelled on the large-scale events held in Aldershot and Tidworth, but were still sizeable enough to require the commitment of a large amount of resources. For example, the 1936 Simla Tattoo had at least three bands performing, all requiring lighting up at different times in the 'Grand Finale', with intricate arrangements demanded of the Royal Engineers (Fig. 8.4)[51]:

---

[50] 'Band Notes', *The "One and All": The Journal of the Duke of Cornwall's Light Infantry*, 1: 2, May (1930), p. 100.
[51] E. McDonald, 'Floodlighting for Military Tattoos', *The Royal Engineers Journal*, L: March (1936), p. 94.

As each band in turn struck up, a proportion of the lights would lift on to it and lead it up to its position in mass, where the remaining lights would equalise over the assembles bodies, while the first light lifted again to lead in another party.[52]

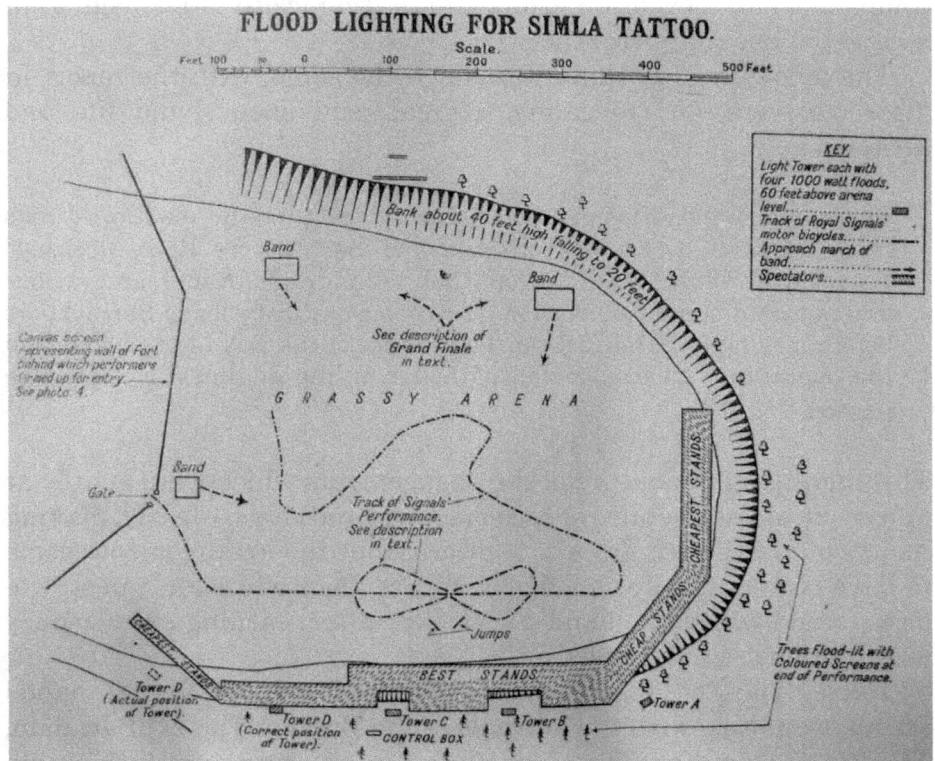

Figure 8.4
Layout for 1935 Silver Jubilee Tattoo, Simla, India

Although for some tattoos in India the 'massed bands' would not consist of large numbers (for the 1937 Mandalay Tattoo the Band of the 1st King's Royal Rifle Corps was the only band[53]), the great effort put into the Simla Tattoo emphasises the importance placed upon big events that aimed to demonstrate the power of the Britishness brand.

Whilst in Barrackpore, the 1DCLI band performed at the Tollygunge Races, Barrackpore Races, Calcutta Races, Darjeeling Races, Calcutta Rowing Club, Begg Dunlop Hall, Empire Theatre,

---

[52] *Ibid.*
[53] *The Bands of The King's Royal Rifle Corps,*
<http://www.krrcassociation.com/krrc_bandandbugles/bands_krrc.pdf> p. 7 [accessed 12th March 2014].

Angus Mills and Victoria Gardens, Darjeeling, as well as a regular engagement at the Barrackpore Club every Wednesday. Their programme also included the annual King's Birthday Parade in Darjeeling, in West Bengal, after the Battalion Headquarters and two companies had moved to Lebong Hill Station (close to Darjeeling) to escape the heat of Barrackpore.[54]

The following year there was much the same, with the report in *The "One and All"* revealing a great deal about band life and attitudes:

> Regarding Band Engagements, history as already mentioned has repeated itself: Calcutta, Tollygunj and Barrackpore Race Meetings, Barrackpore Club, "Begg-Dunlop" Club, St Andrew's Dinner, and various others too numerous to mention. 1930 being our last year in Barrackpore before moving to Bareilly is our last chance of raking in the shekels and the opportunity of engagements, though trying at times, must not be missed.[55]

This highlights the nature of the engagements which were mainly at officer-patronised venues at race meetings and clubs. Clearly, making money out of the officers was a priority but the arrangement seems to have been mutually beneficial; officers, their wives and guests are entertained whilst the band gets looked after, earning extra money in salubrious surroundings.

These types of engagement were characteristic for all bands serving overseas, with the journals of the Band of The 2nd Battalion, The King's Own Yorkshire Light Infantry, reporting much the same in the cantonments, and also in Burma, with extensive use of the Dance Band.[56] Senior Non-Commissioned Officers were also occasionally entertained, with the Dance Band of the Royal Dragoons (1st Dragoons) performing once a month for the sergeants' mess dance,[57] but the emphasis for bands' engagements was as a show of Britishness by the officers.

---

[54] 'Band Notes', The "One and All": *The Journal of the Duke of Cornwall's Light Infantry*, 1: 1, November (1929), p. 13.
[55] *Ibid.*, p. 99.
[56] W. K. Grainger, *The Life and Times of a Regimental Band: A History of The Bands of The King's Own Yorkshire Light Infantry*. The Rifles Office, Pontefract, 1995, MS, pp. 136-49.
[57] Mays, *Fall Out the Officers*, p. 169.

When the band was required to undertake support to military duties it was done begrudgingly, which was publicly stated in the DCLI regimental journal:

> The comforts of [military] camp life did not appeal to us. We do not pretend to be able to understand these things and although we took no part in "Rearguard Actions" and other obtuse happenings we were busily occupied in charming the savage breasts of the soldiery on their daily return from the fray.[58]

This attitude could not have endeared the infantry soldiers to the band but it was accepted that the band's work was quite different. The officers were happy for the battalion band to be utilised as a symbol of Britishness as this would have increased their own standing and reputation within society in India.

Nevertheless, as the Second World War loomed, it seems that music began to take on a subordinate role, as reported by the Band of the 2nd Battalion The Oxfordshire and Buckinghamshire Light Infantry (52nd Foot) whilst serving at Bareilly, in India:

> The Band have just completed their (new) Musketry Course, and...there has been considerable activity of late in connection with "Duties in Aid of Civil Power" – some serious and some purely practice. In fact what with the "real thing" and various schemes, everyone has had quite a busy time and [band] practice has been rather the exception than the rule.[59]

This was a trend that was not uncommon throughout the British army serving overseas as the Second World War drew closer. 'Wilkie' Brown, serving as a bandsman with the 1st Battalion the Argyll and Sutherland Highlanders in Palestine, 1939 describes how 'the band was ceasing to function as a band and although I had the use of the accordion whilst off-duty we were required for numerous duties'.[60]

Bands in India were very much a part of the British culture that made a clear statement of authority. As a soft power tool they were integral to political power relationships between the various British cantonments and the Indian administrations, and through overt displays at tattoos and parades the bands were indispensable in the

---

[58] 'Band Notes', The "One and All": *The Journal of the Duke of Cornwall's Light Infantry*, 1: 2, May (1930), p. 100.
[59] 'Band, 52nd.', *Journal of the Oxfordshire and Buckinghamshire Light Infantry*, XV: 85, May (1939), p. 107.
[60] A. W. Brown, *A Memoir: from Music to Wars* (Aberdeen: A W Brown, 2001), p. 33.

maintenance of British influence. Towards the end of the 1930s when bands in India, and elsewhere, were required to undertake other military duties this may have, unsuspectingly, resulted in a loss of power with the Indian population through a diversion of resources.

Shanghai 1927

China had long been a country in which European powers and the United States had shown an interest. Furthermore, it was also an area of Japanese expansion and a potential cause of friction with Western nations. Although there had been cooperation in the Boxer Rebellion (1898-1900) by the Eight Nation Alliance (Britain (including Australian and Indian troops), United States, Germany, France, Austria-Hungary, Italy, Russia, and Japan), there was much suspicion between nations with the subsequent Russo-Japanese war in 1904-5 culminating in Japan's expansion of influence. Tensions in China between powers also most likely contributed to the diplomatic fault lines that appeared in the run-up to the First World War.[61]

One city in China, Shanghai, started the interwar period as a haven for Europeans, Americans, and Japanese alike but increasingly saw violent confrontation between warring Chinese factions, a Sino-Japanese conflict, and was eventually overrun by the Japanese in 1941. The Treaty of Nanjing in 1842 had made Shanghai a self-governing treaty port, administered by foreign nationals, despite being sovereign Chinese territory. A city of over a million people it had 60,000 resident foreigners by the early 1930s, and a vibrant music scene with at least two orchestras, theatre ensembles, and military-style bands run by the various expatriate communities.[62] Throughout the 1920s and 1930s Shanghai was a very unstable place, despite being a centre for finance and residence of a great many expatriates, including holding large amounts of money for White Russian armies.[63]

---

[61] G. P. Gooch and H. Temperley (eds), *British Documents on the Origins of the War 1898-1914: Vol. II The Anglo-Japanese Alliance and the Franco-British Entente* (London: HMSO, 1927). See for example pp. 152-3 for reports of deteriorating Anglo-German relations in China.
[62] H. Yang, 'Diaspora, Music and Politics: Russian Musical Life in Shanghai during the Inter-war Period', in P. Fairclough (ed.) *Twentieth-Century Music and Politics: Essays in Memory of Neil Edmonds* (Farnham: Ashgate, 2013), pp. 262 & 270.
[63] P. Y. Aisin-Gioro, *From Emperor to Citizen: The Autobiography of Aisin-Gioro Pu Yi*, trans. W. J. F. Jenner (Beijing: Foreign Languages Press, 1989 [1965]), p. 191.

In February 1927, in this precarious environment, to protect the Shanghai International Settlement against attack by warring Kuomintang and Communist Party factions, a combined British and Indian Army force of approximately a division's strength of 13,000 troops was sent to Shanghai.[64] Other nations provided troops to the 'Shanghai Defence Force' (Shaforce), including the United States Marines, but they did not contribute to the maintenance of law and order.[65] The British involvement was the most numerous and active, with troops from Britain as well as a whole brigade deploying from India, the 20th Indian Infantry Brigade, including approximately 3,000 British troops, 4,000 Indian troops and followers, and 1,300 animals.[66] At least two British battalions, the 2nd Battalion the Durham Light Infantry and the 2nd Battalion the Gloucestershire Regiment (Fig. 8.5), deployed with their bands, and part of the initial show of strength upon arrival was the sight of the troops marching through Shanghai with the Gloucesters' band playing, Colours flying and bayonets fixed.[67]

The British military continued to send its bands to Shanghai throughout the deployment with the Band of The Border Regiment also present in the city.[68] As the troops continued to arrive, headed

---

[64] P. Chow, 'British Interests and Policy towards China, 1922-1927' (PhD thesis, London School of Economics, 2011), p. 191.
<http://etheses.lse.ac.uk/228/1/chow_British_Opinion_and_Policy.pdf> [accessed 5th March 2014].

[65] TNA WO/191/9, 'HQ North China Command General Staff 1928 May-July, Appendix E, Foreign Forces in North China (Approximate Numbers), G. S. 'I', Shanghai 31st May 1928'; G. Kennedy, 'Imperial Networks, Imperial Defence, and Perceptions of American Influence on the British Empire in the Inter-war Period: The Case of the 27th Earl of Crawford and Balcarres', *Canadian Journal of History* (Vol. 47, No. 3, Winter 2012), p. 577.

[66] TNA WO/191/34, 'Secret War Diaries of DADSSI'.

[67] TNA WO/191/33, 'Secret War Diary of 2nd Bn Gloucestershire Regiment From 20 Jan 1927 To 28 Feb 1927 Volume I, 14 2 27 1100hrs'. A Pathé newsreel shows the 2nd Battalion Gloucestershire Regiment band marching with troops in Shanghai: <http://www.britishpathe.com/video/a-demonstration-of-force/query/Shanghai> [accessed 10th September 2013]. The 2nd Battalion The Durham Light Infantry, coming from Sialkot in India via Calcutta and Hong Kong, paraded with the Gloucesters but the band did not have their instruments with them – the instruments arrived (along with three band boys) on the S. S. *Rasula* on 1 March 1927 (see TNA WO/191/12, 'Secret War Diary of 2nd Bn The Durham Light Infantry Volume I, 1st March 1927').

[68] The Bandmaster of The Border Regiment, O. W. Geary, arranged a selection of regimental music while he was there called 'Chinese Airs' and in 2007 remained a piece to be played on regimental dinner nights before the marches, see *The*

by their bands, the *Shanghai Times* reported how 'the populace gazed with mixed feelings of admiration and wonder'[69] – exactly the sort of soft power effect that was intended by the British in staging such events.

Figure 8.5
The Band of the 2nd Battalion, The Gloucestershire Regiment in India c1928, the year after it was deployed to Shanghai as part of a British display of strength and confidence during the crisis there (Soldiers of Gloucestershire Museum)

During the five-month deployment there was heavy street fighting and several attempts by Chinese troops to break through into the settlement. These were repulsed but the situation remained tense. Remarkably though, to celebrate the king's birthday, for two nights in the first week of June it was decided to hold other audacious performances: a Trooping of the Colour (Fig. 8.6) and full military tattoo at the settlement's racecourse (Fig. 8.7).

Regimental Handbook of The Duke of Lancaster's Regiment, Section IX, p. 2 (Preston, 2007)
<http://www.army.mod.uk/documents/general/Regimental_handbook.pdf> [accessed 1st July 2014].
[69] Quoted in J. Ambler (ed.), *'Bagged' in World War 2: Two Tales of Royal Marines Prisoners of War: Part 1 – The Fallace Story*. Special Publication No 24 (Portsmouth: Royal Marines Historical Society, 2001), p. 20.

Soft Power Influence Overseas 263

Figure 8.6
'The King's Birthday'. 2nd Battalion, The Gloucestershire Regiment, Shanghai, 1927 (Soldiers of Gloucestershire Museum)

Figure 8.7
'The Devil's Tattoo', Shanghai Race Course, 1927 (Soldiers of Gloucestershire Museum)

Well over 10,000 people attended each performance at the Shanghai Tattoo,[70] whose programme included music that would not have been out of place at one of the popular 'Searchlight Tattoos' that were being performed in Britain at the time. The repertoire for the tattoo included Tchaikovsky's 'Overture 1812', 'Evening Hymn', the 'Last Post' and 'God Bless the Prince of Wales',[71] which even in Britain was considered 'propaganda at its most potent and beguiling'.[72]

The anti-British Chinese element throughout Shanghai had no choice but to be bystanders to the display of apparent imperial might.[73] This was as much a statement of authority by the British as a practical musical event, and the Gloucesters' war diary further confirms the effect of the mission on the Chinese, who were found to be distributing 'seditious' material.[74] Advertisements in the local Chinese press urged Chinese not to attend as, they claimed, British soldiers had not been paid and the tattoo was a way of raising money for the soldiers who were said to be 'oppressing our people'.[75] The event had become known among Chinese communists as the 'Devils Tattoo' and they tried to counteract it by publishing their own propaganda:

> The Shanghai Tattoo is not intended as a birthday compliment to his B---.[sic] Majesty. In reality it is a vulgar, arrogant, provocative display of pride and force on the part of the local authorities and British militarists. In their ignorant fear and rage they hope thereby to intimidate the Chinese into the continued acceptance of British Imperialism. Like a cat hunching its back when confronted by an enemy; trying to make itself look more ferocious and powerful than it really is; the Shanghai die-hards and British military braves have arranged this Tattoo so as to strike fear

---

[70] TNA WO/191/4, 'Shanghai Defence Force and HQ North China Command, General Staff, 1927 June, War Diary, June 3rd'.
[71] '2nd Battalion in Shanghai' <http://www.soldiersofglos.com/1927/05/19/2nd-battalion-in-shanghai/> [accessed 29th November 2017].
[72] Richards, *Imperialism and Music*, p. 245.
[73] Simon Frith, 'Music and Everyday Life', in Martin Clayton, Trevor Herbert and Richard Middleton (eds), *The Cultural Study of Music: A Critical Introduction*, 2nd ed. (Abingdon: Routledge, 2012), p. 151.
[74] TNA WO/191/33, '4 6 27 In the Field'.
[75] TNA WO/191/4, 'Daily Intelligence Report No. 18, 7.6.27'.

and terror, by a display of men and munitions, into the hearts of Chinese workers and nationalists.[76]

The response among the local Chinese population in the aftermath of the both the King's Birthday Parade and the tattoo was varied, with the Political Department of the Nationalist Army on the Eastern Front deciding to set up their own celebrations of nationalist victories with music, dances, boxing and theatrical performances 'doubtless inspired by the [British] military pageants'.[77] For example, on 11 June the Chinese military band played 'God Save the King' followed by 'Rule Britannia' at the Chinese racecourse at Yanglepoo. As noted by the daily intelligence report for 13 June 1927, 'the playing of these tunes synchronised with the arrival of an officer of Shaforce at the meeting.'[78] Given that this was indeed a political reaction to the King's Birthday Parade, the author of this report demonstrated his misunderstanding of the situation in his further assessment that 'the incident is not believed to have any political significance, the Chinese band probably imagined they were playing ordinary rag-time'.

The tattoo performed by the British military bands is a clear instance of military music being used in a soft power influencing role in support of the hard power provided by additional troops. Their performances were designed to bolster the confidence of the British of the Shanghai International Settlement, with the Chinese responding by putting on their own cultural events. The Chinese efforts to put on shows, however, only demonstrated their limited capability and the show of strength by the British was enough to stop any serious attacks on the settlement. Influence was achieved with a soft power mission effect by averting hard power conflict with a proxy resource. After this successful action, British army bands continued to accompany regiments to Shanghai and maintained a high profile presence.[79]

Southern Africa 1931

Soft power influence by a band without other military resources, and purely for diplomatic purposes, was that which made front-page news

---

[76] Quoted in '2nd Battalion in Shanghai' <http://www.soldiersofglos.com/1927/05/19/2nd-battalion-in-shanghai/> [accessed 29th November 2017].
[77] TNA WO/191/4, 'Daily Intelligence Report No. 19, 6-7-27'.
[78] TNA WO/191/4, 'Daily Intelligence Report No. 22, 13.6.27'.
[79] See for example, J. C. Kemp, *The History of the Royal Scots Fusiliers: 1919-1959* (Glasgow: Robert MacLehose & Co/Glasgow University Press, 1963), p. 14.

in January 1931, when the Band of the Grenadier Guards embarked on what was to be a highly successful tour of Southern Africa, including the Union of South Africa and the colony of Southern Rhodesia. Bands had toured overseas before and represented Britain at several exhibitions and festivals – the Band of the 2nd Battalion Argyll and Sutherland Highlanders led by Bandmaster Ricketts (composer of the march 'Colonel Bogey'), for instance, had performed for the New Zealand and South Seas Exhibition held at Dunedin between November 1925 and May 1926, and played twice daily to the more than 3 million visitors who attended the event.[80] Furthermore, the Band of the Coldstream Guards had visited Canada in 1926 and made a great impression.[81] Even so, the Grenadier Guards Band tour had extra significance for the two countries visited.

With respect to South Africa, the tour came less than five years after the Balfour Declaration of 1926, which gave dominions autonomy over legislation, and only months before the Statute of Westminster was passed in Britain, as a result of which the British monarch remained as head of state, but all laws thereafter were passed internally. Furthermore, the Second Boer War had ended only thirty years before and by the late 1920s Afrikaner and Anglophile relations in South Africa had become strained again. Afrikaner nationalism was on the rise as the Afrikaners became more powerful, and as a result there were changes in the relationship with Britain and British interests, which manifested themselves in different ways. For example, in South Africa the 1927 Nationality and Flag Act dropped 'God Save the King' as the national anthem.

Southern Rhodesia, meanwhile, had rejected a union with South Africa in a 1922 referendum, only becoming a British colony in 1923 after the non-renewal of the British South Africa Company's Charter by the British government, and in 1930 the Land Apportionment Act codified racial division of land in Southern Rhodesia. The whole region, therefore, was potentially problematic for Britain in political terms, for different reasons: South Africa was an important ally to keep as a dominion and Southern Rhodesia needed propping up as a new colonial administration. The 1931 Grenadier Guards Band tour

---

[80] J. Trendell, *Colonel Bogey to the Fore: A Biography of Kenneth J. Alford* (Dover: Blue Band, 1991), pp. 44–45.
[81] J. Gleeson, *Pomp and Circumstance: The Band of the Coldstream Guards, A History 1685-2017*, 2nd edn (London: Regimental Headquarters Coldstream Guards, 2018), pp. 169-173.

to South Africa and Southern Rhodesia was a significant factor in addressing these challenges for the maintenance of British interests.[82]

As a brand, the Grenadier Guards epitomised Britishness to all those with British connections living abroad. Apart from the image they presented, the sound of the band would have been like nothing the African public had heard before: the Grenadier Guards Band under George Miller was one of the best professional bands in Britain, it had a fantastic reputation and the local Southern African bands would have not rivalled it in terms of sound and technical ability. There had been no previous visit to Southern Africa by such an accomplished band and the impact of the music must not be underestimated, as was witnessed in the example of the 'Native Musicians' from the Northern Rhodesia Police Band at Livingstone who were impressed by the standard of performance.[83]

The uniforms were particularly noticed by the local press and widely reported upon, such as on the front page of the *Natal Witness* (Fig. 8.8):

> The Grenadier Guards Arrive in Maritzburg; Wild Scenes of Welcome; "Big Hats Made of Black Fluff"; Military Memories Reawakened; City Goes Mad with Delight.[84]

This emphasises the point that the British brand was not just about the music but the visual symbol of scarlet and bearskin. The iconography of the scarlet jackets and bearskins in particular is evident in the Southern African press with great significance placed upon the link with London:

---

[82] 'Diary of Captain George Miller, 1931', Museum of Army Music, Kneller Hall, A.3.1 Item 1026.491A GREN GDS.
[83] *Bulawayo Chronicle*, 'Grenadier Guards Band Tour a Real Triumph; British Sentiment Revived by Sight of the Red Coats; Patriotic Fervour Awakened in Southern Rhodesia', 30 March 1931. The high standard of the band can be heard on a re-issue of recordings from the period on the following CD: The Band of the Grenadier Guards, *Historic Grenadiers: Britain's Oldest Military Band* (recorded 1926–40), Lieutenant Colonel George John Miller (Beulah, 2008).
[84] *Natal Witness*, 4 March 1931.

As the Guards swung round into Gardiner Street a roar rose from the 20,000 men, women and children. The scene was a glimpse of London set in Durban sunshine.[85]

The text is typical of the reporting throughout South Africa and highlights the importance of the band's presence and what it represented:

The King's Band arrived in Maritzburg yesterday, and was given an uproarious welcome. With their vivid scarlet uniforms, faced with gold braid, the bandsmen were an imposing sight as they marched down Church Street to the City Hall playing "Some Talk of Alexander." All the way from the station to the City Hall the route was lined with thousands of people. Flags were flying on most business premises.[86]

Figure 8.8
'The Grenadier Guards Arrive in Maritzburg; Wild Scenes of Welcome; "Big Hats Made of Black Fluff"; Military Memories Reawakened; Thousands See Pride of Britain'. The Natal Witness, Pietermaritzburg, Wednesday, March 4, 1931 (George Miller Diary, MAM)

Furthermore, newspapers reported concerts attended by 30,000 people in the Afrikaner strongholds of Johannesburg and Bloemfontein, with crowds bigger than that for Test matches at the Wanderers cricket ground.[87]

---

[85] *Natal Mercury*, 'Durban Looks Like London; Huge Crowd Sees Guards March; Cheers Drown the Band; 30,000 Admirers; Cars Abandoned in Mid-Street', 6 March 1931.
[86] *Ibid*.
[87] Rand Daily Mail, 2 March 1931.

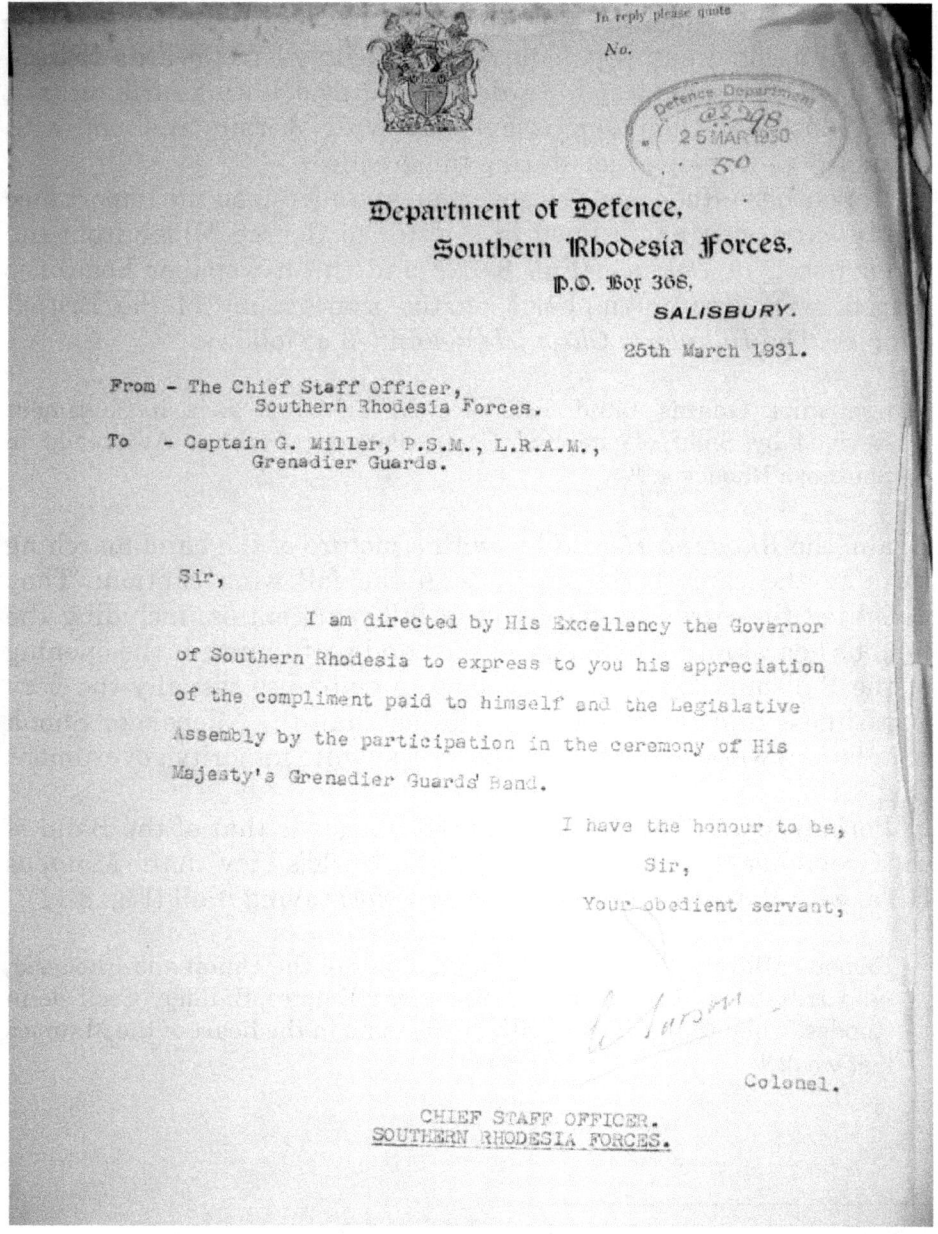

Figure 8.9
The Grenadier Guards Band tour was appreciated at the highest levels of the Southern Rhodesian government (George Miller Diary, MAM)

Pathé newsreels of the time show the sheer scale of the size of the surging crowds when the band marched through the streets in Cape Town and Johannesburg. This wave of patriotism towards Britain may have gone some way towards persuading doubting Afrikaners in the 1930s that their sympathies lay with Britain and not with Germany as it re-emerged during the decade.[88]

In Southern Rhodesia, the government understood the importance of the band visit as outlined in a letter to George Miller from the Department of Defence (Fig. 8.9),[89] and the newspaper headlines placed even greater emphasis on the iconography of the British Empire. The *Bulawayo Chronicle* headlined as follows:

> Grenadier Guards Band Tour a Real Triumph; British Sentiment Revived by Sight of the Red Coats; Patriotic Fervour Awakened in Southern Rhodesia.[90]

Again, the *Rhodesia Herald* led with a picture of the band marching through the capital, Salisbury, with the following caption: 'They delighted the crowd by parading in full regimentals, including the famous bearskin.'[91] The image of the band performing at the opening of the Salisbury Parliament seemed to epitomise visually the very Britishness that the Rhodesians (rather than the Ndebele or Shona population) were so keen to promote as a white minority government (Fig 8.10).

Perhaps one of the most important images is that of the Band of the Grenadier Guards performing at the World's View in the Matopos Hills, with the caption from the *Cape Times* saying it all (Fig. 8.11):

> Famous Military Band, at present on a tour of the Union and Rhodesia, paid tribute to the memory of the great Empire Builder, Cecil John Rhodes, when they laid a wreath on his tomb in the heart of the Matopos last week.[92]

---

[88] Several Pathé newsreels cover the tour, for example:
<http://www.britishpathe.com/video/band-of-his-majestys-grenadier-guards/query/Grenadier+Guards+South+Africa> [accessed 10th September 2013].
[89] The date stamp has the incorrect year, it should read the same as the letter (1931).
[90] *Bulawayo Chronicle*, 30 March 1931.
[91] *Rhodesia Herald*, 24 March 1931.
[92] *Cape Times*, 7 April 1931.

Figure 8.10
'"Stand at Ease." – The guard of honour outside Cecil Square, Salisbury, while awaiting the arrival of the Governor to open the Parliament of Southern Rhodesia last month. The band of the Grenadier Guards, who were touring Rhodesia at the time, are seen providing a programme of music suitable to the occasion.' Cape Times, Thursday, April 9, 1931 (George Miller Diary, MAM)

In this case, the military band clearly created a strong sense of the power of the British brand, deployed as an influencing tool on behalf of British interests that were very important at the time.

The first full-time military band in South Africa had been the Band of the South African Police, raised in 1913, at the same time as the police force, but it was perhaps the impact of the Grenadier Guards Band tour that galvanised the Union Defence Force into the raising of the first Permanent Force Band in 1934.[93]

Exploring issues in the sixth supplementary research theme (military music in marketing, propaganda, and diplomacy, at home and abroad), through factors in the political and sociological domains, has uncovered how British army bands participated in, and influenced, various military and diplomatic episodes through direct involvement, and also as a reputational asset and symbol of power.

---

[93] J. M. M. Imrie, *The Military Band in South Africa* (Simonstown: The South African Navy Printing Press, 1976), pp. 49 & 65.

Figure 8.11
'Grenadier Guards at the "World's View." Famous Military Band, at present on a tour of the Union and Rhodesia, paod tribute to the memory of the great Empire Builder, Cecil John Rhodes, when they laid a wreath on his tomb in the heart of the Matopos last week'. Cape Times, Tuesday, April 7, 1931 (George Miller Diary, MAM)

The case studies in this chapter have revealed how the bands made a significant contribution to British authority and influence, by brand association, in three different administrations of the Empire, at a time of reduced hard-power capability. With the Grenadier Guards Band's tour of Southern Africa in 1931, the brand of a military band 'punched above its weight' and was a major conduit for expressions of Britishness. Furthermore, the brash exhibition of power in Shanghai in 1927 with the staging of a full British military tattoo was a statement of strength over the maintenance of territorial integrity as the Chinese waged war with one another nearby. In India, the bands were an integral part of the administration and function of the establishment which was a symbol of continued British dominance. Through soft power, military bands were effective in portraying Britishness as a reputational asset, enabling the army to achieve disproportionate influence with limited resources.

CHAPTER 9

THE YOUGHAL 'OUTRAGE':
POLITICAL APPROPRIATION OF MILITARY BANDS AND THE
FOUNDING OF THE IRISH FREE STATE

In Ireland, since at least the early twentieth century, military and military-style bands and their music have been important tools in political strategies by contributing to the different cultural associations of the nationalist, republican, and loyalist communities. The study of military bands in Ireland in the interwar period is inextricably linked to the political complexities of the time as music was used to underpin political motives by all sides leading up to Irish independence and beyond. Musical ensembles of some description have frequently been associated with military formations, whether serving Crown forces,[1] or connected to paramilitary nationalist, republican, and loyalist groups. In the interwar period the recurrent strategic use of military music was so strong that it could be recognised as having significant political associations with each group.

The main catalyst for changes in attitudes towards military music in Ireland was the Anglo-Irish war (or Irish War of Independence) in 1919-21 as this phase saw the balance of power shift from a British influenced form of government to that of a partitioned island with an administration in the south being independent and Irish-led, and that in the north continuing to be a Westminster satellite. This episode in particular has shown to be highly emotive and partisan for authors, with analysis of the state of affairs in interwar Ireland being fraught with difficulties due to biased interpretations. Furthermore, the only official British army account, the *Record of the Rebellion in Ireland in 1920-21 and the Part Played by the Army in Dealing with*

---

[1] 'Crown forces' is the term used to refer to police and military forces, both British and Irish, stationed in Ireland. The United Kingdom up until 1921 comprised Great Britain (England, Scotland and Wales) and Ireland and so it would be incorrect to refer to them as 'British forces'. For example, the Royal Irish Constabulary was exclusively Irish until the recruitment of the Auxiliary Division and the 'Black and Tans'.

it, had been withheld from publication for many years,[2] and the published study that would most likely have analysed the Anglo-Irish War from the British army's point of view, Major-General Sir Charles Gwynn's *Imperial Policing*, only gives passing reference to the conflict.[3]

Accordingly, when assessing the impact of events there needs to be careful consideration of what Sheehan calls the 'distorted and fragmented view of the campaign' due to an absence of a British perspective, largely because of reliance by populist and academic writers upon uncorroborated personal memoirs.[4] Sheehan's view is not without its critics, however, who consider it a revisionist approach to a well-trodden and accepted understanding of the conflict, but his analysis has highlighted an imbalance in the presentation of subject matter as well as contradictory versions of events.[5]

In the context of the sixth research theme (military music in marketing, propaganda, and diplomacy, at home and abroad), and placed in the political and sociological domains of the far external environment, this chapter seeks to identify the extent that military music was appropriated for political purposes by all sides and establish how this was used during the conflict and subsequent partition of Ireland. The issue of the targeting of military bands is analysed to determine the significance of military music in Ireland by the British state, the unofficial Irish republican regime that ran in parallel to it, and in the emerging strategic use of army bands by the fledgling Irish Free State that created a distinct Irish military band sound.

The context of music appropriation

The 1801 Union of Great Britain and Ireland was not welcomed by all and there have been violent disturbances in Ireland for centuries. The political appropriation of music was not new in the twentieth century and the symbolism of British uniforms in Ireland, coupled with associated sectarian lyrics, applied to various, often shared

---

[2] TNA WO 141/93, *Record of the Rebellion in Ireland in 1920-21 and the Part Played by the Army in Dealing with it*. This document was originally marked 'Closed until 2022' but was released by the Public Record Office in May 2001.
[3] C. W. Gwynn, *Imperial Policing*, 2nd edn (London: Macmillan, 1939), pp. 8-9.
[4] W. Sheehan, *A Hard Local War: The British Army and the Guerrilla War in Cork, 1919-1921* (Stroud: The History Press, 2011), p. 169.
[5] See for example, 'The Myth of Crossbarry' in Sheehan, *A Hard Local War*, pp. 146-151.

tunes, had evoked reactions throughout the nineteenth century. As agents of the government, British military bands have had political associations with the British identity in Ireland, provoking positive or negative reactions depending upon the nature of the audience, and how strongly groups related to their particular cultural identity. When reviewing the Anglo-Irish war, commentators have recognised that, like the examples given above, psychological factors in Ireland were just as important as 'the shooting',[6] and with their political associations bands in Ireland have been very much a part of this psychological war. The political use of bands in Ireland was not without precedence but the appropriation of music for political purposes in twentieth-century Ireland was important because it brought music into the sphere of military doctrine as a deliberate influencing tool by the Free State government.

This deployment of music in the service of political allegiance in Ireland has re-emerged as a prominent tool in the later twentieth- and early twenty-first century in Ulster,[7] but its roots can be found in the amateur bands and church choirs that were common forms of communal music making in both rural and urban Ireland, and finding themselves at the centre of political controversy depending on with which cultural they identified.[8] For example, in the 1890s there were brass and reed bands with the Catholic Boys' Brigade in Dublin, and bands were also a part of the Gaelic League processions, particularly associated with the trades unions.[9] Republican activists have also used music to support dissent, as witnessed in 1893 by Robert John Buckley, an Englishman travelling in Ireland, who noted that there was 'not a murderer in Ireland whose release would not be celebrated with the blare of brass bands'.[10]

---

[6] W. H. Kautt, *The Anglo-Irish War, 1916-1921: A People's War* (Westport, CT: Praeger, 1999), p. 31.
[7] See, for example, K. Radford, 'Drum Rolls and Gender Roles in Protestant Marching Bands in Belfast', *British Journal of Ethnomusicology*, Vol 10:2, 2001, p. 38 (pp. 37-59); D. MacDonald, *Blood & Thunder: Inside An Ulster Protestant Band* (Cork: Mercier Press, 2010), p. 9.
[8] R. Johnston, 'Music in Northern Ireland since 1921', in J. R. Hill (ed), *A New History of Ireland: Ireland 1921-84: Volume 7* (Oxford: Oxford University Press, 2003), p. 651.
[9] IMA, BMH, WS 889, pp. 12 & 26, Seamus Ua Caomhanaigh.
[10] Quoted in D. B. Scott, 'Irish Nationalism, British Imperialism and the Role of Popular Music', in P. Fairclough (ed.) *Twentieth-Century Music and Politics: Essays in Memory of Neil Edmonds* (Farnham: Ashgate, 2013), p. 240. It is just possible

In pre-conflict times there was a sense of normality for most British army musicians who, on the whole, could mix with the local communities when their services were required. Lance Sergeant Pullinger of the 2nd Battalion, The Manchester Regiment recounts how, when stationed at The Curragh, County Kildare, he was performing at the local Picture House for two shows each evening and earning 5/- a night.[11] But during the First World War the issue of allegiance became prominent and was exacerbated after the partition of 1922. This allegiance to a cultural identity through music had greater impact in Ireland than in other parts of the British Isles because it was an area of conflict where the associated music provoked stark and entrenched views across political fault-lines, with music acting as an *agent provocateur* of the conflict that was to come to a head in 1919-21.[12]

The use of music to emphasise political events appears in Ireland to have been fairly widespread, with some writers even supporting the notion that it was the use of sectarian music that stimulated the political thought in the first place.[13] There is also the suggestion that the musicians themselves were at fault, having 'fallen foul of the divided tradition; extreme positions have been adopted and few have attempted the necessary reconciliation.'[14]

The conflict environment

It is incredibly difficult to estimate the number of British troops in Ireland after the First World War because although the British army was declared to be on 'active' service in Ireland from 1919-21, battalions worked on a 'home' or 'peacetime' footing and continued to provide troops for service overseas, with the strength of a battalion

---

that Buckley was referring to a group of Catholic MPs at Westminster known as 'The Pope's Brass Band', but unlikely in this context.

[11] A. Pullinger, *Reminiscences* (Museum of Army Music, Kneller Hall: MS, 1939), p. 62.
[12] M. J. Grant, R. Möllemann, I. Morlandstö, S. C Münz, and C. Noxoll, 'Music and Conflict: Interdisciplinary Perspectives', *Interdisciplinary Science Reviews*, 35: 2, June, 2010, p. 189.
[13] H. White, 'Nationalism, Colonialism and the Cultural Stasis of Music in Ireland', in White, H. and Murphy, M. (eds.), *Musical Constructions of Nationalism: Essays on the History of European Musical Culture 1800-1945* (Cork: Cork University Press, 2001), p. 258.
[14] J. Ryan, 'The Tone of Defiance', in White, H. and Murphy, M. (eds.), *Musical Constructions of Nationalism: Essays on the History of European Musical Culture 1800-1945* (Cork: Cork University Press, 2001), p. 207.

usually greatly reduced. The military historian, Michael Carver, states that in November 1919 the British army's strength in Ireland was 37,259, with thirty-four infantry battalions, and the three military districts reorganised into two divisions: the 5th at The Curragh encompassing brigades in Dublin and Belfast, and the 6th at Cork. By the end of 1920 Carver suggests that there were 50,000 British troops in Ireland, as well as 10,000 police, comprising the Crown forces.[15] These figures must be taken with caution, though, as battalions were often substantially understrength and the actual number of troops on the ground would have been considerably fewer than the establishment figures. Even as late as December 1920 British army bands were often the only part of a battalion that was consistently stationed in Ireland, and for regiments in the 5th Division area it was 'no exaggeration to state that for short periods, a battalion would consist of its headquarters and the band',[16] with the band being the most high profile aspect of the British army in many areas.

For the Irish Republican Army (IRA) and other revolutionary forces it is even more difficult to establish numbers involved, but perhaps the most reliable figure that should be accepted is from the number of short service military pensions awarded in 1924 to Irish revolutionary veterans by the Free State government: 18,186.[17]

Not all of Ireland was in a continual state of flux and there were areas of the 5th Division that saw hardly any violence. On the other hand, the 6th Division around Cork was very active throughout the conflict and continued to be so during the Civil War. Relations between the British army and local communities varied around the country depending upon the activities of the IRA, the will of the local population to support revolutionary forces, the reputation of the Royal Irish Constabulary (RIC) or Dublin Metropolitan Police (DMP), and the behaviour of the local army units. The dynamics of local relations could change overnight with the handover/takeover of an army battalion and the drive and focus of different personalities – while British army strategy was devised at a higher level, the local

---

[15] R. M. P. Carver, *Britain's Army in the Twentieth Century* (London: Pan, 1999), pp. 138-9. The police comprised Royal Irish Constabulary (RIC) who were all locally-recruited Irish, RIC Temporary Constables ('Black and Tans') who were both British and Irish recruited, and the Auxiliary Division RIC (ADRIC) who were mainly British ex-officers.
[16] W. Sheehan, *Hearts & Mines: The British 5th Division, Ireland, 1920-1922* (Cork: The Collins Press, 2009), p. 6.
[17] M Coleman, 'Military Service Pensions for Veterans of the Irish Revolution, 1916-1923', *War in History*, 20(2), 2013, pp. 202-203 (pp. 201-221).

commander's tactics could vary considerably from barracks to barracks and also over time. It would have been difficult for any part of the Irish population to be disinterested because of the polarity of political standpoints, but it must be considered that the majority of the populace did not want a conflict and that most members of the British army stationed in Ireland, waiting to be de-mobbed after the First World War, were of the same view. In this environment, the British army battalion bands worked to entertain the troops and engage with the local community. There were, however, some issues that could inflame a situation. One was the National Anthem.

The National Anthem

Perhaps the musical example that most polarised political opinion in Ireland was the National Anthem of the United Kingdom of Great Britain and Ireland. Performances in Ireland have always been contentious and there are several historical accounts that underline the precarious position of bands when playing this politically sensitive music and words. In July 1809, the Anglo-Welsh porcelain manufacturer and naturalist, Lewis Dillwyn, noted several political events in his diary when travelling around Ireland with one entry describing how the Cork Militia band had been pelted by a mob while playing *God Save the King*; they were only saved after troops made a bayonet charge at the mob and, as a punishment to the locals, the Colonel of the regiment ordered that the National Anthem be performed every evening along with the loyalist anti-rebel tune, *Croppies Lie Down*.[18]

This was a recurring theme and in the 1870s Bandmaster J. Sidney Jones of the 5th Dragoon Guards was warned that he should not close public concerts in Dublin with *God Save the Queen*, but he ignored the advice:

> The climax was a scene to remember, loyal ladies waving their handkerchiefs, gentlemen their hats, and the party styling themselves Irish Nationalists hooting.[19]

---

[18] Lewis Dillwyn's Visit to Kerry, 1809, <http://www.ucc.ie/celt/published/E800005-001.html> [accessed 8th September 2014].
[19] Quoted in K. Young, *Music's Great Days in the Spas and Watering-Places* (London: Macmillan, 1968), p. 46.

Later in the century, Mr Le Grove, Bandmaster of the 1st Battalion the King's Own Yorkshire Light Infantry, recalled how unwelcome the National Anthem was in one part of Belfast in the 1890s:

> One afternoon we were engaged to play at the Horticultural Society's Gardens; after finishing my programme, I played the Regimental March and the National Anthem as usual. As soon as I had done so, one of the Committee rushed up on to the Band Stand and demanded to know what I meant by playing "that tune", viz, "God Save The Queen", I replied that we were Her Majesty's Regiment and always did so. He replied "You have no right to do so here."[20]

Another account by Lieutenant Mackenzie-Rogan from 1907 with the Band of the Coldstream Guards at the Irish National Exhibition in Dublin further highlights the issue. Mackenzie-Rogan had served in Ireland on several occasions and was acutely aware of the Nationalist feelings of his audiences:

> I spoke a few words of thanks which seemed to touch the crowd, not omitting to say how gratifying it would be to my Colonel and the officers of the regiment to hear of our splendid reception, and winding up by announcing that my band, together with that of the 15th Canadian Light Cavalry, would play "God Save the King."
> "If you will *all* join in and sing it," I added, "the effect will be one which I certainly never forget!"
> That might be seemed a hazardous request to make in Dublin, but I believed in the power of music to awaken the better impulses of the human heart and therefore I was not amazed – as many frankly were – when the ten or fifteen thousand people assembled round us sang the National Anthem so heartily that the two bands were almost drowned by the chorus of voices…a City Councillor rushed up to me: "Oh, Mister Rogan," he exclaimed, "d'ye know what y've been after doing! Ye've had me, a Nationalist, singing 'God Save the King!'"
> "Well," I said, "I hope you don't regret it."
> "No, bedad," he answered, "I'd sing it again under the same circumstances."[21]

Mackenzie-Rogan is not a modest writer and this particular account cannot be corroborated – his stories tend to be unabashedly

---

[20] Quoted in W. K. Grainger, *The Life and Times of a Regimental Band: A History of the Bands of the King's Own Yorkshire Light Infantry*. The Rifles Office, Pontefract, 1995, MS, pp.12-13.
[21] J. Mackenzie-Rogan, *Fifty Years of Army Music* (London: Methuen, 1926), p. 165-6.

self-aggrandising – but it may well have been the case that the power of the musical performance encouraged the Irish Nationalists to join in with the anthem of the (to them) occupying power.

Even after the 1922-3 civil war when Free State bands took on the role of performing the Irish National Anthem there were incidences that had political fallout. One case was when Free State military bands did not perform for the Crown representative, the Governor-General, on several occasions, on the apparent orders of the President of the Executive Council, Éamon de Valera.[22]

Disputes over the National Anthem were particularly significant because of the connection with the military bands, who were obliged to play it, and the associated symbolism of the words and music. It was not a single issue though, as it permeated the whole subject of identity, especially problematic for the army when it needed to recruit soldiers from Ireland.

Recruiting for the British army

Uncoordinated attempts at using bands for recruiting Irish National Volunteers to the British army had initially not been successful, but a synchronised campaign in 1915 led by an advertising expert, Hedley Le Bas, proved very effective. Hedley Le Bas was engaged by the government to market the recruiting campaign for the war and, using the latest marketing techniques, was the driving force behind the famous recruiting poster of Kitchener announcing 'Your King and Country need you'. He was despatched to Ireland in 1915 and began work focusing on specific Irish topics for recruiting, such as replacing 'God Save the King' with 'God Save Ireland' on posters.[23] The campaign was particularly effective in Waterford chiefly because, outside of Ulster, Waterford was the most pro-British (or the least anti-British) city during the First World War, due partly to its economy based upon the army and munitions industries.[24]

---

[22] R. Sherry, 'The Story of the National Anthem', in *History Ireland*, Vol. 4, Issue 1, Spring 1996, <http://www.historyireland.com/20th-century-contemporary-history/the-story-of-the-national-anthem/> [accessed 8th September 2014]. See also G. K. Chesterton, 'Our Note Book', *Illustrated London News*, Issue 4869, Saturday, 13 August 1932, p. 224.

[23] N. Hiley, 'Sir Hedley Le Bas and the Origins of Domestic Propaganda in Britain 1914-1917', *European Journal of Marketing*, Vol. 21, Issue 8, pp. 37-8.

[24] M. Laffan, *The Resurrection of Ireland: The Sinn Féin Party, 1916-1923* (Cambridge: Cambridge University Press, 2004), p. 125. Although this is quite a simplification of the political conditions in Waterford, as there were many local factors affecting loyalties, it is nonetheless broadly accurate.

The Irish nationalist Member of Parliament, John Redmond, had galvanised many of the National Volunteers to join the British army but there was still a significant number of doubters and detractors, particularly those who had broken away to become the Irish Volunteers. Hedley Le Bas, who had served as a Private soldier in Waterford with the 15th Hussars in the 1880s, saw the opportunity to target Waterford for a recruiting campaign and brought together various assets to maximise the effect. Music and bands were important in Waterford public life and the regular band of the 3rd Battalion, The Royal Irish Regiment, was engaged to perform at organised events as a deliberate attempt to entice locals. They paraded through the town each morning and performed concerts in the evenings, and on Sundays, after church parades at both the Roman Catholic cathedral and St Olaf's Protestant church, the band performed near the recruiting office to draw large crowds where it was noted that the band's rendition of a selection of Irish airs was particularly fine.[25] The Royal Hibernian Military School band also played a role in the 1915 recruiting drive, leading parades and performing displays at Warrenpoint, Co. Down, and Kingston (Dun Laoghaire).[26]

This deliberate use of bands by Hedley Le Bas to entice hesitant recruits was especially successful in Waterford because he focused the advertisements on Irish sympathies while the band played Irish music. The Band of the 5th Lancers and the London-based Irish Guards band paraded in Waterford, complete with wolfhound, 'playing ragtime ditties such as "Robert E. Lee" in an effort to attract recruits',[27] but once Hedley Le Bas returned to London his successors in Ireland lacked his command of marketing techniques and although recruiting remained satisfactory with the band of the 4th Battalion Leinster Regiment, by 1917 in Cork there was a serious disturbance at a recruiting meeting where an army band was performing on the Grand Parade and, along with the recruiting team, were pelted with missiles of all types including 'rotten fruit and vegetables and even aging bones from the nearby market'.[28]

---

[25] T. P. Dooley, 'Politics, bands and marketing: army recruitment in Waterford city, 1914-15', *The Irish Sword*, XVIII (1990-1992), pp. 212-214.
[26] H. R. Clarke, *A New History of the Royal Hibernian Military School Phoenix Park, Dublin: 1765-1924* (Wynd Yarm, Cleveland: Howard R. Clarke, 2011), p. 458.
[27] IMA, BMH, WS 1709, pp. 2-4, Michael F. Ryan
[28] IMA, BMH, WS 1741, p. 25, Michael V. O'Donoghue.

Band identity and political allegiance

Any organisation that identified with the bands of the British army would be clearly associated with British authority and this was certainly the case for the two police forces in Ireland. A photograph owned by the Band of the Irish Guards shows the Bands of the Irish Guards, Royal Irish Constabulary, and Dublin Metropolitan Police parading together in Dublin for a recruiting campaign in 1915,[29] and the association of the two Irish police forces for the recruiting of soldiers for the British army would not have been lost on the public. The police were evidently on the side of the Crown forces, with the bands representing their various organisations and signifying their allegiance.

It was not just the police that identified with British forces, but some local civilians through their local bands. For example, when a popular Signals unit were leaving Waterford 'they were played out by the local Barrack Street Brass and Reed Band'.[30] The Cork Barrack Street Band had cordial relations with the local British army bands stationed at Elizabeth Fort and its high musical standard was almost certainly due to the training and guidance provided by the military bandsmen based there.[31] This was not unexpected as the population as a whole had yet to be galvanised towards radical forms of Nationalism, but there were indications that loyalties were changing as civilian bands in Waterford were showing signs of shifts in allegiance in just four years, away from the Crown forces towards the IRA, as by 1919 the Barrack Street Band was parading with the pro-treaty IRA. But even this allegiance was short-lived as the band soon divided between supporters of pro and anti-treaty IRA forces.[32]

A number of civilian bands had already been actively supporting the nationalist cause during World War One, identified by parading with the Irish tricolour flag, causing quite a stir in Kerry and Cork in 1917 and 1918, with up to ten bands at a time attending Nationalist meetings. The Millstreet All-for-Ireland Brass and Reed Band had been operating as a Nationalist band since at least 1914, and as the

---

[29] Irish Guards Band Archive. No reference number. Observed 10th July 2014.
[30] IMA, BMH, WS 1709, pp. 2-4, Michael F. Ryan.
[31] Cork Barrack Street Band, History, <http://corkbarrackstreetband.org/?page_id=11> [accessed 7th September 2014].
[32] Waterford County Museum, 'The Irish War of Independence 1919-21, <http://www.waterfordmuseum.ie/exhibit/web/Display/article/318/8/The_Irish_War_of_Independence_1919__21_Evacuation_of_the_Barracks.html> [accessed 6th September 2014].

bands were essential components of parades, the band instruments were considered valuable assets and removed from club rooms for safekeeping when necessary, to protect against confiscation or destruction by opponents.[33]

Bands that had identified themselves as Irish Volunteer Bands in 1916 had commissioned bandmasters on their strength, for example the list of officers for the 1st Battalion Limerick City includes Lieutenant T. Glynn as bandmaster. The bands were at the forefront of the rebel parades and were the symbol of republican defiance, but they were not always popular. For example, on 23rd May 1915 a column of Irish Volunteers marched through Limerick but was verbally and physically abused by the population who saw them:

> They had been told that these men had cheered and gloated over every disaster that had befallen the Munsters [Royal Munster Fusiliers] in the war which was then raging, and so, their hearts were filled with bitter hatred of the pro-German Sinn Féiners, as they called the Irish Volunteers.
>
> Leading the parade was their band, with Bandmaster Glynn at the front: Altogether, there were about 1,200 in the parade, which started according to schedule, and as, headed by the band of the Limerick [Irish Volunteers] Regiment, they passed through the streets of the city, they should have inspired the respect, if not the admiration, of the citizens. Yet, and it may be difficult for the present generation to realise the fact, they could not have been regarded with more hatred had they been to a man gaolbirds of the vilest type.[34]

There is further evidence that bandmasters played a large part of the Irish Volunteer structure in Ballinagh where the bandmaster, Charlie Fitzpatrick, was 'active'.[35] Bands were clearly an important symbol for the republican movement in the promotion of its opinions and they continued to use them to influence the public after the First World War, when for example, they were planning the parade for Eamon de Valera's return to Dublin in 1919.[36]

---

[33] J. Lane (ed.), *The 'Boys' of the Millstreat Battalion Area: Some Personal Accounts of the War of Independence* (Aubane, Cork: Aubane Historical Society, 2003), pp. 53-55.
[34] IMA, BMH, WS 1700, pp. 13 & 18, Alphonsus J. O'Halloran.
[35] IMA, BMH, WS 393, p. 2, Seamus S. O'Sullivan.
[36] M. Rast, 'Tactics, Politics, and Propaganda in the Irish War of Independence, 1917-1921' (MA thesis, Georgia State University, 2011), pp. 54-55.

Sinn Féin took over bands in some areas, which caused splits, as some of the musicians supported Redmond's National Volunteers who fought with the British army in World War One. Several of the band members left the Bruff Band when the Roger Casement Sinn Féin Club in Bruff took over the Band and appointed a new bandmaster, John Hogan. It was soon leading the Irish Volunteers on parade:

> The band led our Volunteer Company through Sniff from the bridge to the Courthouse and back and played Chopin's Funeral March. Even then we were able to do the slow march with distinction. As we passed by the police barracks, the RIC, in force, were spectators.[37]

IRA man Patrick Coleman described how he was a member of a National Foresters' brass band that was split over the issue:

> During this period [pre-WW1] I became a member of the National Foresters' Brass Band, of which I was the most junior member. On the resignation of the Bandmaster, Mr Jock Campbell, a Scotsman, I was appointed to take his place, which I did until I was captured by the RIC and Black and Tans in Beckette' Mills in January, 1921...I might mention that the complete body of the Foresters were not agreeable to the use of the Band at Sinn Féin functions; as a matter of fact, when we used the Band for the public reception of Senator Ruane, on his release from Sligo gaol, I had to have a few of my Volunteer comrades smuggle out the instruments. This we did and headed the Volunteer parade to the railway station...We used the Band after the formation of the Irish National Volunteers (Redmond's) until the split when I, with a few others, including Stephen Donnelly, Frank Flynn and Denis Sheeran, broke away and formed a Company of the Irish Volunteers in the Town Hall early in 1917.[38]

Thirty-nine members of the Cork Barrack Street Band had volunteered for active war service in the First World War and after the war the band took part in all annual events:

> such as the St Patrick's Day procession, religious functions, parades, political meetings and demonstrations, the Manchester Martyrs' demonstrations, sports events, boat and train outings, promenades and many more.[39]

---

[37] IMA, BMH, WS 1525, p. 14, James Maloney.
[38] IMA, BMH, WS 1683, pp. 1-5, Patrick Coleman.
[39] Cooke, *Cork's Barrack Street Band*, p. 243.

But the band evidently fragmented as some members left the Barrack Street Band in 1922 and joined the nationalist Band of the 10th Battalion at Portabello Barracks, Dublin.[40]

In the civil war, and shortly after, bands sided with their own communities depending on their affiliations, and they could not be hired to perform for the other political persuasions, with one band even refusing to perform for the Free State President of the Executive Council, William Cosgrave.[41] With bands at the centre of political rifts in Ireland and representing both the nationalist and republican causes they became targets as high-profile symbols of their political allegiance.

Bands as targets

Attacks on the nationalist and republican bands became more frequent as the bands' allegiances shifted. The Waterford Barrack Street Brass and Reed Band was assaulted by the IRA in 1922, when 'several instruments were broken and thrown in the river Suir', probably because the same band had headed the Irish National Volunteers parade in the city in January 1914 and had chosen the wrong side in the civil war.[42]

An article in *The Manchester Guardian* in 1921 reported on physical attacks on nationalist bands, specifically the Tumble Hill Drum and Fife Band, which emphasises their political prominence. The silencing of this nationalist band is significant as the sound of the British military band continued in the town:

> The big bass drum was seized and a bayonet put through its heart...[and now] the only music to be heard on the hill is the military band at practice yonder in Victoria Barracks.[43]

---

[40] *Ibid*, p. 244.
[41] F. M Blake, *The Irish Civil War and what it still means for the Irish people* (London: Information on Ireland, 1986), p. 57.
[42] 'A Brief History of the Barrack Street Concert Band', <http://www.barrackstreetband.com/index.php?contentid=history> [accessed 20th July 2014]; T. P. Dooley, 'Politics, bands and marketing: army recruitment in Waterford city, 1914-15', *The Irish Sword*, XVIII (1990-1992), p. 206.
[43] 'Fury's Drum', *The Manchester Guardian*, 1st July 1921.

Civilian bands that identified themselves with nationalism became targets for Crown forces, particularly as it had been noted that on several occasions Irish pipes had accompanied the IRA in ambushes.[44] It was perhaps unsurprising that in 1919, after exercises by Volunteers, the Patrickswell band, which had marched the Volunteers back to town, was attacked by a squad of soldiers who destroyed their instruments and seized a tricolour flag.[45] In another incident, forty-four members of the St James's Band in Dublin were arrested in May 1921 while they were practicing.[46] There were also several occasions when bands of the Irish National Foresters Benefit Society had their instruments confiscated and damaged by the Auxiliary Division Royal Irish Constabulary (ADRIC). The scale of the destruction to one band, the Foresters band at Longford, is shown in a compensation claim presented to the British Government after the Treaty was signed (Fig 9.1).[47]

In 1920, a Foresters band was targeted in Carrickallen with the ADRIC officer in charge reporting that 'I seized and destroyed the articles as a deterrent and this had a great effect on the inhabitants generally and the IRA activities'.[48] It was also testified that the area around 'Carrickallen Co Leitrim was in a very disturbed state and his [the officer's] action had a distinctly quieting effect'.[49]

---

[44] J. McKenna, *Guerrilla Warfare in the Irish War of Independence, 1919-1921* (Jefferson, NC: McFarland, 2011), pp. 203 & 205.
[45] R. O'Donnell (ed.), *Limerick's Fighting Story 1916-21: Told by the Men Who Made It With a Unique Pictorial record of the Period* (Cork: Mercier Press, 2009), p. 315.
[46] 'Forty-Four Bandsmen Arrested', *The Irish Times*, 17th May 1921.
[47] TNA HO/351/170, 'Band instruments taken by military from Irish National Foresters Benefit Society'. 'R. M. Auxiliary' is a probably an error on the document, it should read R. I. C. Auxiliary
[48] *Ibid.*, 'Band instruments taken by military from Irish National Foresters Benefit Society', note dated 12th February 1924.
[49] *Ibid.*

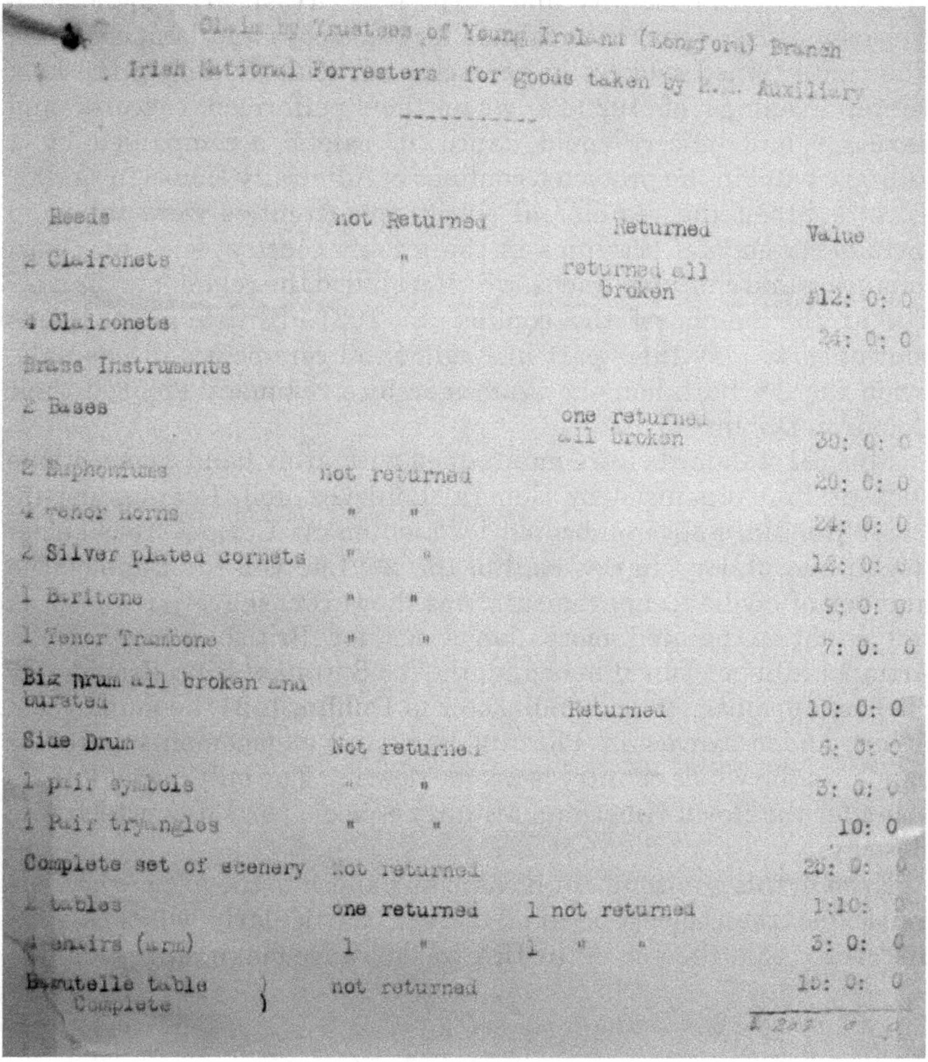

	Claim by Trustees of Young Ireland (Longford) Branch Irish National Forresters for goods taken by R.I.C. Auxiliary		
Reeds	not Returned	Returned	Value
2 Claironets	"	returned all broken	£12: 0: 0
4 Claironets			24: 0: 0
Brass Instruments			
2 Bases		one returned all broken	30: 0: 0
2 Euphoniums	not returned		20: 0: 0
4 Tenor horns	" "		24: 0: 0
2 Silver plated cornets	" "		12: 0: 0
1 Baritone	" "		9: 0: 0
1 Tenor Trombone	" "		7: 0: 0
Big Drum all broken and bursted		Returned	10: 0: 0
Side Drum	Not returned		6: 0: 0
1 pair cymbals	" "		3: 0: 0
1 Pair tryangles	" "		10: 0
Complete set of scenery	not returned		20: 0: 0
2 tables	one returned	1 not returned	1:10: 0
4 chairs (arm)	1 "	1 " "	3: 0: 0
Bagutelle table Complete	not returned		15: 0: 0

Figure 9.1
Irish National Foresters Band (Longford) claim for instruments confiscated by ADRIC during the conflict (TNA)

The Youghal 'outrage'

The fundamental identity and purpose of British army bandsmen was as musicians and entertainers for the troops and local civilians. They entertained soldiers in barracks, particularly during the long winter evenings of 1920-21 when they performed concerts and dances,[50] and officers could dance 'in safety' accompanied by a military band in the protected confines of Admiralty House in Cork.[51] To strengthen the regimental spirit, opportunities were taken to include ceremonial activities in the weekly routine, such as guard mounting and church parades, which included the regimental band.[52] Yet at the height of the conflict, in 1921, British army bands continued to play their part in Regimental ceremony, for example, when the 2nd Battalion the Worcestershire regiment Trooped their Colour in Dublin.[53]

Musical standards were maintained with army band competitions such as that organised by General Lord Grenfell, Commander-in-Chief Ireland, and adjudicated by Lieutenant Colonel Mackenzie-Rogan and Major Charles Hall of the 2nd Life Guards Band.[54] The number of civilian engagements was, however, sharply reduced as the situation became more dangerous for British troops. When Arthur Pullinger joined his band, the 3rd Battalion Rifle Brigade, on his first appointment as bandmaster in Dublin, 1921, he found them living 'under canvas in Phoenix Park…no engagements here for bands, as the whole country is upside down'.[55] The only opportunities being for the Royal Hibernian Military School sports day, which was close by.

Even in this environment it came as a shock to the army when the musicians themselves became targets, particularly when it was discovered that the aim of the IRA was to cause maximum casualties

---

[50] Sheehan, *Hearts & Mines*, p. 275.
[51] W. Sheehan, *British Voices from the Irish War of Independence 1918-1921: The Words of British Servicemen Who Were There* (Cork: The Collins Press, 2007), p. 188.
[52] Sheehan, *Hearts & Mines*, p. 278.
[53] 'Never Shall Thy Glory Fade, 1921', <http://www.britishpathe.com/video/never-shall-their-glory-fade-1/> [accessed 20th May 2014].
[54] Mackenzie-Rogan, *Fifty Years of Army Music*, p. 166.
[55] Pullinger, *Reminiscences*, p. 84.

in its intentional attack on the Band of the 2nd Battalion Hampshire Regiment at Youghal.[56]

It was not uncommon for military bands and other military musical ensembles, such as pipe bands, to march troops to locations in Ireland in full view of the public, even at the height of the conflict, and they did not go unnoticed by the local IRA agitators.[57] Although there were few incidences of anti-personnel mines during the conflict, the IRA's decision to target the Hampshire Regiment band represented one of the most spectacular uses of an anti-personnel improvised explosive device (IED) in what Hart calls 'the bloodiest single ambush of the entire campaign'.[58] There were seven killed and twenty-one injured in a deliberate targeting of the band.

This premeditated targeting of the band, rather than a routine attack on other Crown forces, was the culmination of the harassment of musicians by all sides – republican, nationalist, and Crown forces – but the 'prize' of destroying, or at least immobilising, a band as a particular symbol of British authority by the IRA, raised the stakes, and possibly influenced future military band policy in Ireland. Details of the attack have never been fully investigated and so it is worth examining certain aspects to confirm that the band was indeed the target.

The attack was described in the official accounts of the conflict, the *Historical Records of Rebellion in Ireland 1920-21*:

Hampshire Regiment Band Blown up by a Mine.
A Carefully planned attack on the Hampshire Regiment was carried out on 31st May at Youghal, where a mine in a wall was exploded as they were marching to the range. The full force of the explosion was felt by the band, who had seven killed and 21 wounded. The only sign of the attackers was two men seen running away in the distance, and the wonderful account of the battle written up afterwards by the rebels merely goes to show that they themselves were really ashamed of the tactics which they had been compelled to resort to.[59]

---

[56] W Sheehan, *Hearts & Mines*, p. 4. Reported in *The Irish Times*, Wednesday 1 June 1921, as 'An Appalling Outrage'. Youghal is pronounced 'Yawl'.
[57] IMA, BMH, WS 1367, p. 18, Joseph Aherne.
[58] P. Hart, *The I.R.A. at War 1916-1923* (Oxford: Oxford University Press, 2003), p. 193.
[59] TNA WO 141/93, Record of the Rebellion in Ireland in 1920-21 and the Part Played by the Army in Dealing with it: Volume IV, Part II, 6th Division, p. 194.

This rather short report belies the impact of the event and does little to reveal the circumstances. Although reported at the time,[60] there are several accounts of the attack itself but not all agree on the detail. It is generally accepted, however, that the use of an IED was a new feature of rebel methods.[61] One often quoted version states that the IED was detonated under a lorry in which the band was travelling,[62] but this is incorrect as it is known that the band was marching in front of its regiment to the local rifle range (Fig. 9.2).[63]

Figure 9.2
Band Marching from the Range at Youghal – earlier in May 1921 (The Royal Hampshire Regiment Museum)

---

[60] For example, *The Manchester Guardian*, 1 June 1921, 'Military Band Blown Up in Ireland: Six Soldiers Killed and Twenty-One Wounded'.
[61] TNA WO 141/93, Record of the Rebellion in Ireland in 1920-21 and the Part Played by the Army in Dealing with it: Volume I, Operations, Chapter VI, p. 42; see also T. O'Reilly, *Rebel Heart: George Lennon: Flying Column Commander* (Cork: Mercier Press, 2009), p.149.; W. H. Kautt, *Ambushes and Armour: The Irish Rebellion 1919-1921* (Sallins, Co. Kildare: Irish Academic Press, 2010), p. 178.
[62] See for example <http://irishmedals.org/british-soldiers-kia.html> [accessed 10th July 2014].
[63] Sgts' Mess scrapbook, n. p.

The rebel accounts referred to in the *Historical Records* cannot be traced but there are two known witness versions of the incident and its aftermath, but both were written sometime afterwards. Vice Admiral H. T. Baillie Grohman, then a younger officer in the Royal Navy serving aboard the minesweeper HMS Truro on coastguard support and anti-smuggling duties, wrote his personal memoirs 51 years after the event.[64] He mistakes the names of regiments in his account but was sure of the ghastly aftermath:

> I had just anchored of Youghal on the South coast when a loud explosion occurred on the shore not far from the town…There was a rifle range outside the town, to which the troops marched twice a week with bands playing. On this occasion, a land mine had been exploded under the troops on the march with heavy casualties especially amongst the band. An electric lead was traced to a nearby haystack where two women were hiding…When I came to the scene within an hour of the explosion I found a sad and bloody spectacle on the road. Most of the victims were young bandsmen.[65]

Nothing further is known of the women – or if they were even there.

The other narrative is of the IRA preparation for the attack, and the deed itself, as described by the former Irish Volunteers Vice Commandant of the 4th Battalion, Cork No. 1 Brigade, Patrick Whelan, but again it was a retrospective report from 1956 and there are several discrepancies as Whelan was not actually present.[66] Even so, he names two IRA men, Paddy O'Reilly and Thomas Power, from the Youghal company as those who carried out the attack.[67] Despite Whelan's description it is very difficult to be sure if this is accurate as it is possible that names may have been substituted to allow false IRA pension claims.[68] But Paddy O'Reilly and Thomas Power later died while serving on opposite sides in the civil war: Tommy was

---

[64] Quoted in Sheehan, *British Voices*, p. 81.
[65] *Ibid*, pp. 78-9.
[66] IMA, BMH, WS 1449, pp. 58-60, Commandant Patrick J. Whelan.
[67] *Ibid*.
[68] See the reference in P. Cockburn's, *The Broken Boy* (ebook: Random House, 2010), n. p.:
<http://books.google.co.uk/books?id=8vkkSXsUS1MC&pg=PT110&lpg=PT110&dq=Youghal+rifle+range&source=bl&ots=jgPmwwch0w&sig=rZCi18yvHWTbcph2yCtiJrgbUHY&hl=en&sa=X&ei=dB3RU4XXKaKp7Abd2YGYCA&ved=0CEoQ6AEwBw#v=onepage&q=Youghal%20rifle%20range&f=false> [accessed 24th July 2014].

killed by Irregulars as a Lieutenant in the National Army and Paddy was executed by the National Army, ostensibly for carrying arms:

> On 25 January 1923, two young men [Patrick O'Reilly and Michael Fitzgerald] from the anti-Treaty 1st Cork Brigade who had been captured in Waterford a month previously, were executed by firing squad in Waterford city on the orders of the Free State authorities...Although the official reason for the execution was for bearing arms and waging war against government forces, some noted that these two men had carried out the bomb attack on British forces in Youghal in May 1921.[69]

Again, the story can be confusing as in this description an unknown Michael Fitzgerald is implicated.

One particular irony is that the mine was probably made using an empty Royal Artillery shell case discarded at Fort Carlisle and used by fishermen at Ballinacurra as ballast. The shell case was packed with four different explosives, including gelignite, and electronically (battery) controlled by a switch.[70] A critical point about the explosion was that once the switch was turned to 'on' then it would be activated immediately and so there would be no doubt as to the target, even though the wire was about one hundred and fifty yards long. There were two routes out of the town down to the range, which the Hampshires alternated, and it was not until the fourth occasion that the column passed over the mine and it was detonated.

Patrick Whelan, although not present, suggests that if Paddy O'Reilly had pressed the trigger later then there would have been more casualties in the main body of the column. There can have been no doubt, however, who was to take the main brunt of the explosion as the band was playing at the time and there was a clear line of sight (Fig. 9.3).[71] Even if an advanced guard had been placed forward of the marching column there would have been little chance of seeing the explosives.

---

[69] O'Reilly, *Rebel Heart*, pp. 204-5 and IMA, BMH, WS 1449, p. 60, Commandant Patrick J. Whelan. Whelan does not mention Michael Fitzgerald's involvement in the Youghal attack.
[70] O'Reilly, *Rebel Heart*, p.149.
[71] Sgts' Mess scrapbook, n. p.

Figure 9.3
Scene of the Ambush at Youghal 31st May 1921 (The Royal Hampshire Regiment Museum)

One of the most shocking features of the attack was the age of some of the victims, being band boys, with another sad consequence that Private Whitear, who was wounded in the attack, had had his brother, who also served in the band, murdered by the IRA in Cork in January.[72] Compensation was paid to survivors after the truce,[73] but understandably, the band took some time to recover from the attack, both physically (Fig. 9.4)[74] and mentally.

Figure 9.4
Damaged Band Instruments after the Mine Explosion (The Royal Hampshire Regiment Museum)

---

[72] 'British Soldiers killed Ireland 1919-21', <http://www.cairogang.com/soldiers-killed/list-1921.html> [accessed 28th November 2017].
[73] *The Irish Times*, 22 October 1921, 'Before the Truce: Dreadful Deeds Recalled', reported that £32,833 was awarded in connection with the incident.
[74] Sgts' Mess scrapbook, n. p.

Zehle's march *Viscount Nelson*, the piece being played when the IED exploded, was not performed again by this band or its successors. One former member of the regimental band from the 1980s recalled the continued legacy:

> Viscount Nelson was never played again by the Hampshire Regiment …The march card had a large red cross marked on it from corner to corner – you may argue why not just destroy them but this was in the day of double sided marches and this 'marking' played its own part in remembering the event and those that had been killed and injured…there wasn't an annual memorial service but the band respected the tradition of not playing the march and band members held their ground when challenge[d] on massed gigs – usually resulting in the march being changed…the history was passed onto new members as part of their indoctrination to the band.[75]

An undated handwritten note in the Hampshire Regimental Journal asks whether the attack was in retaliation for the 'Fight at Clonmult' on 20th February 1921, where twelve IRA men had been killed and four captured.[76] In a debate in the House of Commons the day after the attack it was speculated that the reason may have been as retaliation for military reprisals against properties in the nearby Galtee valleys.[77] The main reason, however, was considered by the Hampshire regiment to be that the band was most popular in the town with the local population and that it was targeted deliberately to put an end to the socialising:

---

[75] N. P. Morgan, *Hants_Band_Youghal*, 'Private e-mail message'; 13th May 2014. Lieutenant Colonel Morgan served as a bandsman in the Band of The Royal Hampshire Regiment from 1979-90. The Army Reserve Band of the Princess of Wales's Royal Regiment continues the tradition in the twenty-first century by not playing *Viscount Nelson* http://www.queensroyalsurreys.org.uk/new_music/06.shtml [accessed 7th July 2014]. See also R. Holmes, *Soldiers: Army Lives and Loyalties from Redcoats to Dusty Warriors* (London: Harper Press, 2011) p, 493.
[76] *The Hampshire Regimental Journal*, June 1921, p. 89. Written in the copy at Searles House, Hampshire Regiment Museum, Winchester.
[77] 'Military Operations, Ireland', *Hansard*, HC Deb, 1 June 1921, Vol. 142, cc1157, http://hansard.millbanksystems.com/commons/1921/jun/01/military-operations-ireland-1#column_1157 [accessed 28th November 2017].

For the two previous weeks the band had played every day for the townsfolk of Youghal and it had been very popular; it had accordingly been marked down for destruction by the I.R.A.[78]

Soon after the attack a Court of Inquiry held at Cork Barracks also accepted the evidence that the band was popular with the Youghal population and that

> this cold-blooded murder was deliberately planned on account of the popularity of the Band and Regiment, that the murderer knew the Band was unarmed and contained many young boys, and that no attack was made on anybody except the band.[79]

The band had been heavily involved in battalion life up until the attack and the bandmaster, Mr Orbinski, was keen to ensure that appropriate music was performed when required, as the 2nd Battalion Sgts' Mess noted: 'Special mention must be made to Mr Orbinski's Orchestra, which contributes excellent and suitable music with necessary Jazz effects during the dance'.[80] The bandmaster's attention to detail and pride in performing popular music that was appreciated by all could have been a factor in having such a high profile influence to soldiers and local civilians alike.

It would seem probable that the Hampshire Regiment band was specifically targeted because of its influence on the local community, promoting the 'soft' side of the British army, while the rest of the battalion had been having some considerable success against the IRA. The band itself, as a symbol of the battalion, then became a victim of the escalation. The deliberate attack on the band made it difficult for civilian bands in the area, particularly the Corkhill Pipe Band, who had learnt to play their instruments with the previously locally billeted Scottish regiments, and had cordial relations with the British army – whilst paradoxically also being affiliated to the IRA. It is unlikely that Corkhill Pipe Band members had any involvement

---

[78] D. S. Daniell, *Regimental History: The Royal Hampshire Regiment: Volume Three 1918-1954* (Aldershot: Gale & Polden, 1955), p. 11.
[79] *The Hampshire Regimental Journal*, July 1921, pp. 114-115. Also reported in *The Irish Times*, 14 June 1921, 'The Murder of Hampshire Bandboys: Evidence at Military Inquiry'.
[80] *The Hampshire Regimental Journal*, April 1921, p. 57.

in the attack but they were immediately targeted by Crown forces who threatened to burn their instruments if they came across them.[81]

The particular significance of the Youghal 'outrage' was that it brought to the forefront the issue of bands as icons of political allegiances. Previous altercations involving bands, including stone throwing and the destruction of instruments, were the precursors that prepared the ground for escalation and made the scale of the IED attack seem inevitable. The revulsion shown towards the incident perhaps indicates that the IRA went too far, but the importance of bands (and their music) as political symbols was understood by the Free State government in-waiting.

The military music of the Irish Free State

The commander of the military forces of the provisional government after the Anglo-Irish war, General Mulcahy, would have been fully aware of the Youghal incident and the significance of the IRA's choice of target. Whether or not it directly influenced his judgement, he became particularly keen on incorporating music into the Irish National Army, seeing it as more than just a fighting force but as an exponent of national ideals, and the attack would have confirmed his position. The importance given to music, integral to his nationalist vision, resulted in an inspirational decision to create a Defence Force School of Music, in conjunction with the formation of a Gaelic-speaking battalion.[82] General Mulcahy was clear in his intentions:

> I want, in the first place, bands for the Army, I want to have bands that will disperse music and musical understanding in the highest terms to the people.[83]

His colleague, General Eoin O'Duffy, agreed that bands were good value and that they were an essential part of *esprit de corps*.[84] He was also keen on promoting the use of bands in the new Irish army, telling

---

[81] C. Parker, '100 Years of the Youghal Pipe Band', http://www.youghalonline.com/2014/03/13/youghal-pipe-band-centenary-concert/ [accessed 8th September 2014].
[82] M. G. Valiulis, *Portrait of a Revolutionary: General Richard Mulcahy and the Founding of the Irish Free State* (Lexington: Kentucky University Press, 1992), pp. 238-9.
[83] Quted in Valiulis, *Portrait*, p. 238.
[84] E. O'Halpin, *Defending Ireland: The Irish State and its Enemies Since 1922* (Oxford: Oxford University Press, 1999), p.96.

a visiting American officer that a 'good band and snappy turnout' was a worthy political argument for maintaining the army.[85]

To help develop the status and effectiveness of the band, General Mulcahy enlisted the help of Professor John Larchet, a notable musician working in Dublin, to recruit a full-time military music director from outside Ireland who was experienced in training bands.[86] The political situation would not allow a British bandmaster to be appointed and so it was decided to seek expertise from overseas.[87] The French were in no position to help after the First World War, but Germany was more amenable, particularly after the military reductions from the Treaty of Versailles had resulted in many bandmasters being made redundant. Contact was made with Professor Grawert, Director of the Royal School of Military Music in Berlin, and it was decided to recruit Fritz Brase, a very successful bandmaster in the German army.[88] As head of the Irish Army's School of Music at Beggar's Bush Barracks, Dublin, Fritz Brase was given the rank of colonel and set about training what was to be known as the No. 1 Band. He was a hard taskmaster — shown by his denial in even allowing the band to take their habitual 'smoke' breaks in rehearsals[89] — but by 1926 the Army School of Music establishment had grown to a total of 219 personnel, including 190 musicians in five bands and twenty-nine staff at the Headquarters.[90]

While there is no direct evidence that the Irish authorities deliberately set out to antagonise the British with the engagement of a former enemy as its head of music, it had the effect of setting Irish

---

[85] Quoted in O'Halpin, *Defending Ireland*, p. 96.

[86] J. J. Ryan, 'Nationalism and Music in Ireland' (PhD Thesis, National University of Ireland, St Patrick's College, Maynooth, 1991), pp. 376-7.

[87] Although at the same time the Free State army did consider it appropriate to use British artillery pieces to shell Rory O'Connor, the leader of the IRA, and his men, when they were occupying the Four Courts in Dublin. See, for example, D. Walder, *The Chanak Affair* (London: Hutchinson, 1969), p. 165.

[88] R. Hawkins, 'Brase, Wilhelm Fritz', in J. McGuire and J. Quinn (ed), *Dictionary of Irish Biography*. (Cambridge, 2009). http://dib.cambridge.org/viewReadPage.do?articleId=a0903 [accessed 19th May 2014]. J. M. Doyle, 'Music in the Army', in A. Fleischmann (ed.) *Music in Ireland: A Symposium* (Cork: Cork University Press, 1952), p. 65.

[89] *Wilhelm Maestro*. RTÉ Radio 1, 'Documentary on One'. Written and presented by J. J. Ryan. 19th March 1989. http://www.rte.ie/radio1/doconone/podcast-wilhelm-maestro-irish-army-school-of-music-band-no-1.html [accessed 20th May 2014].

[90] W. J. Brennan-Whitmore (ed), *Defence Forces Saorstát Éireann 1926: Army List and Directory* (Dublin: "An t-Óglác, 1926; repr. Uckfield: The Naval and Military Press, 2007), p. 123.

military music on a separate path that would distinguish it from that of the British army. The need to have a distinct identity was probably accelerated by the continued presence of British iconography in several quarters. As late as 1922, the Royal Hibernian Military School band had marched in Dublin, along with 5,000-6,000 troops, for the Kings' Birthday parade, with the band playing *British Grenadiers* and standing out from the drab khaki uniforms of the troops with their scarlet tunics, even though the War Office had decreed in 1920 that service dress should be worn by all regiments of the line on full dress occasions.[91] Furthermore, the ex-Service community paraded each Armistice Day in Dublin with clashes between the local British Legion and Nationalists whenever the Union Flag was flown or the British National Anthem sung.[92]

One of the first acts of Colonel Brase was to order low pitched ('New Philharmonic' pitch) instruments from Germany in March 1923, with enough to fill two bands, one of forty-two and the other of thirty-six. With the successful recruitment of musicians from civilian bands, police bands, and from the recently disbanded Irish Regiments of the British army, a third and fourth band were resourced with instruments from Germany.[93] This would have had the instant effect of altering the sound from that of the British military band, creating an audible and visual difference with the British regimental bands in Northern Ireland. The brighter sounding rotary-valved trumpets replaced the softer cornet sound associated with the British military and brass bands, with the difference in instruments evident in photographs from 1930 (Fig. 9.5) and on a contemporary British Pathé newsreel.[94]

Brase still maintained his German connections – he is still listed in 1926 as 'Royal Musical Director'[95] – which also meant that it took some time for him to accept saxophones in the band as, although by the 1920s they were standard in British military bands, saxophones were not officially accepted into the German military until 1940,[96]

---

[91] Clarke, *A New History*, p. 474-5.
[92] A. Gregory, *The Silence of Memory: Armistice Day 1919-1946* (Oxford: Berg, 1994), p. 132.
[93] Doyle, 'Music in the Army', p. 66.
[94] 'No. 1 Army Band Conducted by Col. Fitz Brase, 1930',
<http://www.britishpathe.com/video/no-1-army-band-conducted-by-col-fitz-brase> [accessed May 20th 2014].
[95] Brennan-Whitmore, *Defence Forces Saorstát Éireann*, p. 73.
[96] J. J. Ryan. Personal communication. 30th June 2014; S. Cottrell, *The Saxophone* (Yale: Yale University Press: 2013), p. 124.

with Brase's reticence further differentiating the Irish Free State and British sounds.

Figure 9.5
Irish Army No 1 Band with German low-pitched instruments (Defence Forces School of Music (Republic of Ireland))

By 1924 Brase was recording with the No. 1 Band and his work was clearly making an impact on the Free State military, as chronicled in its Journal *An t-Óglác*,[97] and their reputation was reaching Britain by 1925 with *The Bandmaster* journal reporting the No. 1 Band as 'a splendid combination of the pick of Ireland's very best musicians...engaged almost daily throughout the year'.[98]

The Free State lacked a full-time orchestra and with a shortage of civilian wind instrumentalists, the army bands were the main suppliers of brass and woodwind players to the orchestra that would occasionally put on concerts.[99] Brase had a significant influence on the Free State's musical activities and was involved in setting up the Dublin Philharmonic at about the same time as the 2RN orchestra

---

[97] There are several references to the bands' activities in the Christmas 1924 edition, *An t-Óglác*, Vol. II, No. 23 (New Series.), December 20, 1924, pp. 4, 10, 16 & 18.
[98] 'Irish Band News', *The Bandmaster*, Vol. 1, No. 9, November 1925, p. 141.
[99] J. J. Ryan, 'Music in Independent Ireland since 1921', in J. R. Hill (ed), *A New History of Ireland: Ireland 1921-84: Volume 7* (Oxford: Oxford University Press, 2003), p. 632.

was formed. Both orchestras could not function without army players and the Philharmonic's first concert was billed as being in conjunction with the Army No. 1 Band.[100] By the 1930s the army musicians regularly joined with Radio Éireann musicians to present concerts under the umbrella of the Dublin Philharmonic Society,[101] and the Free State military bands were also employed for broadcasting.[102] As a member of the Broadcasting Advisory Committee in the Irish Free State, Colonel Brase,[103] unlike Colonel Somerville as a member of the BBC's MAC, was a practicing musician and had far more credibility on musical matters.

One of the conditions that Colonel Brase imposed when accepting the post was that he could bring an assistant, and when this was granted he brought with him to Ireland Friedrich Sauerzweig, former Bandmaster of the 2nd Foot Artillery in Greifswald, who was to become the first instruction officer for military music in the Irish army (Fig. 9.6).[104]

The influence of the four Free State military bands on the musical life in Ireland was considerable as, with the small broadcasting orchestra, they were the only professional music ensembles in the country. Furthermore, the army bands were the only real source of trained conductors and they soon produced home-grown musicians who became bandleaders, such as Lieutenant Arthur Duff.[105] The development of music in the Free State was acknowledged as being largely down to the hard work and skill of Fritz Brase and his influence also extended to Northern Ireland where he was a regular visitor, invited to conduct the Belfast Wireless Symphony Orchestra and adjudicate at musical gatherings.[106]

---

[100] R. Pine, *Music and Broadcasting in Ireland* (Dublin: Four Courts Press, 2005), p. 35.
[101] F. Sheil, *Missing a Beat: Bridging Ireland's Orchestral Gaps: A Review of Orchestral Provision in Ireland* (Dublin: The Arts Council, 2010), p. 11
[102] Pine, *Music and Broadcasting in Ireland*, p. 331
[103] *Ibid*, pp. 34 & 56.
[104] Doyle, 'Music in the Army', p. 66.
[105] Ryan, 'Music in Independent Ireland', p. 635; J. J. Ryan, 'Duff, Arthur Knox', in J. McGuire and J. Quinn (ed), *Dictionary of Irish Biography*. (Cambridge, 2009). (<http://dib.cambridge.org/viewReadPage.do?articleId=a2804>) [accessed 20th May 2014].
[106] R. Stanley, 'A formative force: the BBC's role in the development of music and its audiences in Northern Ireland, 1924-39' (PhD Thesis, Queen's University, Belfast, 2012), pp. 279 & 320; R. Johnston, 'Music in Northern Ireland since 1921', in J. R. Hill (ed.), *A New History of Ireland: Ireland 1921-84: Volume 7* (Oxford: Oxford University Press, 2003), p. 655.

Figure 9.6
Fritz Brase (left) and Friedrich Sauerzwig (Defence Forces School of Music (Republic of Ireland))

For the British army bands in Northern Ireland there must have been some envy of the military bands in the south due to a tense situation in the north: British army bands stationed there could not always be relied upon to contribute regularly to community music making, as disturbances were sometimes preventing them attending on concert nights.[107] This was in marked difference to the Free State army bands, as for them, General Mulcahy had ensured that the performance of military music was given primacy.

The German influence was to remain throughout the 1930s with an Irish military band marching at the Irish Military Tattoo at Ballsbridge, near Dublin, in 1935 with German instruments, including a bell-lyre, a trademark German marching instrument.[108] But unfortunately Colonel Brase's activities in the 1930s became a

---

[107] Johnston, 'Music in Northern Ireland since 1921', p. 653.
[108] 'Irish Military Tattoo, 1935', <http://www.britishpathe.com/video/irish-military-tattoo/> [accessed 20th May 2014].

cause of concern for the Free State authorities as he was also a leading Nazi Party member in Ireland. Colonel Brase was heavily involved in the Nazi *Auslandsorganisation*,[109] and had been made a professor by Adolf Hitler, being well placed at the highest echelons of Irish cultural organisations.[110] Given the choice by the Irish army authorities to leave the army or the *Auslandsorganisation*, Brase chose to stay in the army, but his reputation was tarnished.[111] Nevertheless, while the appointment of Brase and Sauerzweig was criticised by some who saw the foreigners as interlopers,[112] the quality of their work is undeniable and they shaped an independent military band sound that was unique in the British Isles at the time.

The appropriation of military and military-styled bands and their music by various political entities led to the bands being targeted by the various belligerents as symbols of rebellion, or of Crown forces. Despite the high-profile use of bands in Ireland the British army gave no official recognition to music as a political influencing tool, but the active use of music by Irish paramilitaries, and the understanding of the utility of the influence of British bands on the local population, resulting in an IED attack on the Hampshire Regiment band, were undoubtedly factors that steered the Free State army to formalise music as part of its military doctrine. General Mulcahy's creation of a credible and professional military music organisation would not have been possible without the appropriation of music by the various formal and informal political factions, including the military, in the first quarter of the twentieth century in Ireland. He was not the first to understand the use of music – and its influence – but he was a pioneer in appropriately harnessing it as a soft power effect in military doctrine.

Investigating the role of military music in propaganda and diplomacy in Ireland in the early decades of the twentieth century has exposed the extent to which music was an integral part of conflict, and appropriated by belligerents on all sides. Whether as a symbol of the Crown or rebellion, military bands were seen as the embodiment of the cause they represented and were susceptible to confrontation and assault by opposing factions, culminating in the extreme violence

---

[109] D. O'Donoghue, 'State within a State: The Nazis in Neutral Ireland', *History Ireland*, 14, 6, Nov-Dec (2006), pp. 35-39.
[110] The *Auslandsorganisation* leader in Ireland was Dr Adolf Mahr, curator of the National Museum.
[111] J. P. Duggan, *Neutral Ireland and the Third Reich* (Dublin: Gill and Macmillan, 1985), pp. 14 & 63.
[112] Ryan, 'Nationalism and Music in Ireland', p. 378.

of the IED attack on the Hampshire Regiment band. When the British army and its bands left, the Free State army filled the void with its own distinct bands that were so important in representing the Nationalistic ideals of General Mulcahy's vision. Political factors in the external environment fundamentally altered the way music in Ireland was performed and received, and ultimately led to the formation of a distinct musical tradition.

APPENDIX 1

Broadcasts (excluding outside broadcasts) by staff bands from January 1932 to September 1933.[1]

BROADCASTS from LONDON STUDIOS.

GRENADIER GUARDS	January 1932.	10th.	London Regional.
Conductor:-	February 1932.	21st.	-do- Daventry
Capt. G. Miller.	March 27th. 1932.		National.
	July 10th. 1932.		-do-
	November 1932	6th.	London Regional.
	November 1932	13th.	-do- -do-
	December 1932.	25th.	Daventry National.
	March 14th. 1933.		London
	March 27th. 1933.		Regional.
	August 5th. 1933.		Daventry
	September 1933	9th.	National. -do-
	September 1933.	24th.	London Regional.
ROYAL AIR FORCE.	February 1932.	10th.	London Regional.
Conductor:-	March 18th. 1932.		Daventry
	June 24th. 1932.		National.
Flt-Lieut.	July 17th. 1932.		London
O'Donnell.	August 1932.	14th.	Regional. -do-
	August 1932.	23rd.	Daventry National. -do-

---

[1] BBC WAC R27/209/1 Music General Military Bands File 1A 1933-1934. Attachment to 'BBC Internal Memo: Military Bands.' Dated 31st Oct. 1933.

	October 23rd. 1932.	London Regional.
	November 26th. 1932.	-do-
	January 7th. 1933.	Daventry National.
	January 29th. 1933.	London Regional.
	February 25th. 1933.	-do- -do- -do-
	April 14th. 1933.	Daventry National.
	May 27th. 1933.	
	August 6th. 1933.	-do-
	August 20th. 1933.	
<u>COLDSTREAM GUARDS</u>.	August 9th. 1932.	London Regional.
<u>ROYAL MARINES</u>.	April 18th. 1932.	Midland Regional.
Portsmouth.	February 6th. 1933.	London Regional.
Conductor:-		
Lieut. V. Dunn.		
<u>ROYAL MARINES</u>.	Once in 1932, Dated ?	
Chatham Div.		

APPENDIX 2

Colonel Somerville's list to the BBC of army bands graded 'outstanding' by Kneller Hall in 1933.[1]

List of outstanding Bands recommended to perform for the B.B.C.
- -

4th/7th. Dragoon Guards.
Irish Guards.
1st. Bn. The Border Regt.
1st. Bn. The Oxfordshire and Buckinghamshire Light Infantry.
1st. Bn. The Royal Scots.
2nd. Bn. The South Wales Borderers.
1st. Bn. The Green Howards.
11th. Hussars.
R.A., Portsmouth.
Grenadier Guards.
Scots Guards.
Royal Engineers. Mil. Band.
Royal Engineers. Orchestra.
Life Guards.
Royal Horse Guards.
2nd. Bn. The Gloucestershire Regt.
1st. Bn. The King's Own Yorkshire Light Infantry.
2nd. Bn. The Royal West Kents.
2nd. Bn. Royal Fusiliers.
2nd. Bn. The Somerset Light Infantry.
2nd. Bn. The Queen's Royal Regiment.
2nd. Bn. The Royal Scots Fusiliers.
2nd. Bn. The North Staffordshire Regt.
2nd. Bn. The Seaforth Highlanders.
1st Bn. The Lancashire Fusiliers.
7th. Hussars.

---

[1] BBC WAC R27/209/1 Music General Military Bands File 1A 1933-1934. Attachment to 'BBC Internal Circulating Memo: Military Bands.' Dated 31st Oct. 1933.

R.A., Woolwich. (Orchestra only)
2nd. Bn. The Bedfordshire and Hertfordshire Regt.
2nd. Bn. The Dorsetshire Regt.
2nd. Bn. The East Yorkshire Regt.
2nd. Bn. The Middlesex Regt.
Royal Inniskilling Fusiliers.

APPENDIX 3

Colonel Jervis's 'order of merit' army band list sent to the BBC in 1934, notable for its absence of staff bands.[1]

<u>Order of Merit, June, 1934.</u>

<u>Outstanding.</u>
    1st Bn The Border Regiment.
    2nd Bn The South Wales Borderers.
    1st Bn The Royal Scots.
    1st Bn The Oxford & Buckinghamshire Light Infantry.
    4th/7th Dragoon Guards.
    11th Hussars (P.A.O.)

<u>Very Good.</u>
    1st Bn The Green Howards.
    The Queen's Bays.
    3rd The King's Own Hussars.
    2nd Bn The King's Royal Rifle Corps.
    2nd Bn The East Yorkshire Regiment.
    2nd Bn The Royal Fusiliers.
    2nd Bn The North Staffordshire Regiment.
    2nd Bn The Royal Scots Fusiliers.
    2nd Bn The Q.O. Royal West Kent Regiment.
    7th Queen's Own Hussars.
    1st Bn The King's Own Yorkshire Light Infantry.
    2nd Bn The Gloucestershire Regiment.
    2nd Bn The Buffs.
    1st Bn The Royal Sussex Regiment.
    2nd Bn The Somerset Light Infantry.

<u>Other fine Bands.</u>
    2nd Bn The Dorset Regiment.
    The Royal Scots Greys.
    1st Bn The Argyll & Sutherland Highlanders.
    2nd Bn The Gordon Highlanders.
    2nd Bn The King's Own Royal Regiment.

---

[1] BBC WAC R27/209/1 Music General Military Bands File 1A 1933-1934. Attachment to letter to Mr Eckersby from Colonel Jervis. Dated 5 Aug. 34.

2nd Bn The King's Shropshire Light Infantry.
1st Bn The Lancashire Fusiliers.
2nd Bn The Northumberland Fusiliers.
1st Bn The Durham Light Infantry.

APPENDIX 4

Walton O'Donnell's BBC audition reports for three bands in Northern Ireland.[1]

Scripted text and strikethrough denotes handwritten additions on originals. O'Donnell's reports were handwritten but are presented typed in this Appendix.

Band. 2nd. Bn North Staffordshire Regiment.

Programme for B.B.C. Audition. 13th.June.1935.

1.	March.	"The Staffordshire Knot".	Duthoit.
2.	Overture.	"Oberon".	Weber.
3.		"Schon Rosmarin".	Kreisler.
4.		"Lyric Suite".	Greig.
5.		"Carissima".	Elgar.
6.	Hungarian Dances.	(5 & 6)	Brahms.

Conductor. H.Johnson.A.R.C.M.

-:-:-:-:-:-:-:-:-:-:-:-:-:-:-:-:-:-:-:-

---

[1] BBC WAC R27/209/1 Music General Military Bands File 1B 1935. Attached documents to 'B.B.C. Mr. B. Walton O'Donnell Northern Ireland Regional Offices to Music Executive. Head Office. Private & Confidential.' Dated 13th June, 1935.

2nd. Batt: North Staffordshire Regt.

This band consists of 26 performers. The bandmaster reported that the oboe player was in hospital. Programme attached.

The bandmaster had evidently taken a good deal of trouble to make the most of his material which was a little weak, technically, in the woodwind section. "Oberon" overture stretched the clarinets + had to be eased up when the difficulties came along. The result was inclined to be patchy particularly as the conductor was a little inclined to "play to the gallery".

However there were many points of artistic playing, good attention being given to tone-quality, nuances and balance. Tuning was rather shaky. With more technical accomplishment in the woodwind section this would be a first-class little band.

With reference to the tuning – the bandmaster rightly called for attention to it at the end of each item – but he apparently left it to the players themselves to make the adjustments + generally nothing was done.

I consider this band comes into category B + might be broadcast in a not too exacting programme.

B. Walton O'Donnell

<u>Belfast.</u>

Jun 13th. 1935.

Band of the 2nd Bn. The King's Royal Rifle Corps.

Programme for B.B.C. Audition 13th June 1935.

1. Overture   "Euryanthe"   Weber
2. Selection   "Reminiscences of Rossini"   arr. Godfrey
3. Trombone Solo   "The Swan"   Saint-Saens
4. Toccata Marziale   Vaughan Williams
5. An Original Suite (for Military Band)   Gordon Jacob
   1. March.   2. Intermezzo.   3. Finale.
6. ~~Xylophone Solo~~   ~~"Skeleton Dance"~~   ~~Abbey~~
7. ~~Selection from "The Merry Widow"~~   ~~Lehar~~

Regimental March   "Lutzow's Wild Hunt"

GOD SAVE THE KING

Conductor: Bandmaster D. McBain.

2nd. Battn. – King's Royal Rifle Corps.
———

The band consists of 30 performers.
Programme attached.
An excellent band, well trained + playing well within its capabilities. The work was consistently good + solid, the music was honestly dealt with, + there was no need for camouflage or cheap showmanship. There were some excellent young soloist [sic] (Bb clarinet + trombone) in a band which contained good young musicians generally.
The bandmaster is to be congratulated on his material + the widest care he has exercised over their musical and general discipline – his work is that of a real and serious musician. The tuning, tone quality, precision + musicianship of the band were all very good.
At least one of the best Line Bands I have heard – certainly should have appeared before some on the Kneller Hall "outstanding" list.
I would place this band among leaders of category B.

B. Walton O'Donnell

<u>Belfast.</u>

Jun 13th. 1935.

VICTORIA BARRACKS,
BELFAST,
6th June, 1935.

The British Broadcasting Corporation,
31 Linen Hall Street,
Belfast.

Herewith suggested programme of the Leicestershire Regiment for audition on 13th June, 1935:-

1. March   -   *Szabadi*   *Massenet*
                  ~~TITANEN.~~   ~~Stork.~~

2. Overture -   *Phoebie*   *Massenet*
                  ~~LUSTSPIEL.~~   ~~Kela-Bela.~~

3. Selection -   DOLLAR   Leo Fall.
                  PEINCESS.

4. Valse   -   THE GRENADIER.   Waldteufal.

5. DANCES.   -   TWO RUSSIAN.   Tchaikswsky.   [sic]

6. ~~Ballet~~   ~~EGYPTIAN.~~   ~~Luigini.~~
   Hungarian Dances Nos 5+6   -   *Brahms*

J Brownlow
for Bandmaster,
2nd Bn. The Leicestershire Regiment.

2nd. Batt: Leicestershire Regt.

This band consisted of 25 performers. The bandmaster reported that the Tenor Saxophone player was in hospital.
Programme attached.
The tuning of the band was rather bad at the commencement, particularly in the woodwind, + became worse. Little attention seemed to be paid to it.
Tone quality of the clarinets not very good – that of the oboe quite bad (evidently a beginner).
Balance of the band was fair (woodwind carried the burden generally) but there was little variety in colouring, + the band was quite definitely struggling with the technical difficulties.
The standard of accomplishment throughout was rather low – tuning, tone, technique + musicianship requiring a good deal of attention – there were too many wrong notes + wrong metrics undetected.
I would place this band not very high in category C + cannot really recommend it for broadcasting on its musical merits.

B. Walton O'Donnell

Belfast.

Jun 13th. 1935.

APPENDIX 5

Internal 1941 BBC memo rejecting the Kneller Hall band grading system.[1]

Confirming our conversation the other day, would you please consider the advisability of our ceasing to be ruled by Kneller Hall authorities over the matter of deciding to which Service Bands we grant auditions…I think that we should be allowed to decide for ourselves which, if any, we audition…[O]ur decision would chiefly be guided by previous knowledge of the Conductor, since we have found in the past that where a good band exists in a Line Regiment, it is usually because there is a good conductor, whereas Kneller Hall's gradings were, to some extent, ruled by the "spit and polish" aspect of the band, its instruments and its library – not a very effective way of judging a band's fitness to broadcast.

We feel it would be a good opportunity now to throw off the yolk of Kneller Hall – a yoke that, so far as we can gather, was imposed on us as a sop to their authorities when their suggestion of complete dictatorship as to which bands we broadcast was squashed.

---

[1] BBC WAC R27/209/5 Music General Military Bands File 2C 1941-1942. 'BBC Internal Memo – Glasgow: Service Band Auditions, Routine.' From Mr. Denis Wright to Mus. Ex. (Bristol), Copy to: Mr. P.S.G. O'Donnell, dated 21st January 1941.

APPENDIX 6

[Issue CCCLXXII]

[FOR OFFICIAL USE ONLY]

ARMY COUNCIL INSTRUCTION–544

Addendum to the issue CCCLXXII for week
ending 19th December, 1928

544   Pitch of Instruments of Army Bands

1. The circular forming the Appendix to this A.C.I. was issued to all units at home. The replies to this circular show that a large majority of the Army Bands at home are in favour of the change of pitch. The Army Council have therefore decided to authorize the change, and paragraph 1376, King's Regulations, 1928, is being amended accordingly.

2. This decision is based upon the conviction that a change does not necessitate more than the substitution of low pitch wood-wind for high pitch, and the provision of slides to tone down the brass instruments, and that the change can be effected for the amount set forth in the Appendix.

3. In order to expedite the change and minimize the period of musical confusion resulting from the maintenance of two pitches, commanding officers of those units who agreed to make the change under one or other of the headings in the circular letter are instructed to proceed with the change as quickly as possible. Other units will take steps to conform as and when their particular circumstances admit.

4. With regard to high-pitch instruments no longer required, those in reasonably good condition can e sent to the Commandant, Kneller Hall, to be used as a pool to maintain bands which are able to make the change only gradually.

5. After receipt of this A.C.I. no unit stationed at home, including the Rhine, will purchase any high-pitch instrument without first receiving the authority of the Commandant, when it should be possible to issue to them part-worn instruments.

6. Units sending instruments to Kneller Hall will be credited on paper with the value of the instruments despatched, and should they be re-issued, will be paid the amount realized. The present market value of an old high pitch instrument, if in good condition, is about £1.

7. Units stationed where massed band performances are regularly undertaken at certain times of the year will retain their high pitch instruments until the occasion of massed band performances is passed for the year 1929, when they will take action as detailed above.

8. Units will make their own arrangements with the instrument makers as to the terms they are able to afford. It will be found that firms are ready to offer all reasonable latitude with regard to payment by instalments.

(103/Gen./5101 (A.G. 4).)

By Command of the Army Council

[*signed*]

The War Office
19th *December*, 1928.

(B28/191)   12074   12/28   W.O.P. 4040

APPENDIX

To Officers Commanding all units at home

1. Recent correspondence on the subject of the proposed alteration of the military band pitch from the old Philharmonic to the new Philharmonic pitch (commonly referred to as "sharp" and "flat" pitch) shows that a large majority of units are in favour of the change, provided that some method, better suited to the finances of a number of bands than that suggested, can be arranged. The matter has therefore been further investigated and a new scheme formulated.

2. In order that the War Office may have adequate information on which to base general instructions on the subject, I have been directed to ascertain certain facts, prior to any decision being given.

The particulars required are as follows :–

On the assumption that the Army pitch is to be changed from "sharp" to "flat" during the financial year April, 1929, to March, 1930–

> (i) Are you prepared to finance the change from band funds already in your possession on a cash payment basis? The cash cost of equipping a band of 35 with new wood wind, and conversion of brass by slides, varies from £313 to £390, according to the firm employed.
>
> (ii)   (a)   If your band is unable to pay cash, are you prepared to agree to the sum of £15 per quarter being deducted from the quarterly band allowance payable to you until the credit price has been paid? The credit price, on these terms, is approximately £50 more that the cash price above quoted.
>
> (b) Alternatively, are you prepared for larger quarterly reductions that £15, if so, what amount?

It will be understood that the quicker the amount is paid off, the more closely will the total payable approximate to the cash price.

3. It is appreciated that units are differently situated in this respect and that factors which present no difficulty in one case, assume formidable proportions in another.

The scheme now under consideration has therefore been framed in such a way that units who are in a position to pay cash can be authorized to carry out the conversion under their own arrangements; whilst those who are less fortunately situated shall be enabled to do the same thing under an arrangement which shall not impose on them a liability serious enough to impair the maintenance of the band during the period of payment.

4. A variety of other points in connection with this subject will probably occur to you, but the majority can be overcome by the temporary retention of the old sharp pitch instruments until such time as the conversion of the home bands has been completed.

It is estimated that this can be done within one year.

I shall be glad therefore if you will inform me as to questions in paragraph 2 of this letter so that a definite decision on the subject may be reached at an early date.

APPENDIX 7

An anonymous humorous poem about the change to low pitch published in *The Leading Note* in 1929 (Vol. 1, 3, August, p. 26).

The reference to 'mechanized' relates to the army's mechanization of cavalry to armour at the same time.

NB The text is of its time and contains phrases that are now considered offensive.

A.C.I 544/1928,

Converting Army Bands in the future from high to low pitch, the pitch of Civilian and Continental Orchestras. Present brass instruments in use, to be sent to instrument makers for conversion; wood wind instruments cannot be converted and will be sent to Kneller Hall for scrapping, to be replaced by new ones purchased at Regimental expense!

* * *

The edict is out in an A.C.I.
That our Army Bands are pitched too high;
The Horn, Euphonium, booming Bass,
And others (ommited for lack of space,
Including the Cornet and Bass Trombone),
Have got to be lowered a semitone;
And those that resound with wind through wood
Have got to be scrapped, for they're no more good;
The Oboe; Saxophone, Clarinet,
Are beyond the skill of the musical Vet.;
So we've pensioned them off as useless–all–
To eat out their hearts at Kneller Hall.

Folks say it's a thoroughly eerie sight,
At Kneller Hall, at the dead of night;
When the old wood winds come stealing out
From lumber and store room and peer about,

Round the Barrack Square, e're they start to play,
Some illicit high pitched roundelay;
No longer their dulcet tones are drowned
By that blaring–braying–brassy sound
Of the Cornet, Euphonium, Bass Trombone,
Who, just for a paltry semitone,
Have allowed their insides to be rent apart
By the Surgeons of Hawkes and Rudall Carte.

To tell the truth we are not surprised,
For we know we're bund to be mechanized;
And the tone of the band must be lowered to suit
The motor's mournful minor toot;
The latest research, too, tends to show,
That the next Great War will be pitched quite low,
The rattle of the Vickers, the scream of the shell,
Have all to be flattened down as well;
The stridence of battle will thus, you see,
Be exchanged for a flat pitched symphony;
Nad they'll be no room, you must understand,
In a flat pitched scrap, for a high pitched band.

The greatest boon we can see in this
Complete meta–musical–ninphosis,
I'd that now we can join in a massed band show
With the Wog, the Chink or the Esquimaux;
(Whose double Basses are made, I hear,
From the hindmost slopes of a polar bear);
The Bands of the Dago; the Finn or Russ,
No longer can boast they are flatter than us;
Though we beggar our funds, to please Kneller Hall,
We must strive to become just as flat as them all;
No longer we'll stand isolated, alone,
Form the musical world by a mere semitone.

BIBLIOGRAPHY

Archives

BBC Written Archives Centre
BBC WAC R8/119/1 Artists Policy Musicians Union Light Orchestras and Military Bands File 1 1934-1936
BBC WAC R8/119/2 Artists Policy Musicians Union Light Orchestras and Military Bands File 2 1937-1946
BBC WAC R27/209/1 Music General Military Bands File 1A 1933-1934
BBC WAC R27/209/1 Music General Military Bands File 1B 1935
BBC WAC R27/209/2 Music General Military Bands File 1B 1935
BBC WAC R27/209/3 Music General Military Bands File 2A 1936-1937
BBC WAC R27/209/4 Music General Military Bands File 2B 1938-1940
BBC WAC R27/209/5 Music General Military Bands File 2C 1941-1942
BBC WAC R29/148 ORCH GEN BBC Wireless Military Band
BBC WAC R29/146/1 ORCH GEN BBC Wireless Military Band

The British Library
SoundServer, C1395

Imperial War Museum Sound Archives

837	20468
10454	22077
12708	22165
12713	24691
19989	

Irish Military Archives

BMH, WS 393	BMH, WS 1683
BMH, WS 889	BMH, WS 1700
BMH, WS 1367	BMH, WS 1709
BMH, WS 1449	BMH, WS 1741
BMH, WS 1525	

King's College London
Basil Liddell Hart Archives, LH15/3/13
Kirke 5/1

London Metropolitan Archives
LMA/4647/D/03/01/008
LMA/4647/D/03/01/010
LMA/4647/D/03/01/011
LMA/4647/D/03/02/001
LMA A/FWA/C/D1000/1 Newport Market Refuge
LMA CLSD-2
LMA CLSD/31
LMA CLSD/252

The National Archives

CO/15885
HO/144/1173/215639
HO/351/170
MEPO 2/4290
T/161/105/7
WO/32/3906
WO/32/3913
WO/32/3914
WO/32/3915
WO/32/3916
WO/32/3920
WO/32/4488
WO/32/8685

WO/32/11071
WO/32/14914
WO/141/93
WO/143/23
WO/143/26
WO/143/73
WO/191/4
WO/191/9
WO/191/12
WO/191/33
WO/191/34
Works/16/110

Books, articles, and other printed sources

Adkins, H. E., *Treatise on the Military Band* (London: Boosey & Co., 1931).

Aisin-Gioro, P. Y., *From Emperor to Citizen: The Autobiography of Aisin-Gioro Pu Yi*, trans. W. J. F. Jenner (Beijing: Foreign Languages Press, 1989 [1965]).

Ahrendt, R., Ferraguto, M. and Mahiet, D. (eds), *Music and Diplomacy from the Early Modern Era to the Present* (New York: Palgrave Macmillan, 2014).

Allen, C. (ed.), *Plain Tales From the Raj: Images of British India in the Twentieth Century* (London: Deutsch, 1975).

Ambler, J. (ed.), *'Bagged' in World War 2: Two Tales of Royal Marines Prisoners of War*. Special Publication No 24 (Portsmouth: Royal Marines Historical Society, 2001).

Ambler, J., *The Royal Marines Band Service*. Special Publication Number 28 (Southsea: The Royal Marines Historical Society, 2003).

Ambler, J., *The Royal Marines Band Service: Volume 2*. Special Publication Number 37 (Portsmouth: The Blue Band, 2011).

Ambler, J., *World War I Remembered: Royal Marines Buglers and Musicians at War*. Special Publication Number 47 (Portsmouth: The Royal Marines Historical Society/The Royal Marines Band Service, 2019).

Ambler, S., *A Musical Ride: The Story of the Staff Band of the Royal Corps of Transport. With a concise history of the Band's predecessors* (Stilton: MRA Publishing, 2010).

Andrews, F., *Brass Band Cylinder and Non-microgroove Disc Recordings: 1903-1960* (Winchester: Piccolo Press, 1997).

Andrews, F., *The British Record Industry during the Reign of Edward VII: 1901-1910*, The City of London Phonograph and Gramophone Society Reference Series No. 3 (London: CLPGS, 2010).

Andrews, F., *A History of the Marketing of Sound Recordings in Britain: 1890-1903*, The City of London Phonograph and Gramophone Society Reference Series No. 16 (London: CLPGS, 2012),

Ansell, M., *Soldier On: An Autobiography by Colonel Sir Mike Ansell* (London: Peter Davies, 1973).

Bailey, M., *The Chance of a Lifetime: The Story of The Shaftesbury Homes and Arethusa* (Cirencester: Dianthus, 1996).

Bailey, M., "He Who Has Ears to Hear, Let Him Hear': Christian Pedagogy and Religious Broadcasting During the Inter-War Period', *Westminster Papers in Communication and Culture*, Vol. 4(1), 2007, pp. 4-25.

Bailey, P., 'The Politics and Poetics of Modern British Leisure', in *Rethinking History*, 3:2, 1999, pp. 131-175.

Bannister, R., 'Watching Paint Dry: Musical Meaning in a Military Ceremony', *Australian Defence Force Journal*, No. 106, May/June, 1994, pp. 33-40.

Bannister, R., 'How are we to write our music history? Perspectives on the historiography of military music', in *Musicology Australia*, 25:1, 2002, pp. 1-21.

Banton, M., *Administering the Empire, 1801–1968: A Guide to the Records of the Colonial Office in The National Archives of the UK* (London: Institute of Historical Research/The National Archives, 2008).

Barty-King, H., *The Drum: A Royal Tournament Tribute to the Military Drum* (London: The Royal Tournament, 1988).

Batten, J., *Joe Batten's Book: The Story of Sound Recording, Being the Memoirs of Joe Batten, Recording Manager* (London: Rockliff, 1956).

Bayazitova, R. and Bangura, A. K., 'Cultural Integration: Effect of Music on Cultures', in *Journal of International Diversity* (Vol. 2012, No. 3, September 2012), pp.102-12.

The B. B. C. Handbook 1929 (London: 1929).

The BBC Year Book 1931 (London: BBC, 1931).

The B. B. C. Year-Book 1932 (London: BBC, 1932)

Beckett, I. F. W., *Britain's Part-Time Soldiers: The Amateur Military Tradition 1558-1945*, 2nd edn (Barnsley: Pen & Sword Military, 2011).

Beevor, A., *Inside the British Army* (London: Chatto & Windus, 1990).

Binns, P. L., *A Hundred Years of Military Music: being the story of the Royal Military School of Music Kneller Hall* (Gillingham, Dorset: The Blackmore Press, 1959).

Bion, W. R., *War Memoirs: 1917-19*, ed. F. Bion (London: Karnac, 1997).

Blaikley, D. J., *Acoustics in Relation to Wind Instruments. A Course of Three Lectures Delivered at The Royal Military School of Music, Kneller Hall, by D. J. Blaikley. With an Appendix on Musical Pitch* (London: Boosey & Co, 1890).

Blake, F. M., *The Irish Civil War and what it still means for the Irish people* (London: Information on Ireland, 1986).
Bloom, R. W., 'Propaganda and active measures', in R. Gal & A. D. Mangelsdorff (eds.) *Handbook of Military Psychology* (San Francisco, CA: John Wiley, 1991), pp. 693-710.
Boden, A., (ed.), *Stars in a Dark Night: The Letters of Ivor Gurney to the Chapman Family* (Gloucester: Alan Sutton, 1986).
Bond, B., *British Military Policy between the Two World Wars* (Oxford: Clarendon, 1980)
Bond, B. and Murray, W. 'The British Armed Forces, 1918-39', in A. R. Millett & W. Murray (eds), *Military Effectiveness Volume 2: The Interwar Period*, new (2nd) edn (Cambridge: Cambridge University Press, 2010), pp. 98-130.
Bonner, R., 'Ballincollig: Three Band Boys, Marie Lindsay and Others', *Military Historical Society Bulletin*, Vol. 59, Pt. 235, February, 2009, pp. 121-132.
Bower, M., *The Will to Manage: Corporate Success Through Programmed Management* (New York: McGraw-Hill, 1966).
Boyle, S., 'Organizational Identity or Esprit De Corps? The Use of Music in Military and Paramilitary Style Organisations', paper presented at the 3rd International Critical Management Studies Conference, Lancaster, 7-9 July 2003.
Boyle, S., 'And the Band Played On: Professional Musicians in Military and Service Bands', *International Journal of Arts Management*, 6, 3, Spring, 2004, pp. 4-12.
Bowers, P., *State and ceremonial funerals*, United Kingdom, House of Commons Library, Parliamentary and Constitution Centre, SN/PC/06600, 31 July 2013.
Boycott, J. A. G., *The Elements of Imperial Defence: A Study of the Geographical Features, Material Resources, Communications, and Organization of the British Empire* (Aldershot: Gale & Polden, 1931).
Brennan-Whitmore, W. J., (ed.), *Defence Forces Saorstát Éireann 1926: Army List and Directory* (Dublin: An t-Óglác, 1926; repr. Uckfield: The Naval and Military Press, 2007).
Brereton, J., *Chain Mail: The History of The Duke of Lancaster's Own Yeomanry* (Chippenham: Picton, 1992).
Braggs, S., and Harris, D., *Sun, Sea and Sand: The Great British Seaside Holiday* (Stroud: Tempus, 2006).
Briggs, A., 'The Welfare State in Historical Perspective', *European Journal of Sociology*, Vol. 2, No. 2, 1961, pp. 221-258.
Briggs, A., *Governing the BBC* (London: BBC, 1979).

Briggs, A., *The BBC: The First Fifty Years* (Oxford: Oxford University Press, 1985).

Briggs, A., *The History of Broadcasting in the United Kingdom: Volume I: The Birth of Broadcasting* (Oxford: Oxford University Press, 1995).

Briggs, A., *The History of Broadcasting in the United Kingdom: Volume II: The Golden Age of Wireless* (Oxford: Oxford University Press, 1995).

British Standards Institution, *British Standard Specification: Musical Pitch*. B.S. 880:, 1950.

Brown, A. W., *A Memoir: from Music to Wars* (Aberdeen: A. W. Brown, 2001).

Calder, J., Pigott, M., and Bruce, A., *The Queen's Birthday Parade: Trooping the Colour* (n. p.: Julian Calder Publishing, 2015).

Callery, P., 'Part 2: 1901 Census (families and pupils)' and 'Part 3: 1911 Census (families and pupils)' in G. H. O'Reilly (ed), *History of the Royal Hibernian Military School Dublin* (Dún Laoghaire, Co. Dublin: Genealogical Society of Ireland, 2001), pp. 37 & 55.

Cannadine, D., 'The Context, Performance and Meaning of Ritual: The British Monarchy and the 'Invention of Tradition', c.1820-1977', in E. Hobsbawm and T. Ranger (eds), *The Invention of Tradition* (Cambridge: Cambridge University Press (Canto)), 1992; repr. of 1983 edn).

Carl Fischer Military Band Music (New York: Carl Fischer, 1920).

Carver, M. *Britain's Army in the 20th Century* (London: Macmillan, 1998).

Casson, C., *Blowing My Own Trumpet: Memoirs of a Yorkshire Bandsman* (Stroud: The History Press, 2008).

Chance, W., *Children Under the Poor Law: Their Education Training and After-Care Together with a Criticism of the Report of the Departmental Committee on Metropolitan Poor Law Schools* (London: Swan Sonnenschein, 1897).

Chase, L., 'Modern Images and Social Tone in Clacton and Frinton in the Interwar Years', *International Journal of Maritime History*, 1997, Volume 9, Issue 1, pp. 149-170.

Chow, P., 'British Interests and Policy towards China, 1922-1927' (PhD thesis, London School of Economics, 2011).

Christopher, M., Payne, A. F. T., and Ballantyne, D., *Relationship Marketing: Bringing Quality, Customer Service and Marketing Together* (Oxford: Butterworth Heinemann, 1991).

Clarke, H. R., *A New History of the Royal Hibernian Military School Phoenix Park, Dublin: 1765-1924* (Wynd Yarm, Cleveland: Howard R. Clarke, 2011).

Cloughley, B., *Trumpeters: The Story of the Royal Artillery Boy Trumpeters* (Bognor Regis: Woodfield, 2008).

Cockerill, A. W., *Sons of the Brave: The Story of Boy Soldiers* (London: Leo Cooper/Secker & Warburg, 1984).

Cockerill, A. W., *The Charity of Mars: A History of the Royal Military Asylum (1803-1892)* (Cobourg, Ontario: Black Cat Press, 2002).

Coleman, M., 'Military Service Pensions for Veterans of the Irish Revolution, 1916-1923', *War in History*, 20(2), 2013, pp. 201-221.

Cook, N., 'Methods for analysing recordings', in N. Cook, E. Clarke, D. Leech-Wilkinson and J. Rink (eds.), *The Cambridge Companion to Recorded Music* (Cambridge: Cambridge University Press, 2009), pp. 221-245.

Cooke, R. T., *Cork's Barrack Street Silver and Reed Band: Ireland's oldest amateur musical institution* (Cork: Quality Books, 1992).

Copeland, P., *Sound Recordings* (London: The British Library, 1991).

Cowl, C. and Craik, S. H., *Henry George Farmer: a Bibliography*, (Glasgow: Glasgow University Libraries, 1999).

Crewdson, R., *Apollo's Swan and Lyre: Five Hundred Years of the Musicians' Company* (Woodbridge: Boydell, 2000).

Crook, J., *The Very Thing: The Memoires of Drummer Richard Bentinck, Royal Welch Fusiliers, 1807-1823* (London: Frontline Books, 2011).

Curtis, J., *Bands of Hope: A Study of Military Bands in the Twentieth Century*. 2010. MS.

Daniell, D. S., *Regimental History: The Royal Hampshire Regiment: Volume Three 1918-1954* (Aldershot: Gale & Polden, 1955).

Davin, A., *Growing Up Poor: Home, School and Street in London 1970-1914* (London: Rivers Oram Press, 1996).

Dawson, S., 'Working-Class Consumers and the Campaign for Holidays with Pay', *Twentieth Century British History*, Vol. 18, No. 3, 2007, pp. 277-305.

Day, T., *A Century of Recorded Music: Listening to Musical History* (New Haven: Yale University Press, 2000).

Dean, C. (ed.), *Music Programmes from the Sovereigns' Birthday Parades Trooping the Colour 1864-2008* (n.p.: International Military Music Society, 2008).

Dean, C. (ed.), *Supplement to Music Programmes from the Sovereigns' Birthday Parades 1864-2008* (n.p.: n.d).

Dean, C., 'The Great Annual Occasions' in C. Dean and G. Turner (eds), *Sound the Trumpets Beat the Drums: Military Music through the 20th Century* (Tunbridge Wells: Parapress, 2002), pp. 46-69.

Dean, C., 'Tattoos and Pageants' in C. Dean and G. Turner (eds), *Sound the Trumpets Beat the Drums: Military Music through the 20th Century* (Tunbridge Wells: Parapress, 2002), pp. 135-166.

Dean, C., *Jiggs: A Biography of Lieutenant Colonel C. H. Jaeger, OBE, Mus Bac, LRAM, ARCM, psm* (Tunbridge Wells: Parapress, 2013).

Dean, C., *The Band of the Welsh Guards – A Centenary* (London: Band of the Welsh Guards, 2016).

Dean, C., *The Royal Military School of Music, Kneller Hall 1857-2017* (London: The Kneller Hall Club, 2017).

Dean, C., and Turner, G. (eds), *Sound the Trumpets Beat the Drums: Military Music through the 20th Century* (Tunbridge Wells: IMMS/Parapress, 2002).

Debussy, C., 'Open-Air Music', in *Three Classics in the Aesthetics of Music: Monsieur Croche the Dilettante Hater*, trans. B. N. Langdon Davies (New York: Dover, 1962; repr. of 1928 edn), pp. 1-71.

Dethlefs, G. and Schadewitz, M., *Messenger of Peace and Send Sword: Citizens and Soldiers* (Münster, Germany: Stadtmuseum Münster, 1995).

Docherty, P., *The Khyber Pass: A History of Empire & Invasion* (New York: Sterling, 2008).

Doctor, J., *The BBC and Ultra-Modern Music, 1922-1936* (Cambridge: Cambridge University Press, 2000).

Dooley, T. P., 'Politics, bands and marketing: army recruitment in Waterford city, 1914-15', *The Irish Sword*, XVIII (1990-1992), pp. 205-219.

Down, A., *History of T. J. Down's Bands: From February, 1905 to December, 1936* (Warrington: J. Walker, 1938).

Doyle, J. M., 'Music in the Army', in A. Fleischmann (ed.) *Music in Ireland: A Symposium* (Cork: Cork University Press, 1952).

Duggan, J. P., *Neutral Ireland and the Third Reich* (Dublin: Gill and Macmillan, 1985).

Durie, A., 'The Scottish Seaside Resort in Peace and War, c. 1880-1960', *International Journal of Maritime History*, 1997, Vol. 9, Issue 1, pp. 171-186.

Edward Duke of Windsor, *A King's Story: The Memoirs of H.R.H. the Duke of Windsor K.G.* (New York: Putnam, 1951; repr. with an introduction by Philip Ziegler, London: Prion, 1998).

Edwards, T. J., *Military Customs*. 5th edn (Aldershot: Gale and Polden, 1961).

Ehrlich, C., *The Music Profession in Britain since the Eighteenth Century: A Social History* (Oxford: Clarendon, 1985).

Eiden, H., 'The Resorts Between the Wars' in Thornton, C. C. (ed.), *A History of the County of Essex: Clacton, Walton, and Frinton: North-East Essex Seaside Resorts*, The Victoria History of the Counties of England, Volume XI (Woodbridge: Institute of Historical Research/Boydell & Brewer, 2012), pp. 126-173.

Eisenberg, E., The Recording Angel: Music, Records and Culture from Aristotle to Zappa (London: Picador, 1988).

Emden, R. van, *Boy Soldiers of the Great War*, rev. edn (London: Bloomsbury, 2012).

Fahey, L. and Narayanan, V. K., *Macroenvironmental Analysis for Strategic Management* (St Paul: West Publishing, 1986).

Farmer, H. G., *Memoirs of the Royal Artillery Band: Its Origin, History and Progress* (London, Boosey & Co, 1904).

Farmer, H. G., *History of the Royal Artillery Band: 1762–1953* (London: Royal Artillery Institution, 1954).

Farmer, H. G., 'Irish Bandsmen in the British Army', *The Irish Sword*, V: 18, Summer, 1961, p. 58.

Fennell, F., *Basic Band Repertory: British Band Classics from the Conductor's Point of View* (Evanston, Ill: The Instrumentalist, 1980).

Finnegan, R., *The Hidden Musicians: Music-Making in an English Town*, rev. edn (Middletown: Wesleyan University Press, 2007).

Freeman, R. E., *Strategic Management: A Stakeholder Approach* (Boston, MA: Harper Collins, 1984).

Frith, S., *Performing Rites: Evaluating Pop Music* (Oxford: Oxford University Press, (1996).

Forsyth, C., *Orchestration*. 2nd edn (London: Macmillan, 1935).

Fosler-Lussier, D., 'Music Pushed, Music Pulled: Cultural Diplomacy, Globalization, and Imperialism', *Diplomatic History* (Vol. 36, No. 1, January 2012), pp. 53-64.

Fraser, M., *Weapons of Mass Distraction: Soft Power and American Empire* (Toronto: Key Porter, 2003).

Frith, S., 'Music and Everyday Life', in Clayton, M., Herbert, T. and Middleton, R. (eds), *The Cultural Study of Music: A Critical Introduction*, 2nd edn (Abingdon: Routledge, 2012), pp. 149-58

From Bandstand to Monkey Run (Sheffield: Sheffield City Library, 1989).

Gaisberg, F. W., *Music on Record* (London: Robert Hale, 1946).

Galeota, J., 'Cultural Imperialism: An American Tradition', *The Humanist* (May/June 2004), pp. 22-4 & 46.

Galloway, W. J., *Musical England* (London: Christophers, 1910).

Gaskell, G., *Everybody's Musical Companion: Containing Interesting Facts on Instruments of the Full of Symphony Orchestra. The Military Band. The Brass Band. National Anthems. Some Music Journals. Tales of the Tunes. Diplomas and Certificates. Do You Know? Opera. Regimental Marches. The World's Great Musicians* (Southport: Hugh Rigg, 1949).

Gibson, C., *Army Childhood: British Army Children's Lives and Times* (Oxford: Shire, 2012).

Giddings, R., 'Delusive seduction: Pride, pomp, circumstance and military music', in J. M. MacKenzie (ed.), *Popular Imperialism and the Military, 1850-1950* (Manchester: Manchester University Press, 1992).

Gienow-Hecht, J. C. E., *Sound Diplomacy: Music and Emotions in Transatlantic Relations, 1850-1920* (Chicago: Chicago University Press, 2009).

Gledhill, J., 'Coming of Age in Uniform: the Foundling Hospital and British Army Bands in the Twentieth Century', *Family and Community History*, Vol. 13/2, November, 2010, pp. 114-127.

Gleeson, J., *Pomp and Circumstance: The Band of the Coldstream Guards, A History 1685-2017*, 2nd edn (London: Regimental Headquarters Coldstream Guards, 2018).

Godfrey, D., *Memories and Music: Thirty-five Years of Conducting* (London: Hutchinson, 1924).

Gooch, G. P. and Temperley, H. (eds), *British Documents on the Origins of the War 1898-1914: Vol. II The Anglo-Japanese Alliance and the Franco-British Entente* (London: HMSO, 1927).

Goodman, J. and Jacobs, A., 'Musical literacies in the English inter-war secondary classroom', in *Paedagogica Historica*, Vol. 44, Nos. 1-2, February-April 2008, pp. 153-166.

Gore, J., *Send More Shrouds: The V1 Attack on the Guards' Chapel, 1944* (Barnsley: Pen & Sword Military, 2017).

Grainger, W. K., *The Life and Times of a Regimental Band: A History of the Bands of the King's Own Yorkshire Light Infantry*. The Rifles Office, Pontefract, 1995, MS.

Gramit, D., 'The Business of Music on the Peripheries of Empire: A Turn-of-the-Century Case Study', in C. Bashford and R. Montemorra Marvin (eds) *The Idea of Art Music in a Commercial World, 1800-1930* (Woodbridge: Boydell, 2016), pp. 274-296.

Grant, M. J., Möllemann, R., Morlandstö, I., Münz, S. C., and Noxoll, C., 'Music and Conflict: Interdisciplinary Perspectives', *Interdisciplinary Science Reviews*, 35: 2, June, 2010, pp. 183-198.
Gray, F., *Designing the Seaside: Architecture, Society and Nature* (London: Reaktion, 2006).
Green, L., *City of Ely Military Band: Golden Jubilee Celebrating 50 musical years 1962-2012* (Ely: SHBB Publishing, 2012).
Gregory, A., *The Silence of Memory: Armistice Day 1919-1946* (Oxford: Berg, 1994).
Gregory, A. H., 'The roles of music in society: the ethnomusicological perspective', in D. J. Hargreaves and A. North (eds), *The Social Psychology of Music* (Oxford: Oxford University Press, 1997), pp. 107-140.
Greig, J. (ed.), *The Musical Educator: A Library of Instruction by Eminent Specialists: Volume The Fifth* (Edinburgh: T. C. & E. C. Jack, Grange Publishing, 1895).
Grube, D., 'How can 'Britishness' be Re-made?' *The Political Quarterly* (Vol. 82, No. 4, October-December 2011), pp. 628-35.
Gwynn, C. W., *Imperial Policing*, 2nd edn (London: Macmillan, 1939).
Hailstone, A., *The British Bandsman Centenary Book – a social history of Brass Bands* (Baldock: Egon, 1987).
Hammond, D. B., 'Soft Powering the Empire: British Military Bands, Influence and Cultural Imperialism in the Twentieth Century', *The RUSI Journal*, Vol. 158, Issue 5, 2013, pp. 90-96.
Hammond, D. B., 'Band Corporal John Shaul VC', *Fanfare: The Journal of the Corps of Army Music*, 2016, pp. 134-137.
Hargreaves, D. J., and North, A., 'Experimental aesthetics and everyday music listening', in Hargreaves, D. J. & North, A. (eds), *The Social Psychology of Music* (Oxford: Oxford University Press, 1997), pp. 84-103.
Harley, J., 'Music at the English Court in the Eighteenth and Nineteenth Centuries', *Music & Letters*, Vol. 50, No. 3 , July, 1969.
Harris, J. P., 'Obstacles to innovation and readiness: the British Army's experience 1918-1939', in W. Murray and R. H. Sinnreich (eds) *The Past as Prologue: The Importance of History to the Military Profession* (New York: Cambridge University Press, 2006), pp. 195-216.
Harrison, I., 'Achieving Unity of Purpose in Hybrid Conflict – HQ ARRC: Capability Experimentation: Part 1', *British Army Review*, No. 148, Winter 2009/2010, pp. 55-56.
Hart, P., *The I.R.A. at War 1916-1923* (Oxford: Oxford University Press, 2003).

Hassan, J., *The Seaside, Health and the Environment in England and Wales since 1800* (Aldershot: Ashgate, 2003).

Haynes, B., *A History of Performing Pitch: The Story of "A"* (Lanham, Maryland: Scarecrow Press, 2002).

Herbert, T., 'Farmer's Contribution to the Study of Military Music', in C. Cowl and S. H. Craik, *Henry George Farmer: a Bibliography*, (Glasgow: Glasgow University Libraries, 1999), pp. xvii-xxi.

Herbert, T., 'God's Perfect Minstrels', in *The British Brass Band: A Musical and Social History* (Oxford: Oxford University Press, 2000).

Herbert, T. and Barlow, H., *Music and the British Military in the Long Nineteenth Century* (Oxford: Oxford University Press, 2013).

Higham, R., *Armed Forces in Peacetime: Britain, 1918-1940, a case study* (London: G. T. Foulis & Co, 1962).

Higham, R., 'The Development of the Royal Air Force, 1909-1945', in R. Higham (ed.), *A Guide to the Sources of British Military History* (London: Routledge & Kegan Paul, 1972), pp. 422-451.

Hiley, N., 'Sir Hedley Le Bas and the Origins of Domestic Propaganda in Britain 1914-1917', *European Journal of Marketing*, Vol. 21, Issue 8, pp. 30-46.

Hills, R. J. T., *The Royal Horse Guards (The Blues)* (London: Leo Cooper, 1970).

Hoby, C., *Military Band Instrumentation: A Course for Composers and Students* (London: Oxford University Press, 1936).

Holmes, R., *Soldiers: Army Lives and Loyalties from Redcoats to Dusty Warriors* (London: HarperPress, 2011).

Howe, J., *A Conductor's Journey* (Eastbourne: J. H. Publishing, 2002).

Howard, H. J., *Military Brass vs. Civilian Academics at the National War College: A Clash of Cultures* (Lanham, Maryland: Lexington Books, 2011).

Hyman, R., and Hyman, N., *The Pump Room Orchestra Bath: Three Centuries of Music and Social History* (Salisbury: Hobnob Press, 2011).

Inkster, D., *Union Cinemas Ritz: A Story of Theatre Organs and Cine-Variety* (Hove: Wick), 1999

Imrie, J. M. M., *The Military Band in South Africa* (Simonstown: The South African Navy Printing Press, 1976).

International Organization for Standardization, *Acoustics – Standard tuning frequency (standard musical pitch)*. First edition – 1975-01-15. ISO 16-1975 (E).

Jackson, M. W., *Harmonious Triads: Physicists. Musicians, and Instrument Makers in Nineteenth-Century Germany* (Cambridge, Massachusetts: MIT, 2006).

Jacob, G., *The Composer and his Art* (London: Greenwood, 1955).

Johnson, G., 'Managing Strategic Change: Strategy, Culture and Action', in Susan Segal-Horn (ed.), *The Strategy Reader*, 2nd edn (Malden, MA: Blackwell, 2004), pp. 279-92.

Johnston, R., 'Music in Northern Ireland since 1921', in J. R. Hill (ed.), *A New History of Ireland: Ireland 1921-84: Volume 7* (Oxford: Oxford University Press, 2003).

Jones, D., *Bullets and Bandsmen: The Story of a Bandsman on the Western Front* (Salisbury: Owl Press, 1992).

Jones, R. A., '"Banding Together": Power, Identity and Interaction within the Concert and Contest Performance Contexts of the Brighouse and Rastrick Brass Band' (PhD thesis, Sheffield University, 2007).

Kautt, W. H., *The Anglo-Irish War, 1916-1921: A People's War* (Westport, CT: Praeger, 1999).

Kautt, W. H., *Ambushes and Armour: The Irish Rebellion 1919-1921* (Sallins, Co. Kildare: Irish Academic Press, 2010).

Kaye, G. W. C., 'International Standard of Musical Pitch', *Nature*, vol. 142, November 5, 1938, pp. 820-21.

Kaye, G. W. C., 'International Standard of Concert Pitch', *Nature*, no. 3630, May 27, 1939, pp. 905-906.

Kappey, J. A., *Military Music: A History of Wind-Instrumental Bands* (London: Boosey and Co, 1894).

Keegan, J., 'The Interwar Years', in R. Higham (ed.), *A Guide to the Sources of British Military History* (London: Routledge & Kegan Paul, 1972), pp. 452-469.

Kelsey, J., 'Foundling Hospital Boys' Band'. Lecture given at The Foundling Museum, London, 1st February 2015.

Kemp, J. C., *The History of the Royal Scots Fusiliers: 1919-1959* (Glasgow: Robert MacLehose & Co/Glasgow University Press, 1963),

Kennedy, G., 'Imperial Networks, Imperial Defence, and Perceptions of American Influence on the British Empire in the Inter-war Period: The Case of the 27th Earl of Crawford and Balcarres', *Canadian Journal of History* (Vol. 47, No. 3, Winter 2012), pp. 567-95.

Kendrick, I., *More Music in the Air: The Story of Music in the Royal Air Force* (Ruislip: RAF Music Services, 2011).

Khan, S. S., *When Military Wages Peace: Military Bands in Diplomace, War & Statecraft* (New Delhi, India: Pentagon Press, 2019).

Kim, P. H. and Shin, H., 'The Birth of "Rok": Cultural Imperialism, Nationalism, and the Glocalization of Rock Music in South Korea, 1964–1975', *positions* (Vol. 18, No. 1, Spring 2010), pp. 199-230.

Kohli, M., *The Golden Bridge: Young Immigrants to Canada, 1833-1939* (Toronto: Dundurn, 2003).

Kolkowski, A., Miller, D., and Blier-Carruthers, A., 'The Art and Science of Acoustic Recording: Re-enacting Arthur Nikisch and the Berlin Philharmonic Orchestra's landmark 1913 recording of Beethoven's Fifth Symphony', *Communications (Science Museum Group Journal)*, Spring 2015 (10.15180; 150302 Research), pp. 1-46.

Ladapo, O. A., 'Martial Music at Dawn: Introit for Coups d'État', in M. J. Grant and F. J. Stone-Davis (eds), *The Soundtrack of Conflict: The Role of Music in Wartime and in Conflict Situations* (Hildesheim, Germany: Georg Olms, 2013).

Laffan, M., *The Resurrection of Ireland: The Sinn Féin Party, 1916-1923* (Cambridge: Cambridge University Press, 2004).

Lambert, C., *Music Ho! A Study of Music in Decline* (London: Hogarth, 1985 [1934]).

Lane, J., (ed.), The 'Boys' of the Millstreat Battalion Area: Some Personal Accounts of the War of Independence (Aubane, Cork: Aubane Historical Society, 2003).

Laubach, F., 'The Military Band', in J. Greig (ed.) *The Musical Educator: A Library of Instruction by Eminent Specialists: Volume The Fifth* (Edinburgh: T. C. & E. C. Jack, Grange Publishing, 1895), pp. 77-100.

Leech-Wilkinson, D., 'Recordings and histories of performance style', in N. Cook, E. Clarke, D. Leech-Wilkinson and J. Rink (eds.), *The Cambridge Companion to Recorded Music* (Cambridge: Cambridge University Press, 2009), pp. 246-262.

LeMahieu, D. L., 'The Gramophone: Recorded Music and the Cultivated Mind in Britain Between the Wars', *Technology and Culture*, Vol. 23, No. 3, 1982, pp. 372-391.

Levine, L. W., *Highbrow/Lowbrow: The Emergence of Cultural Hierarchy in America* (Cambridge, Massachusetts: Harvard University Press, 1988).

Liddle, P., *Captured Memories 1900-1918: Across the Threshold of War* (Barnsley: Pen & Sword, 2010).

Limbrick, G. J., *The Children of the Homes: A century of Erdington Cottage Homes* (Birmingham: WordWorks, 2012).
Lindsay, W. A., *And the Band Plays On: The Biography of Ernie Waites M.B.E. as told to Wally Lindsay* (Sale: Wilshere, 1994).
Lloyd, S., *Sir Dan Godfrey: Champion of British Composers* (London: Thames, 1995).
Lowerson, J., *Amateur Operatics: A Social and Cultural History* (Manchester: Manchester University Press, 2005).
Luvaas, J. *The Education of an Army: British Military Thought, 1815-1940* (London: Chicago University Press, 1964).
Lynn, K. S., *Charlie Chaplin and His Times* (New York: Simon & Schuster, 1997).
MacDonald, D., *Blood & Thunder: Inside An Ulster Protestant Band* (Cork: Mercier Press, 2010).
MacDonald, M., *John Foulds: his life in music* (Rickmansworth: Triad Press, 1975).
Maciejewski, R., *Beechholme: A Children's Village* (Banstead: Banstead History Research Group, 2010).
Mackenzie-Rogan, J., *Fifty Years of Army Music* (London: Methuen, 1926).
Magdalen Green Bandstand: 1890-1990 (Dundee: West End Community Council Blackness Library, 1990).
Mallinson, A, *The Making of the British Army: From the English Civil War to the War on Terror* (London: Bantam, 2009).
Mandel, C., *A Treatise on the Instrumentation of Military Bands; Describing the Character and Proper Employment of Every Musical Instrument Used in Reed Bands* (London: Boosey and Sons, 1859).
Manual of Ceremonial (London: HMSO, 1935).
Marshall, P. J., 'Introduction: The World Shaped by Empire', in Marshall, P. J. (ed.), *The Cambridge Illustrated History of the British Empire* (Cambridge: Cambridge University Press, 1996), pp. 7-13.
Marshall, P. J., 'Imperial Britain', in Marshall, P. J. (ed.), *The Cambridge Illustrated History of the British Empire* (Cambridge: Cambridge University Press, 1996), pp. 318-37.
Martland, P., *Recording History: The British Record Industry, 1888-1931* (Lanham: Scarecrow, 2013).
Mason, H. B., *Memoirs of a Gunner Bandsman: 1907-1932* (Orpington: Mason, 1978).
Masters, J., *Bugles and a Tiger: A Personal Adventure* (London: Michael Joseph, 1956).

Mays, S., *Fall Out the Officers* (London: Eyre & Spottiswoode, 1969).
Mays, S., *Reuben's Corner: An English Country Boyhood* (London: Eyre Methuen, 1969; repr. 1980).
Mays, S., *The Band Rats* (London: Peter Davies, 1975).
Mays, S., *The First and the Last* (London: Janus, 1975).
May, T., *Remembering the Past – Looking to the Future: 100 Years of Queen Victoria School* (Oxford: Gresham Books/Queen Victoria School, 2008).
McKenna, J., *Guerrilla Warfare in the Irish War of Independence, 1919-1921* (Jefferson, NC: McFarland, 2011).
McKibben, R. *Classes and Cultures: England, 1918-1951* (Oxford: Oxford University Press, 1998).
Military and Orchestral Band Instruments (London: Boosey & Co, 1929).
Military Band Instruments (London: Hawkes & Son, 1927).
Miller, G. J., *The Military Band* (London: Novello and Company, 1912).
Miller, G. J., *The Piping Times in Peace and War: Being the Autobiography of a Royal Musician in Five Reigns*. Museum of Army Music, n.d., MS.
Mitchell, J. C., *From Kneller Hall to Hammersmith: The Band Works of Gustav Holst* (Tutzing: Verlegt Bei Hans Schneider, 1990).
Mitchell, J. C., 'J. A. C. Sommerville [sic] and the British Band in the Era of Holst and Vaughan Williams' in F. J. Cipolla and D. Hunsberger (eds.), *The Wind Ensemble and its Repertoire: Essays on the Fortieth Anniversary of the Eastman Wind Ensemble* (Rochester, New York: Rochester University Press, 1994).
Mitchell, R. K., Agle, B. R. and Wood, D. J., 'Towards a theory of stakeholder identification and salience: defining the principle of who and what really counts,' *Academy of Management Review*, 22, 4, 1997, pp. 853–86.
Moore, B. C. J., *An Introduction to the Psychology of Hearing*, 3rd edn (London: Academic Press, 1989).
Morgan, N. J., and Pritchard, A., *Power and Politics at the Seaside: The Development of Devon's Resorts in the Twentieth Century* (Exeter: University of Exeter Press, 1999).
Motion, A., *The Lamberts: George, Constant & Kit* (London: Hogarth, 1987).
Murdoch, L., *Imagined Orphans – Poor Families, Child Welfare, and Contested Citizenship in London* (New Brunswick, New Jersey: Rutgers University Press, 2006).

Murray, D., *Music of the Scottish Regiments* (Edinburgh: Mercat, 2001 [1994]).
Myers, A., 'Brasswind Manufacturing at Boosey & Hawkes, 1930-59', *Historic Brass Society Journal*, 1, 3, 2003, pp. 55-72.
Nalden, C., *Half and Half: The Memoirs of a Charity Brat 1908-1989* (Tauranga, New Zealand: Moana Press, 1989).
Napier, R., *From Horses to Chieftains: With the 8th Hussars 1934-1959*, 2nd edn (Bognor Regis, West Sussex: Woodfield, 2002).
Nettels, R., *The Orchestra in England: A Social History* (London: Jonathan Cape, 1946).
Nichols, R. H., and Wray, F. A., *The History of the Foundling Hospital* (London: Oxford University Press (Humphrey Milford), 1935).
Norris, J., *Marching to the Drums: A History of Military Drums and Drummers* (Stroud: Spellmount, 2012).
Nott, J., *Music for the People: Popular Music and Dance in Interwar Britain* (Oxford: Oxford University Press, 2002).
Nye Jr, J., *Soft Power: The Means to Success in World Politics* (London: Public Affairs, 2004).
Nye, Jr., J. S. and Wang, J. 'Hard Decisions on Soft Power: Opportunities and Difficulties for Chinese Soft Power', *Harvard International Review* (Vol. 31, No. 2, Summer 2009), pp. 18-22.
Oakley, D., *Fiddler on the March: A Biography of Lieutenant Colonel Sir Vivian Dunn KCVO OBE FRAM Royal Marines* (London: Royal Marines Historical Society, 2000).
Olatunji, M., *European styled Military Music in Nigeria: Its Theme, Style and Patronage System* (Saarbrücken, Germany: VDM, 2011).
Oldfield, P., *Victoria Crosses on the Western Front August 1914-Apri 1915: Mons to Hill 60* (Barnsley: Pen & Sword Military, 2014).
O'Donnell, R., (ed.), *Limerick's Fighting Story 1916-21: Told by the Men Who Made It With a Unique Pictorial record of the Period* (Cork: Mercier Press, 2009).
O'Donoghue, D., 'State within a State: The Nazis in Neutral Ireland', *History Ireland*, 14, 6, Nov-Dec (2006), pp. 35-39.
O'Halpin, E., *Defending Ireland: The Irish State and its Enemies Since 1922* (Oxford: Oxford University Press, 1999).
O'Reilly, G. H., 'The Royal Hibernian Military School', *Genealogical Society of Ireland*, 3: 4, Winter, 2002, p. 248.
O'Reilly, T., *Rebel Heart: George Lennon: Flying Column Commander* (Cork: Mercier Press, 2009).
Paine, J., 'A Bibliography of British Military Music', *Journal of the Royal United Service Institute*, Feb 1, 73, 1928, pp. 334-341.

Palmer, R., *"What a Lovely War!": British Soldiers' Songs from the Boer War to the Present Day* (London: Michael Joseph, 1990).

Panayi, P., 'The settlement of Germans in Britain during the nineteenth century', *IMIS Beiträge*, 2000, 14, pp. 25-44.

Patmore, D. N. C., 'Selling sounds: Recordings and the record business', in N. Cook, E. Clarke, D. Leech-Wilkinson and J. Rink (eds.), *The Cambridge Companion to Recorded Music* (Cambridge: Cambridge University Press, 2009), pp. 120-139.

Patmore, D. N. C., 'Commerce, Competition and Culture: The Classical Music Recording Industry, 1923-1932', *ARSC Journal*, vol. 46, no. 1, 2015, pp. 43-65.

Pearton, M., *The LSO at 70: A History of the Orchestra*. London: Victor Gollancz, 1974).

Pennanen, R. P., 'Tattoos, Neo-Traditions and Entertainment – The Roles of Military Bands in Habsburg Bosnia and Herzegovina (1878-1918)', in M. Schramm (ed.) *Militärmusik zwischen Nutzen und Mißbrauch* (Bonn: Militärmusikdienst der Bundeswehr, 2011), pp. 17-25.

Pennington, J. W., *Pick Up Your Parrots and Monkeys...and Fall in Facing the Boat: The Life of a Boy Soldier in India* (London: Cassell, 2003).

Perrin, W. G., 'Notes on the Development of Bands of the Royal Navy: I. To the End of the 17th Century.', *The Mariner's Mirror*, Vol 9, No 1, 1923, pp. 2-10.

Perrin, W. G., 'Notes on the Development of Bands of the Royal Navy: II. The Decline and Fall of the Trumpeter.', *The Mariner's Mirror*, Vol 9, No 2, 1923, pp. 46-47.

Perrin, W. G., 'Notes on the Development of Bands of the Royal Navy: III.– Unofficial Bands.', *The Mariner's Mirror*, Vol 9, No 3, 1923, pp. 78-83.

Perrin, W. G., 'Notes on the Development of Bands of the Royal Navy: IV.– Introduction of Band Ratings.', *The Mariner's Mirror*, Vol 9, No 4, 1923, pp. 103-109.

Perrin, W. G., 'Notes on the Development of Bands of the Royal Navy: V.– Training the Bandsmen.', *The Mariner's Mirror*, Vol 9, No 5, 1923, pp. 105-107.

Perrin, W. G., 'Notes on the Development of Bands of the Royal Navy: VI.– Half Measures.', *The Mariner's Mirror*, Vol 9, No 5, 1923, pp. 147-149.

Perrin, W. G., 'Notes on the Development of Bands of the Royal Navy: VII.– Improvements in Pay.', *The Mariner's Mirror*, Vol 9, No 6, 1923, pp. 180-183.

Perrin, W. G., 'Notes on the Development of Bands of the Royal Navy: VIII.– The Establishment of the Royal Naval School of Music.', *The Mariner's Mirror*, Vol 9, No 7, 1923, pp. 202-208.

Philip, R., *Early Recordings and Musical Style: Changing Tastes in Instrumental Performance* (Cambridge: Cambridge University Press, 1992).

Philip, R., *Performing Music in the Age of Recording* (New Haven: Yale University Press, 2004).

Philip, R., 'Brass Playing Before Globalization', in Brass Scholarship in Review: Proceedings of the Historic Brass Society Conference, Cité de la Musique, Paris, Bucina, No. 6, 2006, pp. 275-288.

Pine, R., *Music and Broadcasting in Ireland* (Dublin: Four Courts Press, 2005).

Pitfield, S. S., 'British Music for Clarinet and Piano 1880 to 1945: Repertory and Performance Practice' (PhD thesis, Sheffield University, 2000).

Pond, C., *Lyings in state*, United Kingdom, House of Commons Library, Parliamentary and Constitution Centre, SN/PC/1735, 12 April 2002.

Porter, M. E, Competitive Strategy: Techniques for Analysing Industries and Competitors (New York: The Free Press, 1980).

Prahms, W., *Newcastle Ragged and Industrial School* (Stroud, Gloucestershire: Tempus, 2006).

Pronay, N., 'British Newsreels in the 1930s: 1. Audience and Producers', in *History (Film Section)* (ed. J. A. S. Grenville), 1971, Vol. 56(188), pp. 411-417.

Pronay, N., 'British Newsreels in the 1930s: 2. Their Policies and Impact', in *History (Film Section)* (ed. J. A. S. Grenville), 1971, Vol. 57(189), pp. 63-72.

Pugh, G., *London's Forgotton Children: Thomas Coram and the Foundling Hospital* (Stroud: The History Press, 2007; repr. 2013).

Pugh, G., 'London's Forgotten Children: Thomas Coram and the Foundling Hospital'. Transcript of lecture given at Gresham College, 12 March 2012.

Pullinger, A., *Reminiscences*. Museum of Army Music, 1939, MS.

Purtell, S. A. (2011). 'In tune with the times': The history of performing pitch in Melbourne (PhD thesis, University of Melbourne, 2011).

Quane, M., 'The Royal Hibernian Military School Phoenix Park, Dublin: Part II', *Dublin Historical Record*, Vol. 18, No. 2, March, 1963, p. 48.
Rabbitts, P. A., *Bandstands* (Oxford: Shire, 2011).
Rabbitts, P. A, *Bandstands of Britain* (Stroud: The History Press, 2014).
Radford, K., 'Drum Rolls and Gender Roles in Protestant Marching Bands in Belfast', *British Journal of Ethnomusicology*, Vol 10:2, 2001, pp. 37-59.
Ranson, E., *British Defence Policy and Appeasement Between the Wars, 1919-1939* (London: The Historical Association, 1993).
Range, M., *Music and Ceremonial at British Coronations: From James I to Elizabeth II* (Cambridge: Cambridge University Press, 2012).
Range, M., *British Royal and State Funerals: Music and Ceremonial since Elizabeth I* (Martlesham: Boydell & Brewer, 2016).
Rapp, W. M., *The Wind Band Masterworks of Holst, Vaughan, and Grainger* (Galesville: Meredith Music, 2005).
Rast, M., 'Tactics, Politics, and Propaganda in the Irish War of Independence, 1917-1921' (MA thesis, Georgia State University, 2011).
Rau, P., *English Modernism, National Identity and the Germans, 1890-1950* (Farnham: Ashgate, 2009).
Regimental Standing Orders of The Manchester Regiment: By Order of The Colonel Commanding, 1st June, 1930 (Aldershot: Gale & Polden, 1930).
Regimental Standing Orders. Grenadier Guards (London: Army & Navy Stores, 1939).
Reily, S. A., 'The Localization of the Civic Wind and Brass Band in Minas Gerais, Brazil', in M. Schramm (ed.) *Militärmusik zwischen Nutzen und Mißbrauch* (Bonn: Militärmusikdienst der Bundeswehr, 2011), pp. 119-136.
Reynolds, B., *Music While You Work: An Era in Broadcasting* (Lewes, East Sussex: Book Guild, 2006).
Richards, J. *Imperialism and Music: Britain 1876–1953* (Manchester: Manchester University Press, 2001).
Roberts, R., 'The Corporation as impresario: the municipal provision of entertainment in Victorian and Edwardian Bournemouth', in J. K. Walton and J. Walvin (eds.) *Leisure in Britain: 1780-1939* (Manchester: Manchester University Press, 1983), pp. 137-157.
Rose, K., *King George V* (London: Weidenfeld and Nicolson, 1983).

Royal Horse Guards: Standing Orders (Aldershot: Gale & Polden, 1938).

Rudd, L. C., *A Short Account of the Duke of York's Royal Military School, Dover (Founded 19th June, 1801)* (Dover: The Duke of York's Royal Military School, 1924).

Russell, D., *Popular Music in England, 1840-1914: A social history*. 2nd edn (Manchester: Manchester University Press, 1997).

Russell, D., "What is Wrong with Brass Bands?': Cultural Change and the Band Movement, 1918-c.1964', in T. Herbert (ed.), *The British Brass Band: A Music and Social History* (Oxford: Oxford University Press, 2000), pp. 68-121.

Russell, J. F., and Elliot, J H., *The Brass Band Movement* (London: J. M. Dent and Sons, 1936).

Ryan, J. J., 'Nationalism and Music in Ireland' (PhD thesis, National University of Ireland, St Patrick's College, Maynooth, 1991).

Ryan, J., 'The Tone of Defiance', in White, H. and Murphy, M. (eds.), *Musical Constructions of Nationalism: Essays on the History of European Musical Culture 1800-1945* (Cork: Cork University Press, 2001), pp. 197-211.

Ryan, J. J., 'Music in Independent Ireland since 1921', in J. R. Hill (ed), *A New History of Ireland: Ireland 1921-84: Volume 7* (Oxford: Oxford University Press, 2003).

Sant, J., *Albert W. Ketèlbey 1875-1959 From the Sanctuary of his Heart: Reflections on the life of the Birmingham born composer* (Sutton Coldfield: Manifold, 2000).

Saunders, N., *The Poppy: A Cultural History from Ancient Egypt to Flanders Fields to Afghanistan* (London: Oneworld, 2013).

Scott, D. B., 'Irish Nationalism, British Imperialism and the Role of Popular Music', in P. Fairclough (ed.) *Twentieth-Century Music and Politics: Essays in Memory of Neil Edmonds* (Farnham: Ashgate, 2013).

Scott, J. L., 'The Evolution of the Brass Band and its Repertoire in Northern England' (PhD thesis, Sheffield University, 1970).

Scowcroft, P. L., *British Light Music: A personal gallery of 20th-century composers* (Binsted, Dance Books, 2013 [1997]).

Seashore, C. E., *The Psychology of Music* (New York: Dover, 1967 [1938]).

Self, G., *Light Music in Britain since 1870: A Survey* (Aldershot: Ashgate, 2001).

Sheehan, W., *British Voices from the Irish War of Independence 1918-1921: The Words of British Servicemen Who Were There* (Cork: The Collins Press, 2007).

Sheehan, W., *Hearts & Mines: The British 5th Division, Ireland, 1920-1922* (Cork: The Collins Press, 2009).

Sheehan, W., *A Hard Local War: The British Army and the Guerrilla War in Cork, 1919-1921* (Stroud: The History Press, 2011).

Sheil, F., *Missing a Beat: Bridging Ireland's Orchestral Gaps: A Review of Orchestral Provision in Ireland* (Dublin: The Arts Council, 2010).

Sheldon, N., 'Civilising the Delinquent and the Neglected: The Role of the Industrial School,' *History of Childhood Colloquium*, 21 June 2008, Oxford.

Sheldon, N., 'The musical careers of the poor: the role of music as a vocational training for boys in British care institutions 1870-1918', *History of Education*, Vol. 38, No. 6, November, 2009, pp. 747-759.

Shirer, W. L., *The Rise and Fall of the Third Reich: A History of Nazi Germany* (London: Book Club Associates, 1984 [1960]).

Shorter, G., *"Play Up Dukies": Duke of York's Royal Military School 1801-1986* (Leatherhead, Surrey: The Duke of York's Royal Military School, Old Boys Association, 1987).

Singleton, G., *Music in Blue* (Maidenhead: Eagle & Lyre, 2007).

Smith, R. L. (ed.), *Debussy on Music* (London: Secker and Warburg, 1977).

Stanley, R., 'A formative force: the BBC's role in the development of music and its audiences in Northern Ireland, 1924-39' (PhD thesis, Queen's University, Belfast, 2012).

Statler, K. C., 'The Sound of Musical Diplomacy', *Diplomatic History*, Vol. 36, No. 1, January, 2012, pp. 71-75.

Stewart, S., *The Central London District Schools 1856-1933: A Short History* (Hanwell, London: Hanwell Community Association, 1980).

Stockwell, A., 'Power, Authority, and Freedom', in Marshall, P. J. (ed.), *The Cambridge Illustrated History of the British Empire* (Cambridge: Cambridge University Press, 1996), pp. 147-84.

Stokes, M. 'Globalization and the Politics of World Music', in Clayton, M., Herbert, T. and Middleton, R. (eds), *The Cultural Study of Music: A Critical Introduction*, second edition (Abingdon: Routledge, 2012), pp. 107-16

Street, O. W. 'The Clarinet and its Music', in *Proceedings of the Musical Association*, 42nd Session, 1915-1916, pp. 89-115.

Street, S. and Carpenter, R., *The Bournemouth Symphony Orchestra: A Centenary Celebration* (Wimborne, Dorset: Dovecote, 1993).

Sutherland, H., *They Blow Their Trumpets* (London: P. R. Macmillan, 1959).
Sutton, J. (ed.), *Wait for the Waggon: The Story of the Royal Corps of Transport and its Predecessors 1794-1993* (Barnsley: Leo Cooper, 1998).
Talam, J., 'Meterhane and their influence on Bosnian folk music', in M. Schramm (ed.) *Militärmusik zwischen Nutzen und Mißbrauch* (Bonn: Militärmusikdienst der Bundeswehr, 2011), pp. 9-16.
Tanner, J., *Instruments of Battle: The Fighting Drummers & Buglers of the British Army from the Late 17th Century to the Present Day* (Oxford: Casemate, 2017).
Taylor, A. J. P., *English History 1914-1945* (Harmondsworth: Pelican, 1970).
Taylor, P., 'Music in the Parks', in C. Dean and G. Turner (eds), *Sound the Trumpets Beat the Drums: Military Music through the 20th Century* (Tunbridge Wells: Parapress, 2002), pp. 78-92.
The Drummer's Handbook. AC 71333 (D/DAT/13/28/2), Ministry of Defence, 1985.
The General Annual Report on the British Army for the Year Ending 30th September, 1923, with which is incorporated the Annual Report on Recruiting, Prepared by Command of the Army Council. Presented to Parliament by Command of His Majesty (London: HMSO, 1924).
The King's Regulations and Orders for the Army (London: HMSO, 1912; 1923; 1928; 1935; 1940).
Thomson, G. P. C., 'The Ceremonial and Political Roles of Village Bands, 1846-1974', in W. H. Beezley, C. E. Martin, and W. E. French (eds) *Rituals of Rule, Rituals of Resistance: Public Celebrations and Popular Culture in Mexico* (Lanham, Maryland: Rowman & Littlefield Publishers, 1994), pp. 315-316.
Thornton, R. K. R. (ed.), *Ivor Gurney: War Letters* (Manchester: Carcanet, 1983).
Tomlinson, J. *Cultural Imperialism: A Critical Introduction* (London: Continuum, 2002).
Trendell, J., *Colonel Bogey to the Fore: A Biography of Kenneth J. Alford* (Dover: Blue Band, 1991).
Trezise, S., 'The recorded document: Interpretation and discography', in N. Cook, E. Clarke, D. Leech-Wilkinson and J. Rink (eds.), *The Cambridge Companion to Recorded Music* (Cambridge: Cambridge University Press, 2009), pp. 186-209.
Troup, J., *The Life that Jack Lived: Experiences of a Norfolk soldier and policeman* (Dereham: Larks Press, 1997).

Turner, A. W., *The Last Post: Music, Remembrance and the Great War* (London: Aurum, 2014).

Turner, G. and Turner, A. W., *Cavalry and Corps: The History of British Military Bands, Vol. 1* (Staplehurst, Kent: Spellmount, 1994).

Turner, G. and Turner, A. W., *Guards and Infantry: The History of British Military Bands, Vol.2* (Staplehurst, Kent: Spellmount, 1996).

Turner, G. and Turner, A. W., *The Trumpets Will Sound: The Story of the Royal Military School of Music Kneller Hall (Tunbridge Wells: Parapress, 1996)*

Turner, G. and Turner, A. W., *Infantry and Irish: The History of British Military Bands, Vol. 3* (Staplehurst, Kent: Spellmount, 1997).

Valiulis, M. G., *Portrait of a Revolutionary: General Richard Mulcahy and the Founding of the Irish Free State* (Lexington: Kentucky University Press, 1992).

Vasiljević, M., 'A 'Quiet African Episode' for The Serbian Army in the Great War: The Band of the Cavalry Division and Dragutin F. Pokorni in North Africa (1916–1918)', *New Sound*, 43, I, 2014, pp. 123-156.

Vasiljević, M., 'Stanislav Binički (1872–1942) in the Great War: Preserving National Identity and Musical Links with the Homeland', in Milanović, B., (ed.), *On The Margins of the Musicological Canon: The Generation of Composers Petar Stojanović, Petar Krstić and Stanislav Binički* (Belgrade: Serbian Musicological Society, 2019), pp. 301-319.

Vasiljević, M., and Abramović, V., 'Cultural Diplomacy, Preservation and Construction of National Identity: Dragutin F. Pokorni in North Africa During the Great War', in B. Andrić (ed.), *Proceedings from the International Conference 'Elite in the Great War', Novi Sad 27-28. October 2016* (Novi Sad, 2016), pp. 542-553.

Vasiljević, M., and Dajc, H., 'Between Courtly, Civil and Military Service: Military Musicians in the Principality and Kingdom of Serbia, *Istraživanja, Journal of Historical Researches*, 28, 2017, pp. 118-133.

Vaughan, W. A., *Regimental History Flash* (Leeds: E. J. Arnold, 1943).

Walder, D., *The Chanak Affair* (London: Hutchinson, 1969).

Walton, K., *The British seaside: Holidays and resorts in the twentieth century* (Manchester: Manchester University Press, 2000).

Walvin, J., *Beside the Seaside: A Social History of the Popular Seaside Holiday* (London: Allen Lane Penguin, 1978).
Watson, D. (ed.), *The Wordsworth Dictionary of Musical Quotations* (Ware: Wordsworth, 1994).
Weir, C., *Village and Town Bands* (Aylesbury: Shire, 1981).
Westminster Abbey Memorial Service for Members of the Household Cavalry who Died during the War 1914-1918 (n. p., 1919; repr. The Naval and Military Press, 2003).
Wetherell, E., *Gordon Jacob: A Centenary Biography* (London: Thames Publishing, 1995).
White, H., 'Nationalism, Colonialism and the Cultural Stasis of Music in Ireland', in White, H. and Murphy, M. (eds), *Musical Constructions of Nationalism: Essays on the History of European Musical Culture 1800-1945* (Cork: Cork University Press, 2001), p. 257-271.
White, H., *One and All: A History of the Duke of Cornwall's Light Infantry 1702–1959* (Padstow: Tabb House, 2006).
White, W.C., *Military Band Arranging: A Practical Study for Schools and Private Study* (New York: Carl Fischer, 1924).
Whitty, H. M. (ed.), *The Story of the Royal Army Service Corps 1939-1945* (London: G. Bell and Sons, 1955).
Williams, N. T. St J., *Tommy Atkins' Children: The Story of the Education of the Army's Children 1675-1970* (London: HMSO, 1971).
Wisdom, N. and Hall, W., *My Turn* (London: Arrow, 1992).
Wilson, L. M. B., *Regimental Music of the Queen's Regiment* (n.p., 1980).
Wilson, D. A., 'Consequential Controversies', *The Annals of the American Academy of Political and Social Science*, Vol. 502 (Universities and the Military), March 1989, pp. 40-57.
Wood, S., *Those Terrible Grey Horses: An Illustrated History of the Royal Scots Dragoon Guards* (Oxford: Osprey, 2015).
Wood, W., *The Romance of Regimental Marches* (London: William Clowes, 1932).
Worthington, E. C., 'The modernisation of wind playing in London orchestras, 1909-1939: A study of playing style in early orchestral recordings' (PhD thesis, York University, 2013).
Wright, A. G., and Newcomb, S. P., *Bands of the World* (Evanston, Illinois: The Instrumentalist, 1970).
Wyrall, E., *The History of the Duke of Cornwall's Light Infantry 1914-1919* (London: Methuen, 1932; repr. Uckfield, East Sussex: The Naval and Military Press, 2003).

Yang, H., 'Diaspora, Music and Politics: Russian Musical Life in Shanghai during the Inter-war Period', in P. Fairclough (ed.) *Twentieth-Century Music and Politics: Essays in Memory of Neil Edmonds* (Farnham: Ashgate, 2013), pp. 260-277.

Young, K., *Music's Great Days in the Spas and Watering-Places* (London: Macmillan, 1968).

Zealley, A. E., Ord Hume, J., and Somerville, J. A. C., *Famous Bands of the British Empire* (London, J. P. Hull, 1926).

THE AUTHOR

Educated at the London College of Music and York and Cambridge Universities, and as a performer with the National Youth Jazz Orchestra, David has had a diverse career, taking him across the world as a French horn player and conductor. After four years in Southern Africa working for the Bophuthatswana Arts Council, his subsequent time in the British army saw him live in Germany and Gibraltar, serve in the Balkans, Falkland Islands, Canada, Cyprus, Kenya, and lead soldiers on Operations in Afghanistan.

With the Household Cavalry, David led the mounted band on the Queen's Birthday Parade in 2014, and he continued to work in the state arena as Director of Music, The Countess of Wessex's String Orchestra, responsible for the music at Buckingham Palace, Windsor Castle, and Holyrood Palace for Investitures, State Banquets, and other royal events. As an army reservist David is now Director of Music of The Band of The Royal Yeomanry (Inns of Court & City Yeomanry). As a civilian he is a French horn player and conductor, and a director of the management consultancy Get Psyched Up!

David has five degrees and holds Fellowships from the principal British music conservatoires. Following on from an MBA with the Open University, David's PhD research combined his interests in music, strategy, and history, and forms the basis of this book.

David has participated in sports throughout his career, notably football and rugby, and has also enjoyed 'adventure' travelling – such as canoeing on the Zambezi and completing the Trans-Siberian Railway. He now loves spending his spare time on the Essex coast with his wife, Kate, their teenage twin daughters, Jane and Elizabeth, and two large labradoodles.

www.ingramcontent.com/pod-product-compliance
Lightning Source LLC
Chambersburg PA
CBHW050550170426
43201CB00011B/1643